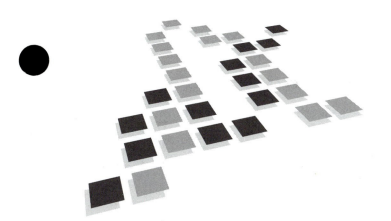

A Stata Companion
to Political Analysis

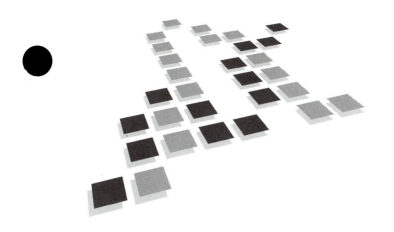

A Stata Companion to Political Analysis

Second Edition

Philip H. Pollock III
University of Central Florida

CQ PRESS

A Division of SAGE
Washington, D.C.

CQ Press
2300 N Street, NW, Suite 800
Washington, DC 20037

Phone: 202-729-1900; toll-free, 1-866-4CQ-PRESS (1-866-427-7737)

Web: www.cqpress.com

Credits: Datasets on the CD: nes2008.dta: selected variables obtained from the 2008 American National Election Study, Inter-university Consortium for Political and Social Research (ICPSR), University of Michigan; gss2006.dta: selected variables obtained from the 2006 General Social Survey, ICPSR, University of Michigan; world.dta: selected variables obtained from Mike Alvarez, Jose Antonio Cheibub, Fernando Limongi, and Adam Przeworski. See Alvarez, Cheibub, Limongi, and Przeworski, *Democracy and Development: Political Institutions and Well-Being in the World, 1950–1990* (Cambridge, UK: Cambridge University Press, 2000); world.dta: selected variables obtained from Pippa Norris, John F. Kennedy School of Government, Harvard University; states.dta: selected variables obtained from Gerald C. Wright, Indiana University. See Robert S. Erikson, Gerald C. Wright, and John P. McIver, *Statehouse Democracy* (Cambridge, UK: Cambridge University Press, 1993).

Cover design: Auburn Associates Inc.
Typesetting: C&M Digitals (P) Ltd.

♾ The paper used in this publication exceeds the requirements of the American National Standard for Information Sciences—Permanence of Paper for Printed Library Materials, ANSI Z39.48-1992.

Printed and bound in the United States of America

14   13   12   3   4   5

Paperback ISBN 978-1-60871-671-5

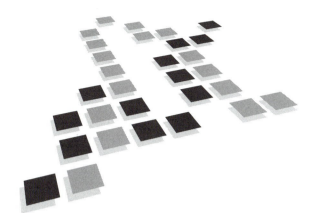

Contents

Commands Covered

describe; codebook *varname*; set more off; File→Log→Begin; search *keyword*; help *command_name*; which *package_name*; ssc install *package_name*

Commands Covered

tabulate *varname*; summarize *varname*, detail; sktest *varname*; histogram *varname*, d percent; histogram *varname*, percent; sort *varname*; list *varname*; The Graph Editor Recorder

A Closer Look

Chapter 3 Transforming Variables   **43**

Commands Covered

recode, generate ( ); generate, recode( ); xtile, nquantiles ( ); generate; tabulate, generate ( ); label variable; label define; label values; drop; aorder

A Closer Look

Chapter 4 Making Comparisons   **59**

Commands Covered

tabulate *dep_var indep_var*, column; tabulate *indep_var*, summarize (*dep_var*); format; _gwtmean, *dep_var_mean=dep_var* [if], by (*indep_var*); if; twoway (line *dep_var indep_var*, sort); replace; graph bar (mean) *dep_var*, over (*indep_var*)

A Closer Look

A Closer Look

Chapter 5 Making Controlled Comparisons   93

Commands Covered

bysort *cntrl_var*: tabulate *dep_var indep_var*, col; tabulate *cntrl_var indep_var*, summarize (*dep_var*); graph bar *dep_var*, over (*cntrl_var*) over (*indep_var*); twoway (line *dep_var indep_var* if *cntrl_var*==value1, sort) (line *dep_var indep_var* if *cntrl_var*==value2, sort)

Chapter 6 Making Inferences about Sample Means   121

Commands Covered

ttest *varname* = *testvalue*; ttest *varname*, by(*group_var*); robvar *varname*, by(*group_var*)

Chapter 7 Chi-square and Measures of Association   137

Commands Covered

(tabulate option) chi2; (tabulate option) V; somersd *indep_var dep_var*; lambda *dep_var indep_var*

Chapter 8 Correlation and Linear Regression   157

Commands Covered

correlate *varlist*; regress *dep_var indep_var(s)*; twoway (*scatter dep_var indep_var*) (lfit *dep_var indep_var*)

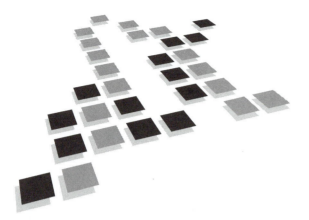

Figures

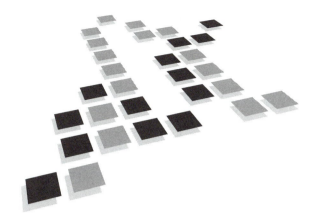

Preface

Like the book that preceded it, this edition of *A Stata Companion to Political Analysis* provides a guided tour of Stata's two most popular attractions: command-line data analysis and graphics. On the command-line side of things, adopters of the earlier edition will find the same step-by-step coverage of basic Stata commands—from data description commands to data analysis and post-estimation procedures. All syntax is the same for Stata 11, with which this book was written, as for Stata 7, 8, 9, or 10—or, I am confident, for any earlier or future releases of Stata. Stata's enduring adherence to backwards compatibility is a reassuring principle and, so, the first edition was not rendered suddenly obsolete by some capricious change in the Stata command language.

Stata graphics are a different story. Shortly after the publication of the first edition, which was written for Stata 8/9, Stata 10 appeared, featuring Stata's first graphics editor in nearly 20 years.[1] Whereas releases 8 and 9 added drop-down functionality to Stata's command-driven graphics capabilities—menu selections and text entries are echoed to the command queue—Stata 10's Graph Editor is a genuine game-changer. A novice can achieve a presentation-quality result by requesting a bare-bones graph in the Command window and adding content- and appearance-enhancing features in the Graph Editor. This edition of the *Companion* thoroughly covers the Graph Editor. In another graphics-related change, I deemphasize the use of bar charts and place new emphasis on the construction of line charts, a graphic form that communicates relationships (especially complex relationships) with great clarity. For all their graphs, bar or line, students follow a three-step protocol: generate indicator variables (for graphing categorical variables) or group means (for graphing interval variables); obtain the basic graph in the Command window; and hone their work product in the Graph Editor.

CHAPTER ORGANIZATION AND DATASETS

This book instructs students in the use of Stata for constructing meaningful descriptions of variables and performing substantive analysis of political relationships. The chapters cover all major topics in data analysis: descriptive statistics (Chapter 2), transforming variables (Chapter 3), cross-tabulation and mean comparisons (Chapter 4), controlled comparisons (Chapter 5), statistical inference (Chapter 6), chi-square and measures of association (Chapter 7), correlation and linear regression (Chapter 8), dummy variables and interaction effects (Chapter 9), and logistic regression (Chapter 10). A final chapter (Chapter 11) describes several doable research projects and lays out a framework for a well-organized research paper.

The CD that accompanies this book contains four datasets: selected variables from the 2008 American National Election Study (nes2008) and the 2006 General Social Survey (gss2006), as well as datasets on the 50 states (states), and 191 countries of the world (world). Because the 2008 ANES over-sampled African American and Latino respondents, students are instructed in how to weight the dataset to achieve results that are representative of the electorate.

Each chapter is written as a tutorial, taking students through a series of guided examples in which they perform the analysis. The figures and annotated command-line screen shots allow students to check their work along the way. This book contains more than 40 end-of-chapter exercises, all of which are based on the datasets, and all of which give students opportunities to apply their new skills—and to discover the meaning of their findings and learn to interpret them. After completing this book, students will have become competent Stata users, and they will have learned a fair amount about substantive political science, too. Adopters may obtain a complete set of the do-files that I used to construct the guided examples and the exercises. Instructors may find these files useful for recreating the graphics, performing the exercises, or for trouble-shooting students' difficulties with the examples or exercises.

DIFFERENT RELEASES OF STATA

This book was written with Stata/SE 11.0 and may be used productively with Stata 10. Because of its heavy reliance on the Graph Editor, this book is not intended to be used with Stata 9 or earlier. Although all the datasets are well within the generous limitations of Stata/SE and Stata/IC, Small Stata users will only be able to analyze the world dataset and the states dataset, and so will find limited usefulness here.

ACCOMPANYING CORE TEXT

Instructors will find that this book makes an effective supplement to any of a variety of methods textbooks. However, it is a particularly suitable companion to my own core text, *The Essentials of Political Analysis*. The textbook's substantive chapters cover basic and intermediate methodological issues and ideas: measurement, explanations and hypotheses, univariate statistics and bivariate analysis, controlled relationships, sampling and inference, statistical significance, correlation and linear regression, and logistic regression. Each chapter also includes end-of-chapter exercises. Students can read the textbook chapters, do the exercises, and then work through the guided examples and exercises in *A Stata Companion to Political Analysis*. The idea is to get students in front of the computer, experiencing political research firsthand, early in the academic term. An instructor's solutions manual, free to adopters, provides solutions for all the textbook and workbook exercises.

ACKNOWLEDGMENTS

I would like to thank the anonymous reviewers for many helpful suggestions. I am especially grateful to Jan Leighley of the University of Arizona for class-testing the first edition of this book. Special thanks to the authors of three Stata packages that play important roles in this volume: Roger Newson of the Respiratory Epidemiology and Public Health Group, National Heart and Lung Institute at Imperial College London (somersd); Nicholas J. Cox, Department of Geography, Durham University, UK (lambda); and David Kantor, Institute for Policy Studies, Johns Hopkins University (_gwtmean).

I have been very fortunate indeed to have a publisher with the prestige of CQ Press, and I gratefully acknowledge the encouragement and professionalism of everyone involved with this project: Charisse Kiino, editorial director; Nancy Loh, editorial assistant; Gwenda Larsen, production editor; Paul Pressau, production manager; and Amy Marks, copy editor.

NOTES

1. In December 1989, Stata released a graphics editor, Stage 1.0, which was written in one month and never updated. See Nicholas J. Cox, "A Brief History of Stata on Its 20th Anniversary," *The Stata Journal* 5 (2005): 2–18.

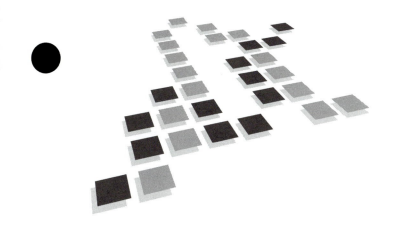

A Stata Companion
to Political Analysis

Getting Started

For this introduction you will need

- Access to a Microsoft Windows–based computer
- The CD that accompanies this workbook
- A USB flash drive or other portable media

As you have learned about political research and explored techniques of political analysis, you have studied many examples of other people's work. You may have read textbook chapters that present frequency distributions, or you may have pondered research articles that use cross-tabulation, correlation, or regression analysis to investigate interesting relationships between variables. As valuable as these learning experiences are, they can be enhanced greatly by performing political analysis firsthand—handling and modifying social science datasets, learning to use data analysis computer software, obtaining your own descriptive statistics for variables, setting up the appropriate analysis for interesting relationships, and running the analysis and interpreting your results.

This book is designed to guide you as you learn these valuable practical skills. In this volume you will gain a working knowledge of Stata, powerful data analysis and graphics software used widely in academic institutions. Stata will perform a great variety of statistical analysis procedures, from basic descriptive statistics to multivariate modeling, and it will construct a wide array of graphic images, from simple bar charts and histograms to sophisticated graphic overlays. In this book you will learn to use Stata's command language for virtually all the data analyses that you perform and the graphs you create, and you will learn to use Stata's Graph Editor to add content and style to your graphs. Although this book assumes that you have practical knowledge of the Windows operating system and that you know how to perform elemental file-handling tasks, it also assumes that you have never heard of Stata and that you have never used a computer to analyze data of any kind. By the time you complete the guided examples and the exercises in this book, you will be well on your way to becoming a Stata aficionado. The skills you learn will be durable, and they will serve you well as you continue your educational career or enter the business world.

This book's chapters are written in tutorial fashion. Each chapter contains several guided examples, and each includes exercises at the end. You will read each chapter while sitting in front of a computer, doing the analysis described in the guided examples, analyzing the datasets that accompany this text. Each data analysis procedure is described in step-by-step fashion, and the book has many figures that show you what your computer screen should look like as you perform the procedures. Thus, the guided examples allow you to develop your skills and to become comfortable with Stata. The end-of-chapter exercises allow you to apply your new skills to different substantive problems.

In Chapter 1 you will learn how to navigate in Stata—how to obtain information about a dataset, how to keep track of your work by using a log file, how to print output, how to use Stata's extensive help system, and how to install statistical modules that you will be using. Chapter 2 demonstrates how to obtain and interpret frequency distributions and how to create bar charts and histograms. Chapter 3 covers data transformations in Stata—recoding variables and generating new variables that you will want to add to your data files. In Chapter 4 you will explore and apply cross-tabulation analysis and mean comparison analysis—again learning to add graphic support to the relationships you analyze. In Chapter 5 you will learn to make controlled comparisons, producing and interpreting tabular and graphic output for the relationship between a dependent variable and an independent variable, controlling for a third variable. In Chapter 6 you will use Stata to obtain the information you need to establish the boundaries of random sampling error and to assess the statistical significance of an empirical relationship. In Chapter 7 you will learn how tests of significance and measures of association add statistical support to your cross-tabulation analyses. In Chapter 8 you will learn correlation and linear regression, and Chapter 9 shows how to use linear regression to model and estimate complex relationships. Chapter 10 describes how to perform logistic regression, a technique that has gained widespread use in political research—and a technique that Stata performs with greater power and flexibility than does any other data analysis software. Finally, in Chapter 11 we will consider some of the challenges you might face in finding and collecting your own data, and we will offer some suggestions on how best to organize and present your original research.

DATASET CD

An accompanying CD contains four datasets that you will analyze using Stata. Insert the CD into your computer's drive and let's take a preliminary look at the datasets (Figure I-1).

1. **gss2006**. This dataset has selected variables from the 2006 General Social Survey, a random sample of 4,510 adults aged 18 years or older, conducted by the National Opinion Research Center and made available through the Inter-university Consortium for Political and Social Research (ICPSR) at the University of Michigan.[1] Some of the scales in gss2006 were constructed by the author. These constructed variables are described in the appendix (Table A-1).

2. **nes2008**. This dataset includes selected variables from the 2008 American National Election Study, a random sample of 2,323 citizens of voting age, conducted by the University of Michigan's Institute for Social Research and made available through ICPSR.[2]

3. **states**. This dataset includes variables on each of the fifty states. Most of these variables were compiled by the author. See the appendix, Table A-2.

4. **world**. This dataset includes variables on 191 countries. These variables are based on data compiled by Pippa Norris, John F. Kennedy School of Government, Harvard University, and made available to the scholarly community through her Web site.[3] A complete description of world appears in the appendix (Table A-3).

As you work your way through this book, you will modify these datasets—recoding some variables, computing new variables, and otherwise tailoring the datasets to suit your purposes. You will need to make personal copies of the datasets and store them on a removable drive, such as a USB flash drive.

 DO THIS NOW: Before proceeding, copy the datasets from the accompanying CD to a personal USB drive or other portable media.

When you begin each chapter's guided examples, or when you do the exercises, you will want to insert your personal media into the appropriate computer drive. Stata will read the data from the drive. If you make any changes to a dataset, you can save the newly modified dataset directly to your personal media. If you have modified a dataset during a data analysis session, it is important that you copy the dataset to your personal media so that you can take the modified dataset with you!

Figure I-1   Datasets on the CD

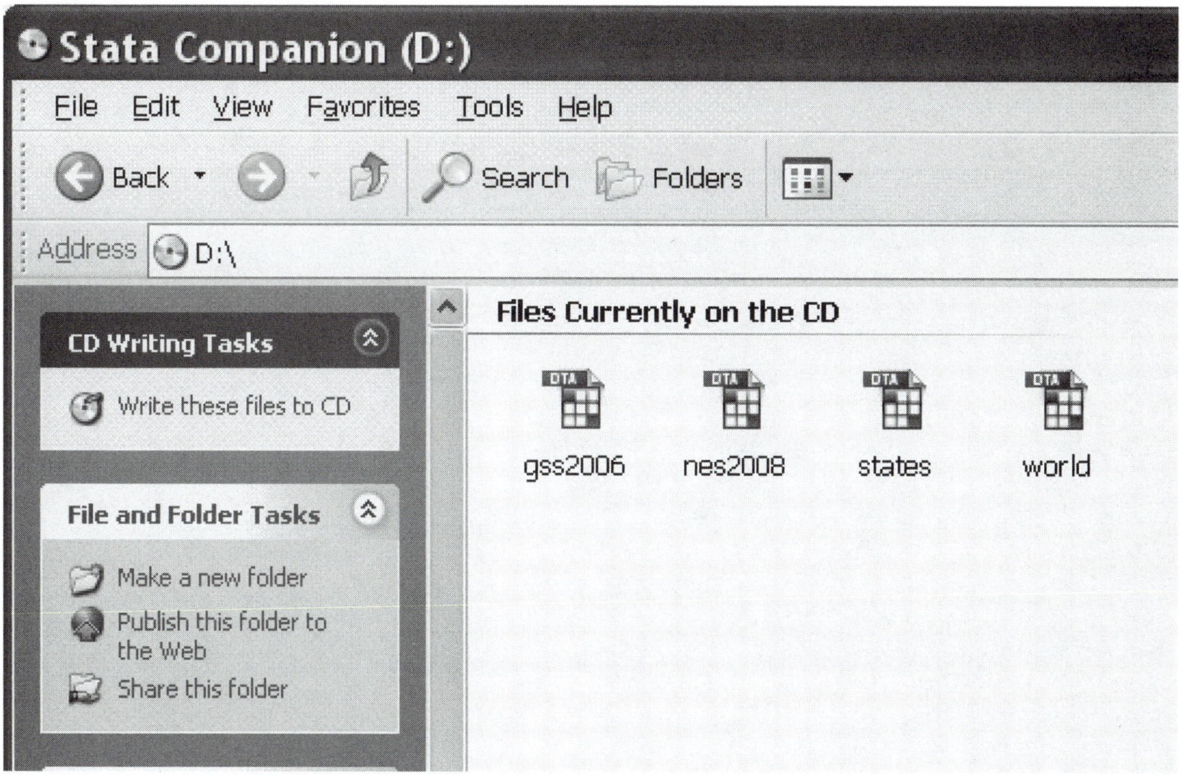

NOTES

1. Gss2006 was created from the General Social Survey 1972–2006 Cumulative Data File. James A. Davis, Tom W. Smith, and Peter V. Marsden. General Social Surveys, 1972–2006 [Cumulative File] [Computer file]. ICPSR04697-v2. Chicago: National Opinion Research Center [producer], 2007. Storrs, Conn.: Roper Center for Public Opinion Research, University of Connecticut/Ann Arbor, Mich.: Inter-university Consortium for Political and Social Research [distributors], 2007-09-10.
2. The American National Election Studies (ANES; www.electionstudies.org). The ANES 2008 Time Series Study [dataset]. Stanford University and the University of Michigan [producers]. These materials are based on work supported by the National Science Foundation under grants SES-0535334, SES-0720428, SES-0840550, and SES-0651271, Stanford University, and the University of Michigan.
3. www.pippanorris.com.

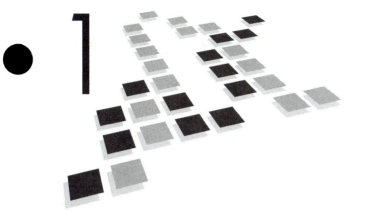

1

Introduction to Stata

In this chapter you will learn these Stata basics:

- How to obtain information about data and variables
- How to create a log file (a file that saves your commands and results)
- How to print output and how to copy/paste output into Word
- How to use Stata's help system
- How to install a statistical module

Let's open one of the datasets, gss2006, and see what the Stata interface looks like. Start Stata as you would start any program. Once Stata loads, click the Open File icon, locate gss2006 on your computer, and open the dataset.[1] Consider Stata's opening window—or windows, to be more precise (Figure 1-1). There are four windows: Command, Results, Review, and Variables. The user types a command in the Command window, presses the Enter key, and views the output in the Results window. The Review window keeps a record of each command that has been entered. Clicking on a previous command in the Review window returns the command to the Command window, where it can be rerun or edited. (Pressing the Page Up key returns the most recently entered command to the Command window.) The Variables window displays the names of all the variables in the current dataset. These variables, of course, are the objects we want to analyze when we type commands in the Command window.

OBTAINING INFORMATION ABOUT A DATASET

The describe command provides descriptive information about a dataset. Click in the Command window, type "describe" (without the quotes), and press Enter. Stata tells us that gss2006 has 4,510 observations and 203 variables (Figure 1-2). It fills the screen with basic information about the dataset's variables, including each variable's name and label. The "more" message at the bottom of the screen informs us that the command produced additional results, which Stata will display when prompted to do so. To scroll through long output line by line, press Enter. To see the next screen, click the Go button on the menu bar (see

Figure 1-1 Stata's Opening Interface

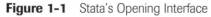

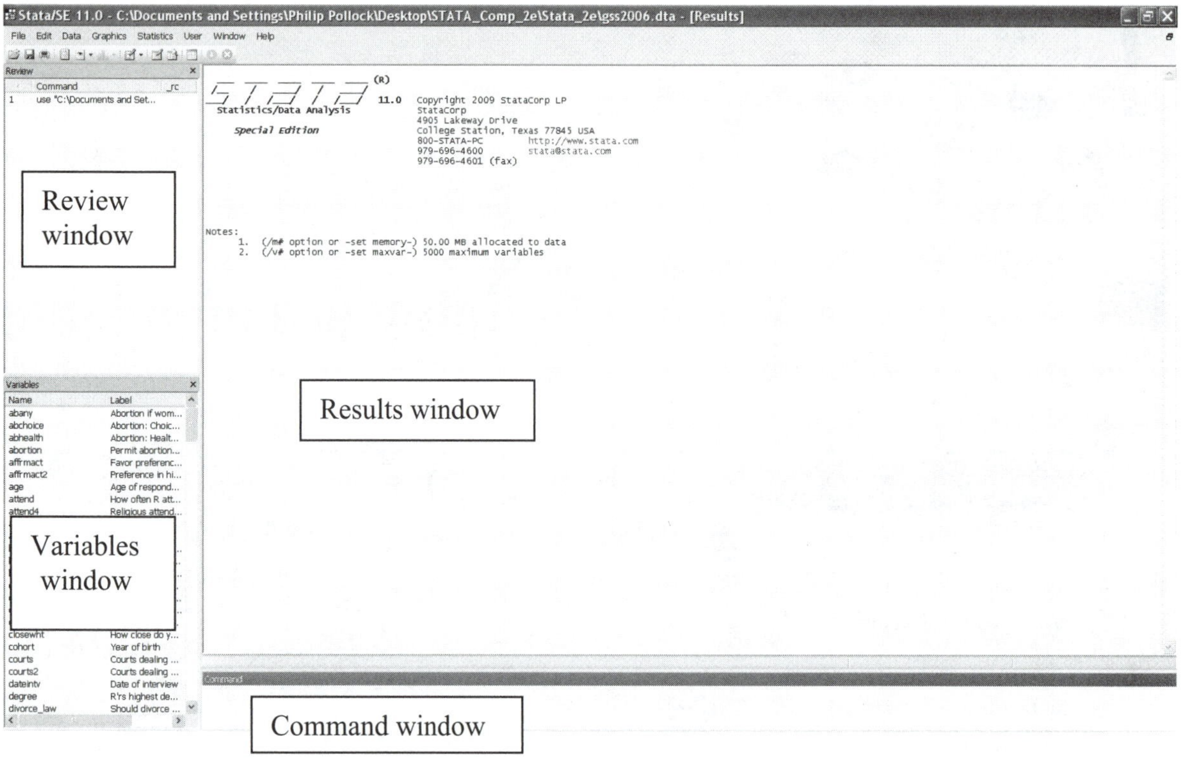

Figure 1-2 Results from the describe Command

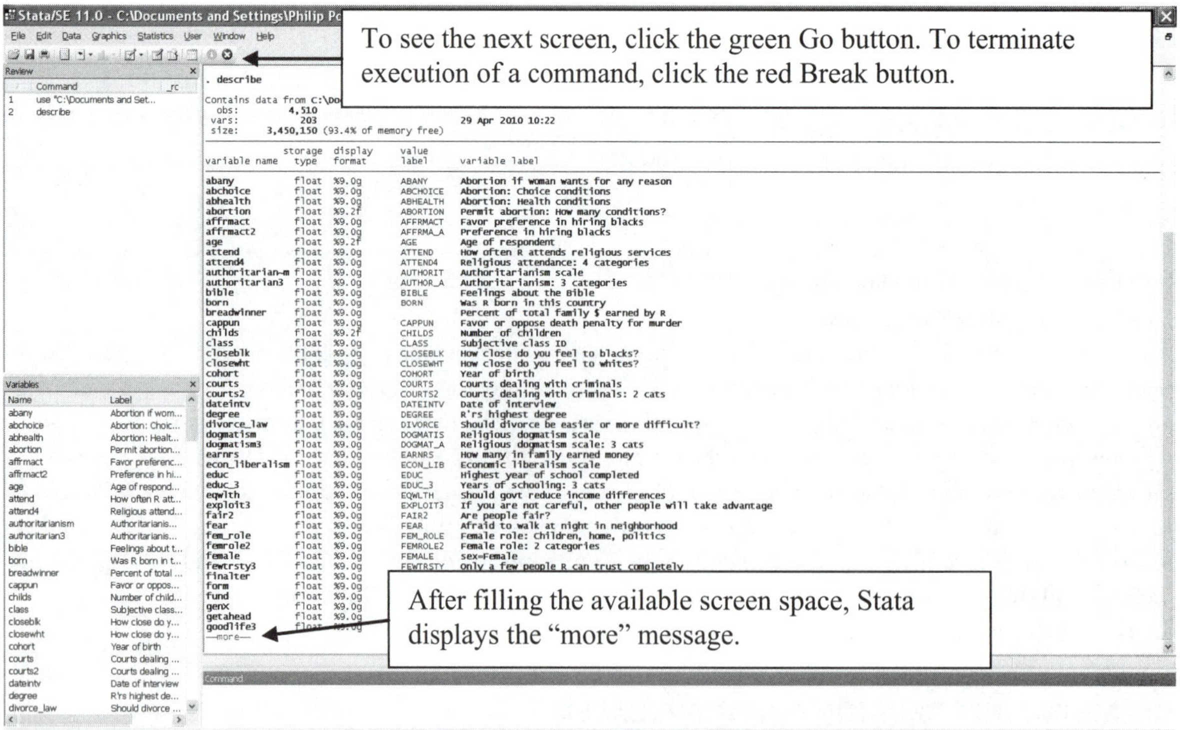

Figure 1-2) or press any key except the Enter key. To end the command without seeing more results, click the Break button on the menu bar or press Ctrl and Break (at the same time) on the keyboard.[2]

By default, Stata will pause long output and display the "more" message. Perhaps you like this default. Perhaps you don't. To switch off the default—that is, to instruct Stata to scroll through all the output without pausing—type "set more off" and press Enter. To reinstate the default, type "set more on" and press Enter.

OBTAINING INFORMATION ABOUT VARIABLES

The codebook command provides information about the variables in a dataset. The general syntax of the codebook command is as follows:

codebook *varname*

For example, suppose we want Stata to display specific coding and labeling information for the variable attend. Click in the Command window and type "codebook attend". (Or, you can type "codebook" and then click attend into the Command window.) Consider the output (Figure 1-3). Along the top line of results, Stata displays the variable's name, "attend", and its label, "How often R attends religious services". (In the idiom of survey research, "R" means "respondent.") Below, codebook offers a fair amount of detail, including (under "Freq.") the number of respondents falling into each category of the variable.

Note the entries beneath "Numeric" and "Label." In storing information and running analyses, Stata relies on numbers, not words. So when Stata looks at the attend variable, it sees that some respondents are coded 0, some are coded 1, some are coded 3, and so on. When a case does not have a valid code on a variable, it has the missing-value designator ".", which tells Stata to exclude the case from any analyses. As long as a variable has numeric codes, Stata will analyze it.[3] To understand a variable in human language, therefore, we need a set of value labels—descriptive words that tell us what each numeric code means. Thus, all respondents coded 0 on attend "Never" attend religious services, while those coded 7 attend "Every week." In Chapter 3 you will learn how to supply value labels for any new variables you create.

Here is a special note about codebook, which may come in handy when you want more detailed information about variables in nes2008. In compiling nes2008 from variables contained in the 2008 American National Election Study, the author changed the original variable names to make them more descriptive. For example, in the original 2008 ANES, V083215x is the variable that reports each respondent's age, and V085086 records his or her opinions about abortion. In creating nes2008, the author renamed V083215x "age" and V085086 "abort_rights." To find out the original variable names for any variable in nes2008, run codebook with the "notes" option:

codebook *varname*, **notes**

With the original variable names in hand, you can retrieve question-wording information by searching the 2008 American National Election Study codebook, available online at http://www.electionstudies.org/studypages/2008prepost/2008prepost.htm.

Figure 1-3 Results from the codebook Command

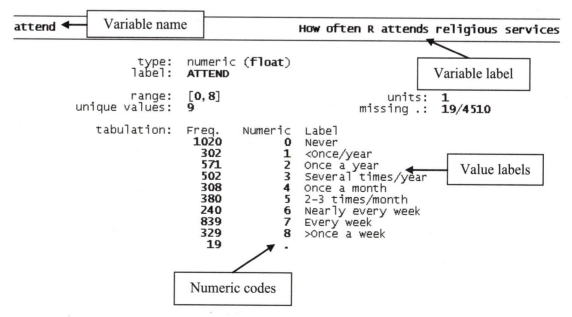

CREATING AND VIEWING A LOG FILE

Unlike most data analysis packages, Stata does not automatically save your work to an output file. This is not a huge disadvantage, because Stata permits the user to select desired output and print it directly from the Results window. (This procedure is discussed below.) Even so, a log file is a good idea. To begin a log file, click File→Log→Begin, as shown in Figure 1-4. Find a suitable location, name the file, and click Save. Stata will now record everything, including commands that are typed in the Command window and output that appears in the Results Window.[4] From within Stata, you can open and view log files, including the current log, by clicking File→Log→View. Ordinarily, Stata correctly assumes that you want to view the active log file. If Stata is remiss, you can browse to the current log's location. Of course, using the File→Log menu, you can suspend, resume, and close log files.

Figure 1-4   Beginning a Log File

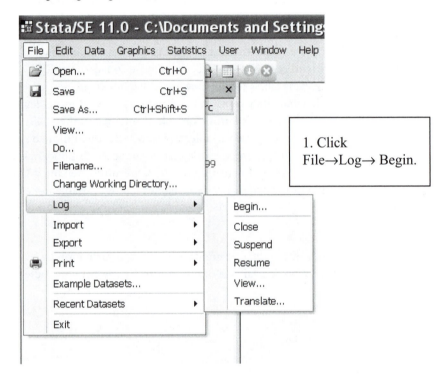

You also can type comments, which of course will be recorded in the log. Comments take the form "* *This is a comment*"—that is, an asterisk followed by the typed comment. The "*" signals the beginning of a comment. Stata will not try to handle such statements as commands.

PRINTING RESULTS AND COPYING OUTPUT

Any tabular or text output can be selected and printed directly from the screen or from a log file. (In the next chapter, we describe how to print graphs.) To illustrate, we will use the tabulate command to obtain a frequency distribution of the variable bible, which measures respondents' feelings toward the Bible. (The tabulate command is covered in Chapter 2.) Type the command "tabulate bible" and press Enter (Figure 1-5). Stata produces tabular output displaying the desired frequency distribution. To print the table: select it, right-click on the selection, and then click Print. In the Print window, click the Selection radio button. (The All button is Stata's default assumption, but you rarely want to print all the output you have produced during a session.) When the Output Settings window appears, uncheck all the boxes along the top of the window (see Figure 1-5).

Figure 1-5 Sending Results to the Printer

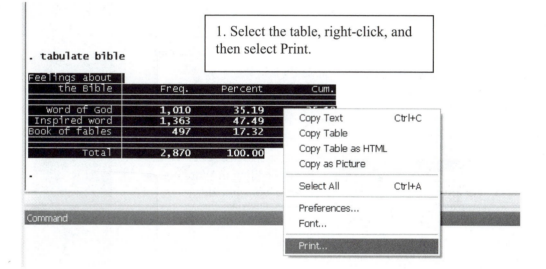

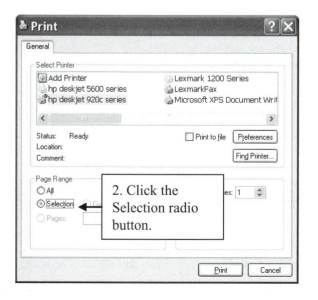

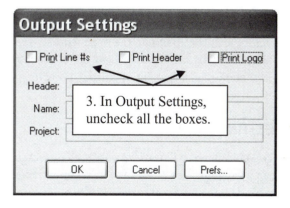

Figure 1-6   Copying and Pasting Results into Word

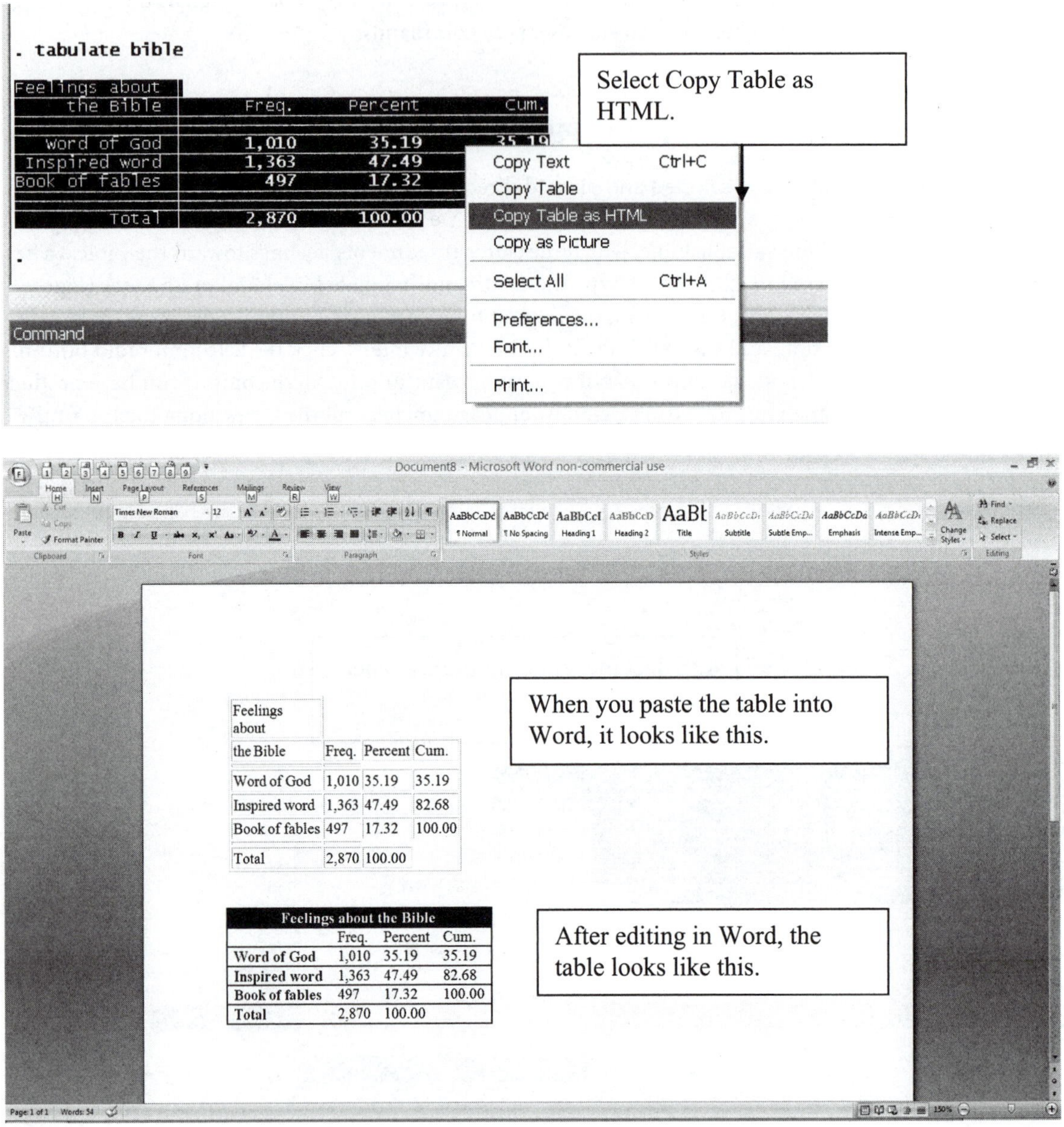

You can copy/paste output into a word processor, too, but (truth be told) this is one of Stata's less satisfactory features. To obtain the most workable result: select the tabular output, right-click, and choose Copy Table as HTML, as shown in Figure 1-6. When pasted into a Word document, the table is editable but not of presentation quality. A bit of editing, however, produces a presentable result.

GETTING HELP

Two commands will retrieve potentially useful information. Use the search command if you don't know or can't remember the name of a Stata command—or if you want to delve into Stata's resources on a particular topic. Use the help command to view Stata command syntax.

The syntax of the search command is as follows:

search *keyword*

Suppose we are interested in doing probit analysis, a specialized modeling technique, and we want access to Stata's information on the topic. Typing the command "search probit" returns about 10 pages of output, including hyperlinks to descriptions of every probit-related Stata command, links to frequently asked questions (FAQs), examples of probit analysis, and references to technical reports and bulletins.[5]

The syntax of the help command is as follows:

help *command_name*

The command "help probit" retrieves specific syntax information—that is, how to type the probit command and what options can be used.

The help command also shows you permissible abbreviations for Stata commands. Consider the describe command, which has a longish name. Can this command be abbreviated? Type "help describe". Stata displays the requested information in a separate window, the Viewer (Figure 1-7). In addition to a

Figure 1-7 The help Command

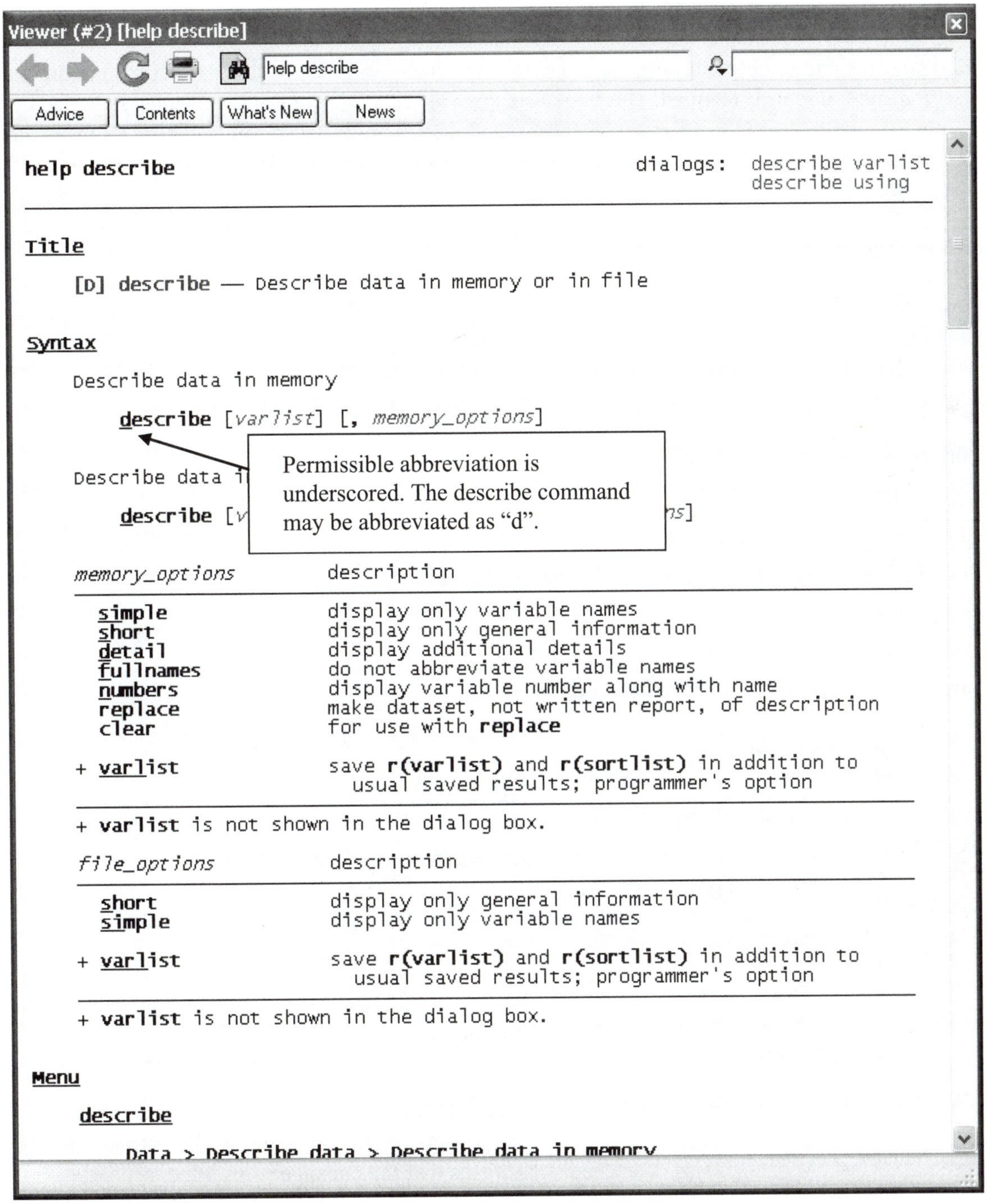

raft of information on options and useful links to command elements, Stata communicates—by way of underlined letters—the minimum acceptable command abbreviation. As Figure 1-7 points out, instead of typing "describe", we can simply type "d", and Stata will know that we mean "describe". Because "d" is the shortest acceptable abbreviation for "describe," each of the following is also acceptable: d, de, des, desc, descr, descri, describ, and (of course) describe. If none of the letters in the command syntax is underlined, then the command may not be abbreviated.

Stata follows three rules in determining abbreviations. First, the more commonly used commands, such as the describe command, generally have shorter acceptable abbreviations. Second, commands that are destructive of data may not be abbreviated. The recode command, discussed in Chapter 3, is an example of a destructive command. Third, commands that are implemented as ado-files (external program files that Stata must access) do not have abbreviations. For example, because the codebook command is implemented as an ado-file, it may not be abbreviated.

INSTALLING STATISTICAL MODULES

Stata is powerful and flexible software that can perform virtually any analytic task. However, sometimes a special statistical module is required. This book uses three modules: _gwtmean (in Chapter 4), lambda (Chapter 7), and somersd (also Chapter 7). If these modules are not installed, you will need to install them now. Use the which command to find out if these packages are already installed. The general syntax for the which command is as follows:

which *package_name*

For example, to check on _gwtmean, you would type "which _gwtmean"; for lambda, "which lambda"; and for somersd, "which somersd". If Stata finds the program, it will display basic information, such as the program's local path and release date. If Stata cannot find the program, it will tell you so. In that case, install each package using the ssc command. The syntax for the ssc command is as follows:

ssc install *package_name*

The ssc command prompts Stata to access the Statistical Software Components (SSC) archive, locate the module, and install it on your computer.[6] Figure 1-8 displays the command sequence for installing _gwtmean. Follow Figure 1-8's example for _gwtmean, lambda, and somersd.[7]

Figure 1-8 Installing a Statistical Module

```
. which _gwtmean
command _gwtmean not found as either built-in or ado-file
r(111);
```

> The "which _gwtmean" command confirms that the package is not installed.

```
.
.
. ssc install _gwtmean
checking _gwtmean consistency and verifying not already installed...
installing into c:\ado\plus\...
installation complete.
```

> The "ssc install _gwtmean" command installs the package.

```
.
.
. which _gwtmean
c:\ado\plus\_\_gwtmean.ado
*! version 1.0.0  6-5-2001
```

> The "which _gwtmean" command this time confirms that the package is installed.

EXERCISES

For the following exercises, you will use dataset nes2008. Click File➔Open, locate nes2008 on your computer, select it, and click Open.

1. Run the describe command. According to the results, nes2008 has (fill in the blanks) _____

    observations and _____ variables.

2. Dataset nes2008 contains the variable, camp_attent. Run "codebook camp_attent".

    A. What is the variable label for camp_attent? _____

    B. Respondents who paid a moderate amount of attention to the campaign have what numeric code on camp_attent? (circle one)

    1   2   3   4   5

    C. According to the codebook results, how many respondents have missing values on camp_attent?

    _____

3. Obtain tabular output for camp_attent. Type "tabulate camp_attent."

    A. Print the table.

    B. Copy/paste the table into a blank Word document. Edit the table for appearance and readability. Print the Word document.

4. In Chapter 2, you will learn how to interpret output from the summarize command. Which of the following are acceptable abbreviations for the summarize command (circle all that apply)?

    su   sum   summ   summa   summar   summari   summariz

This concludes the exercises for this chapter. After exiting Stata, be sure to take your removable media with you.

NOTES

1. Stata's default memory allocation permits the user to open any data file of up to 1 MB (Intercooled Stata) or 10 MB (Stata/SE) in size. This default is adequate for all the datasets included with this book. For larger datasets, however, you may need to change this allocation by running the set memory command. For more information about Stata's memory management, type "help memory" in the Command window. On pages 10–12 of this chapter we take a closer look at Stata's help system.
2. To obtain basic information about a dataset (and suppress variable-specific information), use the short option "describe, short".
3. Some variables do not have numeric codes but, rather, are recorded as words. Thus, a dataset might contain the variable named friends, which takes on the values "Aileen," "Bruce," "Charisse," and "Doug." Variables that are recorded as words are called string variables. Although Stata will analyze string variables, strings are not covered in this book.
4. Stata will write log files in two formats: *.smcl (the default, which stands for Stata Markup and Control Language) and *.log (ASCII text). When viewed from within Stata, logs written in SMCL appear as the original commands and output appeared. ASCII logs can be opened and understood by any word processing software. With the translate command, the user can convert SMCL files to ASCII files (and vice versa).
5. Another help-related command, findit, casts an even wider net than the search command. The findit command is equivalent to running search with the all option.
6. According to Stata, the Statistical Software Components (SSC) archive "has become the premier Stata download site for user-written software on the web." The SSC archive is maintained by the Boston College Department of Economics and is provided by http://repec.org.
7. The lambda module was written by Nicholas J. Cox, Department of Geography, Durham University, United Kingdom. The somersd module was written by Roger Newson, Respiratory Epidemiology and Public Health Group, National Heart and Lung Institute at Imperial College London, United Kingdom. See Newson, "Parameters behind 'Nonparametric' Statistics: Kendall's tau, Somers' D and Median Differences," *The Stata Journal* 2:1 (2002): 45–64. The_gwtmean module was written by David Kantor, Institute for Policy Studies, Johns Hopkins University, Baltimore, Maryland.

2

Descriptive Statistics

Analyzing descriptive statistics is the most basic—and sometimes the most informative—type of analysis you will do. Descriptive statistics reveal two attributes of a variable: its typical value (central tendency) and its spread (degree of dispersion or variation). The precision with which we can describe central tendency for any given variable depends on the variable's level of measurement. For nominal-level variables we can identify the *mode*, the most common value of the variable. For ordinal-level variables, those whose categories can be ranked, we can find the mode and the *median*—the value of the variable that divides the cases into two equal-size groups. For interval-level variables, we can obtain the mode, median, and arithmetic *mean*, the sum of all values divided by the number of cases.

Finding a variable's central tendency is ordinarily a straightforward exercise. Simply read the computer results and report the numbers. Describing a variable's degree of dispersion or variation, however, often requires informed judgment.[1] Here is a general rule that applies to any variable at any level of measurement: A variable has no dispersion if all the cases—states, countries, people, or whatever—fall into the same value of the variable. Using ordinary language, we might describe such a variable as "homogeneous." A variable has maximum dispersion if the cases are spread evenly across all values of the variable. The number of cases in one category equals the number of cases in every other category. In this circumstance, we would describe the variable as "heterogeneous."

INTERPRETING MEASURES OF CENTRAL TENDENCY AND VARIATION

Central tendency and variation work together in providing a complete description of any variable. Some variables have an easily identified typical value and show little dispersion. For example, suppose you were to ask a large number of U.S. citizens what sort of economic system they believe to be the best: capitalism, communism, or socialism. What would be the modal response, the economic system preferred by most people? Capitalism. Would there be a great deal of dispersion, with large numbers of people choosing the alternatives, communism or socialism? Probably not. In other instances, however, you may find that one value of a variable has a more tenuous grasp on the label "typical." And the variable may exhibit more dispersion, with the cases spread out more evenly across the variable's other values. For example, suppose a large sample of voting-age adults were asked, in the weeks preceding a presidential election, how interested they are in the campaign: very interested, somewhat interested, or not very interested. Among your own acquaintances you probably know a number of people who fit into each category. So even if one category, such as "somewhat interested," is the median, there are likely to be many people at either extreme: "very interested" and "not very interested." This would be an instance in which the amount of dispersion in a variable—its degree of spread—is essential to understanding and describing it.

These and other points are best understood by working through some guided examples using gss2006. In the examples that follow, you will learn to use a variant of Stata's versatile tabulate command, which produces frequency distributions for nominal, ordinal, or interval variables. You also will use the summarize command to obtain descriptive statistics for interval-level variables. Finally, in this chapter you will learn to use histogram, a command that creates graphic displays. Open gss2006 and let's get started.

DESCRIBING NOMINAL VARIABLES

In this section you will obtain a frequency distribution for a nominal-level variable, zodiac, which records respondents' astrological signs. But first we will review the codebook command, introduced in Chapter 1. In the Command window, type "codebook zodiac".

Stata responds:

```
zodiac                                              Respondent's Astrological Sign
-------------------------------------------------------------------------------------

              type:  numeric (float)
             label:  ZODIAC

             range:  [1,12]                           units:  1
     unique values:  12                            missing .:  157/4510

          examples:  3       Gemini
                     5       Leo
                     8       Scorpio
                     10      Capricorn
```

Zodiac carries the variable label "Respondent's Astrological Sign." It has 12 unique numeric codes, each of which has a nonnumeric value label. Respondents who are coded 3 on zodiac, for example, are labeled "Gemini," those coded 5 are labeled "Leo," and so on.

Now we will ask Stata to produce a frequency distribution of zodiac. In the Command window, type "tab zodiac". (Alternatively, you can type "tab" and click zodiac from the Variables window into the Command window.) The Results window displays a frequency distribution of respondents' astrological signs (Figure 2-1). The value labels for each astrological code appear in the left-most column, with Aries occupying the top row of numbers and Pisces the bottom row.[2] There are three columns of numbers, labeled "Freq." (frequency), "Percent," and "Cum." (cumulative percent). What does each column mean? The frequency column shows raw frequencies, the actual number of respondents having each zodiac sign. Percent is the percentage of respondents in each category of the variable. So, for example, 340 of the 4,353 respondents, or 7.81 percent, have Aries as their astrological sign. Finally, the cumulative percent column reports the percentage of cases that fall in *or below* each value of the variable. For ordinal variables, as we will see, the cumulative percent column can provide valuable clues about how a variable is distributed. But for nominal variables, which cannot be ranked, this column provides no information of value.

Consider the percent column more closely. What is the mode, the most common astrological sign? For nominal variables, the answer to this question is (almost) always an easy call: Simply find the value with the highest percentage of responses. Virgo is the mode. Does this variable have little dispersion or a lot of dispersion? Again study the percent column. Apply the following rule: A variable has no dispersion if the cases are concentrated in one value of the variable; a variable has maximum dispersion if the cases are

Figure 2-1 Obtaining a Frequency Distribution (nominal variable)

```
. tab zodiac

Respondent'
        s
Astrologica
  l Sign        Freq.      Percent      . Cum.

     Aries        340        7.81        7.81
    Taurus        364        8.36       16.17
    Gemini        388        8.91       25.09
    Cancer        375        8.61       33.70
       Leo        387        8.89       42.59
     Virgo        393        9.03       51.62
     Libra        383        8.80       60.42
   Scorpio        322        7.40       67.82
Sagittarius       321        7.37       75.19
  Capricorn       362        8.32       83.51
   Aquarius       356        8.18       91.68
    Pisces        362        8.32      100.00

     Total      4,353      100.00
```

2. In the Results window, Stata produces a frequency distribution for zodiac.

Command

tab zodiac

1. In the Command window, type "tab zodiac". Alternatively, type "tab" and then click zodiac from the Variables list into the Command window. Press Enter.

spread evenly across all values of the variable. Are most of the cases concentrated in Virgo, or are there many cases in each value of zodiac? Since respondents show great heterogeneity in astrological signs, we would conclude that zodiac has a high level of dispersion.

DESCRIBING ORDINAL VARIABLES

Next, you will analyze and describe two ordinal-level variables, one of which has little variation and the other of which is more spread out. Scroll through the Variables list until you find these variables: helppoor and helpsick. Each of these is a 5-point ordinal scale. Helppoor asks respondents to place themselves on a scale between 1 ("The government should take action to help poor people") and 5 ("People should help themselves"). Helpsick, using a similar 5-point scale, asks respondents about government responsibility or individual responsibility for medical care.

In the Command window, type the command "tab1 helppoor helpsick" and press Enter. Why "tab1" instead of plain "tab"? When requesting frequency distributions for more than one variable in the same tabulate command, you must specify "tab1". If you go with plain "tab", Stata thinks you want a *cross*-tabulation of the listed variables—a perfectly legitimate analytic goal, but not one that suits our current purposes. (Using tabulate to perform cross-tabulation analysis is covered in Chapter 4.[3])

Back to the analysis at hand. Running "tab1 helppoor helpsick" produces two frequency distributions, one for helppoor and one for helpsick (Figure 2-2). First let's focus on the frequency distribution for helppoor. How would you describe its central tendency and dispersion? Because helppoor is an ordinal

Figure 2-2 Obtaining Frequency Distributions (ordinal variables)

```
. tab1 helppoor helpsick

-> tabulation of helppoor
```

Poor: Govt help or people help selves?	Freq.	Percent	Cum.
Govt help	369	18.85	18.85
2	204	10.42	29.26
Agree with both	915	46.73	76.00
4	261	13.33	89.33
Help selves	209	10.67	100.00
Total	1,958	100.00	

```
-> tabulation of helpsick
```

2. Two frequency distributions appear in the Results window.

Medical care: Govt help or people help selves?	Freq.	Percent	Cum.
Govt help	665	33.86	33.86
2	367	18.69	52.55
Agree with both	634	32.28	84.83
4	166	8.45	93.28
Help selves	132	6.72	100.00
Total	1,964	100.00	

Command

tab1 helppoor helpsick

1. In the Command window, type "tab1". Click helppoor and helpsick from the Variables window into the Command window. Press Enter.

variable, we can report both its mode and its median. Its mode, clearly enough, is the response "Agree with both," the option chosen by 915 respondents, or 46.73 percent of the sample. What about the median? This is where the cumulative percent column ("Cum.") of the frequency distribution comes into play. *The median for any ordinal (or interval) variable is the category below which 50 percent of the cases lie.* Is the first category, "Govt help," the median? No, this code contains fewer than half the cases. How about code 2, the next higher category? No, again. According to the cumulative percent column, only 29.26 percent of the cases fall in or below this response category. It is not until we notch up in rank, to "Agree with both," that the cumulative percentage exceeds the magic number of 50 percent. Because more than 50 percent of the cases fall in or below "Agree with both" (the cumulative percentage is equal to 76.00 percent), "Agree with both" is the median.

Does helppoor have a high or low degree of dispersion? If helppoor had a high level of variation, then the percentages of respondents in each response category would be roughly equal, much like the zodiac variable that you analyzed earlier. So roughly one-fifth of the cases would fall into each of the five response categories: 20 percent in "Govt help," 20 percent in response category "2," 20 percent in "Agree with both," 20 percent in response category "4," and 20 percent in "Help selves." If helppoor had no dispersion, then all the cases would fall into one value. That is, one value would have 100 percent of the cases, and each of the other categories would have 0 percent. Which of these two scenarios comes closest to describing the actual distribution of respondents across the values of helppoor? The equal-percentages-in-each-category, high-variation scenario? Or the 100-percent-in-one-category, low-variation scenario? It seems clear that helppoor is a variable with a relatively low degree of dispersion. "Agree with both," with 46.73 percent of the cases, contains more than twice as many cases as its nearest rival ("Govt help") and about four times as many as the other, even more thinly populated responses. What is more, both the mode and the median fall within the same category: "Agree with both."

Now turn your attention to the frequency distribution for helpsick. What is the mode? The most common response is "Govt help," containing 33.86 percent of the cases. So "Govt help" is the mode. Use the cumulative percent column to find the median. Is the first value, "Govt help," the median? No, this value contains only about a third of the cases. Now go up one value to the category labeled "2" on the 5-point ordinal scale. Is this the median? Yes, it is. According to the cumulative percent column, 52.55 percent of the cases fall in or below this value. So "Govt help" is the mode, but the median falls within response category 2, which lies a bit more toward the "Help selves" side of the variable.

Which variable, helppoor or helpsick, has higher variation? Notice that, unlike helppoor, respondents' values on helpsick are more spread out, with sizable numbers of cases falling in the first value ("Govt help") and the middle category ("Agree with both"). Indeed, these two quite different responses are close rivals for the distinction of being the modal opinion on this issue. And, unlike helppoor, helpsick's mode and median are different, providing a useful field mark of higher variation. Thus helpsick has more variation—greater dispersion—than helppoor.

DESCRIBING INTERVAL VARIABLES

We now turn to the descriptive analysis of interval-level variables. An interval-level variable represents the most precise level of measurement. Unlike nominal variables, whose values stand for categories, and ordinal variables, whose values can be ranked, the values of an interval variable *tell us the exact quantity of the characteristic being measured*. For example, age qualifies as an interval-level variable since its values impart each respondent's age in years.

Because interval variables have the most precision, they can be described more completely than can nominal or ordinal variables. For any interval-level variable, we can report its mode, median, and arithmetic average, or *mean*. In addition to these measures of central tendency, we can make more sophisticated judgments about variation. Specifically, we can determine if an interval-level distribution is *skewed*. What is skewness and how do you know it when you see it?

Skewness refers to the symmetry of a distribution. If a distribution is not skewed, the cases tend to cluster symmetrically around the mean of the distribution, and they taper off evenly for values above and below the mean. If a distribution is skewed, by contrast, one tail of the distribution is longer and skinnier than the other tail. Distributions in which a small number of cases occupy extremely high values of an interval variable—distributions with a skinnier right-hand tail—are said to have a *positive skew*. By the same token, if the distribution has a few cases at the extreme lower end—the distribution has a skinnier left-hand tail—then the distribution has a *negative skew*. Skewness has a predictable effect on the mean. A positive skew tends to pull the mean upward; a negative skew pulls it downward. However, skewness has less effect on the median. Since the median reports the middle-most value of a distribution, it is not tugged upward or downward by extreme values. *For badly skewed distributions, it is a good practice to use the median instead of the mean in describing central tendency.* A step-by-step analysis of a gss2006 variable, age, will clarify these points.

In obtaining descriptive information for a nominal or an ordinal variable, tab (or tab1) is the command of choice. The tab command also is useful for describing an interval-level variable, providing that the variable has, say, thirty or fewer values. (For several of the exercises at the end of this chapter, you will use tab to help describe interval variables.) For an interval variable with many unique values, such as age, tab is somewhat less informative. Typing "tab age" in the Command window elicits this response from Stata:

Age of respondent	Freq.	Percent	Cum.
18	19	0.42	0.42
19	47	1.05	1.47
20	50	1.11	2.58
21	52	1.16	3.74
22	72	1.60	5.34
23	63	1.40	6.75
24	61	1.36	8.10
25	74	1.65	9.75
26	83	1.85	11.60
27	86	1.91	13.51
28	80	1.78	15.29
29	79	1.76	17.05
30	84	1.87	18.92
31	67	1.49	20.41
32	97	2.16	22.57
33	88	1.96	24.53
34	91	2.03	26.56
35	80	1.78	28.34
36	105	2.34	30.68
37	89	1.98	32.66
38	94	2.09	34.75
39	95	2.11	36.87
40	95	2.11	38.98
41	94	2.09	41.07
42	99	2.20	43.28
43	95	2.11	45.39
44	100	2.23	47.62
45	79	1.76	49.38
46	90	2.00	51.38
47	110	2.45	53.83
48	109	2.43	56.26
49	97	2.16	58.41
50	93	2.07	60.49
51	76	1.69	62.18
52	78	1.74	63.91
53	89	1.98	65.89
54	96	2.14	68.03
55	86	1.91	69.95
56	68	1.51	71.46
57	58	1.29	72.75
58	81	1.80	74.55
59	78	1.74	76.29
60	75	1.67	77.96
61	57	1.27	79.23
62	58	1.29	80.52
63	62	1.38	81.90
64	56	1.25	83.15
65	42	0.93	84.08
66	53	1.18	85.26
67	45	1.00	86.26
68	41	0.91	87.18
69	42	0.93	88.11
70	41	0.91	89.02
71	39	0.87	89.89
72	48	1.07	90.96
73	29	0.65	91.61
74	33	0.73	92.34
75	39	0.87	93.21
76	31	0.69	93.90
77	33	0.73	94.63
78	28	0.62	95.26
79	22	0.49	95.75
80	27	0.60	96.35
81	25	0.56	96.91
82	21	0.47	97.37
83	19	0.42	97.80
84	17	0.38	98.17
85	18	0.40	98.58
86	17	0.38	98.95
87	7	0.16	99.11
88	11	0.24	99.35
89 or older	29	0.65	100.00
Total	4,492	100.00	

The cumulative percent column leads us directly to the median age: 46 (cumulative percentage, 51.38). But locating the modal age is a chore.[4]

Although tab may (or may not) be a valuable descriptive tool for interval-level variables, summarize will always fill the bill. Go ahead and type "sum age" in the Command window and press Enter:

```
. sum age
```

Variable	Obs	Mean	Std. Dev.	Min	Max
age	4492	47.14159	16.89426	18	89

Stata tells us the number of respondents or observations in the data ("Obs"), the mean age, the standard deviation of the distribution ("Std. Dev."), and the minimum and maximum observed values. By running summarize on its defaults, you can get a quick and concise profile of any interval variable in the dataset. But because we are after a more detailed description, we will need to append an option to the summarize command.

Make sure that the Command window is highlighted. Do this: Press the Page Up key, returning the previous command, "sum age," to the command line. Now modify "sum age" to read "sum age, detail" or "sum age, d". The detail option, not surprisingly, instructs Stata to provide a fuller description of the variable. Press Enter and consider the Results window (Figure 2-3). We now have a wealth of information about age. The mean age is about 47 years. The median age, 46 years, also is displayed. Notice the two left-hand columns of numbers, under the heading "Percentiles." Percentiles are synonymous with cumulative percentages. So, the left-most column displays cumulative percentages in ascending order ("1%, 5%, 10%, . . . 99%"). The next column lists corresponding values of the age variable. Thus the pairing "25%   34" can be read, "25 percent of respondents are age 34 or younger." And the pairing "50%   46" means, "50 percent of respondents are age 46 or younger." The median is the same as the 50th percentile. To find the median of an interval-level variable, run summarize with the detail option and look for the value of the variable that is associated with "50%" in the percentiles column.

All right, we have discovered that the mean age, at 47.14159, is higher than the median age of 46. What does this comparison tell us about the skewness of the distribution? When a distribution is perfectly symmetrical—no skew—its mean will be equal to its median and it will have a skewness equal to zero. If the mean is lower than the median—that is, if a few extremely low values pull the mean down, away from the center of the distribution—the distribution has a negative skew. If the mean is higher than the median, as is the case with our current analysis, the distribution has a positive skew. Thus it comes as no shock that Stata has reported a positive value for the skewness statistic: .3841628, or about .38.

Just about all distributions will have some degree of skewness. How much is too much? The Stata command sktest can help us decide whether a variable is significantly skewed. The syntax for the sktest command is as follows:

sktest *varname*

For the gss2006 variable age, type "sktest age" and press Enter:

```
. sktest age
```

Skewness/Kurtosis tests for Normality

Variable	Obs	Pr(Skewness)	Pr(Kurtosis)	adj chi2(2)	joint Prob>chi2
age	4.5e+03	0.0000	0.0000	.	0.0000

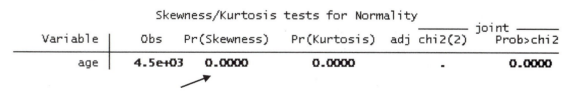

Focus on the value beneath the label, "Pr(Skewness)." Here is a rule: If the Pr(Skewness) value is less than .05, then the distribution is significantly skewed, and you should use the median as the best measure of

Figure 2-3 Obtaining Summary Information (interval variable)

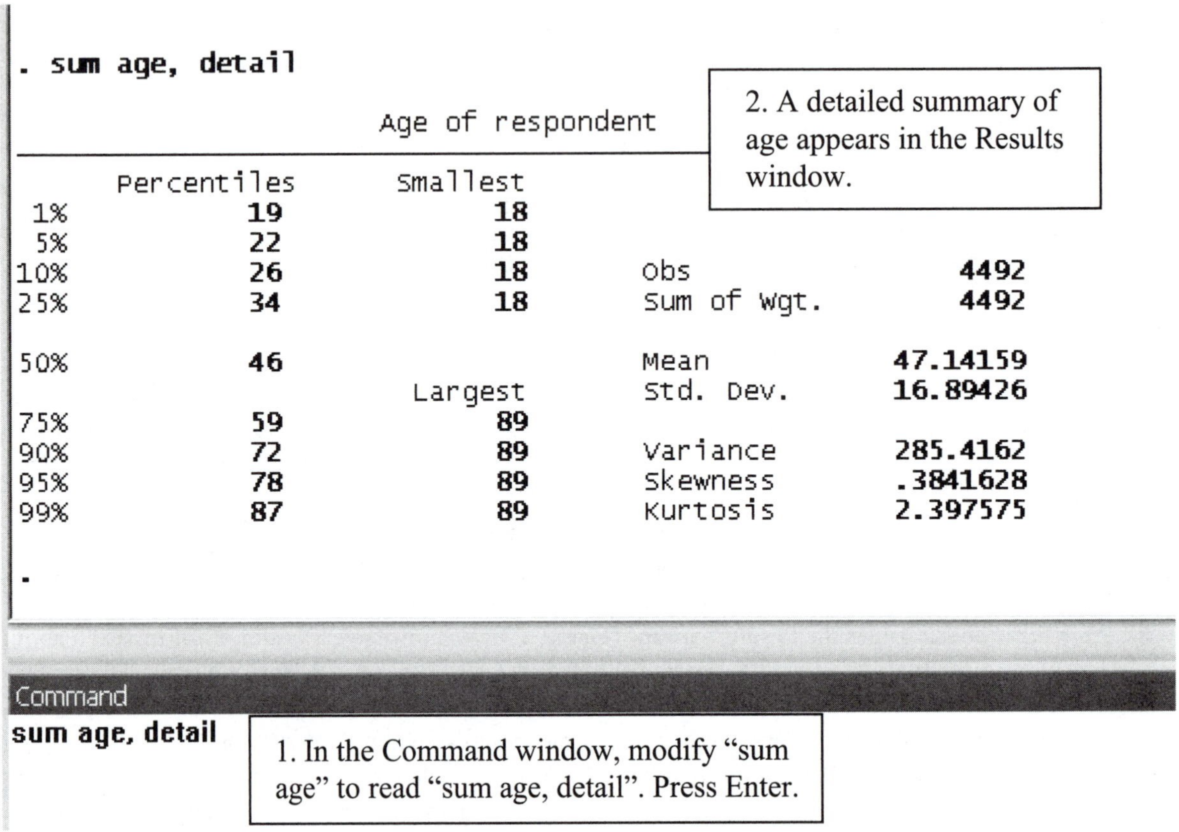

```
. sum age, detail

                            Age of respondent          2. A detailed summary of
                                                        age appears in the Results
          Percentiles     Smallest                      window.
    1%         19             18
    5%         22             18
   10%         26             18         Obs                   4492
   25%         34             18         Sum of wgt.           4492

   50%         46                        Mean              47.14159
                            Largest      Std. Dev.         16.89426
   75%         59             89
   90%         72             89         Variance          285.4162
   95%         78             89         Skewness          .3841628
   99%         87             89         Kurtosis          2.397575

.
```

Command

sum age, detail   1. In the Command window, modify "sum age" to read "sum age, detail". Press Enter.

central tendency. If the Pr(Skewness) value is equal to or greater than .05, then the distribution is not significantly skewed. Use the mean as the best measure of central tendency.[5] In the case of the age variable, there must be a number of cases in the upper reaches of this variable that have pulled the mean off the exact fifty-fifty center, creating a distribution that is significantly skewed. In this situation, the median should be used to describe the central tendency of the distribution.[6]

OBTAINING BAR CHARTS AND HISTOGRAMS

Thus far you have learned to wring a fair amount of information out of a dry handful of numbers: the mode, median, mean, skewness, and the standard error of skewness. Visual displays can add richness and nuance to these numerical descriptions of central tendency and variation. Two related types of graphs provide appropriate support for descriptive statistics. For nominal and ordinal variables, a *bar chart* is used. A bar chart displays each value of a variable and shows you the percentage of cases that fall into each category. Bar charts can also be used for interval variables that have a manageable number of values—generally 30 or fewer. For an interval variable with many values, a *histogram* is generally a better choice. A histogram is similar to a bar chart, but instead of displaying each discrete value, it collapses categories into ranges (called bins), resulting in a compact display.

Stata's histogram command will produce either a bar chart or a histogram. (Confusingly, Stata also has a bar chart command: graph bar. The graph bar command will come into play in Chapter 4, when we consider how to depict the relationship between two variables.) In the next section, we will create a bar chart of zodiac using the histogram command and Stata's enormously flexible Graph Editor. For the zodiac example, we will start with the finished product and then demonstrate how it was built. We then create a histogram of age—again using the command line to frame a bare-bones graph and deploying the Graph Editor to add essential content and style.

Creating Bar Charts

Figure 2-4 displays a finished bar chart of zodiac. Several features are worth noting. First, the y-axis records the percentage of respondents falling into each category of zodiac. The use of percentages makes the chart directly analogous to zodiac's frequency distribution, which you analyzed earlier. There are 12 tick marks along the x-axis, one for each category of zodiac. The ticks are labeled using zodiac's value labels, from "Aries" (numeric code 1 on zodiac) to "Pisces" (code 12). Because each tick is labeled—and because some of the label names, such as "Sagittarius" and "Capricorn," are pretty long—the value labels appear in smallish font, and they are angled at 45 degrees. These adjustments help to make the labels readable. Plus, they don't run into each other, as they would if they were displayed horizontally along the axis.

Let's build the bar chart, roughing it out from the Command window and honing it in the Graph Editor. Consider the command: "hist zodiac, d percent". The term "hist" is an acceptable abbreviation for the histogram command, and "zodiac" names the variable we are graphing. When we use histogram to produce a bar chart of a nominal or an ordinal variable (or an interval variable having 30 or fewer values), we must include the two options that appear to the right of the comma: "d percent". In what ways do these options modify Stata defaults? The term "d" stands for "discrete" data. By default, the histogram command assumes we wish to graph an interval-level variable with many unique values (continuous data), not a nominal- or an ordinal-level variable (discrete data). Because zodiac is a nominal variable,

Figure 2-4   Bar Chart of a Nominal Variable

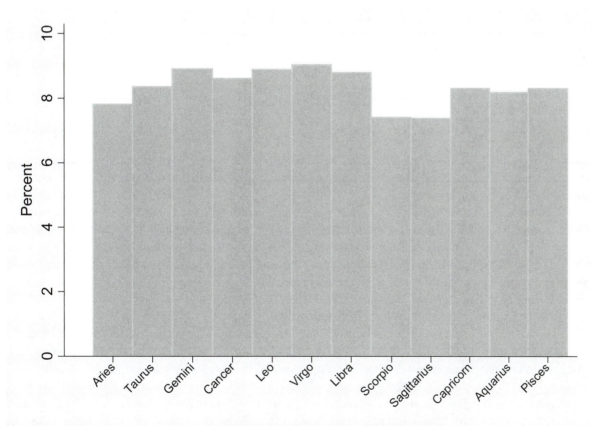

Figure 2-5 Obtaining a Bar Chart of a Nominal Variable

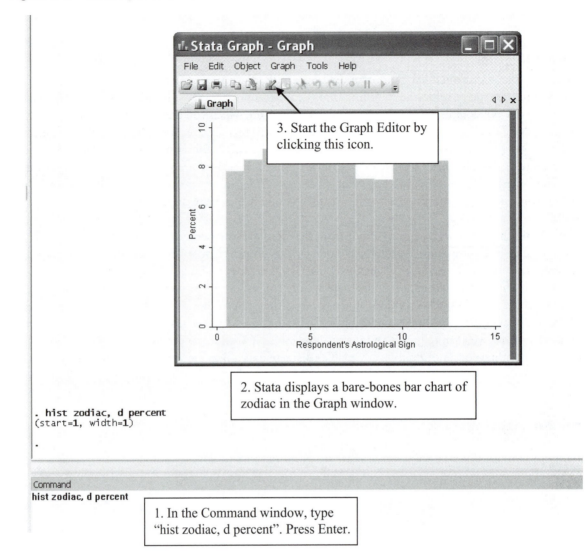

we need to specify "d" for discrete. The term "percent" tells Stata that we want the bars to represent the percentages of respondents in each category of zodiac. (By default, Stata will graph densities, not percentages.)

Click in the Command window. Type "hist zodiac, d percent" and press Enter. In short order, a bar chart appears in a separate window above the Results window, as shown in Figure 2-5. A comparison of the raw product (Figure 2-5) with the final product (Figure 2-4) shows that several features are already in place. The axis titles ("Respondent's Astrological Sign" and "Percent") are acceptable, and the y-axis tick marks are nicely scaled and legible. And, of course, the 12 bars represent the percentages of respondents falling into each category of zodiac. However, the x-axis value labels ("0," "5," "10," and "15") are default-driven nonsense. Let's ask the Graph Editor to remedy this situation.

To open the Graph Editor, click the Start Graph Editor icon on the graph toolbar, as shown in Figure 2-5. Take a few minutes to take stock of the editing environment (Figure 2-6). Notice the Tools Toolbar along the left margin of the graph. For most editing purposes, the Pointer tool default (which, clearly enough, is just the mouse) will be the main vehicle for navigating the Graph Editor. In a nutshell, here is how the editor works: The user selects an object for editing, which the editor outlines in red. The Contextual Toolbar, the main workhorse for most tasks, displays the editable features of the selected object. To make revisions, the user clicks drop-downs or types text on the Contextual Toolbar. For objects that already

Figure 2-6 Graph Editor

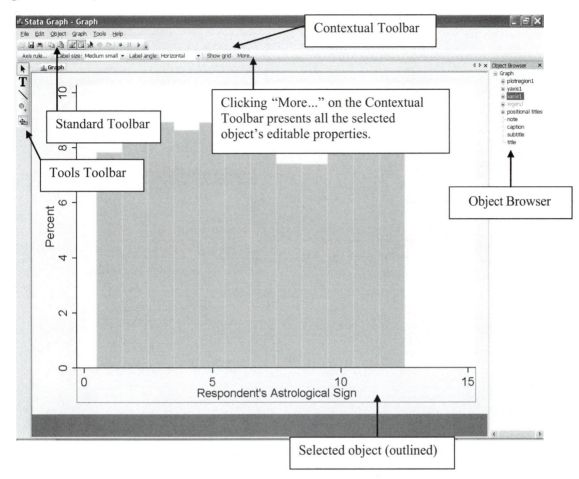

exist within the graph, you can select them with the mouse by simply clicking on them. The Object Browser, which occupies the right-hand margin of the editor, may be used to select existing objects or to add content, such as text, titles, and notes. For example, because we want to add value labels and tick marks to the x-axis—one small-font, diagonally angled label for each bar—we first would bring the mouse to the Object Browser and click on "xaxis1," which is already highlighted in Figure 2-6. Stata selects the x-axis elements, outlining them in red. The Contextual Toolbar responds to our choice by showing us the elements we can change quickly (Axis rule, Label size, Label angle) and those that require some extra clicks (the More button, which displays Extended Properties). In this example, we will go ahead and make all the desired changes by clicking More and working with Extended Properties.

On the Contextual Toolbar, click More. Because the x-axis is selected in the Object Browser, clicking More will open the Axis properties window (Figure 2-7). There are two panels, Axis rule and Global properties. In the Axis rule panel, we must convince Stata to give us 12 tick marks, one for each value of zodiac. This seemingly innocuous request requires familiarity with an obscure bit of Stata-speak. First, click the radio button next to Range/Delta, which wakes up three boxes: Minimum value, Maximum value, and Delta (Figure 2-8). What does Stata mean by Range/Delta? Stata needs to be micromanaged. We've got to tell it the exact format for the x-axis labels. Using the variable's numeric codes (not its value labels), we must specify the first coded value to be labeled, the last coded value to be labeled, and the increment ("delta") to use (label every value? every other value? every fifth value? . . . and so on). Zodiac's first numeric code is 1 (labeled "Aries") and its last numeric code is 12 (labeled "Pisces"). And because we want each value of zodiac to be labeled—no label is to be skipped!—we would specify a Delta value of 1. So, for zodiac, we would type "1" in the Minimum value box, "12" in the Maximum

Figure 2-7 Axis properties Window

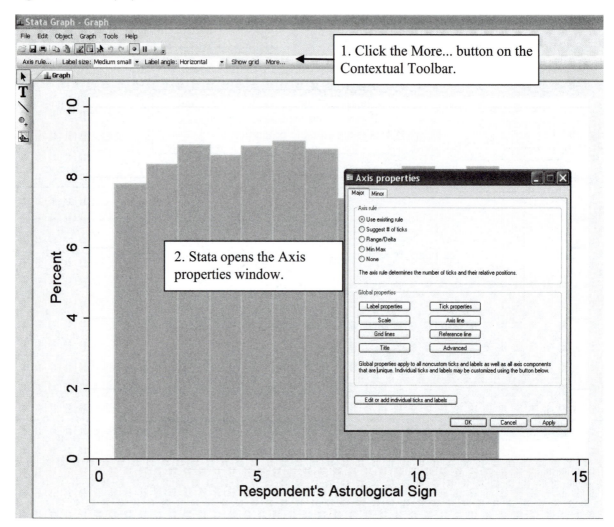

value box, and "1" in the Delta box, as shown in Figure 2-8. Click Apply. Stata labels each value of zodiac with its numeric code.

Now for some less esoteric fare. In the Global properties panel, click the Label properties button (Figure 2-9). By default, Stata will label the x-axis values with numeric codes, not value labels. Request value labels by clicking the Use value labels checkbox, step 2 in Figure 2-9. While we are here, let's go ahead and obtain the desired font size (Small) and label angle (45 degrees), as shown in Figure 2-9. Click Apply. Stata replaces zodiac's numeric codes with its value labels, angled at a very readable 45 degrees. Clicking OK closes the Axis label properties pop-up and returns us to the Axis properties window. To view the edited product, click OK (Figure 2-10). Not too bad.

Do this: Save the graph by clicking the Save file icon. (Refer to Figure 2-10.) Find an appropriate location and pick a descriptive name, such as "zodiac." Stata will supply the .gph extension. The graph can be reopened by clicking File→Open→[file of type]*.gph from the Stata main menu. (If you are running Stata 10: File→Open Graph.) Stop the Graph Editor by clicking the Graph Editor icon (Figure 2-10). Do you want to copy the image to a word processor, or send it to the printer? Right-click on the graph and make a choice. (The Graph Editor Recorder, activated by the user during editing sessions, offers an alternative method for recording, saving, and retrieving your work. See "A Closer Look" for a description of the Graph Editor Recorder.)

Figure 2-8 Changing the Axis Rule for the x-axis

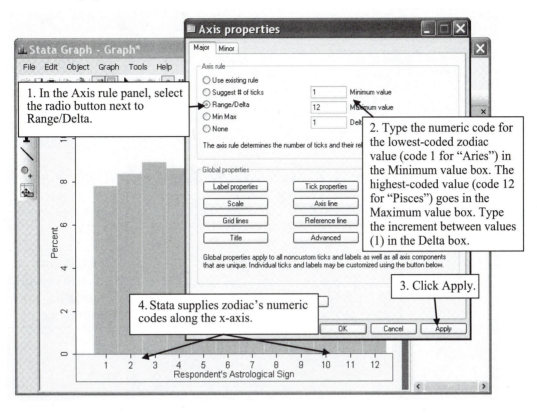

Figure 2-9 Changing the Axis Label Properties for the x-axis

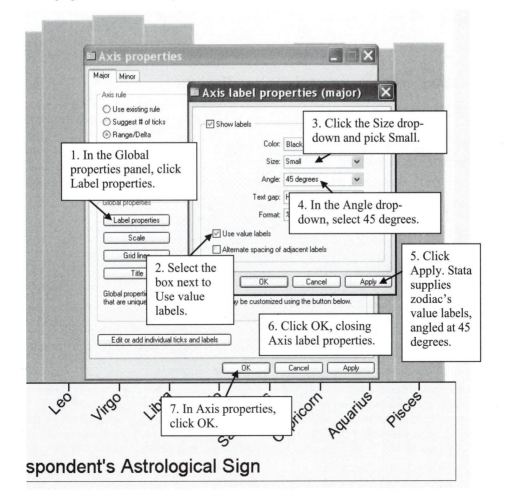

Figure 2-10 Edited Bar Chart

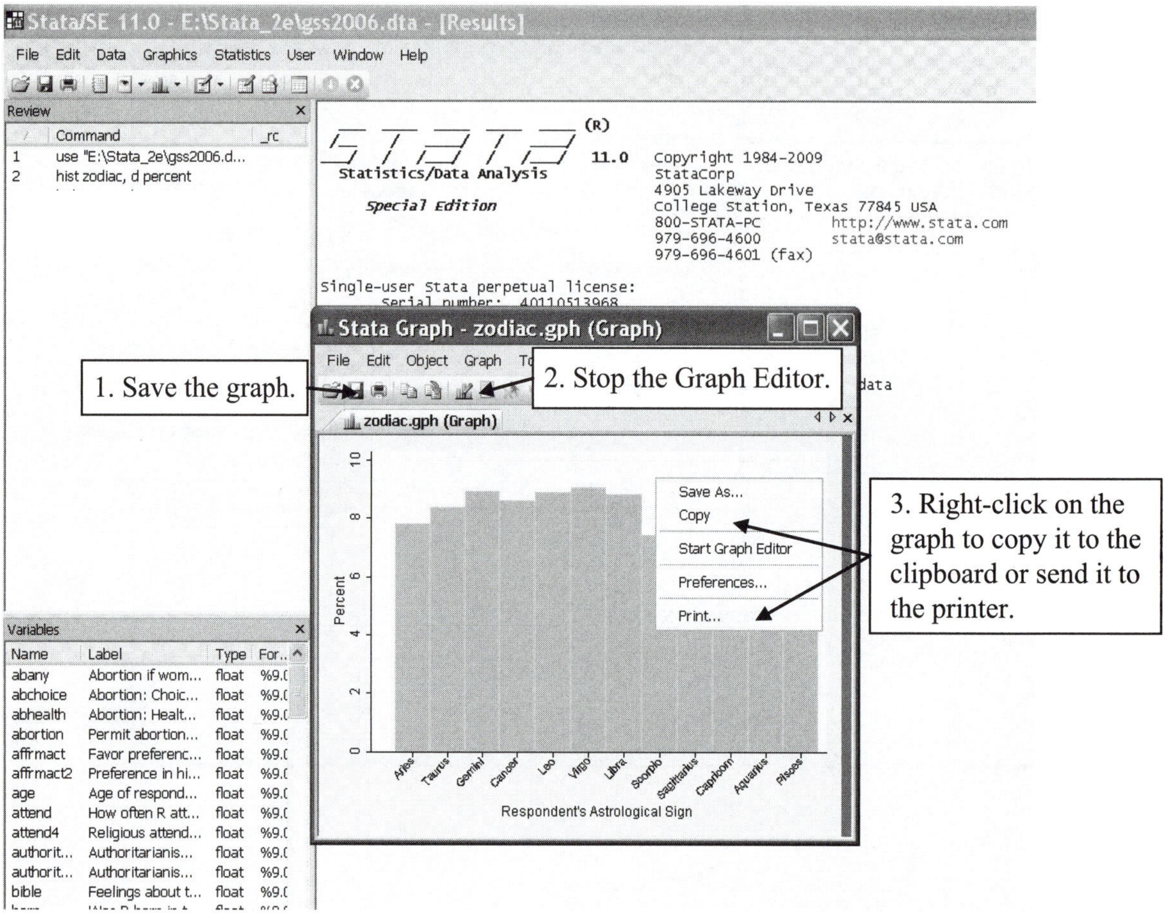

A **Closer Look** **Graph Editor Recorder**

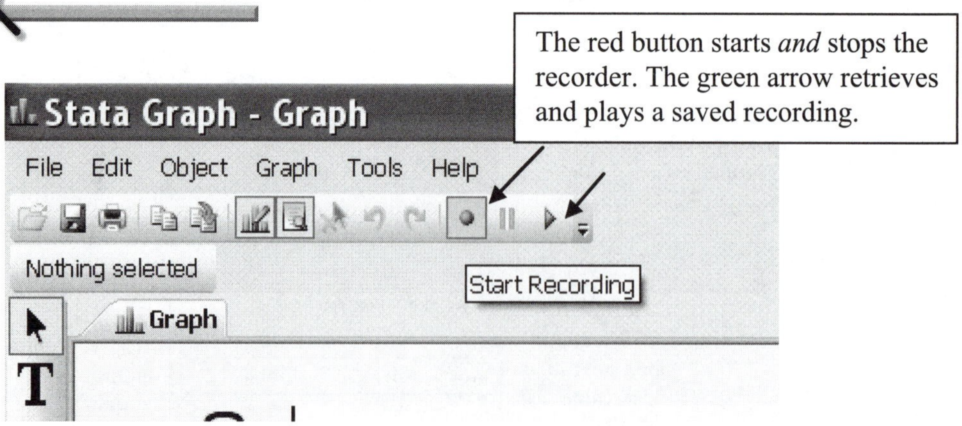

The red button starts *and* stops the recorder. The green arrow retrieves and plays a saved recording.

The Graph Editor Recorder, as its name suggests, keeps a save-able and retrievable record of the edits you make to your graphs. Certainly, the recorder is a handy way to capture all your changes to a specific graph: Switch it on when you start the editor and switch it off (and save the recording) before you stop the editor. This feature also provides an efficient way to record generic preferences that you want to apply to any new graph. For example, suppose you like small font labels and prefer blue bar chart bars to Stata's default. Start the Graph Editor and click the red recording button. After making the generic edits (font sizes, bar colors, or labeling conventions), stop recording and save the record, giving it a descriptive file name. To apply these preferences to a new graph, start the Graph Editor and click the green arrow. By retrieving the earlier recording—Stata will anticipate this step—you can automatically apply the earlier edits to the current project.

Figure 2-11 Obtaining a Histogram of an Interval Variable

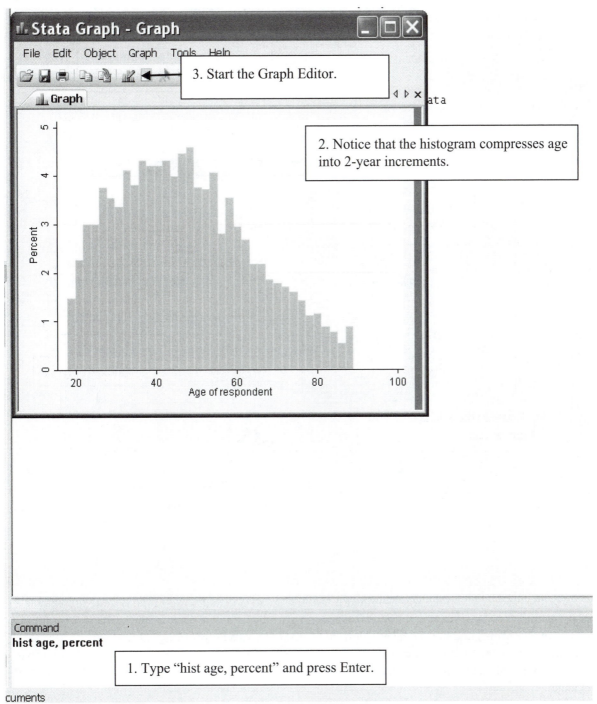

Creating Histograms

Now let's create a histogram of age, again obtaining a crude beginning from the command line and a refined outcome from the Graph Editor. Click in the Command window. Because age is an interval-level variable (in Stata's lexicon, a continuous variable), we drop the "d" from the options list: "hist age, percent". Type the command and press Enter. (Refer to Figure 2-11.) Notice that the histogram's graphic signature—combining adjacent values of a variable—results in a compact, readable display. One can easily locate the center of the distribution (46–47 years of age). And the skinny right-hand tail reaffirms the presence of the positive skew we found in our numerical analysis.

Figure 2-12 Changing the Axis Rule for a Histogram

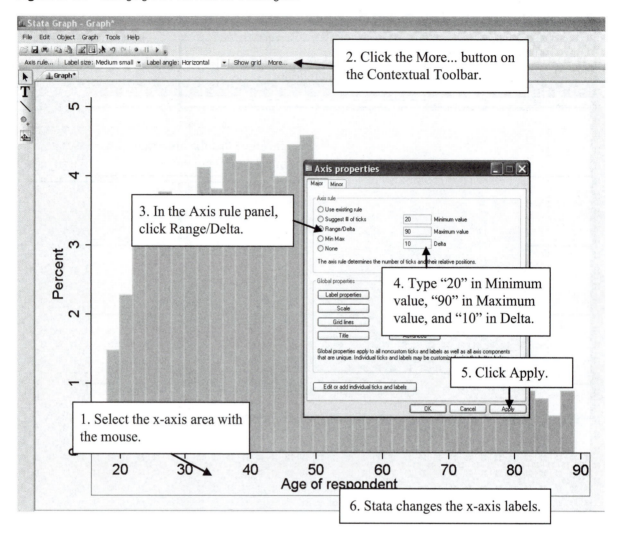

For the product of a three-word command running on Stata defaults, this graph is quite presentable as is. A curmudgeon, however, might find two aspects to grumble about: the x-axis labels (this is a common source of complaint) and the bland bar color. Currently, the x-axis ranges from "20" to "100" in 20-year increments. Suppose we prefer that it range from "20" to "90" in 10-year increments. Suppose further that we plan to print in color, and so prefer a bolder color for the bars. Start the Graph Editor, and let's make the changes.

Select the x-axis in the Object Browser, or simply click in the x-axis area with the mouse (Figure 2-12). Click More on the Contextual Toolbar. Here we are once again—in the Axis properties window. (Refer to Figure 2-12.) What syntax would be appropriate for the Range/Delta boxes? Remember that we want the x-axis to range from 20 to 90 in 10-year increments: "20," "30," "40," . . . "90." Therefore, type "20" in Minimum value, "90" in Maximum value, and "10" in Delta. Click Apply. Looks right. Click OK. The Range/Delta routine is getting to be old hat.

To change the bar color, click on any bar. Stata selects all the bars (Figure 2-13). On the Contextual Toolbar, click More. This opens the Bar properties window. Click the Color drop-down, make a choice, and click Apply. Do you like what you see? Click OK. Save the graph and stop the Graph Editor. Our command-line work produced a serviceable result, but the edited version is even better (Figure 2-14).

Figure 2-13   Changing the Bar Color in Bar properties

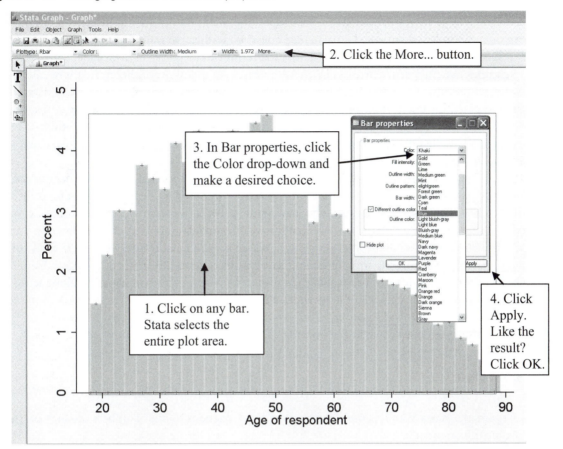

Figure 2-14   Edited Histogram

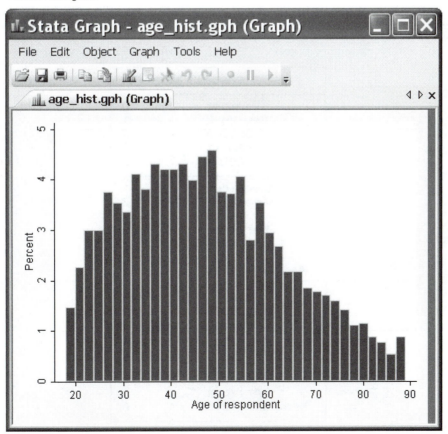

OBTAINING CASE-LEVEL INFORMATION WITH SORT AND LIST

When we analyze a large survey dataset, as we have just done, we generally are not interested in how respondent x or respondent y answered a particular question. Rather, we want to know how the entire sample of respondents distributed themselves across the response categories of a variable. Sometimes, however, we gather data on particular cases because the cases are themselves inherently important. The states dataset (50 cases) and the world dataset (191 cases) are good examples. With these datasets, we may want to push the descriptions beyond the relative anonymity of a tabulate analysis or a summary command and find out where particular cases "are" on an interesting variable. Stata's sort and list commands are readymade for such elemental insights. Before beginning this guided example, close gss2006 and open states.

Suppose that we are interested in studying state laws that regulate abortion. The states dataset contains the variable abortlaw, which records the number of restrictions imposed by each state, from no restrictions (a value of 0 on abortlaw) to 10 restrictions (abortlaw value of 10). If we were to run "tab abortlaw", we would find that one state has 0 restrictions, two states have 10, and a fair amount of variation exists among states. But exactly which states are the least restrictive? Which are the most restrictive? Where does your state fall on the list? By enlisting the sort command, we can sort states on the basis of abortlaw, from lower values to higher values.[7] The list command will then display the sorted values of abortlaw along with, at our request, the name of each state. (The states dataset contains the variable state, which records the states' names.)

With the states dataset open, click in the Command window, and type this command:

`sort abortlaw`

Stata silently sorts the states from low numbers of abortion restrictions to high numbers of abortion restrictions. Now type this command:

`list state abortlaw`

Stata responds by giving us a table reporting which states go with which values of abortlaw:

state	abortlaw
Vermont	0
New York	1
Oregon	1
Hawaii	1
Washington	1
Connecticut	1
New Hampshire	2
Maine	3
Maryland	3
California	3
Massachusetts	4
New Jersey	5
Alaska	5
Minnesota	5
North Carolina	5
New Mexico	5
Wyoming	5
Colorado	5
Arizona	5
West Virginia	6

Nevada	6
Montana	6
Illinois	6
Iowa	6
Florida	7
Delaware	7
Texas	7
Pennsylvania	7
Kansas	7
Virginia	8
Alabama	8
Tennessee	8
Utah	8
Wisconsin	8
Indiana	8
Mississippi	8
Idaho	9
Louisiana	9
Georgia	9
South Dakota	9
Ohio	9
Rhode Island	9
Arkansas	9
Michigan	9
Missouri	9
Oklahoma	9
South Carolina	9
Nebraska	9
Kentucky	10
North Dakota	10

Vermont has no restrictions; a varied group of states (New York, Oregon, Hawaii, Washington, and Connecticut) have one restriction. At the other end of the scale, a large contingent of twelve states have nine restrictions each, and two (Kentucky and North Dakota) have ten.

EXERCISES

Before beginning these exercises, make sure that you have a log file open and running.

1. (Dataset: gss2006. Variables: stoprndm, tapphone, wotrial.) We frequently describe public opinion by referring to how citizens distribute themselves on a political issue. *Consensus* is a situation in which just about everyone, 80–90 percent of the public, holds the same position (or very similar positions) on an issue. *Dissensus* is a situation in which opinion is spread out pretty evenly across all positions on an issue. *Polarization* refers to a configuration of opinion in which people are split between two extreme poles of an issue, with only a few individuals populating the more moderate, middle-of-the-road positions. In this exercise you will decide whether consensus, dissensus, or polarization best describes public opinion on each of three civil liberties issues.

The 2006 General Social Survey asked respondents to "suppose [that] the government suspected that a terrorist act was about to happen." Respondents were then asked whether "the authorities should have the right to" do each of three things: stop and search people in the street at random (stoprndm), tap people's telephone conversations (tapphone), or detain people for as long as they want without putting them on trial (wotrial). For each variable, responses are coded 0 (authorities definitely should have the right), 1 (authorities probably should have the right), 2 (authorities probably should not have the right), and 3 (authorities definitely should not have the right). So lower codes denote stronger pro-security opinions and higher codes denote stronger pro-civil-liberties opinions.

A. Open gss2006. Run the command "tab1 stoprndm tapphone wotrial". Refer to the percent column of the frequency distributions of stoprndm, tapphone, and wotrial. In the table that follows, write in the appropriate percent next to each question mark (?):

Should authorities have right?	stoprndm Percent	tapphone Percent	wotrial Percent
Definitely yes	?	?	?
Probably yes	?	?	?
Probably no	?	?	?
Definitely no	?	?	?
Total	100.0	100.0	100.0

B. Examine the percentages in part A. Which of the following statements is supported by your analysis? (check one)

❑ The public is polarized on the question of whether the authorities should have the right to stop and search people in the street.

❑ Dissensus exists on the question of whether the authorities should have the right to detain people for as long as they want without putting them on trial.

❑ On all three civil liberties questions, most people respond, "Probably yes," when asked whether authorities should have the right.

C. Suppose that a group of civil libertarians sought to build a strong pro-civil-liberties consensus on one of these three issues. On which issue would the group stand the best chance of succeeding? (circle one)

Stop and search people   Tap telephone conversations   Detain people without trial

Briefly explain your reasoning. _____

_____

_____

D. Use the histogram command to create a bar chart of the variable you chose in part C. Because you are dealing with a discrete variable, make sure to specify the "d percent" options. In the Graph Editor, make the following changes to the x-axis. (i) Change the axis rule to range from 0 to 3 in increments of 1. (ii) In label properties, specify "Use value labels." (iii) Change label size to small. (Leave the default angle, horizontal, as it is.) Print the bar chart you have created.

2. (Dataset: gss2006. Variable: science_quiz.) The late Carl Sagan once lamented: "We live in a society exquisitely dependent on science and technology, in which hardly anyone knows anything about science and technology." This is a rather pessimistic assessment of the scientific acumen of ordinary Americans. Sagan seemed to be suggesting that the average level of scientific knowledge is quite low and that most people would fail even the simplest test of scientific facts.

Dataset gss2006 contains science_quiz, which was created from 10 true-false questions testing respondents' knowledge of basic scientific facts. Values on science_quiz range from 0 (the respondent did not answer any of the questions correctly) to 10 (the respondent correctly answered all 10).[8]

A. Consider three possible scenarios for the distribution of science_quiz. All three scenarios assume that science_quiz has a median value of 6 on the 10-item scale. In scenario X, science_quiz has no skew. In scenario Y, science_quiz has a positive skew. In scenario Z, science_quiz has a negative skew.

Below are three graphic shells, labeled Scenario X, Scenario Y, and Scenario Z. Sketch a curved line or a set of bar-chart bars within each shell, depicting what the distribution of science_quiz would look like if that scenario were accurate.

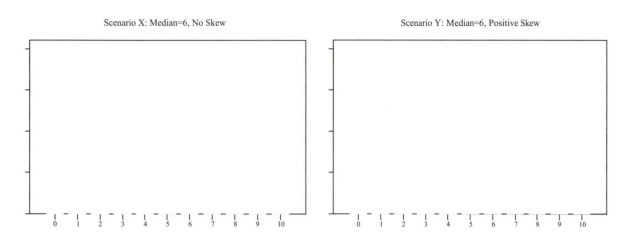

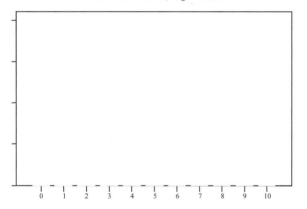

B. Run "tab science_quiz" to obtain a frequency distribution of science_quiz. Fill in the table that follows.

science_quiz	Frequency	Percent	Cumulative Percent
0	?	?	?
1	?	?	?
2	?	?	?
3	?	?	?
4	?	?	?
5	?	?	?
6	?	?	?
7	?	?	?
8	?	?	?
9	?	?	?
10	?	?	100.0
Total	?	100.0	

C. Use histogram to create a bar chart of science_quiz. Make sure to specify the "d percent" options. In the Graph Editor, change the x-axis so that its values range from 0 to 10 in increments of 1. (You could also edit the x-axis title to read, "Number Correct on 10-Item Science Quiz". Though not discussed in this chapter, axis-title changes are accomplished easily by clicking directly on the existing title, typing a new title in the appropriate box on Contextual Toolbar, and pressing Enter.) Print the bar chart.

D. Examine the frequency distribution and the bar chart. Based on your analysis, which scenario does the distribution of science_quiz most closely approximate? (circle one)

Scenario X   Scenario Y   Scenario Z

Briefly explain your reasoning. _____

_____

_____

E. According to conventional academic standards, any science_quiz score of 5 or lower would be an F, a failing grade. A score of 6 would be a grade of D, a 7 would be a C, an 8 a B, and scores of 9 or 10 would be an A. Based on these standards, about what percentage of people got passing grades on science_quiz? (circle one)

About 30 percent   About 40 percent   About 50 percent   About 60 percent

What percentage got a C or better? (circle one)

About 30 percent   About 40 percent   About 50 percent   About 60 percent

3. (Dataset: gss2006. Variable: fem_role). Two pundits are arguing about how the general public views the role of women in the home and in politics.

Pundit 1: "Our society has a sizable minority of traditionally minded individuals who think that the proper 'place' for women is taking care of the home and caring for children. This small but vocal group of traditionalists aside, the typical adult supports the idea that women belong in work and in politics."

Pundit 2: "Poppycock! It's just the opposite. The extremist 'women's liberation' crowd has distorted the overall picture. The typical view among most citizens is that women should be in the home, not in work and politics."

A. Dataset gss2006 contains fem_role, an interval-level variable that measures respondents' attitudes toward women in society and politics. Scores can range from 0 (women belong in the home) to 12 (women belong in work and politics).

If pundit 1 is correct, fem_role will have (circle one)

a negative skew.   no skew.   a positive skew.

If pundit 2 is correct, fem_role will have (circle one)

a negative skew.   no skew.   a positive skew.

If pundit 1 is correct, fem_role's mean will be (circle one)

lower than its median.   the same as its median.   higher than its median.

If pundit 2 is correct, fem_role's mean will be (circle one)

lower than its median.   the same as its median.   higher than its median.

B. (i) Run "sum fem_role, detail". (ii) Run "sktest fem_role". Fill in the table that follows:

Statistics for fem_role	
Mean	?
Median	?
Skewness	?
Pr(Skewness)	?

C. Obtain a bar chart of fem_role by running histogram with the "d percent" options. (Even though we are treating fem_role as an interval variable, the "d" option works nicely for interval variables having fewer than 30 values.) (i) Edit the x-axis to range from 0 to 12 in increments of 1. (ii) Request "Use value labels." (iii) Change the font size to small and the label angle to 45 degrees. (iv) Choose a different bar color. (v) Print the bar chart.

D. Consider the evidence you obtained in parts B and C. Based on your analysis, whose assessment is more accurate? (circle one)

Pundit 1's   Pundit 2's

Citing *specific evidence* obtained in parts B and C, explain your reasoning. _____

_____

_____

_____

_____

_____

_____

4. (Dataset: gss2006. Variable: attend.) The General Social Survey provides a rich array of variables that permit scholars to study religiosity among the adult population. Dataset gss2006 contains attend, a 9-point ordinal scale that measures how often respondents attend religious services. Values can range from 0 ("Never attend") to 8 ("Attend more than once a week").

A. The shell of a bar chart is given below. The categories of attend appear along the horizontal axis. What would a bar chart of attend look like if this variable had maximum dispersion? Sketch inside the axes a bar chart that would depict maximum dispersion.

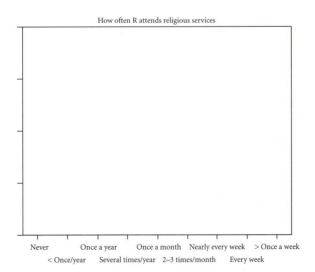

B. What would a bar chart of attend look like if this variable had no dispersion? Sketch inside the axes a bar chart that would depict no dispersion.

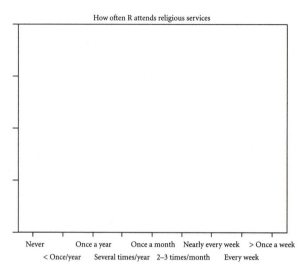

C. Perform a tabulate analysis of attend. Complete the following table:

How often R attends religious services	Frequency	Percent	Cumulative Percent
Never	1,020	?	?
<Once/year	302	?	?
Once a year	571	?	?
Several times/year	502	?	?
Once a month	308	?	?
2–3 times/month	380	?	?
Nearly every week	240	?	?
Every week	839	?	?
>Once a week	329	?	100.00
Total	4,491	100.0	

D. (i) Use histogram to obtain a bar chart of attend. (Remember that attend is a discrete variable.) (ii) Edit the x-axis to range from 0 to 8 in increments of 1. (iii) Request value labels. (iv) Change the size to small and the angle to 45 degrees. (v) Print the bar chart.

E. Based on your examination of the frequency distribution,

the mode of attend is _____.   the median of attend is _____.

F. Based on your examination of the frequency distribution and bar chart, you would conclude that attend has (circle one)

low dispersion.   high dispersion.

5. (Dataset: world. Variable: women09.) What percentage of members of the U.S. House of Representatives are women? In 2009 the value was 16.8 percent, according to the Inter-Parliamentary Union, an international

organization of parliaments.[9] How does the United States compare to other countries? Is 16.8 percent comparatively low, comparatively high, or average for a typical national legislature?

A. World contains women09, the percentage of women in the lower house of the legislature in each of 180 countries. Perform a summary analysis (with detail) on women09. Run sktest on women09.

Statistics for women09	
Mean	?
Median	?
Skewness	?
Pr(Skewness)	?

B. Based on the statistics you obtained, which is the better measure of central tendency to use, the mean or the median? (circle one)

Mean   Median

Briefly explain your answer. _____

_____

_____

C. Examine the results of the summary analysis. Recall that 16.8 percent of U.S. House members are women. Which of the following statements *most accurately describes* the U.S. House? Using the appropriate measure of central tendency, the percentage of women in the U.S. House can be described as (circle one)

"below average."   "average."   "above average."

D. Suppose a women's advocacy organization vows to support female congressional candidates so that the U.S. House might someday "be ranked among the top one-fourth of countries in the percentage of female members." According to the summary analysis, to meet this goal, women would need to constitute about what percentage of the House? (circle one)

about 20 percent   about 30 percent   about 40 percent

E. Create a histogram of women09. Because women09 is an interval-level (continuous) variable, only specify the "percent" option. As you did in Exercise 2, part C, you may wish to modify the x-axis title so that it more clearly describes the results. (A suggestion: "Percentage of Women in Legislature".) Print the histogram.

6. (Dataset: states. Variables: defexpen, state.) Here is the conventional political wisdom: Well-positioned members of Congress from a handful of states are successful in getting the federal government to spend revenue in their states—defense-related expenditures, for example. The typical state, by contrast, receives far fewer defense budget dollars.

A. Suppose you had a variable that measured the amount of defense-related expenditures in each state. The conventional wisdom says that, when you look at how all 50 states are distributed on this variable, a few states would have a high amount of defense spending. Most states, however, would have lower values on this variable.

If the conventional wisdom is correct, the distribution of defense-related expenditures will have (circle one) a negative skew.   no skew.   a positive skew.

If the conventional wisdom is correct, the mean of defense-related expenditures will be (circle one)

lower than its median.   the same as its median.   higher than its median.

B. The states dataset contains the variable defexpen, defense expenditures per capita for each of the 50 states. Perform a summary analysis of defexpen (with detail). Run sktest on defexpen. Fill in the following table:

Statistics for defexpen	
Mean	?
Median	?
Skewness	?
Pr(Skewness)	?

C. Which is the better measure of central tendency? (circle one)

Mean   Median

Briefly explain your answer. _____

_____

D. Obtain a histogram of defexpen. Because defexpen is an interval-level (continuous) variable, only specify the "percent" option. Print the histogram.

E. Based on your analysis, would you say that the conventional wisdom is accurate or inaccurate? (circle one)

The conventional wisdom is accurate.   The conventional wisdom is inaccurate.

F. Run "sort defexpen". Run "list state defexpen". The state with the lowest per-capita defense spending is

_____, with $_____ per capita. The state with the highest per-capita defense

spending is _____, with $_____ per capita.

7. (Dataset: states. Variables: blkpct, hispanic, state.) Two demographers are arguing over how best to describe the racial and ethnic composition of the "typical" state.

Demographer 1: "The typical state is 10.3 percent black and 8.8 percent Hispanic."

Demographer 2: "The typical state is 7.2 percent black and 5.8 percent Hispanic."

A. Run summary (with detail) for blkpct (the percentage of each state's population that is African American) and hispanic (the percentage of each state's population that is Hispanic). Run sktest on blkpct and hispanic. (Hint: Stata will permit you to name more than one variable after the sum and sktest commands. "sum blkpct hispanic, detail" and "sktest blkpct hispanic" are valid commands.) Record the appropriate statistics for each variable in the table that follows:

	blkpct	hispanic
Mean	?	?
Median	?	?
Skewness	?	?
Pr(Skewness)	?	?

B. Based on your analysis, which demographer is more accurate (circle one)?

Demographer 1   Demographer 2

Write a few sentences explaining your reasoning. _____

_____

_____

_____

C. Run sort and list to obtain information on the percentage of Hispanics in each state.

Which five states have the lowest percentages of Hispanics?

_____

_____

_____

_____

_____

Which five states have the highest percentages of Hispanics?

_____

_____

_____

_____

_____

That concludes the exercises for this chapter.

NOTES

1. In this chapter we use the terms *dispersion*, *variation*, and *spread* interchangeably.

2. Unless instructed otherwise, Stata will use a variable's value labels (not its numeric codes) when it displays results. If we wanted Stata to use zodiac's numeric codes, we would enter this command: "tab zodiac, nolabel". The nolabel option suppresses value labels and instead displays the numeric codes.

3. Stata users can tailor the tabulate command to obtain frequency distributions (this chapter's topic), as well as cross-tabulations and mean comparisons (covered in Chapter 4). With the correct options, tabulate can also be used to create new variables. This application is discussed in Chapter 3.

4. The mode of age is 47, with 2.45 percent of the cases. Many interval-level variables have multiple modes. That is, several values may "tie" for the distinction of being the most common. Thus, the description of an interval-level variable usually centers on its median and mean, which generally provide more useful information than its mode.

5. The sktest command tests the working assumption that the distribution is not skewed. The entry under "Pr(Skewness)" reports the probability that this assumption is correct. Thus we would conclude that there is a probability of 0.000 that the distribution of age is not skewed. Chapter 6 covers probabilities or "P-values" in greater detail. The sktest command also tests the kurtosis of a distribution. Kurtosis refers to how "flat" or "peaked" a distribution is. This book does not cover the evaluation of kurtosis.

6. Many demographic variables are skewed, so their median values rather than their means are often used to give a clearer picture of central tendency. One hears or reads reports, for example, of median family income or the median price of homes in an area.

7. A related Stata command, gsort, permits the user to sort in ascending or descending order.

8. Science_quiz was created by summing the number of correct responses to the following questions (all are in true-false format, except for earthsun): The center of the Earth is very hot (General Social Survey variable, hotcore); It is the father's gene that decides whether the baby is a boy or a girl (boyorgrl); Electrons are smaller than atoms (electron); The universe began with a huge explosion (bigbang); The continents on which we live have been moving their locations for millions of years and will continue to move in the future (condrift); Human beings, as we know them today, developed from earlier species of animals (evolved); Does the Earth go around the Sun, or does the Sun go around the Earth? (earthsun); All radioactivity is man-made (radioact); Lasers work by focusing sound waves (lasers); Antibiotics kill viruses as well as bacteria (viruses).

9. See the Inter-Parliamentary Union Web site (www.ipu.org/english/home.htm).

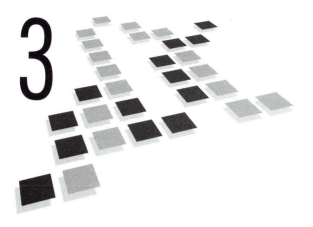

3

Transforming Variables

Commands Covered

recode, generate ( )	Creates a new variable by translating or combining codes of an existing variable
generate, recode ( )	Creates a new variable by combining codes of an existing variable
xtile, nquantiles ( )	Creates a new variable by collapsing an existing variable into categories containing approximately equal numbers of cases
generate	Creates a new variable from the codes of one or more existing variables
tabulate, generate ( )	Creates a set of indicator variables from the codes of an existing variable
label variable	Labels a variable
label define	Creates and names a label that connects a set of numeric codes to a set of value labels
label values	Labels the values of a variable using a previously defined label
drop	Deletes variables from a dataset
aorder	Changes the order in which variables appear in a dataset

Political researchers sometimes must modify the variables they wish to analyze. Generally speaking, there are three situations in which variable transformations become desirable or necessary. In the first situation, a researcher may want to collapse a variable, combining its values or codes into a smaller number of useful categories. For categorical variables, those measured by a handful of nominal or ordinal values, the recode command accomplishes this. Although the recode command may also be used to collapse interval-level variables, you might prefer the simplicity of another procedure—the generate command with the recode function. Another command, xtile, is a quick and efficient way to collapse an interval-level variable into a set of ordinal categories containing equal numbers of cases. In a second situation, a dataset may contain several variables that provide similar measures of the same concept. The researcher may wish to combine the codes of different variables, creating a new and more precise measure. Stata's generate command is designed for this task. In a third set of (more specialized) circumstances, the researcher may wish to transform a nominal or an ordinal variable into a set of new indicator variables. To graph relationships between categorical variables (covered in Chapter 4), indicator variables are required. Stata's omnicompetent tabulate command, with the right option, will create indicator variables.

With this arsenal of Stata commands at your disposal, you can modify any variable at any level of measurement—nominal, ordinal, or interval. But you should exercise vigilance and care. Here are three rules:

1. Before transforming a variable, obtain a frequency distribution.
2. After transforming a variable, check your work.
3. Properly label any new variables that you create.

We will follow these rules as we work through several examples. The variables you modify or create in this chapter (and in this chapter's exercises) will become permanent variables in the datasets. After you complete each guided example and each exercise, be sure to save the dataset.

A WORKBOOK CONVENTION: WEIGHTING THE NES2008 DATASET

All of this chapter's guided examples use nes2008. Before proceeding, you need to learn about a feature of nes2008 that will require special treatment throughout the book. In gathering interview data, the American National Election Study "oversampled" African American and Latino respondents. These larger-than-normal subsamples are valuable resources for researchers, because they allow us to obtain better estimates of the attitudes and behaviors of these groups. As a consequence, however, the survey data are not representative of the electorate as a whole. For some Stata commands, including recode and generate, this lack of representativeness does not matter. For most Stata commands, however, the oversamples produce incorrect results. Fortunately, survey designers included the necessary corrective in the 2008 dataset: a weight variable. A *weight variable* adjusts for the distorting effect of oversampling and calculates results that accurately reflect the makeup of the electorate. Therefore, to obtain correct results *you must specify the weight variable whenever you analyze the nes2008 dataset.* The first guided example demonstrates how to perform this simple yet essential procedure.

TRANSFORMING CATEGORICAL VARIABLES

Dataset nes2008 contains marital, a demographic variable that measures marital status in six categories: married (coded 1), divorced (coded 2), separated (coded 3), widowed (coded 4), never married (coded 5), and partnered-not married (coded 6). This is a perfectly fine variable, and we do not want to alter or destroy it. But suppose we wish to use marital to create a new variable that collapses respondents into two categories: married (code 1) or not married (codes 2 through 6). The recode command will accomplish this goal. Following the first rule of data transformations, we will run tabulate on marital, which will tell us what the new, collapsed variable should look like. Stata's tabulate command permits weights. Because nes2008 needs to be weighted, we must specify a weight variable in the tab command. Note the special stipulation, "[aw=w]", appended to the following tab command:

```
tab marital [aw=w]
```

The term "aw" is an acceptable Stata abbreviation for "aweight"—telling Stata to use an analytic weight in analyzing the data. And "w" is the minimalist name the author assigned to nes2008's weight variable.[1] With the exception of certain data transformation commands, such as recode and generate, your analyses of nes2008 will include the term "[aw=w]".

Click in the Command window, type "tab marital [aw=w]", and press Enter, as shown in Figure 3-1. Stata displays the weighted frequencies (distractingly, to multi-decimal-point precision) and the correct percentages in each category of marital. (For illustrative purposes, Figure 3-1 also displays the unweighted frequency distribution. As you can see, the unweighted numbers are pretty far off the mark.) According to the frequency distribution, 50.08 percent of the sample is married. This means that the rest of the sample, 49.92 percent, must fall into the other five values of marital. The two numbers, 50.08 and 49.92, will help us verify that we performed the recode correctly.

Now let's use marital to create a new variable, named married. Respondents who are married will be coded 1 and labeled "Yes" on married. Unmarried respondents will be coded 0 and labeled "No." Any respondents who have missing values on marital will have a missing value on married. Consider this recoding protocol:

Marital Status	Existing Numeric Code (marital)	New Numeric Code (married)
Married	1	1
Divorced	2	0
Separated	3	0
Widowed	4	0
Never married	5	0
Partnered-not married	6	0
(missing)	.	.

Figure 3-1 An Unweighted and a Weighted Frequency Distribution

. `tab marital`

> This unweighted frequency distribution is incorrect. For example, it greatly underestimates the number of married respondents.

SUMMARY: Marital status	Freq.	Percent	Cum.
1. Married	975	42.24	42.24
2. Divorced	371	16.07	58.32
3. Separated	102	4.42	62.74
4. Widowed	218	9.45	72.18
5. Never married	604	26.17	98.35
6. Partnered, not married {VOL}	38	1.65	100.00
Total	2,308	100.00	

. `tab marital [aw=w]`

SUMMARY: Marital status	Freq.	Percent	Cum.
1. Married	1,155.9489	50.08	50.08
2. Divorced	298.156623	12.92	63.00
3. Separated	67.5080556	2.92	65.93
4. Widowed	180.8455111	7.84	73.76
5. Never married	569.3673357	24.67	98.43
6. Partnered, not married {VOL}	36.1735513	1.57	100.00
Total	2,308	100.00	

> 2. Stata displays adjusted frequencies, accompanied by correct percentages.

Command

tab marital [aw=w]

> 1. Type "tab marital [aw=w]". The term "aw" means "analytic weight," and "w" is the name of the nes2008 weight variable.

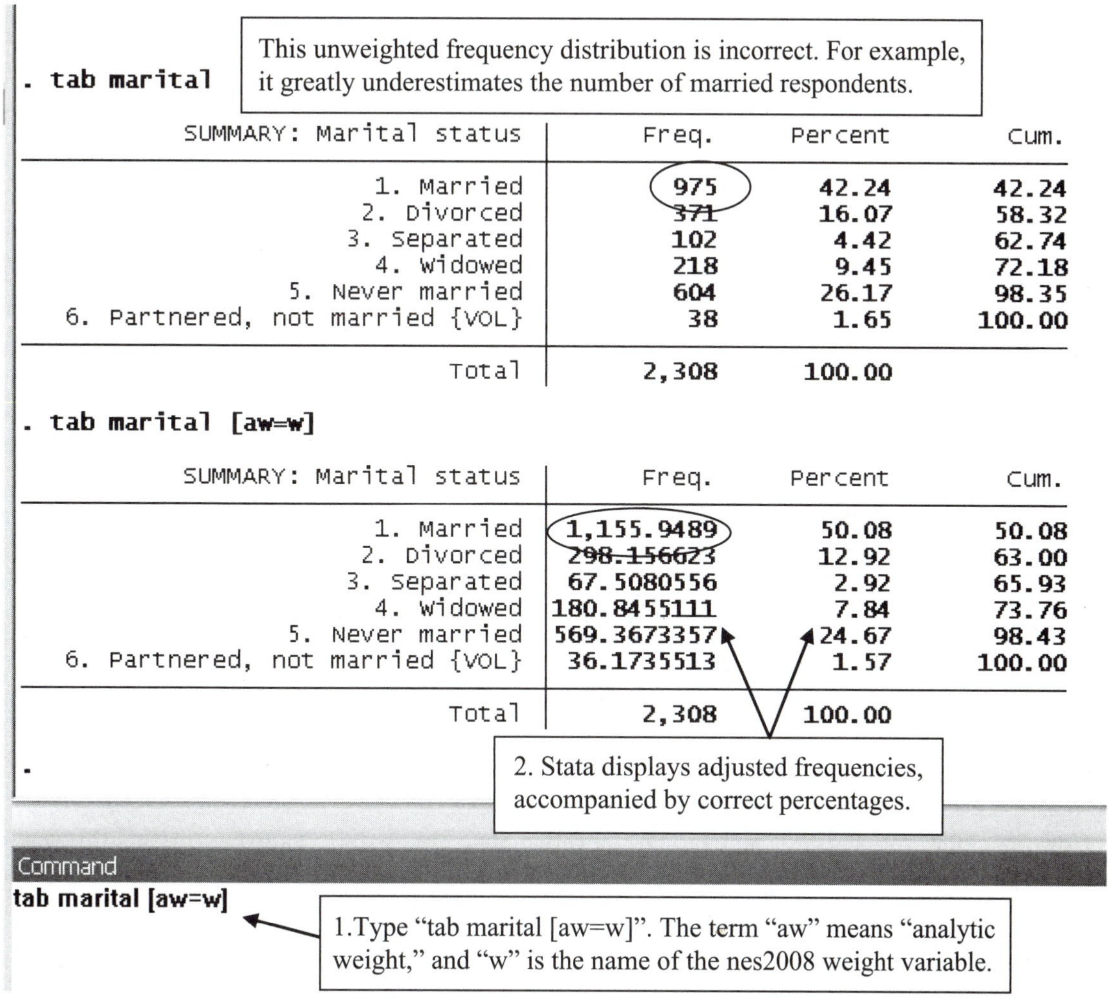

We know the name of the existing variable (marital) and the name of the new variable (married), and we know the rule for transforming the existing numeric codes into the new numeric codes: existing code 1 = new code 1; existing code 2 through code 6 = new code 0. And note that any respondent who has a missing value on marital (which appears as a "." in the dataset) will be assigned a missing value on married. The general syntax for the recode command is as follows:

recode *old_var (old_code(s) = new_code "value label"), gen(new_var)*

Applying this syntax to the marital-into-married recode:

recode marital (1=1 "Yes") (2/6=0 "No") (.=.), gen(married)

The first part of the syntax tells Stata how to translate or combine the original codes. For example, the statement (1=1 "Yes") says that each respondent coded 1 on marital is to be coded 1 on the new variable, and that the new numeric code is to be labeled "Yes." The "gen" part of the syntax tells Stata the name of the new variable. The statement "gen(married)" instructs Stata to create or generate a new variable, named married, and to add this new variable to the dataset. By specifying this option we ensure that the original variable, marital, remains unchanged.

Here are five noteworthy facts about the recode command. First, Stata's syntax for combining codes is a bit eccentric. In combining codes, be sure to use a slash (as in "2/6") and not a dash ("2-6"). Second, it is a good practice always to use quotation marks to enclose the new variable's value labels. Quotation marks will always work and will never annoy Stata.[2] Third, whenever you run recode, *always generate a new variable*. This is important. Stata will not second-guess you. If you run recode without generating a new variable, Stata will replace the existing variable, destroying its codes. Fourth, make sure to recode missing values on the original variable into missing values on the new variable. That is, the recode syntax should always include the argument "(.=.)". The fifth fact was mentioned earlier: For recode (and for generate), do not use the weight variable.

Back to the recode at hand. In the Command window, type the recode command (as shown above) and press Enter. Stata reports an error-free run:

```
. recode marital (1=1 "Yes") (2/6=0 "No") (.=.), gen(married)
(1333 differences between marital and married)
```

But did the recode work correctly? This is where the second rule of data transformations—the check-your-work rule—takes effect. Always run tab on the newly created variable to ensure that you did things right. Run the command "tab married [aw=w]":

```
. tab married [aw=w]
```

RECODE of marital (SUMMARY: Marital status)	Freq.	Percent	Cum.
No	1,152.0511	49.92	49.92
Yes	1,155.9489	50.08	100.00
Total	2,308	100.00	

Yes, our new variable classifies 50.08 percent as married and 49.92 percent as unmarried. So the new variable, married, checks out.

However, notice the clunky default variable label that Stata has used: "RECODE of marital (SUMMARY: Marital status)." Let's follow the third rule of data transformations and give married a better label, such as "Is R married?" The general syntax for labeling a variable is as follows:

label var *varname "variable label"*

Relabel married by using the following command, just as you see it printed here:

label var married "Is R married?"

Stata says nothing, which generally is a good sign. Just to make sure, run tab on married one last time:

```
. label var married "Is R married?"

. tab married [aw=w]
```

Is R married?	Freq.	Percent	Cum.
No	1,152.0511	49.92	49.92
Yes	1,155.9489	50.08	100.00
Total	2,308	100.00	

All is well. Before going to the next guided example, save nes2008.

TRANSFORMING INTERVAL VARIABLES

Once you become familiar with the recode command, you will probably find yourself using it to collapse any variable at any level of measurement. That's fine. The existing variable may be nominal level, such as marital. Or it may be ordinal level. For example, it might make sense to collapse four response categories such as "strongly agree/agree/disagree/strongly disagree" into two, "agree/disagree." At other times the original variable is interval level, such as age or income. Recode will always work. With Stata, however, there is usually more than one way to accomplish a desired goal. When working with interval-level variables, the generate command with the recode function is a powerful and parsimonious alternative to recode. (Another command, xtile, can be used to collapse a variable into categories containing approximately equal numbers of cases. See "A Closer Look" for a discussion of the xtile command.)

The nes2008 dataset contains the variable yob, which records the year of birth for each respondent. Our goal here is to collapse yob into three theoretically useful categories: respondents born in 1949 or before, those born between 1950 and 1965, and those born between 1966 and 1990 (the birth year of the youngest respondents). How do we proceed? First, of course, we need a frequency distribution of yob. Run "tab yob [aw=w]":

Birthdate Year	Freq.	Percent	Cum.
1915	1.98101889	0.09	0.09
1917	6.705179131	0.29	0.38
1918	4.79957349	0.21	0.59
1919	2.83173932	0.12	0.72
1920	2.08250206	0.09	0.81
1921	7.26153854	0.32	1.13
1922	7.31877267	0.32	1.45
1923	6.80606316	0.30	1.75
1924	11.6857442	0.51	2.26
1925	7.4105669	0.33	2.59
1926	9.2140903	0.40	2.99
1927	14.0269485	0.62	3.61
1928	18.9048315	0.83	4.44
1929	12.7479211	0.56	5.00
1930	26.3634433	1.16	6.15
1931	12.8252322	0.56	6.72
1932	16.2792548	0.71	7.43
1933	12.6443405	0.56	7.99
1934	14.68269336	0.64	8.63
1935	20.5248661	0.90	9.53
1936	21.583347	0.95	10.48
1937	20.6790884	0.91	11.39
1938	23.9290461	1.05	12.44
1939	20.0979578	0.88	13.32
1940	18.0458205	0.79	14.12
1941	24.8470892	1.09	15.21
1942	32.14608489	1.41	16.62
1943	24.529555	1.08	17.70
1944	33.0369589	1.45	19.15
1945	24.8498861	1.09	20.24
1946	34.974028	1.54	21.77
1947	28.214612	1.24	23.01
1948	33.2637977	1.46	24.47
1949	41.8533075	1.84	26.31
1950	39.509606	1.74	28.05
1951	50.182816	2.20	30.25
1952	27.53629308	1.21	31.46
1953	36.2378734	1.59	33.05
1954	43.0644127	1.89	34.94
1955	49.90503602	2.19	37.14
1956	37.9062524	1.66	38.80
1957	43.2754696	1.90	40.70
1958	48.6726548	2.14	42.84
1959	45.9096363	2.02	44.85
1960	54.8630268	2.41	47.26
1961	56.5340023	2.48	49.75
1962	50.6507772	2.22	51.97
1963	47.6672126	2.09	54.07
1964	34.5656986	1.52	55.58
1965	30.9965081	1.36	56.94
1966	42.3592247	1.86	58.80
1967	39.4692525	1.73	60.54
1968	39.5521565	1.74	62.28
1969	33.927833	1.49	63.77
1970	33.8922739	1.49	65.25
1971	43.0117733	1.89	67.14
1972	37.9582923	1.67	68.81
1973	33.1032823	1.45	70.26
1974	37.3802577	1.64	71.91
1975	29.5546685	1.30	73.20
1976	42.3031891	1.86	75.06
1977	46.4925651	2.04	77.10
1978	40.1381817	1.76	78.87
1979	35.1551197	1.54	80.41
1980	52.824174	2.32	82.73
1981	46.0481774	2.02	84.75
1982	55.456044	2.44	87.19
1983	36.4453342	1.60	88.79
1984	47.8739746	2.10	90.89
1985	49.0408307	2.15	93.04
1986	29.7391565	1.31	94.35
1987	33.5095147	1.47	95.82
1988	38.4865835	1.69	97.51
1989	23.223559	1.02	98.53
1990	33.4304058	1.47	100.00
Total	2,277	100.00	

A Closer Look — The xtile Command

If you want to quickly collapse an interval-level variable into a few manageable categories containing roughly equal numbers of cases, then the xtile command (with the nquantiles option) is the best way to go. The syntax for the xtile command is as follows:

xtile *new_var* = *old_var* [aw=weight_var], nquantiles (#)

Stata will create a new variable by collapsing an existing variable into # categories, in which "#" is a user-specified number. (Special note: xtile permits weights. When running xtile on nes2008, be sure to include "[aw=w]".) Here, for example, is the frequency distribution of nes2008 variable income_r, a measure of the respondent's income:

```
. tab income_r [aw=w]
```

R income	Freq.	Percent	Cum.
1. None or less than $2,999	193.093432	8.89	8.89
2. $3,000 –$4,999	65.6401646	3.02	11.91
3. $5,000 –$7,499	112.34226	5.17	17.08
4. $7,500 –$9,999	109.0263	5.02	22.10
5. $10,000 –$10,999	52.0652522	2.40	24.50
6. $11,000–$12,499	70.6284196	3.25	27.75
7. $12,500–$14,999	110.107263	5.07	32.82
8. $15,000–$16,999	75.2647379	3.47	36.29
9. $17,000–$19,999	86.71113	3.99	40.28
10. $20,000–$21,999	74.5235835	3.43	43.71
11. $22,000–$24,999	103.62984	4.77	48.48
12. $25,000–$29,999	149.489573	6.88	55.36
13. $30,000–$34,999	154.085627	7.09	62.46
14. $35,000–$39,999	133.457068	6.14	68.60
15. $40,000–$44,999	107.592208	4.95	73.56
16. $45,000–$49,999	73.3775022	3.38	76.94
17. $50,000–$59,999	138.917554	6.40	83.33
18. $60,000–$74,999	108.271128	4.98	88.32
19. $75,000–$89,999	77.93369038	3.59	91.90
20. $90,000–$99,999	38.2054091	1.76	93.66
21. $100,000–$109,999	33.4279185	1.54	95.20
22. $110,000–$119,999	19.2154439	0.88	96.09
23. $120,000–$134,999	23.6378165	1.09	97.18
24. $135,000–$149,999	14.8174284	0.68	97.86
25. $150,000 and over	46.53925004	2.14	100.00
Total	2,172	100.00	

(continued)

Let's use this distribution to get an idea of what the recoded variable should look like. To do this, focus on the cumulative percent column. What percentage of the sample falls into the oldest category—born in 1949 or before? That's easy: 26.31 percent. What percentage of the sample falls *in or below* the middle category, people born between 1950 and 1965? Well, 56.94 percent of the sample was born in 1965 or earlier, so 56.94 percent of the sample should fall into the first two categories of the recoded variable. These two cumulative markers, 26.31 percent and 56.94 percent, will help us verify the data transformation.

Now consider the general syntax of the generate command with the recode function:

generate *new_var* = **recode**(*old_var, max_1, max_2,...max_n*)

A Closer Look   The xtile Command   *(continued)*

The following command will create a new variable, income_r3, by collapsing income_r into three ordinal categories with roughly equal numbers of cases:

   For nes2008, the weight variable is required.

xtile income_r3 = income_r [aw=w], nquantiles(3)

Running "tab income_r3 [aw=w]":

```
. xtile income_r3 = income_r [aw=w], nquantiles(3)

. tab income_r3 [aw=w]

3 quantiles
of income_r |     Freq.      Percent       Cum.
------------+----------------------------------
          1 |  788.16783       36.29      36.29
          2 |  701.896821      32.32      68.60
          3 |  681.935349      31.40     100.00
------------+----------------------------------
      Total |     2,172       100.00
```

Similarly, the following command would create a four-category variable from income_r:

xtile income_r4 = income_r [aw=w], nquantiles(4)

```
. xtile income_r4 = income_r [aw=w], nquantiles(4)

. tab income_r4 [aw=w]

4 quantiles
of income_r |     Freq.      Percent       Cum.
------------+----------------------------------
          1 |  602.795829      27.75      27.75
          2 |  599.726127      27.61      55.36
          3 |  468.512405      21.57      76.94
          4 |  500.965639      23.06     100.00
------------+----------------------------------
      Total |     2,172       100.00
```

Stata provides descriptive variable labels (for example, "4 quantiles of income_r"), but you will probably wish to supply value labels for the numeric codes that Stata has assigned to each category of the new variable.[1]

_____

1. The xtile command is a special application of the pctile command. For more information, type "help pctile".

You type the generate command, followed by a name for the new, collapsed variable and an equals sign. Then type "recode" followed immediately by a left parenthesis. *Do not leave a space between the word* recode *and the left parenthesis.* The name of the original variable is the first entry inside the parentheses, followed by a comma. The values of the original variable that define the *upper boundaries* of the collapsed categories come next, separated by commas.

   Apply these syntactical rules to the yob transformation. The oldest age group includes everyone born in or before 1949, so the first upper boundary is 1949. The middle group is bracketed by 1950 at the low end and 1965 at the high end, so the second upper boundary is 1965. The youngest group includes all respondents born from 1966 to 1990, making 1990 the third upper boundary. Therefore, the command is "gen yob3=recode(yob, 1949, 1965, 1990)".

Type the command and let's see if Stata likes it:

No space here.

```
. gen yob3=recode(yob, 1949, 1965, 1990)
(46 missing values generated)
```

Seems fine. Check your work by running "tab yob3 [aw=w]":

```
. tab yob3 [aw=w]
```

yob3	Freq.	Percent	Cum.
1949	599.146899	26.31	26.31
1965	697.477276	30.63	56.94
1990	980.3758248	43.06	100.00
Total	2,277	100.00	

The cumulative percent markers, 26.31 percent and 56.94 percent, are just where they are supposed to be. The yob3 variable checks out. Using the variable name "Three generations," ask Stata to label yob3 by running the label var command, just as it appears here:

label var yob3 "Three generations"

Now, notice that Stata has adopted the boundary maximums ("1949," "1965," and "1990") as default numeric codes for the categories of the new variable. So people in the oldest cohort are coded 1949, those in the middle category are coded 1965, and those in the youngest group are coded 1990. These are not terribly informative codes. Before proceeding to the next example, we will use yob3 to acquire a new skill—how to define and assign labels to the values of a newly created variable.

THE LABEL DEFINE AND LABEL VALUES COMMANDS

Suppose we want to use the label "1949/before" for numeric code 1949 on yob3, "1950-1965" for code 1965, and "1966-1990" for code 1990. What command will instruct Stata to apply these labels to yob3 numeric codes? Actually, two commands are required. The first command, label define, creates and names a label that connects a set of numeric codes to a set of value labels. The second command, label values, tells Stata to label the values of a variable using a previously defined label. Confused? Welcome to Stata's oddly inefficient way of dealing with labels.[3]

First run label define. The syntax of the label define command is as follows:

label define *label_name code_1 "label 1" code_2 "label 2" ... code_n "label n"*

Accordingly, the following command defines a label, which we will name "yob3_label," that connects the numeric codes with the desired value labels:

label define yob3_label 1949 "1949/before" 1965 "1950-1965" 1990 "1966-1990"

Now run label values. The label values command conforms to this syntax:

label values *varname label_name*

The following command tells Stata to label the numeric codes of yob3 using yob3_label:

label values yob3 yob3_label

Did all our typing pay off? Run "tab yob3 [aw=w]":

```
. label var yob3 "Three generations"

. label define yob3_label 1949 "1949/before" 1965 "1950-1965" 1990 "1966-1990"

. label values yob3 yob3_label

. tab yob3 [aw=w]
```

Three generations	Freq.	Percent	Cum.
1949/before	599.146899	26.31	26.31
1950-1965	697.477276	30.63	56.94
1966-1990	980.3758248	43.06	100.00
Total	2,277	100.00	

A flawless set of Stata labels is a thing of uncommon beauty. Save the dataset and let's move to the next example.

CREATING AN ADDITIVE INDEX

We just demonstrated one of the several ways in which the generate command can create new variables. Let's now consider another (and perhaps more typical) use of generate—to create a simple *additive index* from similarly coded variables. Consider a simple illustration. Suppose you have three variables, each of which measures whether or not a respondent engaged in each of the following activities during an election campaign: tried to convince somebody how to vote, put a campaign bumper sticker on his or her car, or gave money to one of the candidates or parties. Each variable is coded identically: 0 if the respondent did not engage in the activity and 1 if he or she did. Now, each of these variables is interesting in its own right, but you might want to add them together, creating an overall measure of campaigning: People who did not engage in any of these activities would have a value of 0 on the new variable; those who engaged in one activity, a code of 1; two activities, a code of 2; and those who engaged in all three activities, a code of 3.

Here are some suggested guidelines for using generate to create a simple additive index. First, before running generate, make sure that each of the variables is coded identically. In the preceding illustration, if the "bumper sticker" variable were coded 1 for no and 2 for yes, and the other variables were coded 0 and 1, the resulting additive index would be incorrect. Second, make sure that the variables are all coded in the same *direction*. If the "contribute money" variable were coded 0 for yes and 1 for no, and the other variables were coded 0 for no and 1 for yes, the additive index would again be incorrect.[4] Third, after running generate, obtain a frequency distribution of the newly created variable. Upon examining the frequency distribution, you may decide to run recode to collapse the new variable into more useful categories. Suppose, for example, that we add the three campaign acts together and get this frequency distribution for the new variable:

Additive index: Number of campaign acts		
Value label	Value	Percentage of sample
Engaged in none	0	60
Engaged in one	1	25
Engaged in two	2	13
Engaged in three	3	2
Total		100

Clearly, it looks like a recode run may be in order—collapsing respondents coded 2 or 3 into the same category.

These points are best understood firsthand. The 2008 American National Election Study asked respondents whether certain internationalist policies should be important U.S. foreign policy goals: helping to bring a democratic form of government to other nations (nes2008 variable, goal_democ), promoting and defending human rights in other countries (goal_humanrights), combating world hunger (goal_hunger), and strengthening the United Nations and other international organizations (goal_UN). For each of these variables, respondents who said that the goal was "very important" are coded 1; those giving other responses are coded 0. We are going to add these variables together, using the expression "goal_democ + goal_human-rights + goal_hunger + goal_UN." Think about this expression for a moment. Perhaps a respondent takes a dim view of internationalism and thinks that none of the four goals is "very important." What would be his or her score on an additive index? It would be 0 + 0 + 0 + 0 = 0. Another, international-minded respondent might say that all four are "very important". For that respondent, 1 + 1 + 1+ 1 = 4. Thus, we know from the get-go that the values of the new variable will range from 0 to 4.

We will ask Stata to generate a new variable, which we will name intism, by summing the codes of goal_democ, goal_humanrights, goal_hunger, and goal_UN. Scroll the Variables window until these four variables are visible. In the Command window, type "gen intism =". Now click goal_democ into the Command window, type a "+" sign, click goal_humanrights into the Command window, type a "+" sign, and so on, until you have typed the following expression:

gen intism = goal_democ + goal_humanrights + goal_hunger + goal_UN

Press Enter. Stata runs the command and deposits our new variable, internationalism, at the bottom of the Variables window. What does the new variable look like? To find out, run "tab intism [aw=w]":

```
. gen intism =  goal_democ + goal_humanrights + goal_hunger + goal_UN
(235 missing values generated)

. tab intism [aw=w]

   intism |       Freq.     Percent        Cum.
----------+-----------------------------------
        0 |   521.10868       24.96       24.96
        1 |  549.787547       26.33       51.29
        2 |  534.036418       25.58       76.86
        3 |  345.594887       16.55       93.42
        4 |  137.472467        6.58      100.00
----------+-----------------------------------
    Total |       2,088      100.00
```

Notice the high variation in respondents' opinions about the importance of international policies. Close to 25 percent of the sample falls into each of the first three values, and the remaining 25 percent occupy the highest two codes. This is an interesting variable that you may want to analyze later. Give intism a descriptive variable label, such as "Internationalism support." In the Command window type:

label var intism "Internationalism support"

Before moving on, use intism to exercise a recently acquired skill, defining and labeling the values of a new variable. Using the label define command, create a label that connects numeric code 0 on intism with value label "Low," code 1 with "Med-low," code 2 with "Medium," code 3 with "Med-high," and code 4 with "High":

label define intism_label 0 "Low" 1 "Med-low" 2 "Medium" 3 "Med-High" 4 "High"

Now run label values, instructing Stata to apply the new label to numeric codes:

label values intism intism_label

Check your work by running "tab intism [aw=w]":

```
. label var intism "Internationalism support"

. label define intism_label 0 "Low" 1 "Med-low" 2 "Medium" 3 "Med-High" 4 "High"

. label values intism intism_label

. tab intism [aw=w]

Internation |
      alism |
    support |       Freq.     Percent        Cum.
------------+-----------------------------------
        Low |   521.10868       24.96       24.96
    Med-low |  549.787547       26.33       51.29
     Medium |  534.036418       25.58       76.86
   Med-High |  345.594887       16.55       93.42
       High |  137.472467        6.58      100.00
------------+-----------------------------------
      Total |       2,088      100.00
```

Well, maybe Stata's two-command system for labeling a variable's values isn't so bad after all.

CREATING INDICATOR VARIABLES

As you are well aware by now, by default the tabulate command will produce a frequency distribution of a variable. In Chapter 4 you will use other applications of tabulate to produce cross-tabulations and to perform mean comparison analyses. Frequency distributions, cross-tabulations, and mean comparisons are standard forms of description and analysis that you will use in just about every research question you address. Stata's tabulate, the "command that does it all," also can be used—in specialized situations—to create new variables from existing variables.

Consider deathpen, a four-category ordinal variable tapping strength of support for (or opposition to) capital punishment. Respondents can "Favor strongly" (coded 1), "Favor not strongly" (coded 2), "Oppose not strongly" (coded 3), or "Oppose strongly" (coded 4). A tabulate run shows how respondents distributed themselves on this issue:

```
. tab  deathpen [aw=w]
```

R favor/oppose death penalty	Freq.	Percent	Cum.
Favor strongly	1,101.1029	51.69	51.69
Favor not strongly	390.995063	18.36	70.05
Oppose not strongly	214.478287	10.07	80.12
Oppose strongly	423.4238	19.88	100.00
Total	2,130	100.00	

Suppose that we want to use deathpen to create a new variable. We would like this new variable to be coded 1 for the 51.69 percent of the sample who "Favor strongly" and coded 0 for individuals who gave any other response—the 48.31 percent who "Favor not strongly," "Oppose not strongly," or "Oppose strongly." Again, we could run recode. But here is a quicker way. Press the Page Up key, returning "tab deathpen [aw=w]" to the Command window. Modify it to read:

tab deathpen [aw=w], gen(deathdum)

Running this command produces a (by now familiar) frequency distribution of deathpen in the Results window. But scroll to the bottom of the Variables window and see what else Stata has done (Figure 3-2). There you will find four new variables, each named sequentially and according to deathdum, the name "handle" we supplied in the generate option: deathdum1, deathdum2, deathdum3, and deathdum4. What do these new variables measure? The first variable, deathdum1, takes on a value of 1 for all respondents falling into the lowest numeric code of deathpen, and a value of 0 for all respondents not falling into the lowest code. Because the lowest code of deathpen is the value for "Favor strongly," Stata assigned a code of 1 to respondents in this category, and a code of 0 to everybody else. Stata then moved to the next-highest numeric code of deathpen (code 2, "Favor not strongly") and created a second variable, deathdum2, which assumes a value of 1 for individuals who gave the "Favor not strongly" response and a value of 0 for all other respondents. Stata generated deathdum3 and deathdum4 in the same way, assigning codes of 1 ("Oppose not strongly") or 0 (all other responses) for deathdum3, and assigning codes of 1 ("Oppose strongly") or 0 (all other responses) for deathdum4. Go ahead and run this command, "tab deathdum1 [aw=w]":

```
. tab  deathdum1 [aw=w]
```

deathpen==Favor strongly	Freq.	Percent	Cum.
0	1,028.8971	48.31	48.31
1	1,101.1029	51.69	100.00
Total	2,130	100.00	

These results show that the percentage of respondents falling into code 1 of the newly generated death-pen1—the "Favor strongly" respondents—matches the percentage of respondents who fall into the "Favor strongly" category of the original variable, 51.69 percent. And notice that Stata has supplied a useful variable label for deathdum1: "deathpen==Favor strongly." Thankfully we won't need to change the variable label or create value labels.

Figure 3-2 Creating Indicator Variables

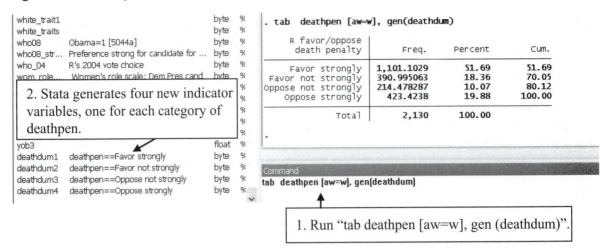

Stata uses the term *indicator variables* for variables such as these—variables that are coded 1 for cases falling into a specific value and coded 0 for cases not falling into that value. Indicator variables, also called dummy variables or binary variables, play key roles in graphing and analyzing complex relationships. In the chapters that follow, you will be making frequent use of the tabulate command with the generate option.

The ease with which Stata generates indicator variables has one small disadvantage: Datasets tend to become overpopulated with superfluous variables. Certainly we want deathdum1 to become a permanent variable in the dataset. But we really have no use for deathdum2, deathdum3, and deathdum4. Let's perform two housekeeping chores. First, use the drop command to get rid of the unwanted variables:

drop deathdum2 deathdum3 deathdum4

Stata deletes the variables without comment. All right, now we will re-alphabetize the variable names in the Variable window. In the Command window, type the following command:

aorder

Stata puts everything neatly in alphabetical order. Before beginning the exercises, be sure to save the dataset.

EXERCISES

For this chapter's exercises you will analyze gss2006. Unlike your analyses of nes2008, when you analyze gss2006 you will not use a weight variable.

1. (Dataset: gss2006. Variable: polviews.) Dataset gss2006 contains polviews, which measures political ideology—the extent to which individuals "think of themselves as liberal or conservative." Here is how polviews is coded:

Value	Value label
1	Extremely liberal
2	Liberal
3	Slightly liberal
4	Moderate
5	Slightly conservative
6	Conservative
7	Extremely conservative

A. Run "tab polviews".

The percentage of respondents who are either "Extremely liberal," "Liberal," or "Slightly liberal" is

(fill in the blank) _____ percent.

The percentage of respondents who are "Moderate" is (fill in the blank) _____ percent.

The percentage of respondents who are either "Slightly conservative," "Conservative," or "Extremely

conservative" is (fill in the blank) _____ percent.

B. (i) Use recode (with the generate option) to create a new variable named polview3. Collapse the three liberal codes into one category (assign this category a code of 1 on polview3), put the moderates into their own category (coded 2 on polview3), and collapse the three conservative codes into one category (coded 3 on polview3). (Don't forget to recode missing values on polviews into missing values on polview3.) (ii) Run tabulate on polview3.

The percentage of respondents who are coded 1 on polview3 is (fill in the blank) _____ percent.

The percentage of respondents who are coded 2 on polview3 is (fill in the blank) _____ percent.

The percentage of respondents who are coded 3 on polview3 is (fill in the blank) _____ percent.

Make sure that the three percentages you wrote down in part B match the percentages you recorded in part A. The numbers may be very slightly different, such as 33.92 versus 33.93, and still be considered a match. If the two sets of numbers match, proceed to part C. If they do not match, you performed the recode incorrectly. If you performed the recode incorrectly, run "drop polview3", review this chapter's discussion of recode, and try the recode again.

C. (i) Run label var and give polview3 this label: "Ideology: 3 categories." (ii) Run label define to create a label named "polview3_label." In the label define command, connect the following numeric codes and value labels: 1 "Liberal" 2 "Moderate" 3 "Conservative." (iii) Run label values to label the values of polview3 using polview3_label. (iv) To ensure that everything worked, run tabulate on polview3. Based on your findings, fill in the numbers next to the question marks (?):

Ideology: 3 categories	Frequency	Percent	Cumulative Percent
Liberal	?	?	?
Moderate	?	?	?
Conservative	?	?	100.0
Total	?	100.0	

2. (Dataset: gss2006. Variables: stoprndm, tapphone, wotrial.) In Chapter 2, you analyzed three civil liberties issues: whether people think that government authorities should have the right to stop and search people on the street (stoprndm), to record telephone conversations (tapphone), or hold suspects without trial (wotrial). Recall that each variable is coded identically from 0 ("Definitely yes," authorities should have the right), 1 ("Probably yes"), 2 ("Probably no," authorities should not have the right), and 3 ("Definitely no"). Thus, higher codes are more pro–civil liberties and lower codes are more pro-security.

A. Imagine creating an additive index from these three variables. The additive index would have scores that range between what two values?

Between a score of _____ and a score of _____.

B. Suppose a respondent takes the strongest pro-security position on two of the issues but takes the "probably yes" position on the third issue. What score would this respondent have?

A score of _____.

C. (i) Use generate to create an additive index from stoprndm, tapphone, and wotrial. Name the new variable civlibs. (ii) Run label var, giving civlibs this label: "Pro-civil liberties scale". (iii) Run tabulate on civlibs. Referring to the Results window, fill in the table that follows. (Record the values of civlibs, the frequencies, and the percentage of respondents in each value. You do not need to record the cumulative percentages.)

civlibs Pro-civil liberties scale		
Pro-civil liberties scale	Frequency	Percent
?	?	?
?	?	?
?	?	?
?	?	?
?	?	?
?	?	?
?	?	?
?	?	?
?	?	?
?	?	?
Total	1,478	100.0

3. (Dataset: gss2006. Variable: cohort.) In one of this chapter's guided examples with nes2008, you used generate (with the recode option) to create yob3 ("Three generations"). In this exercise, you will run generate (with the recode option) to create a similar variable in gss2006. Gss2006 contains cohort, which records the year of birth for each respondent. Just as you did in the guided example, you will collapse cohort into three categories: respondents born in 1949 or before, those born between 1950 and 1965, and those born between 1966 and 1988 (the birth year of the youngest respondents in gss2006).

A. Run tabulate on cohort. To ensure that the data transformation goes according to plan, you will want to record two cumulative percentage markers:

The cumulative percentage for the year 1949 is (fill in the blank) _____ percent.

The cumulative percentage for the year 1965 is (fill in the blank) _____ percent.

B. Create a new variable, named cohort3, using generate (with the recode option). Remember to specify the following upper boundaries: 1949, 1965, and 1988. Stata will label the categories of cohort3 using the three upper boundary values. Run tabulate on cohort3.

The cumulative percentage for code 1949 on cohort3 is (fill in the blank) _____ percent.

The cumulative percentage for code 1965 on cohort3 is (fill in the blank) _____ percent.

Make sure that the two percentages you wrote down in part B match the percentages you recorded in part A. If the two sets of numbers match, proceed to part C. If they do not match, you performed the transformation incorrectly. If you performed the transformation incorrectly, run "drop cohort3", review this chapter's discussion of generate (with the recode option), and try the transformation again.

C. (i) Run label var and give cohort3 this label: "Three generations." (ii) Run label define to create a label named "cohort3_label." In the label define command, connect the following numeric codes and value labels: 1949 "1949/before" 1965 "1950-1965" 1988 "1966-1988". (iii) Run label values to label the values of cohort3 using cohort3_label. (iv) Run tabulate on cohort3. Based on your findings, fill in the numbers next to the question marks (?):

Three generations	Frequency	Percent	Cumulative Percent
1949/before	?	?	?
1950-1965	?	?	?
1966-1988	?	?	?
Total	4,492	100.00	

4. (Dataset: gss2006. Variable: rincom06.) In this chapter you learned to use the xtile command to collapse an nes2008 measure of income into three roughly equal ordinal categories. In this exercise you will use xtile to collapse a very similar variable from gss2006, rincom06. You will collapse rincom06 into rincom06_3, a three-category ordinal measure of respondents' incomes.

A. For guidance, refer back to this chapter's "A Closer Look" box on pages 48–49. Run xtile, using rincom06 to create rincom06_3. Run tabulate on rincom06_3. Referring to the Results window, fill in the numbers next to the question marks (?):

3 quantiles of rincom06	Frequency	Percent	Cumulative Percent
1	1,000	37.47	37.47
2	?	?	?
3	?	?	100.00
Total	2,669	100.00	

B. (i) Run label define to create a label named "rincom_label." In the label define command, connect the following numeric codes and value labels: 1 "Low" 2 "Middle" 3 "High". (ii) Run label values to label the values of rincom06_3 using rincom_label.

5. (Dataset: gss2006. Variable: pornlaw2.) In this chapter you learned to use tabulate (with the generate option) to create indicator variables. In this exercise you will create indicator variables from gss2006 variable, pornlaw2, which measures individuals' opinions about pornography. Respondents thinking pornography should be "Illegal to all" are coded 1, and those saying, "No, not illegal to all," are coded 2.

A. Run "tab pornlaw2".

The percentage of respondents saying "Yes, illegal to all" is (fill in the blank) _____ percent.

The percentage of respondents saying "No, not illegal to all" is (fill in the blank) _____ percent.

B. Run tabulate on pornlaw2 with the generate option. In the generate option, use "porn" as the name handle. Run "tab porn1".

The percentage of respondents coded 1 on porn1 is (fill in the blank) _____ percent.

The percentage of respondents coded 0 on porn1 is (fill in the blank) _____ percent.

C. (i) Use drop to delete porn2 from the dataset. (ii) Run aorder to alphabetize the variables in gss2006.

That concludes the exercises for this chapter. Before exiting Stata, be sure to save the dataset.

NOTES

1. 2008 American National Election Study variable V080101.
2. For single-word value labels, quotation marks are not required. Because we are using the value labels "Yes" and "No," the following syntax also is correct: recode marital (1 = 1 Yes) (2/6 = 0 No) (. = .), gen(married). For multiple-word value labels, quotation marks are required. Quotation marks always work, so it never hurts to use them.
3. If a dataset contains a number of identically coded variables, then Stata's two-command system makes a certain amount of sense. Suppose, for example, that there are 20 variables, var01 through var20, coded 0 or 1, with 0 denoting "No" and 1 denoting "Yes." In this situation, the researcher would need to define only one label (e.g., label define no_yes_label 0 "No" 1 "Yes"), which could then be applied to each of the 20 identically coded variables (label values var01 no_yes_label; label values var02 no_yes_label; etc.).
4. Survey datasets are notorious for "reverse coding." Survey designers do this so that respondents don't fall into response bias, automatically giving the same response to a series of questions. Though you may need to be on the lookout for reverse coding in your future research, none of the examples or exercises in this book will require that you "repair" the original coding of any variables.

4

Making Comparisons

tabulate *dep_var indep_var*, column	Produces a cross-tabulation with column percentages
tabulate *indep_var*, summarize (*dep_var*)	Produces a mean comparison table
format	Changes the level of precision with which results are displayed
_gwtmean, *dep_var_mean=dep_var* [if], by(*indep_var*)	Generates a group mean of a dependent variable for each value of an independent variable
if	A command qualifier that selectively applies a Stata command to a subset of cases
twoway (line *dep_var indep_var*, sort)	Produces a line graph of the mean value of a dependent variable for each value of an independent variable
replace	Changes or replaces the values of an existing variable
graph bar (mean) *dep_var*, over (*indep_var*)	Produces a bar chart of the mean value of a dependent variable for each value of an independent variable

All hypothesis testing in political research follows a common logic of comparison. The researcher separates subjects into categories of the independent variable and then compares these groups on the dependent variable. For example, suppose I think that gender (independent variable) affects opinions about gun control (dependent variable) and that women are less likely than men to oppose gun control. I would divide subjects into two groups on the basis of gender, women and men, and then compare the percentage of women who oppose gun control with the percentage of men who oppose gun control. Similarly, if I hypothesize that Republicans have higher incomes than do Democrats, I would divide subjects into partisanship groups (independent variable), Republicans and Democrats, and compare the average income (dependent variable) of Republicans with that of Democrats.

Although the logic of comparison is always the same, the appropriate method depends on the level of measurement of the independent and dependent variables. In this chapter you will learn how to address two common hypothesis-testing situations. First, we will cover situations in which the independent and the dependent variables are both categorical (nominal or ordinal). Then we will consider instances in which the independent variable is categorical and the dependent variable is interval. In this chapter you also will learn to create line charts and bar charts, which can greatly assist you in interpreting relationships.

CROSS-TABULATION ANALYSIS

Cross-tabulations are the workhorse vehicles for testing hypotheses for categorical variables. A cross-tabulation shows how cases defined by categories of the independent variable are distributed across the categories of the dependent variable. When setting up a cross-tabulation, you must observe the following three rules:

First, put the independent variable on the columns and the dependent variable on the rows. Second, always obtain percentages of the independent variable, not the dependent variable. Third, interpret the cross-tabulation by comparing the percentages of subjects who fall into the same category of the dependent variable.

Consider this hypothesis: In a comparison of individuals, older generations will pay more attention to political campaigns than will younger generations. The dataset nes2008 contains the variable camp_int, which measures respondents' levels of interest in the 2008 campaigns: "High" (coded 1), "Moderate" (coded 2), or "Low" (coded 3). This will serve as the dependent variable. One of the variables that you generated in Chapter 3, yob3, is the independent variable. Recall that yob3 classifies individuals by year of birth: 1949 or before (coded 1), 1950-1965 (coded 2), and 1966-1990 (coded 3). Open nes2008, begin a log file, and let's test the hypothesis.

Stata's omnipresent tabulate command—the command that produces frequency distributions and generates indicator variables—also cranks out cross-tabulations. Following is the general syntax for a bivariate cross-tabulation that heeds the three rules of cross-tab construction:

tabulate *dep_var indep_var [aw=weight_var],* **column**

This syntax is simple and direct. Type "tabulate" or simply "tab" (but *not* tab1), followed by the name of the dependent variable and the name of the independent variable. To ensure that Stata will report percentages of the independent variable, type a comma and then "col" (an acceptable abbreviation for the column option).[1] And with nes2008, of course, you need to specify the weight variable. Applying the syntax to our analysis:

```
. tab camp_int yob3 [aw=w], col
```

Key	
frequency	
column percentage	

Campaign interest	Three generations 1949/befo	1950-1965	1966-1990	Total
High	356.79055 59.57	371.58997 53.32	365.46362 37.29	1,093.844 48.06
Moderate	171.47637 28.63	234.62854 33.67	400.071123 40.82	806.17603 35.42
Low	70.704554 11.80	90.7212368 13.02	214.55404 21.89	375.97983 16.52
Total	598.97148 100.00	696.93974 100.00	980.08878 100.00	2,276 100.00

The presence of weighted frequencies (at and beyond five-decimal precision) creates a confusing clutter of digits. Before we rerun the cross-tabulation and request a cleaner display, let's consider the table at hand. The categories of the dependent variable, camp_int, define the rows of the table, and the independent variable, yob3, is on the columns. In fact, Stata has given us a set of side-by-side frequency distributions of the dependent variable—one for each category of the independent variable—plus an overall frequency distribution for all 2,276 analyzed cases. Accordingly, the table has four columns of numbers. The first column shows the distribution for the 599 respondents born in 1949 or before (we will round up from the weighted frequency of 598.97). The middle column shows how the 697 individuals in the 1950–1965 generation are distributed across camp_int, and the next column depicts the 980 people in the youngest age group. The "Total" column shows the distribution of all 2,276 valid cases across the dependent variable. Each cell reports the column percentage and the raw (weighted) frequency of cases in the cell. To get a clearer view of the column percentages, we can rerun the command, using the nofreq option to suppress frequencies. We'll also include the nokey option, which suppresses the space-consuming key box.

```
. tab camp_int yob3 [aw=w], col nofreq nokey
```

Campaign interest	Three generations			Total
	1949/befo	1950-1965	1966-1990	
High	59.57	53.32	37.29	48.06
Moderate	28.63	33.67	40.82	35.42
Low	11.80	13.02	21.89	16.52
Total	100.00	100.00	100.00	100.00

What do you think? Does the cross-tabulation fit the hypothesis? The third rule of cross-tabulation analysis is easily applied. Focusing on the "High" value of the dependent variable ("Campaign interest") we see a pattern of percentages in the hypothesized direction. A comparison of respondents in the "1949/ before" column with those in the "1950-1965" column reveals a decline from 59.57 to 53.32 in the percentage who have a "High" level of interest, a drop of about 6 percentage points. Moving from the "1950-1965" column to the "1966-1990" column, we find another decrease, from 53.32 percent to 37.29 percent, about a 16-point drop. Do younger people profess lower levels of campaign interest than do older people? Yes, the analysis supports the hypothesis.

MEAN COMPARISON ANALYSIS

We now turn to another common hypothesis-testing situation: a categorical independent variable and an interval-level dependent variable. The logic of comparison still applies—divide cases on the independent variable and compare values of the dependent variable—but the method is different. Instead of comparing percentages, we now compare means.

To illustrate, let's say that you are interested in explaining this dependent variable: attitudes toward Barack Obama. Why do some people give him positive ratings while others rate him lower? Here is a plausible idea: Partisanship (independent variable) will have a strong effect on attitudes toward Barack Obama (dependent variable). The hypothesis: In a comparison of individuals, those who are Democrats will have more favorable attitudes toward Barack Obama than will those who are Republicans.

Dataset nes2008 contains obama_therm, a 100-point feeling thermometer. During the campaign, each respondent was asked to rate candidate Obama on this scale, from 0 (cold or negative) to 100 (warm or positive). This is the dependent variable. The dataset also has partyid7, which measures partisanship in seven ordinal categories, from Strong Democrat (coded 0) to Strong Republican (coded 6). (The intervening codes capture gradations between these poles: Weak Democrat, Independent-Democrat, Independent, Independent-Republican, and Weak Republican.) This is the independent variable. If the hypothesis is correct, we should find that Strong Democrats have the highest mean scores on obama_therm and that mean scores decline systematically across categories of partyid7, hitting bottom among respondents who are Strong Republicans. Is this what happens?

Yet again, tabulate will provide the answer. In using tabulate to perform bivariate mean comparison analyses, the general syntax is as follows:

tabulate *indep_var [aw=weight_var]*, **summarize**(*dep_var*)

The syntax to the left of the comma says that you want Stata to divide cases according to the values of the independent variable. In the current example, partyid7 is the independent variable, so we would begin the command by typing, "tab partyid7". The summarize option (which can be abbreviated "sum") tells Stata to calculate summary statistics of the dependent variable for each category of the independent variable. So our dependent variable, obama_therm, would go inside the parentheses. The completed command, including nes2008's weight variable, for the Barack Obama thermometer:

```
. tab partyid7 [aw=w], sum(obama_therm)
```

Summary Party ID	Summary of Feeling Thermometer: Obama			
	Mean	Std. Dev.	Freq.	Obs.
StrDem	80.89	21.51	431.2529	579
WkDem	68.08	23.33	346.753	391
IndDem	68.74	19.91	397.3017	391
Indep	57.22	23.24	257.1239	257
IndRep	45.04	24.51	264.0854	221
WkRep	40.39	23.02	287.4041	198
StrRep	27.18	21.01	296.7604	227
Total	57.91	28.45	2280.6814	2264

By default, the summarize option will display the mean of the dependent variable ("Mean"), its standard deviation ("Std. Dev."), plus frequencies ("Freq."). For weighted data, Stata also displays the unweighted number of cases in each category of the independent variable ("Obs."). Despite this bumper crop of output, the table remains eminently readable. Even so, if you prefer to focus your attention on the mean values of obama_therm, you may suppress the standard deviation (by adding the nost option), the weighted frequencies (nofreq), and the number of unweighted cases (noobs):

```
. tab partyid7 [aw=w], sum(obama_therm) nost nofreq noobs
```

Summary Party ID	Summary of Feeling Thermometer : Obama Mean
StrDem	80.89
WkDem	68.08
IndDem	68.74
Indep	57.22
IndRep	45.04
WkRep	40.39
StrRep	27.18
Total	57.91

Compared with a cross-tabulation, a mean comparison table is the soul of simplicity. The label of the dependent variable, "Summary of Feeling Thermometer: Obama," appears along the top of the table. The label for the independent variable, "Summary Party ID," defines the left-most column, which shows all seven categories, from the lowest-coded value, Strong Democrat (coded 0), at the top, to the highest-coded value, Strong Republican (coded 6), at the bottom. Beside each partisan category Stata has calculated the mean of obama_therm, displayed at two-decimal-point precision, as in "80.89" for the Strong Democrat mean. (Sometimes you will need to change the number of decimal points that Stata displays in the Results window or in a graphic. The format command is designed for this purpose. See "A Closer Look" for a discussion of the format command.) The bottom row, "Total," gives the mean for the whole sample.

Among Strong Democrats the mean of obama_therm is pretty high—about 81 degrees. Does the mean decline as attachment to the Democratic Party weakens and identification with the Republican Party strengthens? Well, the mean drops sharply among Weak Democrats (who average about 68 degrees), momentarily stalls among Independent-Democratic leaners (68.74), then continues to decline predictably, although the drop is modest between Independent-Republican leaners and Weak Republicans. Strong Republicans, who average close to 27 degrees on the thermometer, have the chilliest response to Obama. On the whole, then, the data support the hypothesis.[2]

VISUALIZING RELATIONSHIPS WITH LINE CHARTS AND BAR CHARTS

We have already seen that bar charts and histograms can be a great help in describing the central tendency and dispersion of a *single* variable. Stata's graphic procedures also come in handy for illustrating relationships *between* variables. Many of the relationships that you will be investigating can be illustrated nicely

A Closer Look   The format Command

Stata will always store numeric data at a high level of precision—up to 16.5 decimal points, depending on a variable's storage type. However, in the interests of clarity or accuracy, you may want to change a variable's display format—that is, the number of decimal points Stata uses when it displays results or creates graphics. Here we describe how to use a *fixed format* specification, one of the three numeric format types recognized by Stata.

Consider three ways of displaying the mean Barack Obama thermometer rating among Strong Democrats: "80.8876," "80.89," and "81." The first number shows four decimal points, the second rounds to two, and the third rounds to the nearest whole number. Stata's default will give you the second display, "80.89," which works for most purposes. But let's suppose you wanted the more precise rendition, "80.8876." In the Command window you would type:

format obama_therm %9.4f

Roughly translated into human language, this command says, "From now on, allow a maximum width of 9 digits for obama_therm, and display 4 digits to the right of the decimal point."

The general syntax begins with "format *varname*", followed by a "%," which signals the beginning of a format specification. You then type a number for the maximum width of the variable ("9" is usually adequate), followed by a period ("."). Finally, type the number of decimals you want displayed, and end the specification with the letter "f."

The command "format obama_therm %9.2f" would tell Stata to display obama_therm with two decimal points, "80.89." The command "format obama_therm %9.0f" would instruct Stata to round to the nearest whole number, "81."

with a bar chart or a line chart. A bar chart is useful for summarizing the relationship between two categorical variables, such as the relationship between generation (yob3) and campaign interest (camp_int). Bar charts are the graphic companions of cross-tabulation analysis. A line chart is useful for depicting the relationship between a categorical independent variable and an interval-level dependent variable, such as the relationship between party identification (partyid7) and ratings of Barack Obama (obama_therm). Line charts are the graphic companions of mean comparison analysis.

To convince Stata to produce precisely the kind of graph you are after, preliminary command-line work is almost always required. Suppose you wanted a line chart depicting the mean values of obama_therm (dependent variable) across the values of partyid7 (independent variable). Stata's twoway command will oblige, but only after you generate a set of group means: mean values of obama_therm for each value of partyid7. Similarly, Stata's graph bar command will produce a bar chart showing the percentage of respondents in each generation (yob3) who have "High" campaign interest (coded 1 on camp_int), but you first need to generate a set of indicator variables.[3] Since you just performed a mean comparison analysis, first we will demonstrate how to create a line chart for the relationship between an interval-level dependent variable and an ordinal independent variable.

Graphing an Interval-level Dependent Variable

Figure 4-1 shows a line chart of the relationship you just analyzed, the relationship between Obama thermometer ratings and party identification. Examine Figure 4-1 for a few moments. This graphic is at once simple and informative. The y-axis records mean values of the dependent variable, the Barack Obama feeling thermometer. The line traces the mean ratings across the values of party identification: approximately 81 degrees for Strong Democrats, 68 degrees for Weak Democrats, and so on, all the way to 27 degrees for Strong Republicans. One can immediately see the negative relationship between the independent and dependent variables—as partyid7 increases from low codes to high codes, mean Obama ratings decline—as well as the curious similarities between the independent leaners and weak partisans of each party. The chart has a descriptive title, the y-axis is labeled clearly, and a source line identifies the data on which the graphic is based. You will want to incorporate these features into any chart you create.

Figure 4-1   Line Chart of the Relationship Between an Interval-level Dependent Variable and a Categorical
Independent Variable

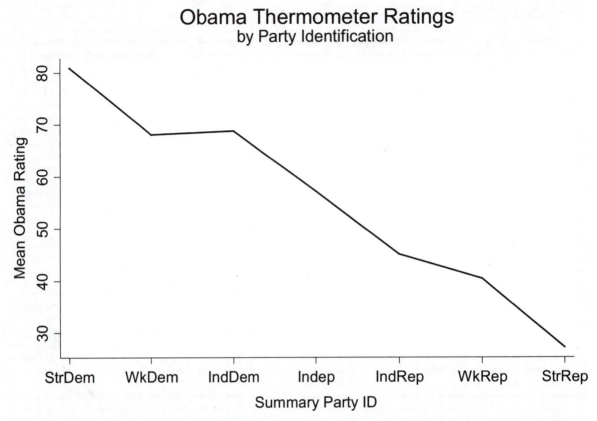

Source: 2008 American National Election Study

As we will see, the line chart in Figure 4-1 can be roughed out in the Command window and refined in the Graph Editor. Before reaching that point, however, we need to generate a new variable that records the mean of obama_therm for each value of partyid7. One of the programs you installed in Chapter 1, _gwtmean, will provide the assistance we need. The _gwtmean command will generate group means, that is, mean Obama thermometer ratings for strong Democrats, weak Democrats, and so on, for each partisan group. The newly generated group means can then be graphed using Stata's twoway command. Now, one of Stata's official commands, egen, also will generate group means (and many other group statistics). But egen does not permit weighted data. Because _gwtmean can be used with or without weights, it is well suited to our purposes. (Before proceeding, find out whether _gwtmean is installed by clicking in the Command window and typing "which _gwtmean". If _gwtmean is not installed, return to Chapter 1 and follow the download and installation instructions.)

The following command will generate a group mean, pid7_obama, that will record mean Obama ratings for each partisan group:

```
_gwtmean pid7_obama = obama_therm if obama_therm!=., by (partyid7)  weight(w)
```

This command has a few unfamiliar features—in fact, the whole thing probably looks a bit strange. For the moment, let's ignore the term "if obama_therm!=." and concentrate on the beginning of the command and the options to the right of the comma. The first part is similar to the generate command: type the command, then type the name of the new variable you want to create, followed by an equals sign, "_gwtmean pid7_obama =". Then type the name of the existing variable from which to generate group means, "obama_therm". Now focus on the options after the comma. The first element, "by (partyid7)", defines the groups for which the group means are to be generated. So, Stata will find the first code of partyid7, code 0 (strong Democrats), and generate a mean Obama rating for all strong Democrats in the dataset. It then moves to the next code, code 1 (weak Democrats), and generates a group mean, and then to code 2, and so on for each value of the variable named in the by() option. If you need to weight the data, as we do with nes2008, type "weight" followed by (in parentheses) the name of the dataset's weight variable. Because nes2008's weight variable has the pithy name "w", you would type, "weight (w)". *Note:* For all official Stata commands, request weights by typing "[aw=w]" on the left-hand side of the comma. For the_gwtmean command, request weights by typing "weight (w)" on the right-hand side of the comma.

Here is a problem with _gwtmean. When Stata encounters a case with a missing value on the variable from which it is creating group means (obama_therm, in the current example) but a nonmissing value on the grouping variable (partyid7), it will go ahead and assign that case a group mean anyway. Suppose a respondent wasn't asked the Obama thermometer question, or refused to answer, or said "don't know." This respondent has a missing value (".") on obama_therm. Suppose further that this same respondent said "strong Democrat" when asked the party identification question. Because this respondent has a missing value on the Obama thermometer, he or she clearly should be treated as missing on the new variable, pid7_obama. However, if not instructed otherwise, Stata will ignore the missing value on obama_therm and assign the respondent the same group mean as all other strong Democrats in the data. (The egen command shares this flaw.)

The remedy: the if qualifier. The statement "if obama_therm!=." says, "Perform this command if obama_therm is not equal to missing." The logical operator "!=" means "not equal to." A few other logical operators: a double-equal sign, "==", means "equal to"; ">" means "greater than"; "<=" means "less than or equal to." The if qualifier, which at the user's discretion will apply virtually any Stata command to a subset of cases, will make frequent appearances in future analyses. (See "A Closer Look" for a discussion of the if qualifier.)

A Closer Look   The if Qualifier

At the user's discretion, most Stata commands can be applied selectively to a subset of cases. Suppose, for example, that we wanted to confine our analysis of the relationship between Obama_therm and partyid7 to women, who are coded 2 on the gender variable. We would type "tab partyid7 if gender==2 [aw=w], sum(obama_therm)". The double-equals sign ("==") is Stata-speak for "equal to." So the qualifier "if gender==2" means "run the command for all cases having a value of 2 on gender." When you use the if qualifier, be sure to type it to the right of the list of variables you are analyzing and to the left of the comma that separates the command from the options list.

Here are some other examples. The command "tab partyid7 if educ_r<12 [aw=w], sum(obama_therm)" would display the obama_therm-partyid7 relationship for respondents having *less than* 12 years of schooling. (The variable, educ_r, records the number of years of education for each respondent.) The command "tab partyid7 if educ_r>=13 [aw=w], sum(obama_therm)" would confine the analysis to those with a value on educ_r *equal to greater than* 13 years of schooling.

You may also use the logical operators "&" (which stands for "and") and "|" (which stands for "or") to subset the cases you wish to analyze. The command "tab partyid7 if gender==2 & educ_r>=13 [aw=w], sum(obama_therm)" would show the relationship for females having 13 or more years of education. The command "tab partyid7 if region==2 | region==4 [aw=w], sum(obama_therm)" would display the relationship for respondents residing in the South (coded 3 on region) or in the West (coded 4 on region).

A list of Stata's most frequently used operators follows:

> greater than	< less than	>= greater than or equal to
<= less than or equal to	== equal to	~= not equal to
!= not equal to	& and	| or

All right, the _gwtmean command, properly qualified and optioned, will generate group means of obama_therm for each value of partyid7 (pid7_obama). Once again, here is the _gwtmean command that you want to type:

```
_gwtmean pid7_obama = obama_therm if obama_therm!=., by (partyid7)  weight(w)
```

Now let's create a basic graph that plots the group means of the Obama feeling thermometer (pid7_obama) for each value of party identification (partyid7). The following command, an application of Stata's versatile twoway command, will draw a graph that uses a line to connect the values of pid7_obama across the values of partyid7:

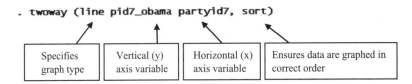

You start by typing the command "twoway" followed by a space and a left parenthesis. The first parenthetical argument requests a line graph, one of seven basic plot types in Stata's twoway repertoire. Then you type the variable that defines the vertical axis (pid7_obama, the group means of the Obama thermometer) and the variable that defines the horizontal axis (partyid7, party identification). Type a comma, followed by the sort option, which instructs Stata to first sort the cases on the x-axis variable. This ensures that Stata will group the cases on partyid7 before it plots mean Obama ratings.

Figure 4-2 shows the crude but editable result of the twoway command. Start the Graph Editor and, if desired, click the Record button. Let's perform four tasks: (1) label the x-axis values using the partyid7

Figure 4-2   Twoway Graph

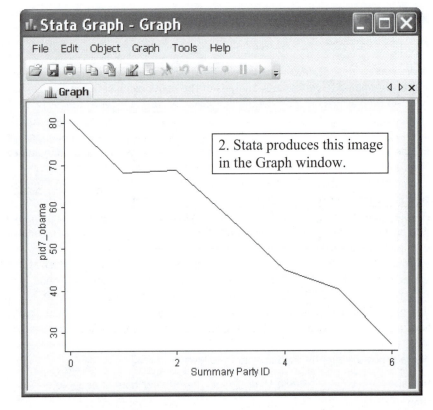

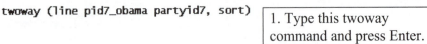

Figure 4-3 Changing Axis Properties

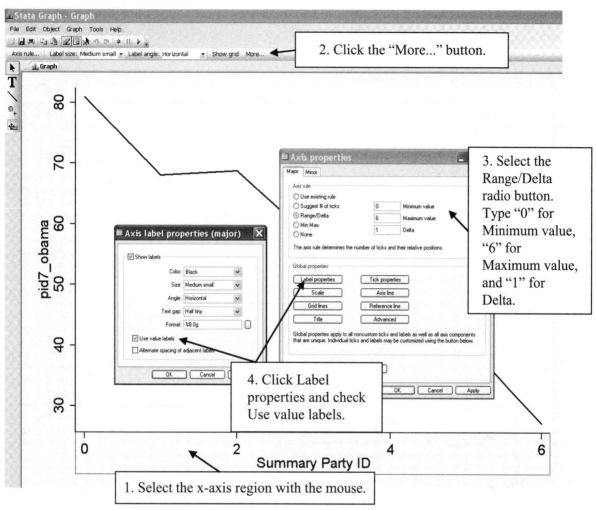

value labels; (2) change the y-axis title; (3) add a chart title, subtitle, and source note; and (4) make the plot line a bit thicker. The first task was covered in Chapter 2, but a quick review won't do any harm. Click in the x-axis region. Click More on the menu bar, opening the Axis properties window, as shown in Figure 4-3. In the Axis rule panel, select the Range/Delta radio button. We want to label every value of partyid7, from 0 ("StrDem") to 6 ("StrRep"). Therefore, type "0" in Minimum value, type "6" in Maximum value, and type "1" in Delta. In the Global properties panel, click Label properties. In the Axis label properties window, check the Use value labels box. Click OK, returning to the Axis properties window. Click OK.

Changing axis titles and adding text elements are easily accomplished. To change the y-axis title, select it with the mouse, as shown in Figure 4-4. Now click in the Text box on the main menu bar and type an appropriate axis title, such as "Mean Obama Rating." The Graph Editor replaces the axis title. To add positional titles—chart title, subtitle, and source note—use the Object Browser, as depicted in Figures 4-5 (title), 4-6 (subtitle), and 4-7 (note). Select the element you want to add, click in the Text box on the main menu bar, and type appropriate text. Finally, change the line thickness by selecting the line and making a choice from the Width drop-down on the main menu bar (Figure 4-8). Given other desired edits—for example, Stata's default font sizes are rather large and may require down-sizing—the final product should look like Figure 4-1. Before exiting the Chart Editor, be sure to save the graph.

Figure 4-4 Changing the Y-axis Title

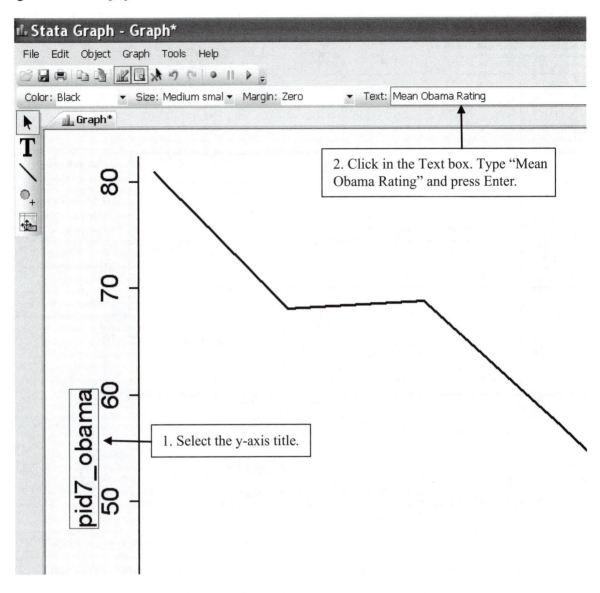

Figure 4-5 Adding a Chart Title

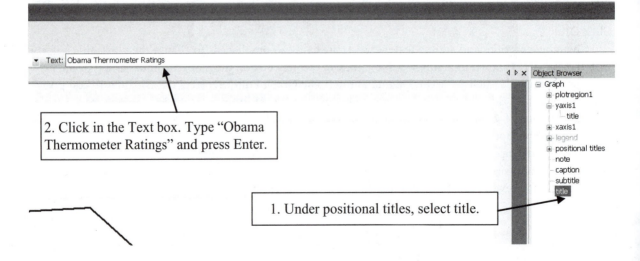

Figure 4-6   Adding a Chart Subtitle

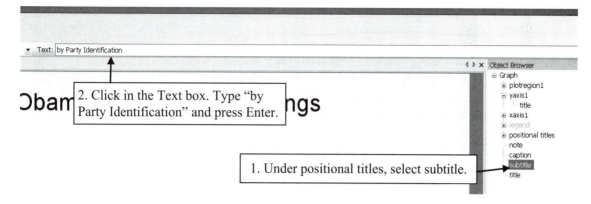

Figure 4-7   Adding a Source Note

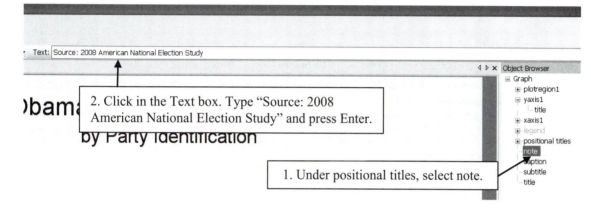

Figure 4-8   Changing the Line Thickness

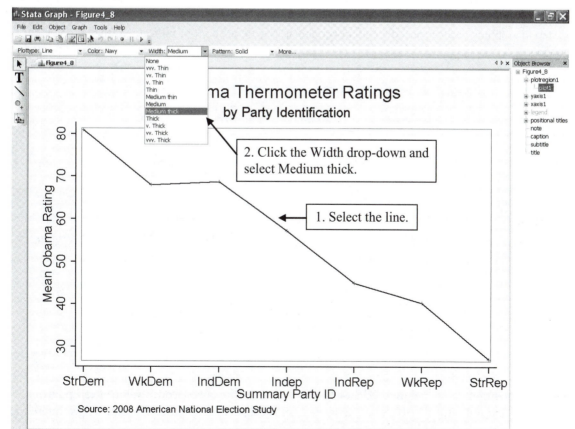

Graphing a Categorical Dependent Variable

As we have just seen, a line chart will concisely summarize the relationship between an interval-level dependent variable and a categorical independent variable. In fact, for clarifying complex relationships between variables of any level of measurement, line charts point the researcher toward the correct interpretation. (This use of line charts is covered in Chapter 5.) Sometimes, however, you may wish to create a bar chart to depict the relationship between two categorical variables, such as the relationship between generation (yob3) and campaign interest (camp_int). Let's run the camp_int-yob3 analysis again and figure out what a bar chart of the relationship should look like:

```
. tab camp_int yob3 [aw=w], col nofreq nokey
```

Campaign interest	Three generations 1949/befo	1950-1965	1966-1990	Total
High	59.57	53.32	37.29	48.06
Moderate	28.63	33.67	40.82	35.42
Low	11.80	13.02	21.89	16.52
Total	100.00	100.00	100.00	100.00

Suppose we would like the bar chart's y-axis to display the percentage of respondents who have a "High" level of campaign interest. The categories of yob3—"1949/before," "1950-1965," and "1966-1990"—will appear along the horizontal axis. Based on the cross-tabulation analysis, we can anticipate what the bar chart will look like. The bar for the oldest generation will stand at 59.57 percent, the middle group at 53.32 percent, and the youngest age cohort at 37.29 percent. We can easily state our graphic goal in human language: "I want to graph the percentage of respondents with 'High' campaign interest across different values of yob3." As is sometimes the case with Stata, however, this human language cannot be translated directly into a single Stata command.

The simple truth is that Stata does not like to graph categorical dependent variables. But Stata *does* like to graph indicator variables, transformations of categorical variables. In Chapter 3 you learned how to run tabulate (with the generate option) to compute a set of indicator variables from a categorical variable. For any categorical variable having K categories, Stata will generate K indicator variables, named sequentially based on the name handle that you supply in the generate option. Each indicator variable will be coded 1 for cases falling into that category of the original variable and coded 0 for cases not falling into that category. The first step in graphing a categorical dependent variable is to generate a set of indicator variables. Type the following:

```
. tab camp_int [aw=w], gen(campdum)
```

Campaign interest	Freq.	Percent	Cum.
High	1,110.0468	47.81	47.81
Moderate	828.228274	35.67	83.47
Low	383.724937	16.53	100.00
Total	2,322	100.00	

Stata produces a frequency distribution in the Results window. Stata also creates three indicator variables—campdum1, campdum2, and campdum3—and lists them at the bottom of the Variables window:

Focus your attention on campdum1. Because "High" interest is the lowest-coded value of camp_int (code 1), the first indicator variable that Stata generates is coded 1 for respondents with "High" interest and coded 0 for respondents who have "Moderate" or "Low" interest.

Now let's demonstrate why Stata likes to work with indicator variables. The following command will return the mean of campdum1 (dependent variable) for each value of yob3 (independent variable):

```
. tab yob3 [aw=w], sum(campdum1) nost nofreq noobs
```

Three generations	Summary of camp_int==High Mean
1949/befo	.59567202
1950–1965	.53317374
1966–1990	.37288828
Total	.48059936

Notice that the mean of attentdum1 for the oldest generation is .5957 (that is, .59567202 rounded to four decimal points). Refer back to our cross-tabulation analysis. What percentage of this generation has "High" interest in the campaigns? 59.57 percent. You can see that the means of our newly created indicator variable, campdum1, are identical to the proportions of respondents in each generation who fall into the "High" interest category of the original variable, camp_int. Remember that a proportion is just a percentage that's been divided by 100. In the cross-tab we found that 53.32 percent of the 1950–1965 group said they had "High" interest, which appears as a mean—a proportion—of .5332 on campdum1. For the youngest cohort the numbers are the same, as well: 37.29 percent and .3729. More generally, *the mean of an indicator variable is equal to the proportion of cases coded 1 on the indicator variable.* Because a code of 1 on campdum1 denotes "High" interest, the means .5957, .5332, and .3729 report the proportions of respondents in each value of the independent variable, yob3, who have "High" interest.

Graphically, percentages are more attractive than proportions. Using Stata's replace command, we can convert campdum1 into percentages:

```
. replace campdum1 = 100*campdum1
(1128 real changes made)

. tab yob3 [aw=w], sum(campdum1) nost nofreq noobs
```

Three generations	Summary of camp_int==High Mean
1949/befo	59.567202
1950–1965	53.317374
1966–1990	37.288828
Total	48.059936

Why use replace instead of generate? (See "A Closer Look" for a discussion of the replace command.)

A Closer Look — The replace Command

Stata's replace command, a special instance of the generate command, can be used to change or replace the values of a variable that already exists. Unlike Stata's devil-may-care attitude toward the recode command—if the user doesn't consciously specify the generate option, the recode command will destroy and replace the original variable—Stata will not permit the generate command to overwrite an existing variable. Suppose you sought to convert campdum1 from a proportion to a percentage; that is, you wanted to multiply campdum1 times 100. If you entered, "generate campdum1=campdum1 * 100", Stata would refuse, saying, "campdum1 already defined." However, if you typed, "replace campdum1=campdum1 * 100", Stata would perform as requested.

With the appropriate indicator variable in hand, we can now run Stata's graph bar command:

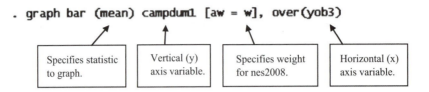

The goal here is to graph mean values of the dependent variable, campdum1, by ("over") values of the independent variable, yob3. Type the two-word command "graph bar", followed by (in parentheses) "mean", one of many different statistics that graph bar will display. Type the dependent (y-axis) variable, followed by the weight stipulation, if appropriate. (We need the weight for nes2008, but not for the other datasets.) Type a comma and name the independent variable in parentheses after the word "over": "over(yob3)".

Figure 4-9 shows the graphic result. Another good beginning. Start the Graph Editor and make these changes: (1) change the y-axis title to "Percentage with 'High' Interest"; (2) in positional titles, add the following chart title: "Percentage with 'High' Campaign Interest"; (3) add this subtitle: "by Generation"; and (4) add this note: "Source: 2008 American National Election Study". Barring any personalized edits you decide to make, the edited bar chart should look similar to Figure 4-10.

Figure 4-9 Bar Chart (unedited)

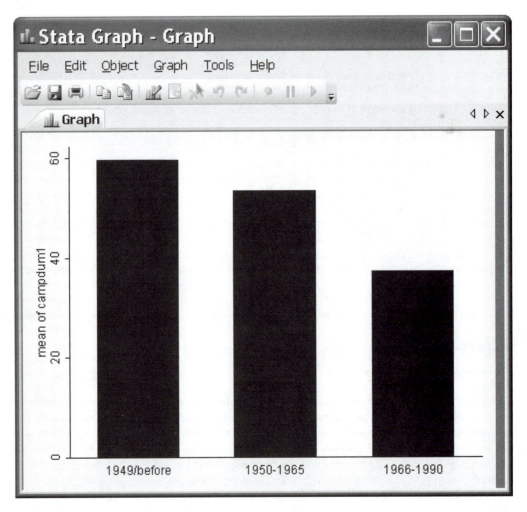

Figure 4-10 Bar Chart (edited)

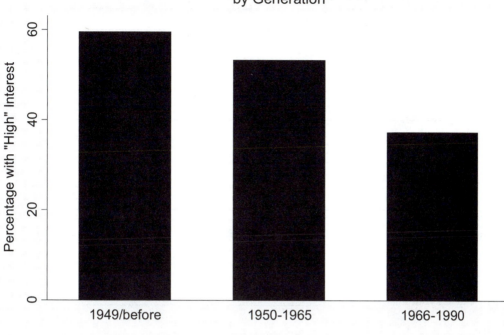

Percentage with "High" Campaign Interest
by Generation

Source: 2008 American National Election Study

EXERCISES

1. (Dataset: nes2008. Variables: medinsur_r, partyid7, [aw=w].) Here is a widely observed difference between Democrats and Republicans: Democrats favor government-funded medical insurance and Republicans prefer private insurance plans. Is this difference borne out by the data? Dataset nes2008 contains the variable medinsur_r, a 7-point scale that measures respondents' opinions on this issue. Respondents indicate their opinions by choosing any position on this scale, from 1 (government plan) at one end to 7 (private plan) at the other end. This is the dependent variable. Use the 7-point party identification scale (partyid7) as the independent variable.

    A. If Democrats are more likely than Republicans to favor government-funded medical insurance, then Democrats will have (check one)

    ❑ a higher mean than do Republicans on medinsur_r.

    ❑ about the same mean as do Republicans on medinsur_r.

    ❑ a lower mean than do Republicans on medinsur_r.

    B. Run tabulate with the summarize option to obtain a mean comparison that shows the mean score on the dependent variable, medinsur_r, for each category of the independent variable, partyid7. (Make sure to weight the data. You might also wish to specify these options: nost, nofreq, noobs.) Write the results in the table that follows:

Summary of Govt/private medical insurance scale: self-placement	
Party ID	Mean
Strong Democrat	?
Weak Democrat	?
Independent-Dem	?
Independent	?
Independent-Rep	?
Weak Republican	?
Strong Republican	?
Total	?

C. Generally speaking, does your analysis support the idea that Democrats are more likely than Republicans to support government-funded medical insurance? (circle one)

Yes   No

Briefly explain your answer. _____

_____

_____

D. Suppose you overheard someone making this claim: "People might say they're 'Independent-Democrats,' but when it comes to opinions about medical insurance, they're closer to 'Independent' than to 'Democrat.'" Based on your analysis, is this claim correct? (circle one)

Yes   No

Briefly explain your answer. _____

_____

_____

Before proceeding to part E, you will need to run the following command, which generates pid7_medinsur, group means of medinsur_r for each partisan category: **_gwtmean pid7_medinsur= medinsur_r if medinsur_r!=., by(partyid7) weight(w)**

E. Create and print a line chart of the relationship between pid_medinsur (y-axis) and partyid7 (x-axis). (i) Run twoway to create the rough product. (ii) Make six refinements in the Graph Editor: Label the x-axis with the values of partyid7; change the y-axis title to read, "Mean Score"; add a chart title, "Medical Insurance Opinions"; add a subtitle, "by Party Identification"; add a source note: "Source: 2008 American National Election Study"; and make the plot line thicker. (iii) Print the chart.

2. (Dataset: nes2008. Variables: gay_marriage3, relig_attend3, gender, libcon3_r, [aw=w].) Should gay couples be legally permitted to marry? This controversial issue has gained center stage in recent elections. In 2004, amendments regarding the legal definition of marriage appeared on the ballot in 11 states. In 2008, three states considered such measures, and a fourth considered whether unmarried couples (including same-sex couples) should be prohibited from adopting or serving as foster parents. One can imagine several

characteristics that divide people on this issue. People who are more religiously observant might be less likely to favor gay marriage than are the less observant. Men may be less likely than women to favor it. Or conservatives might be less open to the idea than are liberals.

Dataset nes2008 contains gay_marriage3, which is coded 1 (yes, gay marriage should be allowed), 2 (no, gay marriage should not be allowed, but civil unions should be permitted), or 3 (no, gay marriage should not be allowed). This is the dependent variable that you will use to test each of the following hypotheses:

Hypothesis 1: In a comparison of individuals, people who have high levels of attendance at religious services will be less likely to favor gay marriage than will people who have lower levels of religious attendance. (The independent variable is relig_attend3.)

Hypothesis 2: In a comparison of individuals, men are less likely than women to favor gay marriage. (The independent variable is gender.)

Hypothesis 3: In a comparison of individuals, conservatives are less likely than liberals to favor gay marriage. (The independent variable is libcon3_r.)

A. Test these hypotheses by obtaining three cross-tabulations, one for each hypothesis. Be sure to request column percentages. This is dataset nes2008, so remember to weight the analysis. Clean things up with the nofreq and nokey options. For example, the following syntax will permit you to test the first hypothesis: "tab gay_marriage3 relig_attend3 [aw=w], col nofreq nokey". In the following spaces, record the percentages who say "Yes" when asked about gay marriage:

	Level of religious attendance		
	High	Middle	Low
Percentage "Yes"	?	?	?
	R gender		
	Male		Female
Percentage "Yes"	?		?
	R self-placement lib-con scale		
	Liberal	Moderate	Conservative
Percentage "Yes"	?	?	?

B. These findings (circle one)

        support Hypothesis 1.   do not support Hypothesis 1.

Briefly explain your reasoning. _____

_____

_____

_____

_____

C. These findings (circle one)

        support Hypothesis 2.   do not support Hypothesis 2.

Briefly explain your reasoning. _____

_____

_____

_____

_____

_____

D. These findings (circle one)

        support Hypothesis 3.   do not support Hypothesis 3.

Briefly explain your reasoning. _____

_____

_____

_____

_____

_____

Perform two tasks before proceeding to part E: (i) Run the following command, which will generate a set of indicator variables (gay_dum1, gay_dum2, gay_dum3) from gay_marriage3: "tab gay_marriage3 [aw=w], gen(gay_dum)". Gay_dum1 records the proportion of respondents saying "Yes" to gay marriage. (ii) Convert the proportion to a percentage by running the replace command: "replace gay_dum1= gay_dum1 * 100".

E. Create and print a bar chart. (i) Run graph bar to create a bar chart of the relationship between gay_dum1 and relig_attend3. The y-axis will depict the mean of gay_dum1 over values of relig_attend3 (x-axis). (Again, don't forget nes2008's weight variable.) (ii) Make four refinements in the Graph Editor: Change the y-axis title to read, "Percentage Favoring Gay Marriage"; add a chart title, "Percentage Favoring Gay Marriage"; add a subtitle, "by Religious Attendance"; and add a source note: "Source: 2008 American National Election Study". (iii) Print the chart.

3. (Dataset: nes2008. Variables: who08, r_econ_past3, [aw=w].) What factors determine how people vote in presidential elections? Political scientists have investigated and debated this question for many years. A particularly powerful and elegant perspective emphasizes voters' *retrospective* evaluations. According to this view, for example, voters whose financial situations have gotten better during the year preceding the election are likely to reward the candidate of the incumbent party. Voters whose economic situations have worsened, by contrast, are likely to punish the incumbent party by voting for the candidate of the party not currently in power. As political scientist V. O. Key once famously put it, the electorate plays the role of "rational god of vengeance and reward."[4] Does Key's idea help explain how people voted in the 2008 election?

A. Test this hypothesis: In a comparison of individuals, those whose personal finances improved during the year preceding the 2008 election were more likely to vote for the candidate of the incumbent party, John McCain, than were individuals whose personal finances worsened. Use these two variables from nes2008: who08 (dependent variable) and r_econ_past3 (independent variable). Obtain a cross-tabulation of the relationship. Record the percentages voting for McCain and Obama in the table that follows:

R better/same/worse off than 1 yr ago				
Pres vote 2008	Better	Same	Worse	Total
McCain	?	?	?	?
Obama	?	?	?	?
Total	100.0	100.0	100.0	100.0

B. What do you think? Are the data consistent with the hypothesis? Write a paragraph explaining your reasoning.

_____

_____

_____

_____

C. _Loss aversion_ is an interesting psychological phenomenon that can shape the choices people make.[5] One idea behind loss aversion is that losses loom larger than commensurate gains. According to this theory, for example, the psychological pain felt from losing $100 is greater than the pleasure felt from gaining $100. Applied to retrospective voting, loss aversion might suggest that the "vengeance" impulse is stronger than the "reward" impulse—that the anti-incumbent-party motivation among those whose financial fortunes worsened will be stronger than the pro-incumbent-party motivation among those whose financial fortunes improved.

With this idea in mind, examine the percentages in the table in part A. What do you think? Do the data suggest that Key's rational god of vengeance is stronger than his rational god of reward? Answer yes or no and write a few sentences explaining your reasoning.

_____

_____

_____

_____

_____

4. (Dataset: nes2008. Variables: voter0408, age5, hispanic, race2, income_r3, contact_GOTV, [aw=w].) In 2008, 131 million Americans voted, 9 million more than in 2004. Who were these newly mobilized voters? The Obama campaign, in particular, staged get-out-the-vote (GOTV) drives among groups that are most likely to stay home on Election Day: young people, Hispanics, African Americans, and the poor. It stands to reason, then, that newly mobilized voters in 2008 will resemble nonvoters in most ways, except one: the newly mobilized were more likely than nonvoters to be contacted by GOTV campaigns. Furthermore, both

nonvoters and new voters will be demographically different from established voters, that is, people who voted in 2004 and 2008. Consider the following hypothetical expectations:

(i)   Newly mobilized voters will be similar to nonvoters in age, Hispanic composition, racial composition, and income.

(ii) Newly mobilized voters and nonvoters will be different from established voters in age, Hispanic composition, racial composition, and income.

(iii) Newly mobilized voters will be more likely than nonvoters to report being contacted during the campaign by GOTV efforts.

The nes2008 dataset contains voter0408, which classifies each respondent as "Nonvoter" (did not vote in 2004 or 2008), "New voter" (voted in 2008 but not in 2004), or "Voter" (voted in both elections).[6] This is the independent variable.

Run five cross-tabulations analyzing the relationship between voter0408 and age5, hispanic, race2, income_r3, and contact_GOTV. (*Note*: You created income_r3 in Chapter 3's "Closer Look" using the xtile command.)

A.   Browse the cross-tabulation results. Write the percentage of each voter type having the attribute listed in the left-hand column. Along the "Percent 18-30 yrs of age" row, for example, write the percentage of nonvoters who are 18-30 years old, the percentage of new voters who are 18-30, and the percentage of voters who are 18-30.

Attribute	Nonvoters	New voters	Voters
Percent 18-30 yrs of age	?	?	?
Percent Hispanic	?	?	?
Percent black	?	?	?
Percent low income	?	?	?
Percent "Yes" contacted	?	?	?

B.   Examine the table in part B. Think about the hypothetical expectations regarding age, Hispanic composition, racial composition, income, and GOTV contact. In what ways are your findings consistent with the expectations? In what ways do your findings depart from expectations?

_____

_____

_____

_____

_____

For Exercises 5–8, you will analyze gss2006. For this dataset, you will not use a weight variable. Because Stata reports unweighted observations in nice round numbers, exercises 5–8 may ask you to record numbers of observations, as well as means and percentages.

5.   (Dataset: gss2006. Variables: polviews, fem_role.) Why do some people hold more traditional views about the role of women in society and politics, whereas others take a less traditional stance? General ideological

orientations, liberalism versus conservatism, may play an important role in shaping individuals' opinions on this cultural question. Thus it seems plausible to suggest that ideology (independent variable) will affect opinions about appropriate female roles (dependent variable). The hypothesis: In a comparison of individuals, liberals will be more likely than conservatives to approve of nontraditional female roles.

The gss2006 dataset contains fem_role, a scale that measures opinions about the appropriate role of women. You analyzed this variable in Chapter 2. Recall that fem_role scores ranges from 0 (women belong in the home) to 12 (women belong in work and politics). That is, higher scores denote less traditional beliefs. This is the dependent variable. The dataset also has polviews, a 7-point ordinal scale measuring ideology. Scores on polviews can range from 1 (extremely liberal) to 7 (extremely conservative). This is the independent variable.

A. According to the hypothesis, as the values of polviews increase, from 1 through 7, mean values of fem_role should (circle one)

decrease.   neither decrease nor increase.   increase.

B. Run tabulate with the summarize option to obtain mean values of fem_role across values of polviews. Specify the nost option. Fill in the table that follows:

Female role: Children, home, politics		
Ideological self placement	Mean	Freq.
Extremely liberal	?	?
Liberal	?	?
Slightly liberal	?	?
Moderate	?	?
Slightly conservative	?	?
Conservative	?	?
Extremely conservative	?	?
Total	?	?

C. Do the results support the hypothesis? Write a few sentences explaining your reasoning.

_____

_____

_____

_____

Before proceeding to part D, run _gwtmean to generate a new variable, named polviews_fem, recording group means of fem_role for each value of polviews. The syntax for _gwtmean is the same as illustrated in this chapter. However, do not include a weight variable.

D. Create and print a line chart of the relationship between polviews_fem (y-axis) and polviews (x-axis). (i) Run twoway to create the rough product. (ii) Make six refinements in the Graph Editor: Label the x-axis with the values of polviews (to enhance readability, set the label angle at 45 degrees and request small labels); change the y-axis title to read, "Mean Score"; add a chart title, "Opinions on Women's Role"; add a subtitle, "by Ideological Self-placement"; add a source note: "Source: 2006 General Social Survey"; and make the plot line thicker. (iii) Print the chart.

6. (Dataset: gss2006. Variables: tvhours, news.) Here are two common media fixtures in our lives: newspapers and television. Are people who consume the printed word also avid consumers of broadcast media? Or is it an either-or proposition, with newspaper readers being less likely than newspaper nonreaders to watch television? There isn't much theory to rely on here, so let's test an exploratory hypothesis: In a comparison of individuals, people who read newspapers more often will spend more hours watching television than will those who read newspapers less often.

A. In this hypothesis, the dependent variable is (fill in the blank) _____,

and the independent variable is (fill in the blank) _____.

B. According to this hypothesis, if one compares people who frequently read a newspaper with people who infrequently read a newspaper, (check one)

❏ the mean number of hours spent watching television will be higher among newspaper readers than among the nonreaders.

❏ the mean number of hours spent watching television will be lower among newspaper readers than among the nonreaders.

C. Run tabulate with the summarize option to test this hypothesis. The gss2006 dataset contains these variables: tvhours and news. The variable tvhours measures the number of hours the respondent watches television each day. The news variable measures how frequently the respondent reads a newspaper during the week. Lower values on news denote less frequent newspaper reading, and higher values on news denote more frequent newspaper reading. Record your results in the table that follows. Write the value labels of the independent variable in the left-most column. Record the mean values of the dependent variable in the column labeled "Mean" and the number of cases in the column labeled "Freq."

Values of independent variable	Mean	Freq.
?	?	?
?	?	?
?	?	?
?	?	?
?	?	?
Total	?	?

D. Examine the mean comparison table. Suppose you wanted to collapse the values of the independent variable into only two categories, "Low" and "High." Your goal is to combine values of the independent variable in such a way that respondents scoring "Low" on the collapsed variable share similar values on the dependent variable, and respondents scoring "High" on the independent variable share similar values on the dependent variable. Based on the analysis you just performed, which values of the independent variable would fall into the "High" category? (circle all that apply)

Never   Less than once/week   Once/week   Few times/week   Every day

7. (Dataset: gss2006. Variables: intrace_2, affrmact2, natrace.) Untruthful answers by survey respondents can create big headaches for public opinion researchers. Why might a respondent not tell the truth to an

interviewer? Certain types of questions, combined with particular characteristics of the interviewer, can trigger a phenomenon called preference falsification: "the act of misrepresenting one's genuine wants under perceived social pressures."[7] For example, consider the difficulty in gauging opinions on affirmative action, hiring policies aimed at giving preference to black applicants. One might reasonably expect people questioned by an African American interviewer to express greater support for such programs than would those questioned by a white pollster. An affirmative action opponent, not wanting to appear racially insensitive to a black questioner, might instead offer a false pro–affirmative action opinion.[8]

The gss2006 dataset contains intrace_2, coded 0 for respondents questioned by a white interviewer and coded 1 for those questioned by a black interviewer. This is the independent variable that will allow you to test two preference falsification hypotheses:

Hypothesis 1: In a comparison of individuals, those questioned by a black interviewer will be more likely to express support for affirmative action than will those questioned by a white interviewer. (The dependent variable is affrmact2, coded 1 for "Support" and 2 for "Oppose.")

Hypothesis 2: In a comparison of individuals, those questioned by a black interviewer will be more likely to say that we are spending too little to improve the condition of blacks than will those questioned by a white interviewer. (The dependent variable is natrace, which is coded 1 for respondents saying, "Too little"; 2 for those saying, "About the right amount"; and 3 for "Too much.")

A. Run two cross-tabulation analyses, one analyzing the relationship between intrace_2 and affrmact2 and one analyzing the relationship between intrace_2 and natrace. Make sure to request column percentages. In the table that follows, record the percentages that "Support" affirmative action and the percentages that say we are spending "Too little" to improve the condition of blacks.

	Interviewer's race	
	White	Black
Percent "Support" affirmative action	?	?
Percent spending "Too little" to improve condition of blacks	?	?

B. These findings (circle one)

        support Hypothesis 1.   do not support Hypothesis 1.

Briefly explain your reasoning. _____

_____

_____

_____

C. These findings (circle one)

        support Hypothesis 2.   do not support Hypothesis 2.

Briefly explain your reasoning. _____

_____

_____

_____

_____

Perform two tasks before proceeding to part D. (i) Generate a set of indicator variables from affrmact2, using the variable handle "affdum." Affdum1 records the proportion of respondents who "Support" affirmative action. (ii) Run the replace command to convert affdum1 from a proportion to a percentage.

D. Create and print a bar chart. (i) Run graph bar to create a bar chart of the relationship between affdum1 and intrace_2. (ii) Make four refinements in the Graph Editor: Change the y-axis title to read, "Percentage Supporting Affirmative Action"; add a chart title, "Percentage Supporting Affirmative Action"; add a subtitle, "by Race of Interviewer"; and add a source note: "Source: 2006 General Social Survey". (iii) Print the chart.

8. (Dataset: gss2006. Variables: science_gw3, partyid_3, polview3.) The following exchange between George W. Bush and Al Gore during the 2000 campaign illustrates a key feature of the global warming debate: Republicans and conservatives do not perceive scientific agreement on the causes of global warming, whereas Democrats and liberals do. Bush said, "I don't think we know the solution to global warming yet and I don't think we've got all the facts before we make decisions." Gore disagreed "that we don't know the cause of global warming. I think that we do. It's pollution, carbon dioxide and other chemicals that are even more potent." Bush persisted: "Some of the scientists, I believe, haven't they been changing their opinion a little bit on global warming? There's a lot of differing opinions. . . ."[9]

At the elite level, at least, the global warming battle line is defined by how much one believes that scientists themselves agree on the issue. Is this line of disagreement evident, as well, among the mass public? Are Democrats more likely to perceive scientific consensus than are Republicans? Are liberals more likely than conservatives to think that scientists agree about the causes of global warming? The gss2006 dataset contains science_gw3, which records respondents' assessments of the extent to which "environmental scientists agree among themselves about the existence and causes of global warming." Responses are coded 1 ("Scientists agree"), 2 ("Middle"), or 3 ("Scientists disagree"). This is the dependent variable. The two independent variables are partyid_3 (coded 1 for Democrats, 2 for independents, and 3 for Republicans) and polview3 (coded 1 for self-described liberals, 2 for moderates, and 3 for conservatives). (You created polview3 in one of the Chapter 3 exercises.)

A. Run the appropriate cross-tabulation analyses and examine the output. Which of the following inferences are supported by your analysis? (check all that apply)

❑ Overall, most respondents think that scientists disagree among themselves about the existence and causes of global warming.

❑ Democrats are more likely than Republicans to think that scientists agree among themselves.

❑ Republicans are more likely than independents to think that scientists agree among themselves.

❑ Liberals are more likely than conservatives to think that scientists agree among themselves.

❑ There is about a 10-point difference between the percentage of liberals who think that scientists agree and the percentage of moderates who think that scientists agree.

❑ There is about a 10-point difference between the percentage of moderates who think that scientists agree and the percentage of conservatives who think that scientists agree.

B. Create a bar chart depicting the relationship between science_gw3 and partyid_3. (*Hint*: You'll need to generate indicator variables from science_gw3. The first indicator variable will record the proportion of respondents who think that scientists agree.) The vertical axis should display the percentage of respondents who think that scientists agree. Give the vertical axis a more descriptive title. Add a title, subtitle, and source note. Make the chart more readable, and make any other desired appearance-enhancing changes. Print the chart.

9. (Dataset: states. Variables: union, region.) Where are unions stronger? Where are they weaker? Consider the following two claims:

Claim 1: States in the northeastern United States are more likely to have unionized workforces than are states in the South.

Claim 2: States in the Midwest and West have levels of unionization more similar to those in the South than to those in the Northeast.

A. The states dataset contains union, the percentage of each state's workforce that is unionized. Another variable, region, is a 4-category census classification of the states. Run a mean comparison analysis. Record your results in the table that follows:

Percentage of workers who are union members		
Census region	Mean	Freq.
Northeast	?	?
Midwest	?	?
South	?	?
West	?	?
Total	?	50

B. Based on your analysis, would you say that Claim 1 is correct or incorrect? How do you know? Check the appropriate box and complete the sentence that follows.

❑ Claim 1 is correct, because _____

_____.

❑ Claim 1 is incorrect, because _____

_____.

C. Based on your analysis, would you say that Claim 2 is correct or incorrect? How do you know? Check the appropriate box and complete the sentence that follows.

❑ Claim 2 is correct, because _____

_____.

❑ Claim 2 is incorrect, because _____

_____.

D. Produce a bar chart of the relationship you just analyzed. The vertical axis will depict the percentage of states' workforces that are unionized. (*Note*: The dependent variable, union, is in graph-ready form, so you do not need to create indicator variables.) Give the vertical axis a more descriptive title, such as "Mean Percentage Unionized". Add a title ("Unionized Workforce"), subtitle ("by Region"), and source note ("Source: States Dataset"). Make any other desired appearance-enhancing changes. Print the chart.

10. (Dataset: states. Variables: cigarettes, cig_tax_3.) Two policy researchers are arguing about whether higher taxes on cigarettes reduce cigarette consumption:

Policy researcher 1: "The demand for cigarettes is highly inelastic—smokers need to consume cigarettes, and they will buy them without regard to the cost. Raising taxes on a pack of cigarettes will have no effect on the level of cigarette consumption."

Policy researcher 2: "Look, any behavior that's taxed is discouraged. If state governments want to discourage smoking, then raising cigarette taxes will certainly have the desired effect. Higher taxes mean lower consumption."

Imagine a line chart of the relationship between cigarette taxes and cigarette consumption. The horizontal axis measures state cigarette taxes in three categories, from lower taxes on the left to higher taxes on the right. The vertical axis records per-capita cigarette consumption. Now consider line charts X, Y, and Z, which follow:

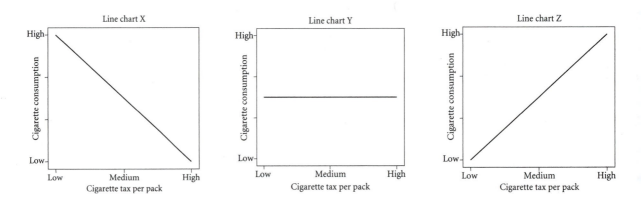

A. If policy researcher 1 were correct, which line chart would most accurately depict the relationship between states' cigarette taxes and cigarette consumption? (circle one)

Line chart X   Line chart Y   Line chart Z

B. If policy researcher 2 were correct, which line chart would most accurately depict the relationship between states' cigarette taxes and cigarette consumption? (circle one)

Line chart X   Line chart Y   Line chart Z

C. The states dataset contains the variables cigarettes and cig_tax_3. Run a mean comparison analysis, using cigarettes as the dependent variable and cig_tax_3 as the independent variable. Record your results in the table that follows:

Summary of Packs bimonthly per adult pop		
Cigarette tax per pack: 3 categories	Mean	Freq.
$.07-$.64	?	?
$.695-$1.36	?	?
$1.41-$2.58	?	?
Total	?	50

Before proceeding to part D, run _gwtmean to generate a new variable, named cig_tax_cigs, recording group means of cigarettes for each value of cig_tax_3. The syntax for _gwtmean is the same as illustrated in this chapter. However, do not include a weight variable.

D. Create and print a line chart of the relationship between cig_tax_cigs (y-axis) and cig_tax_3 (x-axis). (i) Run twoway to create the rough product. (ii) Make these refinements in the Graph Editor: Label the x-axis, using the value labels of cig_tax_3; change the y-axis title to read, "Mean Cigarette Consumption"; add a chart title, "Cigarette Consumption"; add a subtitle, "by Cigarette Taxes"; add a source note: "Source: States Dataset"; and make the plot line thicker. (iii) Print the chart.

E. Examine the mean comparison table and the line chart. Which policy researcher is more correct? (check one)

❑ Policy researcher 1 is more correct.

❑ Policy researcher 2 is more correct.

For Exercises 11–14, you will analyze the world dataset. For this dataset, you will not use a weight variable.

11. (Dataset: world. Variables: enpp3_democ, district_size3, frac_eth3.) Two scholars of comparative politics are discussing possible reasons why some democracies have many political parties and other democracies have only a few:

Scholar 1: "It all has to do with the rules of the election game. Some countries, such as the United Kingdom, have single-member electoral districts. Voters in each district elect only one representative. This militates in favor of fewer and larger parties, since small parties have less chance of winning enough votes to gain the seat. Other countries, like Switzerland, have multi-member districts. Because voters choose more than one representative per district, a larger number of smaller parties have a chance to win representation. It doesn't surprise me in the least, then, that the U.K. has fewer political parties than Switzerland."

Scholar 2: "I notice that your explanation fails to mention the single most important determinant of the number of political parties: social structural heterogeneity. Homogeneous societies, those with few linguistic or religious differences, have fewer conflicts and thus fewer parties. Heterogeneous polities, by the same logic, are more contentious and will produce more parties. By the way, the examples you picked to support your case also support mine: the U.K. is relatively homogeneous and Switzerland relatively heterogeneous. It doesn't surprise me in the least, then, that the U.K. has fewer political parties than Switzerland."

A. Scholar 1's hypothesis: In a comparison of democracies, those having single-member districts will have (circle one)

fewer political parties   more political parties

than democracies electing multiple members from each district.

B. State Scholar 2's hypothesis: _____

_____

_____

_____

_____

C. The world dataset variable enpp3_democ measures, for each democracy, the number of effective parliamentary parties: 1–3 parties (coded 1), 4–5 parties (coded 2), or 6–11 parties (coded 3). Use enpp3_democ as the dependent variable to test each hypothesis. For independent variables, test Scholar 1's hypothesis using district_size3, which measures the number of seats per district: countries with single-member districts are coded 1, countries that average more than one but fewer than six members are coded 2, and countries with six or more members per district are coded 3. Test Scholar 2's hypothesis using frac_eth3, which classifies each country's level of ethnic/linguistic fractionalization as low (coded 1), medium (coded 2), or high (coded 3). Countries with higher codes on frac_eth3 have a higher level of ethnic conflict. Use cross-tabulation analysis to test the hypotheses. In the table that follows, record the percentages of cases falling into the lowest code of the dependent variable, 1–3 parties:

	Average # of members per district		
	Single-member	> 1 to 5 members	6 or more members
Percentage having 1–3 parties	?	?	?
	Level of ethnic fractionalization		
	Low	Medium	High
Percentage having 1–3 parties	?	?	?

D. Which of the following statements best summarizes your findings? (check one)

❑ Scholar 1's hypothesis is supported by the analysis, but Scholar 2's hypothesis is not supported by the analysis.

❑ Scholar 2's hypothesis is supported by the analysis, but Scholar 1's hypothesis is not supported by the analysis.

❑ Both hypotheses are supported by the analysis.

❑ Neither hypothesis is supported by the analysis.

E. Making specific reference to your findings, write a paragraph explaining your choice in part D. _____

12. (Dataset: world. Variables: regime_type3, durable.) The two comparative politics scholars are still arguing, only now they're trying to figure out what sort of institutional arrangement produces the longest-lasting, most stable political system. Also, a third scholar joins the interchange of ideas.

Scholar 1: "Presidential democracies, like the United States, are going to be more stable than are any other type of system. In presidential democracies, the executive and the legislature have separate electoral constituencies and separate but overlapping domains of responsibility. The people's political interests are represented both by the president's national constituency and by legislators' or parliament members' more localized constituencies. If one branch does something that's unpopular, it can be blocked by the other branch. The result: political stability."

Scholar 2: "Parliamentary democracies are by far more stable than presidential democracies. In presidential systems, the executive and legislature can be controlled by different political parties, a situation that produces deadlock. Since the leaders of parliament can't remove the president and install a more compliant or agreeable executive, they are liable to resort to a coup, toppling the whole system. Parliamentary democracies avoid these pitfalls. In parliamentary democracies, all legitimacy and accountability resides with the legislature. The parliament organizes the government and chooses the executive (the prime minister) from among its own leaders. The prime minister and members of parliament have strong incentives to cooperate and keep things running smoothly and efficiently. The result: political stability."

Scholar 3: "You two have made such compelling—if incorrect—arguments that I almost hesitate to point this out: Democracies of any species, presidential or parliamentary, are inherently unstable. Any system that permits the clamor of competing parties or dissident viewpoints is surely bound to fail. If it's stability that you value above all else, then dictatorships will deliver. Strong executives, feckless or nonexistent legislatures, powerful armies, social control. The result: political stability."

The world dataset contains the variable durable, which measures the number of years since the last regime transition. The more years that have passed since the system last failed (higher values on durable), the more stable a country's political system. The variable regime_type3 captures system type: dictatorship, parliamentary democracy, or presidential democracy.

A. Run the appropriate mean comparison analyses. Which of the following inferences are supported by your analyses? (check all that apply)

❑ Parliamentary democracy is the most stable form of government.

❑ On average, parliamentary democracies last about 20 years longer than dictatorships.

❑ Presidential democracies are more stable than dictatorships.

❑ Of the 141 countries included in the analyses, dictatorships are the most prevalent.

❑ Among the 141 countries included in the analyses, the typical regime lasts about 24 years.

B. Produce a bar chart of the relationship you just analyzed. The vertical axis will depict the mean number of years since the last regime transition. (*Note*: The dependent variable, durable, is in graph-ready form, so you do not need to create indicator variables.) Give the vertical axis a more descriptive title, such as "Mean Years since Transition". Add a title ("Political Stability"), subtitle ("by Regime Type"), and source note ("Source: World Dataset"). Make any other desired appearance-enhancing changes. Print the chart.

13. (Dataset: world. Variables: fhrate08_rev, dem_other5.) Why do some countries develop democratic systems whereas others do not? Certainly the transition toward democracy—or away from it—is a complex process. Some scholars emphasize factors internal to countries, such as educational attainment or economic development. Others look to external factors, such as patterns of governance that are prevalent in a country's region of the world. Perhaps governmental systems are like infectious diseases: Similar systems diffuse among countries in close geographic proximity. According to the democratic diffusion hypothesis, countries in regions having fewer democracies are themselves less likely to be democratic than are countries in regions having more democracies.[10]

A. Suppose you had two variables for a large number of countries: a dependent variable that measured democracy along an interval-level scale, with higher scores denoting higher levels of democracy, and an independent variable measuring the number of democracies in each country's region, from fewer democracies to more democracies. According to the democratic diffusion hypothesis, if you were to compare mean values of the dependent variable for countries having different values on the independent variable, you should find (check one)

❑ a lower mean of the dependent variable for countries in regions having fewer democracies than for countries in regions having more democracies.

❑ a higher mean of the dependent variable for countries in regions having fewer democracies than for countries in regions having more democracies.

❑ no difference between the means of the dependent variable for countries in regions having fewer democracies and countries in regions having more democracies.

B. The world dataset contains fhrate08_rev, an interval-level measure of democracy based on the Freedom House rating system. Scores range from 0 (least democratic) to 12 (most democratic).[11] This is the dependent variable. The dataset also has dem_other5, a 5-category ordinal measure that divides countries into five groups, based on the percentage of democracies in each country's geographic region: 10 percent, approximately 40 percent, approximately 60 percent, approximately 90 percent, or 100 percent. This is the independent variable. Run the appropriate mean comparison analysis. Label and record the results in the table that follows:

Percent of other democracies in region: 5 cats	Mean	Freq.
10%	?	?
Approx. 40%	?	?
Approx. 60%	?	?
Approx. 90%	?	?
100%	?	?
Total	?	?

C. Create and print a line chart of the relationship you just analyzed.

D. Examine the mean comparison table and the line chart. Which of the following statements are supported by your analysis? (check all that apply)

❑ Countries in regions having fewer democracies are more likely to be democratic than are countries in regions having more democracies.

❑ The relationship between the independent and dependent variables is positive.

❑ The democratic diffusion hypothesis is incorrect.

❑ Countries in regions having fewer democracies are less likely to be democratic than are countries in regions having more democracies.

❑ The relationship between the independent and dependent variables is negative.

14. (Dataset: world. Variables: decentralization4, effectiveness, confidence.) Are decentralized governments more effective than centralized governments? In decentralized systems, local officials have politically autonomous authority to raise public money and administer government programs. This leads to more effective governance and, the argument goes, inspires confidence among citizens. Centralized systems, remote from local problems and burdened by red tape, may be both less effective and less likely to be viewed positively by citizens. Given these putative benefits, it is little wonder that "policy makers and politicians have frequently pushed for decentralisation as a panacea for the ills of poor governance."[12]

The world dataset variable decentralization4 measures, for each country, the level of decentralization by four ordinal categories, from less decentralization (coded 1) to more decentralization (coded 4). The assessments of a panel of expert observers were used to create the variable effectiveness, which measures government effectiveness on a 100-point scale (higher scores denote greater effectiveness). Confidence, also on a 100-point scale, gauges the degree to which a country's citizens have "a great deal" or "quite a lot" of confidence in state institutions (higher scores denote higher confidence).

A. The world variables will permit you to test two hypotheses about the effects of decentralization on effectiveness and confidence. State the two hypotheses.

Effectiveness hypothesis: _____

_____

_____

_____

Confidence hypothesis: _____

_____

_____

_____

B. Test the hypotheses by comparing means. Write the results in the table that follows:

Level of decentralization	Government effectiveness scale (mean)	Confidence in institutions scale (mean)
Less decentralization	?	?
2	?	?
3	?	?
More decentralization	?	?
Total	?	?

C. The effectiveness hypothesis (circle one)

is supported   is not supported

by the analysis. _____

Explain your reasoning. _____

_____

_____

_____

_____

D. The confidence hypothesis (circle one)

is supported   is not supported

by the analysis. _____

Explain your reasoning. _____

_____

_____

_____

_____

That concludes the exercises for this chapter. After exiting Stata, don't forget to take your removable media with you.

NOTES

1. Stata treats the first-named variable as the row variable and the second-named variable as the column variable. Under this standard setup, the column option will produce percentages of the independent variable. In situations in which the independent variable has many more categories than the dependent variable, the standard setup might create formatting problems, and so you may want to create a cross-tabulation having the dependent variable on the columns and the independent variable on the rows. The following syntax would produce the desired result: tab independent_variable dependent_variable, row. The row option instructs Stata to calculate percentages of the row variable, which in this case is the independent variable.
2. Interestingly, weak Democrats and independent-Democrats often hold similar opinions and attitudes, as do weak Republicans and independent-Republicans. Your future analyses of nes2008 may uncover more examples of these similarities.
3. In executing the graph bar command, Stata automatically calculates group means for the categories of the independent variable. This works well for graphing the relationship between a nominal-level independent variable and an interval-level dependent variable. Line graphs, using the twoway command, are more appropriate for ordinal independent-interval dependent relationships. However, twoway does not automatically calculate group means.

4. V. O. Key, *Politics, Parties, and Pressure Groups*, 5th ed. (New York: Crowell, 1964), 568.

5. George A. Quattrone and Amos Tversky, "Contrasting Rational and Psychological Analyses of Political Choice," *American Political Science Review* 82 (Sept. 1988): 719–736.

6. A fourth category, citizens who voted in 2004 but not in 2008, contains only 86 respondents. This category was set to missing.

7. Timur Kuran, *Private Truths, Public Lies: The Social Consequences of Preference Falsification* (Cambridge: Harvard University Press, 1995), 3.

8. It may have occurred to you that this effect might be greater for white respondents than for black respondents, with white subjects more likely to hide their true preferences in the presence of a black interviewer. An exercise in Chapter 5 will give you a chance to investigate this possibility.

9. From the presidential debate at Wake Forest University, October 11, 2000. In a speech to the Sierra Club on September 9, 2005, Gore again made reference to scientific agreement: "Two thousand scientists, in a hundred countries, engaged in the most elaborate, well organized scientific collaboration in the history of humankind, have produced long-since a consensus that we will face a string of terrible catastrophes unless we act to prepare ourselves and deal with the underlying causes of global warming."

10. See Jeffrey S. Kopstein and David A. Reilly, "Geographic Diffusion and the Transformation of the Postcommunist World," *World Politics* 53 (2000): 1–37. Noting that "[a]ll of the big winners of postcommunism share the trait of being geographically close to the former border of the noncommunist world" (p. 1), Kopstein and Reilly use geographic proximity to the West as the independent variable in testing the democratic diffusion hypothesis. By and large, the authors find "that the farther away a country is from the West, the less likely it is to be democratic" (p. 10).

11. The original Freedom House scale ranges from 1 (most democratic) to 7 (least democratic). The author reversed the coding and rescaled fhrate08_rev so that it ranges from 0 (least democratic) to 12 (most democratic).

12. Conor O'Dwyer and Daniel Ziblatt, "Does Decentralisation Make Government More Efficient and Effective?" *Commonwealth & Comparative Politics* 44 (Nov. 2006): 1–18; this quote from p. 2. O'Dwyer and Ziblatt use sophisticated multivariate techniques to test the hypothesis that decentralized systems are more effective. Interestingly, they find that decentralization produces a higher quality of governance in richer countries but a lower quality of governance in poorer countries.

5

Making Controlled Comparisons

Political analysis often begins by making simple comparisons using cross-tabulation analysis or mean comparison analysis. Simple comparisons allow the researcher to examine the relationship between an independent variable, X, and a dependent variable, Y. However, there is always the possibility that alternative causes—rival explanations—are at work, affecting the observed relationship between X and Y. An alternative cause is symbolized by the letter Z. If the researcher does not control for Z, then he or she may misinterpret the relationship between X and Y.

What can happen to the relationship between an independent variable and a dependent variable, controlling for an alternative cause? One possibility is that the relationship between the independent variable and the dependent variable is spurious. In a spurious relationship, once the researcher controls for a rival causal factor, the original relationship becomes very weak, perhaps disappearing altogether. The control variable does all of the explanatory work. In another possibility, the researcher observes an additive relationship between the independent variable, the dependent variable, and the control variable. In an additive relationship, two sets of meaningful relationships exist. The independent variable maintains a relationship with the dependent variable, and the control variable helps to explain the dependent variable. A third possibility, interaction, is somewhat more complex. If interaction is occurring, then the effect of the independent variable on the dependent variable depends on the value of the control variable. The strength or tendency of the relationship is different for one value of the control variable than for another value of the control variable.

These situations—a spurious relationship, an additive relationship, and interaction—are logical possibilities. Of course, Stata cannot interpret a set of controlled comparisons for you. But it can produce tabular analysis and graphics that will give you the raw material you need to evaluate controlled comparisons.

In this chapter you will learn to use the tabulate command to analyze relationships when the independent variable and control variable are categorical and the dependent variable is categorical or interval-level. Because graphic displays are especially valuable tools for evaluating complex relationships, we will demonstrate how to obtain bar charts and line charts for controlled comparisons. These skills are natural extensions of the procedures you learned in Chapter 4.

CROSS-TABULATION ANALYSIS WITH A CONTROL VARIABLE

We will begin by working through an example with gss2006. This guided example uses one of the variables you created in Chapter 3, polview3.

Consider this hypothesis: In comparing individuals, liberals will be more likely to favor the legalization of marijuana than will conservatives. In this hypothesis, polview3, which categorizes respondents as liberal, moderate, or conservative, is the independent variable. The dataset contains the variable grass, which records respondents' opinions on the legalization of marijuana. (Code 1 is "Legal," and code 2 is "Not legal.") First we will look at the uncontrolled relationship between polview3 and grass. Then we will add a control variable.

Open gss2006 and begin a log file. Go ahead and run the following tabulate command, which will produce a cross-tabulation of grass (dependent variable) by polview3 (independent variable) with column percentages: "tab grass polview3, col".

Should marijuana be made legal?	Ideology: 3 categories			Total
	Liberal	Moderate	Conservat	
Legal	245	247	166	658
	50.72	37.48	26.39	37.15
Not legal	238	412	463	1,113
	49.28	62.52	73.61	62.85
Total	483	659	629	1,771
	100.00	100.00	100.00	100.00

Clearly the hypothesis has merit. Of the liberals, 50.72 percent favor legalization, compared with 37.48 percent of moderates and 26.39 percent of conservatives.

What other factors, besides ideology, might account for differing opinions on marijuana legalization? A plausible answer: whether the respondent has children. Regardless of ideology, people with children may be less inclined to endorse the legalization of an illegal drug than are people who do not have children. And here is an interesting (if complicating) fact: conservatives are substantially more likely to have children than are liberals.[1] Thus, when we compare the marijuana opinions of liberals and conservatives, as we have just done, we are also comparing people who are less likely to have children (liberals) with people who are more likely to have children (conservatives). It could be that liberals are more inclined to favor legalization, not because they are liberal per se, but because they are less likely to have children. By the same token, conservatives might oppose legalization for reasons unrelated to their ideology: they're more likely to have children. The only way to isolate the effect of ideology on marijuana opinions is to compare liberals who do not have children with conservatives who do not have children, and to compare liberals who have children with conservatives who have children. In other words, we need to control for the effect of having children by holding it constant.

Dataset gss2006 contains the variable kids, which classifies respondents into one of two categories: those with children (coded 1 and labeled "Yes" on kids) or those without (coded 0 and labeled "No" on kids). Let's run the analysis again, this time adding kids as a control variable.

We need to ask Stata to produce two cross-tabulations. One cross-tab will show the grass-polview3 relationship for people without children, and the other will show the relationship for people with children. Because of the way Stata handles problems such as this—running a command for one value of a control variable (people without children) and rerunning the command for another value of the variable (people with children)—the dataset must first be sorted on the control variable. Conveniently, the user can request this procedure within the tabulate command. Click the command "tab grass polview3, col" back into the Command window. Make two modifications, as follows:

bysort kids: tab grass polview3, col nokey

The command prefix "bysort kids:" instructs Stata to sort the dataset according to the values of the control variable, kids, and to produce a cross-tabulation of grass and polview3 for each value of the control.[2] (Stata sometimes calls a sorting variable a "by variable." So, in the current example, kids is the by variable.)

Nokey, introduced in Chapter 4, suppresses Stata's space-consuming tabular key, making it easier to view both cross-tabulations in the Results window without scrolling between them. Run the modified command and consider the results:

```
. bysort kids: tab grass polview3, col nokey
```

-> kids = No

Should marijuana be made legal?	Ideology: 3 categories			Total
	Liberal	Moderate	Conservat	
Legal	104	80	44	228
	59.43	45.20	30.56	45.97
Not legal	71	97	100	268
	40.57	54.80	69.44	54.03
Total	175	177	144	496
	100.00	100.00	100.00	100.00

-> kids = Yes

Should marijuana be made legal?	Ideology: 3 categories			Total
	Liberal	Moderate	Conservat	
Legal	139	167	122	428
	45.42	34.72	25.15	33.65
Not legal	167	314	363	844
	54.58	65.28	74.85	66.35
Total	306	481	485	1,272
	100.00	100.00	100.00	100.00

The first cross-tabulation, beneath the label "kids=No," shows the grass-polview3 relationship for people who do not have children. The bottom cross-tabulation shows the relationship for respondents with children, respondents with the value "Yes" on the control variable. (Unless instructed otherwise, Stata will run the command for cases defined as missing on the by variable, as in "kids=.". Generally, these results can be safely ignored. By using the if qualifier, discussed in Chapter 4, the user can dissuade Stata from producing results for cases defined as missing on the by variable: "bysort kids: tab grass polview3 if kids!=. , col nokey".)

What is the relationship between ideology and support for marijuana legalization among respondents who do not have children? For those with children? Is polview3 still related to grass? You can see that ideology is related to marijuana opinions for both values of kids. Among people without children, 59.43 percent of the liberals favor legalization, compared with 45.20 percent of the moderates and 30.56 percent of the conservatives. The more conservative people are, the lower the likelihood that they will favor legalization. The same general pattern holds for people with children: 45.42 percent of the liberals favor legalization, compared with 34.72 percent of moderates and 25.15 percent of conservatives. So, controlling for kids, polview3 is related to grass in the hypothesized way.

One bonus of control tables is that they permit you to evaluate the relationship between the control variable and the dependent variable, controlling for the independent variable. What is the relationship between the control variable, kids, and marijuana attitudes, controlling for ideology? We can address this question by jumping between the top cross-tabulation and the bottom cross-tabulation, comparing marijuana opinions of people who share the same ideology but who differ on the control variable, kids. Consider liberals. Are liberals without kids more likely to favor legalization than are liberals with kids? Yes. Among liberals without children, 59.43 percent favor legalization versus only 45.42 percent for liberals with children. How about moderates? Yes, again. There is a noticeable difference between the percentage of moderates without children who favor legalization (45.20 percent) and that of moderates with children who favor legalization (34.72 percent). For conservatives, too, having children somewhat decreases the likelihood of a pro-legalization response, although here the "kid effect" is much weaker than for moderates or liberals: 30.56 percent versus 25.15 percent.

How would you characterize this set of relationships? Does a spurious relationship exist between grass and polview3? Or are these additive relationships, with polview3 helping to explain legalization opinions and kids adding to the explanation? Or is interaction going on? Is the grass-polview3 relationship different for people without children than for people with children? If the grass-polview3 relationship were spurious, then the relationship would weaken or disappear after controlling for kids. Among respondents without children, liberals, moderates, and conservatives would all hold the same opinion about marijuana legalization. Ditto for people with children: Ideology would not play a role in explaining the dependent variable. Because the relationship persists after controlling for kids, we can rule out spuriousness. Now, it is sometimes difficult to distinguish between additive relationships and interaction relationships, so let's dwell on this question. In additive relationships, the effect of the independent variable on the dependent variable is the same or quite similar for each value of the control variable. In interaction relationships, by contrast, the effect of the independent variable on the dependent variable varies in strength or tendency for different values of the control variable.

Return to the cross-tabulation results. The grass-polview3 relationship has the same tendency for people with and without children: For both values of the control, liberals are more pro-legalization than are conservatives. But notice that this effect is much larger for people without children. As you compare percentages across the "Legal" row, the percentage drops nearly 30 percentage points, from 59.43 percent among liberals to 30.56 percent among conservatives. Now examine the second table, the grass-polview3 relationship for people with children. Here we find a weaker effect of ideology on legalization opinions: from 45.42 percent among liberals to 25.15 percent among conservatives, a drop of about 20 percentage points. So the "ideology effect" is about 30 points for people without children and about 20 points for people with children. Another way of describing this set of interaction relationships is to look at the effect of the control variable, kids, at each value of polview3. As mentioned above, the "kid effect" is sizable for liberals—the pro-legalization percentage is about 15 points lower for liberals with children than for liberals without children. But look at conservatives: having children has a very modest effect (only a 5-point difference) on their opinions. Because polview3 has a much larger effect on grass for one value of the control (respondents without children) than for the other value of the control (respondents with children), this is a set of interaction relationships.

Interaction relationships are quite common. So that you can become comfortable recognizing interaction in cross-tabulations, we will run through another example that is related to the line of analysis we have been pursuing. We just found that having children weakens the effect of ideology on attitudes toward the legalization of marijuana use—a behavior that, theoretically at least, touches upon the parent-child relationship. Let's see whether the same interaction pattern holds for opinions about another behavior that impacts parenting: premarital sex. The gss2006 dataset contains premarsx2, coded 1 for respondents who think it is wrong for "a man and woman to have sex relations before marriage," and coded 2 for respondents who think it is not wrong.

Click the previous command, "bysort kids: tab grass polview3, col nokey", back into the Command window. Except for the dependent variable, our new analysis is the same. Therefore, delete "grass" and type "premarsx2" in its place: "bysort kids: tab premarsx2 polview3, col nokey".

```
. bysort kids: tab premarsx2 polview3, col nokey
```

-> kids = No

Is premarital sex wrong?	Ideology: 3 categories			Total
	Liberal	Moderate	Conservat	
wrong	65 33.33	77 47.24	95 67.86	237 47.59
Not wrong	130 66.67	86 52.76	45 32.14	261 52.41
Total	195 100.00	163 100.00	140 100.00	498 100.00

```
-> kids = Yes
```

Is premarital sex wrong?	Ideology: 3 categories			Total
	Liberal	Moderate	Conservat	
wrong	143	290	345	778
	43.73	52.82	68.45	56.38
Not wrong	184	259	159	602
	56.27	47.18	31.55	43.62
Total	327	549	504	1,380
	100.00	100.00	100.00	100.00

Focus on the percentage of respondents saying "Not wrong." Clearly enough, ideology has a big effect on the dependent variable for people without children, as well as for people with children. As the independent variable changes from "liberal" to "moderate" to "conservative," the "Not wrong" percentages decline. So, just as with grass, the premarsx2-polview3 relationship has the same tendency for both values of the control, kids. Now take a closer look at the size of this effect. For respondents without kids, the drop is on the order of 35 points, from 66.67 percent to 32.14 percent. For respondents with kids, the decline, though still noteworthy, is nonetheless weaker—about 25 points (from 56.27 percent to 31.55 percent). Keep practicing reading the control table and identifying the interaction pattern. Is the "kid effect" the same for liberals and conservatives? No, it is not. There is about a 10-percentage-point difference on the dependent variable between liberals without kids (66.67 percent) and liberals with kids (56.27 percent). For conservatives, by contrast, having children has no discernible effect on the dependent variable: 32.14 percent of those without kids say "Not wrong" compared with 31.55 percent of those with kids. Just as we found with marijuana opinions, the kid effect is larger for liberals than for conservatives.

BAR CHARTS FOR CONTROLLED COMPARISONS WITH A CATEGORICAL DEPENDENT VARIABLE

Take a few moments to examine Figure 5-1, a bar chart of the relationship between marijuana opinions and ideology, controlling for whether respondents have children. The values of the independent variable, polview3, appear along the x-axis: "Liberal," "Moderate," and "Conservative." The y-axis records the percentage of each group falling into the "Legal" category of the dependent variable, grass. There are two bars at each value of polview3. The left-hand bars (the lighter bars in Figure 5-1) show the relationship between grass and polview3 for people without children, and the right-hand bars (darker) depict the relationship for people with children. Notice that, for both sets of bars, the percentages favoring legalization decline as you move across the values of polview3. Note, too, that within each set of bars the without-kids bar is taller than the with-kids bar, revealing the effect of the control variable, kids, on the dependent variable. Finally, as you move from liberal to moderate to conservative, observe the precipitous drop in the heights of the bars for respondents without children and the milder decline among respondents with children. Clearly, this graphic greatly facilitates interpretation of the relationship. To reproduce Figure 5-1, follow three steps:

Step 1. Generate an indicator variable. The dependent variable, grass, is a categorical variable. As discussed in Chapter 4, Stata will graph a categorical dependent variable after it has been transformed into an indicator variable. The following command will generate two indicator variables, grassdum1 and grassdum2: "tab1 grass, gen(grassdum)". The mean of grasssdum1 will tell us the proportion of respondents saying "Legal." Using the replace command, we can convert the proportion to a percentage: "replace grassdum1=grassdum1 * 100".

```
. tab grass, gen(grassdum)
```

Should marijuana be made legal?	Freq.	Percent	Cum.
Legal	672	36.76	36.76
Not legal	1,156	63.24	100.00
Total	1,828	100.00	

```
. replace grassdum1 = grassdum1 * 100
(672 real changes made)
```

Figure 5-1   Bar Chart with a Control Variable

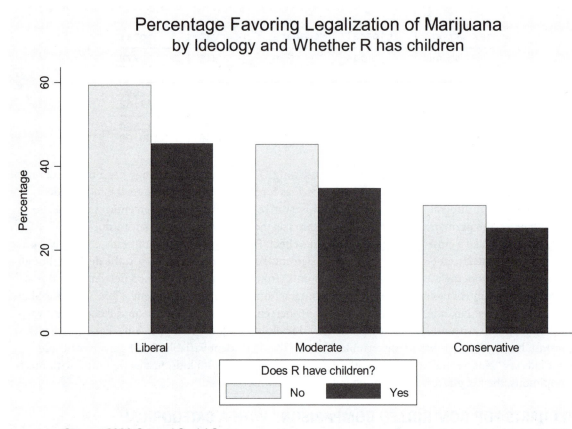

Percentage Favoring Legalization of Marijuana
by Ideology and Whether R has children

Source: 2006 General Social Survey

Step 2. Run the graph bar command. Now we can enlist the graph bar command to create a raw but editable bar chart of the grassdum1-polview3 relationship, controlling for kids:

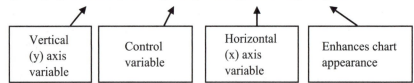

This command adds necessary extensions to the basic graph bar procedure you learned in Chapter 4. Just as in the basic command, the statement to the left of the comma, "graph bar (mean) grassdum1", requests mean percentages of grassdum1 (those saying "Legal") on the vertical axis. Notice that the control variable, kids, is the first-mentioned "over" group, "over(kids)", and the independent variable comes second, "over(polview3)". When Stata sees this ordering, it will first divide cases on the control—respondents with and without children—and then divide further on the basis of the independent variable—liberals with/ without, moderates with/without, and conservatives with/without. The asyvars option is as influential as it is weird. When you specify this option, Stata applies three appearance-enhancing features to its treatment of the control variable: (1) The bars depicting categories of the control variable will touch; (2) the bars will be of different colors; and (3) the bars will be identified by a legend beneath the x-axis. Enter the graph bar command and consider the result (Figure 5-2).

Step 3. Edit the chart. You will always need to add text to unedited graphs, and you may want to change the colors of the bars. Figure 5-3 shows how to use the Object Browser to add five required text elements: a legend title ("Does R have children?"); a chart title ("Percentage Favoring Legalization of Marijuana");

Figure 5-2   Bar Chart with Control Variable (unedited)

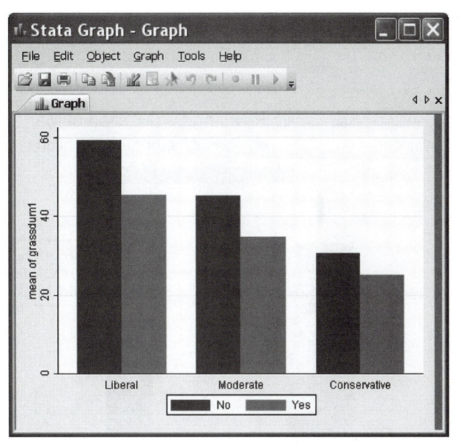

Figure 5-3   Adding Text Elements

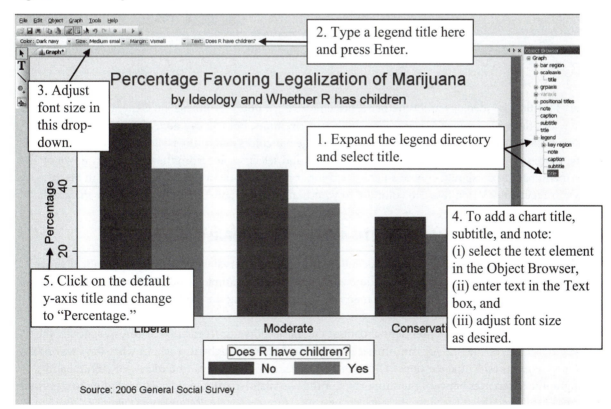

Figure 5-4 Changing Bar Color and Bar Outline

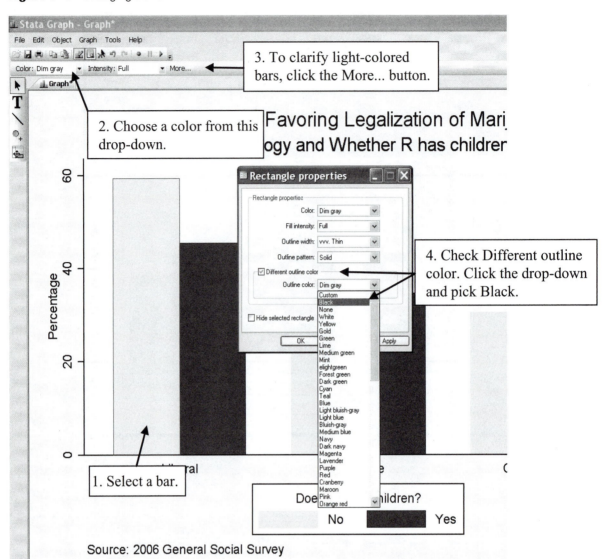

Source: 2006 General Social Survey

a chart subtitle ("by Ideology and Whether R has children"); a note ("Source: 2006 General Social Survey"); and a y-axis title ("Percentage"). Stata favors billboard-size fonts, but you can adjust these as you proceed. (See Figure 5-3, step 3.) Figure 5-4 shows how to change bar colors and outlines. Editing procedures could not be more straightforward than this: click on the bar and select a color from the Color drop-down on the main menu bar. If you should choose a light bar color, it is a good practice to outline the bar in black, as shown in Figure 5-4. When text and color are to your liking (as in Figure 5-5), be sure to save the graph.

MEAN COMPARISON ANALYSIS WITH A CONTROL VARIABLE

We now consider a situation in which the dependent variable is interval level and the independent variable and the control variable are nominal or ordinal. The next guided example, which analyzes nes2008, will use another variable you created in Chapter 3, married. Before beginning this example, save gss2006 and open nes2008.

Many analyses of the 2008 presidential contest emphasized its unprecedented features, especially the successful election of the first African American president.[3] Yet one might also ask: In what ways was 2008 similar to recent presidential elections? Did 2008 see a weakening—or a continuation—of cultural and demographic differences between the supporters of the two major-party candidates? According to a particularly insightful account of the 2004 election, for example, support for the Republican (George W. Bush)

Figure 5-5   Bar Chart with a Control Variable (edited)

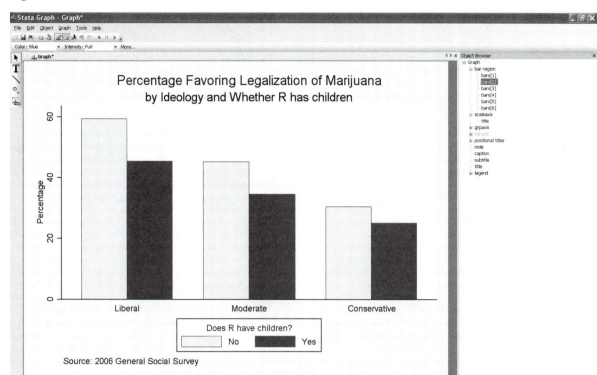

"was particularly high among whites, regular churchgoers, evangelical Christians, residents of smaller communities, married people, those not in union households, those with a family income above $50,000, and southerners."[4] People with a much different profile—non-white, single, secular, less affluent, residing in urban centers—were less favorably disposed toward Bush and more strongly attracted to the Democrat, John Kerry. It is an interesting question whether support for the 2008 Republican nominee, John McCain, was concentrated among the same groups that supported Bush 4 years earlier.

Of course, we know that several of the above-mentioned demographic attributes are related to each other. For example, marital status and religiosity are linked rather closely. According to a cross-tabulation of variables contained in nes2008 (an analysis you are invited to repeat), 60 percent of regular churchgoers are married, compared with only 45 percent of the less observant.[5] Such interrelationships present a challenge for the political researcher. Suppose you wanted to assess the effect of religious attendance (independent variable) on support for McCain (dependent variable). If you were to divide respondents according to their levels of religious attendance and then compare support for McCain, you would also be comparing groups who differ on another variable, marital status. Why so? Because the religiously observant group would have proportionately more married people than would the less observant group. It could be that regular church-goers are more likely to support McCain because they are more likely to be married, not because they frequently attend religious services. Potentially, then, you might confuse the effect of religiosity with the effect of marital status. To isolate the effect of religiosity, you will need to obtain two comparisons—one that looks at the effect of religious attendance on McCain support among unmarried people, and one that shows the effect of religious attendance among married people.

Let's analyze the relationship between religiosity and support for McCain, controlling for marital status. A 100-point feeling thermometer of John McCain, nes2008 variable mccain_therm, is the dependent variable. The independent variable, relig_attendHi, classifies respondents' frequency of religious attendance into two ordinal categories: "Low" (coded 0) and "High" (coded 1).[6] For the control, we will use married, a variable you created in Chapter 3. Recall that unmarried respondents are coded 0 on married and married respondents are coded 1.

Before running the analysis, let's consider the analysis that we would like Stata to produce. We want to see two sets of mean comparisons, one for unmarried people and one for married people. Each set will show mean

McCain thermometer ratings for respondents categorized as "Low" and "High" on relig_attendHi. If religiosity affects McCain support in the expected way, then the mean thermometer values should be higher for high-attenders than for low-attenders. What is more, if married people are stronger McCain supporters than are unmarried people, then mean ratings should be higher among married respondents at each value of relig_attendHi. So, for example, married people who are "Low" on relig_attendHi should give McCain higher ratings than unmarried people who are "Low" on relig_attendHi. There are two ways to make Stata perform this analysis.

The first way is to sort the dataset on the control variable, married, and then request a summary of mccain_therm for each value of relig_attendHi: "bysort married: tab relig_attendHi [aw=w], sum(mccain_therm) nost". This is the same sorting procedure you used in obtaining cross-tabulations with a control variable. And it will work the same way for mean comparisons, producing two mean comparison tables, one for each value of married.

There is a second, more concise way to obtain the results we need. The following command will create a Stata *breakdown table*, a single table of summary statistics for each combination of values of the independent variable and the control variable:

tab married relig_attendHi [aw=w], sum(mccain_therm) nost

In this setup, the control variable is typed first (right after the tab command), followed by the independent variable, a comma, and the summarize option, which will return descriptive statistics on the variable enclosed in parentheses. (By default, the summarize option will report means, standard deviations, and frequencies for each combination of variables named in the tab command. The nost option asks Stata not to report standard deviations.) We obtain the following results:

```
. tab married relig_attendHi [aw=w], sum(mccain_therm) nost

              Means, Frequencies and Number of Observations
                    of Feeling Thermometer: McCain

                Level of religious
     Is R       attendance: 2 cats
   married?       Low        High        Total

       No        44.93      55.33        47.70
               830.7299   301.2552    1131.9851
                   907        395         1302

      Yes        51.84      61.97        55.83
               697.2335   453.0268    1150.2603
                   566        395          961

     Total       48.08      59.32        51.79
              1527.9634   754.282     2282.2454
                  1473        790         2263
```

Breakdown tables are compact and readable. The values of married, which is mentioned first in the syntax ("tab married…"), define the rows. The values of relig_attendHi, which appears second in the syntax ("tab married relig_attendHi…"), define the columns.[7] Table entries are mean McCain thermometer ratings (plus weight frequencies and numbers of observations) for respondents having each combination of married and relig_attendHi. The "Total" row and "Total" column report the overall means of the dependent variable for respondents at each value of relig_attendHi (bottom-most row) and married (right-most column). For example, the mean McCain rating for all respondents categorized as "High" on relig_attendHi, unmarried and married mixed together, is 59.32. All unmarried respondents rated McCain at 47.70, on average.

To evaluate the effect of the independent variable, we would compare mean ratings across the values of relig_attendHi for unmarried and for married respondents. What do these comparisons reveal? Consider respondents who are not married. The mean McCain rating for unmarried, low-attending respondents is 44.93. This mean increases to 55.33 for those in the "High" attendance category. So, for the unmarried, the McCain thermometer gets 10 degrees warmer as we move across the values of the independent variable: 55.33 minus 44.93 equals 10.40. Now shift your attention to married respondents. Here we see a similar pattern: 51.84 for "Low" and 61.97 for "High," an increase of 10.13 in the expected direction. Thus, at both values of the control, as attendance goes up, so do McCain thermometer ratings—an "attendance effect" of 10 degrees, on average.

Notice that, by comparing mean values down the columns, we can see how the control variable, married, affects McCain ratings at each level of the independent variable, relig_attendHi. Among the less observant, for instance, there is a difference of nearly 7 degrees: 44.93 degrees for unmarried individuals compared with 51.84 for married people, a mean difference of 6.91. In fact, this 7-point "marriage effect" also applies to high attenders: 61.97 minus 55.33 equals 6.64—again, very close to 7 degrees. Thus, one would have to say that, controlling for religious attendance, married people are about 7 degrees warmer toward McCain than are unmarried people.

The independent variable, relig_attendHi, continues to have an effect on McCain thermometer ratings after marital status is controlled, so spuriousness is not at work in this set of relationships. As usual, however, the choice between additive relationships and interaction relationships is the more difficult call. Does the mccain_therm-relig_attendHi relationship have the same tendency at both values of the control variable? Yes, it does. For both unmarried and married respondents alike, as attendance increases, McCain ratings go up. Is the size of this effect, a 10.40-degree difference for unmarried and a 10.13-degree difference for married, about the same for each value of the control? Yes, it is. Because the mccain_therm-relig_attendHi relationship has the same tendency and the same magnitude at both values of married, we would characterize this set of relationships as additive.

A further example will help to illustrate the differences between additive relationships and interaction relationships. For this analysis, we will use the same dependent variable (mccain_therm) and the same independent variable (relig_attendHi). Instead of married, for the control we will use the variable race2, which classifies respondents as "White" (coded 1 on race2) or "Black" (coded 2). Click "tab married relig_attendHi [aw=w], sum(mccain_therm) nost" back into the Command window. Delete "married" and type "race2": "tab race2 relig_attendHi [aw=w], sum(mccain_therm) nost".

```
. tab race2 relig_attendHi [aw=w], sum(mccain_therm) nost

          Means, Frequencies and Number of Observations
                of Feeling Thermometer: McCain

  Race: 2 | Level of religious
categories| attendance: 2 cats
          |    Low      High  |    Total
----------+--------------------+----------
    White |  50.21     64.00  |   54.70
          |1225.3853 591.7776 |1817.1629
          |   955       463   |   1418
----------+--------------------+----------
    Black |  37.00     36.87  |   36.95
          | 161.6305 109.1313 | 270.7618
          |   330       236   |    566
----------+--------------------+----------
    Total |  48.67     59.78  |   52.40
          |1387.0158 700.9089 |2087.9247
          |  1285       699   |   1984
```

Focus on the mccain_therm-relig_attendHi relationship within each racial group. Is religious attendance related to McCain ratings among whites? Clearly, there is a sizable effect here. McCain averages 50.21 among low attenders and 64.00 among high attenders, a 14-degree difference. For blacks, by contrast, attendance has no effect: McCain averages 37.00 among low-attending blacks and 36.87 among high-attending blacks, a difference essentially equal to zero. Does the relationship between religiosity and McCain ratings have the same tendency at both values of the control? No. For whites, as attendance goes up, McCain ratings go up; for blacks, as attendance goes up, McCain ratings do not change. This is a sure sign of interaction. Turning the analysis around—looking at the race-McCain relationship separately for "Low" and "High" attenders—leads to the same interpretation. Whereas a 13-degree racial gap exists for the less observant (50.21 minus 37.00), there is a 27-degree racial gap among the more devout (64.00 minus 36.87).

LINE CHARTS FOR CONTROLLED COMPARISONS WITH AN INTERVAL-LEVEL DEPENDENT VARIABLE

Line charts for simple comparisons were covered in Chapter 4. The procedure, in a three-step nutshell: (1) Run _gwtmean to generate group means of the dependent variable for each value of the independent variable; (2) run twoway to graph the group means; and (3) use the Graph Editor to add text and modify

Figure 5-6 Line Chart with a Control Variable

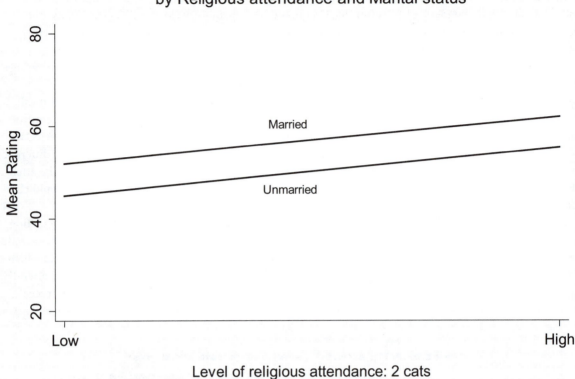

This command is identical to the simple-comparison case, with one exception: the by() option specifies two variables instead of one. When it encounters this command, Stata will create four group means, one for each combination of married and relig_attendHi. Useful fact: Stata doesn't care which variable appears first in the by() option. So, "by(relig_attendHi married)" works just as well as "by(married relig_attendHi)".

Step 2. Run the twoway command. The following command will produce a graph that shows the relationship between mccain_group (vertical axis) and relig_attendHi (horizontal axis) separately for unmarried and married respondents.

---

color and lines. With some minor embellishments and extensions, the same steps apply to line charts for controlled comparisons.

Figure 5-6 shows a line chart for the relationship between McCain ratings and religious attendance, controlling for marital status. Again, appreciate how graphs can help you interpret a set of relationships. The "attendance effect" is captured by the slope of the lines. Reading from left to right, both lines rise 10 degrees. The "marriage effect" is reflected in the distance between the lines. At both values of attendance, the "Married" line is 7 degrees higher than the "Unmarried" line. Parallel lines provide smoking-gun proof of additive relationships. Let's run through the steps that produced Figure 5-6.

Step 1. Generate group means. The following _gwtmean command will generate a new variable, mccain_group, that records the mean values of mccain_therm for unmarried-low attenders, unmarried high-attenders, married low-attenders, and married high-attenders.

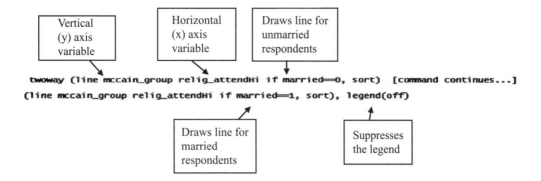

```
twoway (line mccain_group relig_attendHi if married==0, sort) [command continues...]
(line mccain_group relig_attendHi if married==1, sort), legend(off)
```

In effect, this command is two twoway commands in one. The first parenthetical expression uses the if qualifier to create the unmarried line ("if married==0"), and the second creates the married line ("if married==1"). There is less typing than meets the eye. Type the first parenthetical. Copy/paste it onto the end of the command line, and then modify "married==0" to read "married==1". The option "legend(off)" dispenses with the default color-coded legend. We will label the lines using the Graph Editor's Add Text tool. (*Note*: To fit the above command on the printed page, the author broke it into two lines. Be sure to type the command as one long line.)

Step 3. Edit the chart. An unedited Stata graphic is an increasingly familiar sight (Figure 5-7). Start the Graph Editor. Just as with the bar chart you created earlier, use the Object Browser to add text elements: a chart title ("McCain Thermometer Ratings"); a chart subtitle ("by Religious attendance and Marital status"); a note ("Source: 2008 National Election Study"); and a y-axis title ("Mean Rating"). Make sure that the x-axis values, "Low" (coded 0) and "High" (coded 1), are labeled properly. You've done this before.

Figure 5-7 Line Chart with Control Variable (unedited)

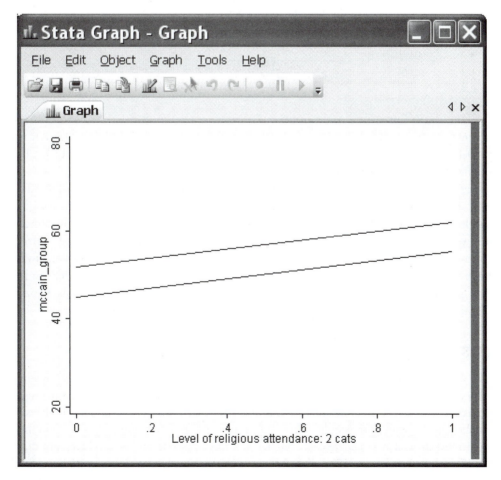

Figure 5-8 Using the Add Text Tool

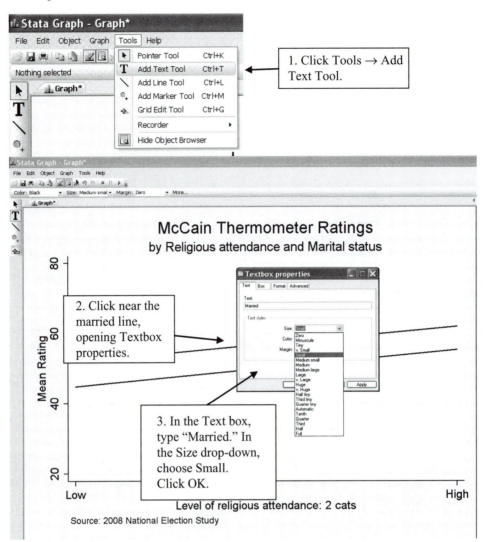

After selecting the x-axis region, click More, which opens the Axis properties window. In Axis rule, select the Range/Delta. The minimum value is 0, the maximum value is 1, and Delta is equal to 1. Click Label properties and check the Use value labels box.

Now for something new: text labels for the lines. On the main menu bar, click Tools→ Add Text Tool (Figure 5-8). The cursor pointer changes into the text tool, a pale vertical line. Because we wish to label the upper-most line (the married line), move the cursor to a position above the line, and click once. This action opens the Textbox properties box, as shown in Figure 5-8. Click in the text box and type "Married." Click the Size drop-down and select Small. Click OK. Stata supplies the requested label above the married line. Repeat the process for the unmarried line. Click below the married line, type "Unmarried" in the text box, select Small, and click OK. Do you want to adjust the positions of the labels? Click Tools→Pointer Tool. The pointer tool allows you to click-hold-drag the labels to more desirable positions.

EXERCISES

1. (Dataset: world. Variables: democ_regime, frac_eth3, gdp_cap2.) Some countries have democratic regimes, and other countries do not. What factors help to explain this difference? One idea is that the type of government is shaped by the ethnic and religious diversity in a country's population. Countries that are relatively homogeneous, with most people sharing the same language and religious beliefs, are more likely to develop democratic systems than are countries having more linguistic conflicts and religious differences. Consider the ethnic heterogeneity hypothesis: In a comparison of countries, those with lower levels of ethnic heterogeneity are more likely to be democracies than are countries with higher levels of ethnic heterogeneity.

A. According to the ethnic heterogeneity hypothesis, if you were to compare countries having lower heterogeneity with countries having higher heterogeneity, you should find (check one)

❑ a lower percentage of democracies among countries having lower heterogeneity.

❑ a higher percentage of democracies among countries having lower heterogeneity.

❑ no difference between the percentage of democracies among countries having lower heterogeneity and the percentage of democracies among countries with higher heterogeneity.

B. The world dataset contains the variable democ_regime, which classifies each country as a democracy (coded 1) or a dictatorship (coded 0). This is the dependent variable. The dataset also contains frac_eth3, which classifies countries according to their level of ethnic heterogeneity: low (coded 1), medium (coded 2), or high (coded 3). This is the independent variable. Run tabulate, testing the ethnic heterogeneity hypothesis. Fill in the percentages of democracies in the table:

	Ethnic heterogeneity		
	Low	Medium	High
Percentage of democracies	?	?	?

C. Based on these results, you could say that (check one)

❑ as ethnic heterogeneity increases, the percentage of democracies increases.

❑ as ethnic heterogeneity increases, the percentage of democracies decreases.

❑ as ethnic heterogeneity increases, there is little change in the percentage of democracies.

D. A country's level of economic development also might be linked to its type of government. According to this perspective, countries with higher levels of economic development will be more likely to be democracies than will countries with lower levels. The world dataset contains the variable gdp_cap2. This variable, based on gross domestic product per capita, is an indicator of economic development. Countries are classified as low (coded 1) or high (coded 2). Use the bysort prefix to obtain a cross-tabulation analysis of the democ_regime-frac_eth3 relationship, controlling for gdp_cap2. Fill in the percentages of democracies in the table:

	Ethnic heterogeneity		
	Low	Medium	High
Low GDP per capita			
Percentage of democracies	?	?	?
High GDP per capita			
Percentage of democracies	?	?	?

E. Examine the relationship between ethnic heterogeneity and democracy in high-GDP countries and low-GDP countries.

Consider the democ_regime-frac_eth3 relationship for low-GDP countries. Examine the difference between the percentage of democracies for "Low" heterogeneity and the percentage of democracies for "High" heterogeneity. This difference shows that the percentage of democracies among "Low" heterogeneity countries is (fill in the blank) _____ percentage points (circle one)

lower than   higher than

the percentage of democracies among "High" heterogeneity countries.

Now consider the democ_regime-frac_eth3 relationship for high-GDP countries. Examine the difference between the percentage of democracies for "Low" heterogeneity and the percentage of democracies for "High" heterogeneity. This difference shows that the percentage of democracies among "Low" heterogeneity countries is (fill in the blank) _____ percentage points (circle one)

lower than   higher than

the percentage of democracies among "High" heterogeneity countries.

F. Think about the set of relationships you just analyzed. How would you describe the relationship between ethno-linguistic heterogeneity and democracy, controlling for GDP per capita (circle one)?

Spurious   Additive   Interaction

Explain your reasoning. _____

_____

_____

_____

_____

_____

Review the three steps for creating bar charts for controlled comparisons with a categorical dependent variable. Perform the first step before proceeding to part G: Generate an indicator variable that is coded 1 for democracies and 0 for non-democracies. The following command will generate two indicator variables from democ_regime, democ_dum1 and democ_dum2: "tab democ_regime, gen(democ_dum)". Because democracies are coded 1 on democ_regime, democ_dum2 will be coded 1 for democracies and 0 for non-democracies. Run the replace command to multiply democ_dum2 by 100: "replace democ_dum2=democ_dum2*100".

G. (i) Obtain a bar chart depicting the mean values of democ_dum2 (the percentage of democracies) for each value of the independent variable, frac_eth3, controlling for gdp_cap2. Remember to specify the control variable, gdp_cap2, as the first over group and the independent variable, frac_eth3, as the second over group. Specify the asyvars option. (ii) Edit the chart. Use the Object Browser to add five text elements: a legend title ("Level of economic development"); a chart title ("Percentage of Democracies"); a chart subtitle ("by Ethnic Heterogeneity and Level of Economic Development"); a note ("Source: World Dataset"); and a y-axis title ("Percentage"). Edit the bar colors and adjust font sizes as you see fit. Save and print the chart.

2. (Dataset: world. Variables: women09, pr_sys, womyear2.) In Chapter 2 you analyzed the distribution of the variable women09, the percentage of women in the lower house of the legislatures in a number of countries. In this exercise you will analyze the relationship between women09 and two variables that could have an impact on the number of women serving in national legislatures.

First consider the role of the type of electoral system. Many democracies have proportional representation (PR) systems. PR systems foster multiple parties having diverse ideological positions—and, perhaps, having diverse demographic compositions as well. Non-PR systems, like the system used in U.S. elections, militate in favor of fewer and more homogeneous parties. Thus you might expect that non-PR countries will have fewer women in their national legislatures than will countries with PR-based electoral systems.

Now consider the role of history and tradition. In some countries, women have had a long history of political empowerment. New Zealand, for example, gave women the right to vote in 1893. In other countries, such as Switzerland (where women were not enfranchised until 1971), women have had less experience in the electoral arena. Thus it seems reasonable to hypothesize that countries with longer histories of women's suffrage will have higher percentages of women in their national legislatures than will countries in which women's suffrage is a more recent development. In this exercise you will isolate the effect of the type of electoral system on the percentage of women in parliament, controlling for the timing of women's suffrage. However, before running any analyses, you will graphically depict different possible scenarios for the relationships you might discover.

Parts A, B, and C contain graphic shells showing the percentage of women in parliament along the vertical axis and the type of electoral system along the horizontal axis. Countries without PR systems are represented by the tick mark on the left, and countries with PR systems, by the tick mark on the right. For each shell, you will draw two lines within the graphic space, a solid line depicting the relationship for countries having a longer history of women's suffrage and a dashed line depicting the relationship for countries having a shorter history of women's suffrage.

A. Draw an additive relationship fitting this description: Countries with PR systems have higher percentages of women in parliament than do countries with non-PR systems, and countries with a longer history of women's suffrage have higher percentages of women in parliament than do countries with a shorter history of women's suffrage. (*Hint*: In additive relationships, the strength and tendency of the relationship is the same or very similar for all values of the control variable.) Remember to use a solid line to depict the relationship for countries having a longer history of women's suffrage and a dashed line to depict the relationship for countries having a shorter history of women's suffrage.

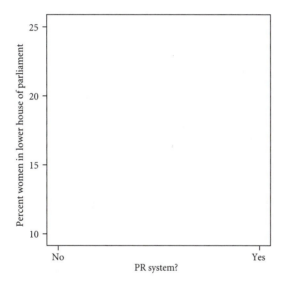

B. Draw a spurious relationship: Type of electoral system has no effect on the percentage of women in parliament; timing of women's suffrage has a big effect on the percentage of women in parliament.

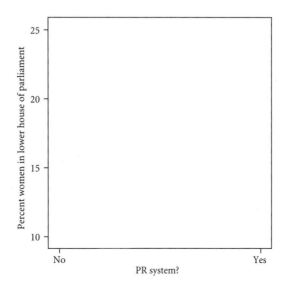

C. Draw a set of interaction relationships fitting this description: For countries with a longer history of women's suffrage, those with PR systems have higher percentages of women in parliament than do countries with non-PR systems. For countries with a shorter history of women's suffrage, the type of electoral system has no effect on the percentage of women in parliament.

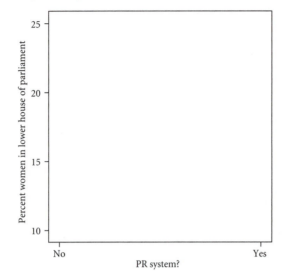

In addition to the dependent variable, women09, the world dataset contains pr_sys, coded 0 for countries with non-PR systems and coded 1 for those having PR systems. Use pr_sys as the independent variable. World also contains womyear2, which measures the timing of women's suffrage by two values: 1944 or before (coded 0) and after 1944 (coded 1). Use womyear2 as the control variable.

D. Run the following command to obtain a breakdown table showing mean values of women09 for each value of pr_sys, controlling for womyear2: "tab womyear2 pr_sys, sum(women09) nost". Refer to the results. In the table below, record the mean values of women09 next of each question mark:

Mean percent of women in lower house of parliament, 2009		
	PR system?	
Women's suffrage	No	Yes
1944 or before	?	?
After 1944	?	?

Review the three steps for creating line charts for controlled comparisons with an interval-level dependent variable. Perform the first step before proceeding to part E: Use the _gwtmean command to generate group means. The following _gwtmean command will generate a new variable, women_group, that records the mean values of women09 for each combination of pr_sys and womyear2: "_gwtmean women_group= women09 if women09!=. , by(womyear2 pr_sys)". (For world, the weight option is not required.)

E. Obtain a line chart of the relationship between women_group and pr_sys, controlling for womyear2. (i) Run twoway. In the first parenthetical expression, use the if qualifier to create the line for countries with a longer history of women's suffrage. *Hint*: The first parenthetical is "(line women_group pr_sys if womyear2==0, sort)". In the second parenthetical expression, use the if qualifier to create the line for countries with a shorter history of women's suffrage. Specify the legend(off) option. (ii) Edit the chart. Use the Object Browser to add text elements: a chart title ("Percentage of Women in Parliament"); a chart subtitle ("by Electoral System and Timing of Women's Suffrage"); a note ("Source: World dataset"); and a y-axis title ("Percentage"). Make sure that the x-axis values, "No" (coded 0) and "Yes" (coded 1), are labeled properly. Click Tools→Add Text Tool. Label the upper line "1944 or Before". Label the lower line "After 1944". Save and print the chart.

F. Examine the table (part D) and the chart (part E). Consider the women09-pr_sys relationship for countries that enfranchised women in 1944 or before. Examine the difference between the means for non-PR countries and PR countries. This difference shows that the mean for PR countries is (fill in the blank) _____ points (circle one)

lower than   higher than

the mean for non-PR countries.

Now consider the women09-pr_sys relationship for countries that enfranchised women after 1944. Examine the difference between the means for non-PR countries and PR countries. This difference shows that the mean for PR countries is (fill in the blank) _____ points (circle one)

lower than   higher than

the mean for non-PR countries.

G. Which of the following best characterizes the women09-pr_sys relationship, controlling for womyear2? (Check one)

❏ The women09-pr_sys relationships have the same tendency and very similar strength at both values of womyear2.

❏ The women09-pr_sys relationships have the same tendency but very different strengths at each value of womyear2.

❏ The women09-pr_sys relationships have different tendencies at each value of womyear2.

H. Review your artistic work in parts A–C. Examine the table (part D) and the line chart (part E). Consider your conclusions in parts F and G. Which possible scenario—the line chart you drew in A, B, or C— resembles most closely the pattern shown in the data? (circle one)

The line chart in A   The line chart in B   The line chart in C

3. (Dataset: nes2008. Variables: voted, memnum2, educ_r3, [aw=w].) Two political analysts are discussing factors that affect turnout in U.S. elections.

Political analyst 1: "I think that the role of voluntary association memberships has been overlooked as an important causal factor. People who belong to community associations, interest groups, or labor unions will interact with other individuals, discuss politics, and become aware of important issues. As a result, they will be more likely to vote than will people who do not belong to any groups."

Political analyst 2: "Your idea is interesting . . . but flawed. We know that education is strongly linked to voter turnout. People with more education are more likely to vote. Plus—and here is the relationship you are over-looking—people with more education are also more likely to join voluntary organizations. So as education goes up, people will be more likely to join groups *and* to vote. But there is no causal connection between belonging to groups and voting."

A. According to political analyst 1, if you were to compare the voter turnout of people who are not members of voluntary groups with that of people who are members, you would find (check one)

❏ that people who are members of voluntary groups are more likely to vote than are people who are not members of voluntary groups.

❏ that people who are members of voluntary groups are less likely to vote than are people who are not members of voluntary groups.

❏ no difference in turnout between people who are members of voluntary groups and those who are not members of voluntary groups.

B. According to political analyst 2, if you were to compare the group memberships of people who have less education with the group memberships of people who have more education, you would find (check one)

❑ that people with more education are more likely to be members of voluntary groups than are people with less education.

❑ that people with more education are less likely to be members of voluntary groups than are people with less education.

❑ no difference in the group membership between people with more education and people with less education.

C. Think about a tabulate analysis showing three cross-tabulations: the relationship between turnout (dependent variable) and group membership (independent variable) for people with low education, medium education, and high education. According to political analyst 2, such an analysis would reveal (check all that apply)

❑ that at each level of education, people who are members of voluntary groups are no more likely to vote than are people who are not members of voluntary groups.

❑ that regardless of group memberships, people with more education are more likely to vote than are people with less education.

❑ that the relationship between voter turnout and group membership is spurious.

D. The nes2008 dataset contains voted (coded 1 for voters and 0 for nonvoters). This is the dependent variable. The independent variable, memnum2, is coded 0 for respondents having no voluntary group memberships and coded 1 for respondents having at least one membership. The control variable, educ_r3, categorizes respondents into three education levels: 0–11 years (coded 1), 12 years (coded 2), and 13 or more years (coded 3). Using the bysort prefix, analyze the voted-memnum2 relationship, controlling for educ_r3. *Reminder*: This exercise uses the nes2008 dataset, so don't forget "[aw=w]". *Recommendation*: Neaten up the output by specifying "nofreq nokey". In the table that follows, record the *percentages who voted*:

Percentages who voted		
	Belong to group?	
Education level	No	Yes
0–11 years	?	?
12 years	?	?
13-more years	?	?

E. Examine the tabular evidence (Part D). Consider the set of relationships you just analyzed. How would you describe the relationship between the independent variable, memnum2, and turnout, controlling for education? (circle one)

Spurious   Additive   Interaction

Explain your reasoning. _____

_____

_____

_____

_____

_____

F. Which political analyst, political analyst 1 or political analyst 2, is more correct? (circle one)

Political analyst 1   Political analyst 2

Explain your reasoning. _____

_____

_____

_____

_____

_____

4. (Dataset: nes2008. Variables: voted_04, voted, contact_GOTV, [aw=w].) The two political analysts are at it again. This time they are discussing the effectiveness of get-out-the-vote (GOTV) campaigns.

Political analyst 1: "GOTV campaigns are a big waste of time and money."

Political analyst 2: "Your dyspepsia is showing. Care to share your reasoning?"

Political analyst 1: "Suppose you were in charge of a GOTV campaign. How would you locate people to contact? Simple: You'd go through voter registration records and identify people who are registered to vote or who voted in the previous election. Well, people who voted in the past election are very likely to vote in the current election, GOTV contact or no GOTV contact. A big waste of time and money. Now, suppose you managed to contact a few habitual nonvoters. People with no history of voting are unlikely to vote in the current election. A friendly 'Don't forget to vote' reminder will have no effect on them. Another big waste of time and money."

Political analyst 2: "Look, GOTV campaigns are a lot more sophisticated than you seem to think. My guess is that individuals' voting histories make little or no difference in whether they are contacted by GOTV mobilizers. Plus, you are way off base on the effect of GOTV contact. People who are contacted are much more likely to vote than are people who are not contacted, past voters and past nonvoters alike."

A. Imagine performing two analyses. The first analysis: the relationship between GOTV contact (dependent variable) and past voting turnout (independent variable). The second analysis: the relationship between current voting turnout (dependent variable) and GOTV contact (independent variable), controlling for past voting behavior (control variable).

   (i) If political analyst 1 is correct, these analyses will show that (check three)

       ❑ past voters are much more likely to be contacted than are past nonvoters.

       ❑ past voters and past nonvoters are about equally likely to be contacted.

       ❑ among past voters, those who are contacted are much more likely to vote than are those who are not contacted.

❏ among past voters, those who are contacted and those who are not contacted are about equally likely to vote.

❏ among past nonvoters, those who are contacted are much more likely to vote than are those who are not contacted.

❏ among past nonvoters, those who are contacted and those who are not contacted are about equally likely to vote.

(ii) If political analyst 2 is correct, these analyses will show that (check three)

❏ past voters are much more likely to be contacted than are past nonvoters.

❏ past voters and past nonvoters are about equally likely to be contacted.

❏ among past voters, those who are contacted are much more likely to vote than are those who are not contacted.

❏ among past voters, those who are contacted and those who are not contacted are about equally likely to vote.

❏ among past nonvoters, those who are contacted are much more likely to vote than are those who are not contacted.

❏ among past nonvoters, those who are contacted and those who are not contacted are about equally likely to vote.

The nes2008 dataset contains three variables: voted_04, coded 0 for respondents who did not vote in the previous presidential election (2004) and coded 1 for respondents who did; contact_GOTV, coded 0 for respondents who were not contacted in 2008 and coded 1 for those who were contacted; and voted, coded 0 for those who did not vote in 2008 and coded 1 for those who voted in 2008. (Also include: "[aw=w]".)

B. Analyze the contact_GOTV-voted_04 relationship to find out whether past voters are more likely to be contacted than are past nonvoters. According to your analysis, _____ percent of past nonvoters were contacted, compared with _____ percent of past voters.

Based on this analysis, you can conclude that (check one)

❏ past voters are much more likely to be contacted than are past nonvoters.

❏ past voters and past nonvoters are about equally likely to be contacted.

C. Analyze the voted-contact_GOTV relationship, controlling for voted_04. In the table that follows, record the *percentages who voted*:

	Anyone talk to R about registering or getting out to vote? (contact_GOTV)	
Did R vote in 2004? (voted_04)	No	Yes
No	?	?
Yes	?	?

D. Examine the tabular results (part C). Based on this analysis, you can conclude that (check two)

❏ among past voters, those who are contacted are much more likely to vote than are those who are not contacted.

❏ among past voters, those who are contacted and those who are not contacted are about equally likely to vote.

❏ among past nonvoters, those who are contacted are much more likely to vote than are those who are not contacted.

❏ among past nonvoters, those who are contacted and those who are not contacted are about equally likely to vote.

E. Consider your findings and conclusions in parts B–D. Which political analyst is more correct, political analyst 1 or political analyst 2? (circle one)

Political analyst 1   Political analyst 2

Explain your reasoning. _____

_____

_____

_____

F. Think for a few minutes about the set of relationships between voted and contact_GOTV, controlling for voted_04. How would you describe this set of relationships? (circle one)

Spurious   Additive   Interaction

Explain your reasoning. _____

_____

_____

_____

_____

5. (Dataset: nes2008. Variables: environ_therm, enviro_jobs_r3, enviro_jobs_imp2, [aw=w]). Who has positive feelings toward environmentalists? Who views this group with greater suspicion? It seems plausible to suggest that ratings of environmentalists are shaped by positions on important environmental issues. For example, we could hypothesize that individuals who favor environmental protection over jobs will give environmentalists higher ratings than will individuals who favor jobs over environmental protection. Yet this relationship may not be the same for everyone. Imagine a group of people for whom the environment-jobs issue is not very important. To be sure, these individuals have positions on the tradeoff—some favor the environment, some take a middle position, and some favor jobs—but the issue, to them, has *low salience*. Contrast these low-salience individuals to a group for whom the environment-jobs tradeoff is very important, for whom the issue has *high salience*. We might expect that the relationship between issue position (environment versus jobs) and ratings of environmentalists will be stronger for high-salience individuals than for low-salience individuals. In this exercise you will test two hypothetical claims:

Claim x: Controlling for issue salience, individuals who favor the environment over jobs will give environmentalists higher ratings than will individuals who favor jobs over the environment.

Claim y: The relationship between environmental-issue position (environment versus jobs) and ratings of environmentalists will be stronger for high-salience individuals than for low-salience individuals.

The nes2008 dataset contains environ_therm, a feeling thermometer of environmentalists. Ratings can range from 0 (negative ratings) to 100 (positive ratings). This is the dependent variable. For the independent variable, use enviro_jobs_r3, coded 1 ("Protect the environment, even if it costs jobs and standard of living"), 2 (middle position), or 3 ("Jobs and standard of living are more important than the environment"). For the control variable, issue salience, use enviro_jobs_imp2, which is coded 0 (the issue is "not very" important) or 1 (the issue is "very/extremely" important).

A. Obtain a breakdown table of the environ_therm-enviro_jobs_r3 relationship, controlling for enviro_jobs_imp2. Record the mean values of environ_therm in the table that follows:

How important is environment/ jobs issue? (enviro_jobs_imp2)	Environment vs. jobs tradeoff (enviro_jobs_r3)		
	Environment	Middle	Jobs
Not very	?	?	?
Very/extremely	?	?	?

B. Does your analysis support Claim x? (circle one)

        Yes, the analysis supports Claim x.   No, the analysis does not support Claim x.

Explain your reasoning. _____

_____

_____

_____

C. Does your analysis support Claim y? (circle one)

        Yes, the analysis supports Claim y.   No, the analysis does not support Claim y.

Explain your reasoning. _____

_____

_____

_____

D. Produce an edited, presentable line chart of the environ_therm-enviro_jobs_r3 relationship, controlling for enviro_jobs_imp2. You will need to (i) run _gwtmean to generate group means; (ii) run twoway to rough out a line chart that shows the relationship between group means (vertical axis) and enviro_jobs_r3 separately for low-salience (enviro_jobs_imp2==0) and high-salience (enviro_jobs_imp2==1) individuals; and (iii) use the Graph Editor to make necessary text edits and appearance enhancements. Save and print the chart.

E. Consider how issue salience affects the relationship between environmental issues and ratings of environmentalists. How would you describe this set of relationships? (circle one)

Spurious   Additive   Interaction

Explain your reasoning. _____

_____

_____

_____

_____

6. (Dataset: gss2006. Variables: natrace, natfare, natsci, intrace_2, race_2.) For an exercise in Chapter 4, you tested for the presence of preference falsification, the tendency for respondents to offer false opinions that they nonetheless believe to be socially desirable under the circumstances. You evaluated the hypothesis that respondents are more likely to express support for government policies aimed at helping blacks (such as "government spending to improve the conditions of blacks") when questioned by a black interviewer than when questioned by a white interviewer. But you did not control for the respondent's race. That is, you did not look to see whether whites are more (or less) likely than blacks to misrepresent their support for racial policies, depending on the race of the interviewer.[8]

Furthermore, it may be that whites, and perhaps blacks as well, will engage in the same preference-falsifying behavior for policies that do not explicitly reference race but that may *symbolize* race, such as "government spending for welfare." Although "welfare" does not mention "blacks," it may be that whites see "welfare" through a racially tinged lens and will respond *as if* the question refers to a racial policy. Of course, some policies, such as "government spending for scientific research," do not evoke such symbolic connections. Questions about these race-neutral policies should not show the same race-of-interviewer effects as questions that make explicit—or implicit—reference to race.[9]

In this exercise you will extend your Chapter 4 analysis in two ways. First, you will analyze the relationship between interviewer race (intrace_2, the independent variable) and three dependent variables: opinions on an explicitly racial policy (natrace, which measures attitudes toward spending to improve the conditions of blacks), a symbolically racial policy (natfare, opinions on spending for welfare), and a race-neutral policy (natsci, spending for scientific research). Second, you will perform these analyses while controlling for respondent's race (race_2).

Based on previous research in this area, what might you expect to find? Here are two plausible expectations:

Expectation 1: For both white and black respondents, the race-of-interviewer effect will be strongest for the explicitly racial policy (natrace), weaker for the symbolically racial policy (natfare), and nonexistent for the race-neutral policy (natsci).

Expectation 2: For the explicitly racial policy (natrace) and for the symbolically racial policy (natfare), the race-of-interviewer effect will be greater for white respondents than for black respondents. For the race-neutral policy (natsci), the race-of-interviewer effect will be the same (close to 0) for both white respondents and black respondents (see Expectation 1).

A. Run the appropriate tabulate analyses. In the table that follows, record the percentages of respondents saying that we are spending "too little" in each of the policy areas. For each policy, obtain the race-of-interviewer effect by subtracting the percentage of respondents saying "too little" when interviewed by a white questioner from the percentage saying "too little" when interviewed by a black questioner. (For example, if 50.0 percent of respondents said we are spending "too little" when questioned by a white and 70.0 percent said "too little" when questioned by a black, then the race-of-interview effect would be 70.0 percent minus 50.0 percent, or 20.0 percentage points.)

Race of respondent	Percent saying we are spending "too little" on:	Race of interviewer		
		White	Black	Race-of-interviewer effect (black % − white %)
White	Improving the conditions of blacks (natrace)	?	?	?
	Welfare (natfare)	?	?	?
	Supporting scientific research (natsci)	?	?	?
Black	Improving the conditions of blacks (natrace)	?	?	?
	Welfare (natfare)	?	?	?
	Supporting scientific research (natsci)	?	?	?

B. Examine the tabular data closely. Among white respondents, would you say that Expectation 1 is or is not supported by the evidence? (circle one)

　　　　　　Expectation 1 is supported.　　　Expectation 1 is not supported.

Explain your reasoning. _____

_____

_____

_____

_____

Among black respondents, would you say that Expectation 1 is or is not supported by the evidence? (circle one)

　　　　　　Expectation 1 is supported.　　　Expectation 1 is not supported.

Explain your reasoning. _____

_____

_____

_____

_____

_____

C. Now compare the race-of-interviewer effects between respondents of different races. That is, compare the race-of-interviewer effect on natrace among white respondents with the race-of-interviewer effect on natrace among black respondents. Do the same for natfare and natsci. Generally speaking, would you say that Expectation 2 is supported or is not supported by the evidence? (circle one)

Expectation 2 is supported.   Expectation 2 is not supported.

Explain your reasoning. _____

_____

_____

_____

_____

D. Produce an edited, presentable bar chart of the relationship between natrace and intrace_2, controlling for race_2. You will need to (i) generate an indicator variable that is coded 1 for respondents saying we are spending "too little" and 0 for respondents giving other responses; (ii) run replace to multiply the indicator variable by 100; (iii) run graph bar to rough out a bar chart showing mean values of the indicator variable by race_2 (first over group) and intrace_2 (second over group); and (iv) use the Graph Editor to make necessary text edits/additions and appearance enhancements. Save and print the chart.

E. It is clear from this exercise that the survey environment can be quite sensitive to extraneous contextual stimuli. On a more sobering note, your findings suggest how the survey environment can be manipulated by cynical, unprincipled pollsters to produce a desired result. Suppose one wanted to "prove" that no discernible racial difference exists on the explicitly racial policy of spending to improve the conditions of blacks. One would (check two)

❑ assign black interviewers to black respondents.

❑ assign black interviewers to white respondents.

❑ assign white interviewers to black respondents.

❑ assign white interviewers to white respondents.

That concludes the exercises for this chapter. After exiting Stata, be sure to take the media containing your datasets with you.

NOTES

1. According to gss2006, 78.3 percent of conservatives have children, compared with 61.8 percent of liberals—almost a 17-percentage-point difference.
2. Alternatively, you can run two separate commands. First sort the dataset, using the sort command: sort kids. Then run tabulate, using the by prefix: "by kids: tab grass polview3, col nokey".
3. Gerald M. Pomper, "The Presidential Election: Change Comes to America," in Michael Nelson (ed.), _The Elections of 2008_ (Washington, D.C.: CQ Press, 2010), 22–44.

4. Gerald M. Pomper, "The Presidential Election: The Ills of American Politics after 9/11," in Michael Nelson (ed.), *The Elections of 2004* (Washington, D.C.: CQ Press, 2005), 42–68; this quote, p. 47.

5. These percentages were obtained from the following analysis: "tab married relig_attendHi [aw=w], col".

6. Respondents who report attending religious services "almost every week" or more frequently are coded 1 and labeled "High." Respondents attending less frequently than "almost every week" are coded 0 and labeled "Low."

7. There is no rule that says the control variable must define the rows and the independent variable must define the columns of a breakdown table. It is a matter of personal preference or, perhaps, readability. If you prefer the independent variable on the rows and the control variable on the columns, simply reverse the order in which they are typed. In the current example, the following command would produce a table showing attend3 on the rows and married on the columns: "tab relig_attendHi married [aw=w], sum(mccain_therm) nost".

8. See Darren W. Davis and Brian D. Silver, "Stereotype Threat and Race of Interviewer Effects in a Survey of Political Knowledge," *American Journal of Political Science* 47 (Jan. 2003): 33–45.

9. There is a large body of literature on "symbolic racism." For an excellent review and analysis, see Stanley Feldman and Leonie Huddy, "Racial Resentment and White Opposition to Race-Conscious Programs: Principles or Prejudice?" *American Journal of Political Science* 49 (Jan. 2005): 168–183.

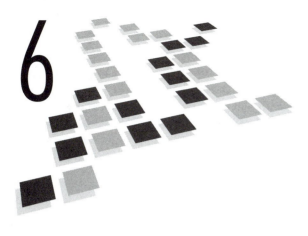

6

Making Inferences about Sample Means

Commands Covered

ttest *varname = testvalue*	Performs a one-sample t test
ttest *varname,* by*(group_var)*	Performs a two-sample t test
robvar *varname,* by*(group_var)*	Tests the assumption that two groups have equal sample variances

Political research has much to do with observing patterns, creating explanations, framing hypotheses, and analyzing relationships. In interpreting their findings, however, researchers often operate in an environment of uncertainty. This uncertainty arises, in large measure, from the complexity of the political world. As we have seen, when we infer a causal connection between an independent variable and a dependent variable, it is hard to know for sure whether the independent variable is causing the dependent variable. Other, uncontrolled variables might be affecting the relationship, too. Yet uncertainty arises, as well, from the simple fact that research findings are often based on random samples. In an ideal world, we could observe and measure the characteristics of every element in the population of interest—every voting-age adult, every student enrolled at a university, every bill introduced in every national legislature, and so on. In such an ideal situation, we would enjoy a high degree of certainty that the variables we have described and the relationships we have analyzed mirror "what is really going on" in the population. But of course we often do not have access to every member of a population. Instead we rely on a sample, a subset drawn at random from the population. By taking a random sample, we introduce random sampling error. In using a sample to draw inferences about a population, therefore, we never use the word *certainty*. Rather, we talk about *confidence* or *probability*. We know that the measurements we make on the sample will reflect the characteristics of the population, within the boundaries of random sampling error.

What are those boundaries? If we calculate the mean income of a random sample of adults, for example, how confident can we be that the mean income we observe in our sample is the same as the mean income in the population? The answer depends on the standard error of the sample mean, the extent to which the mean income of the sample departs by chance from the mean income of the population. If we use a sample to calculate a mean income for women and a mean income for men, how confident can we be that the difference between these two sample means reflects the true income difference between women and men in the population? Again, the answer depends on the standard error—in this case, the standard error of the *difference* between the sample means, the extent to which the difference in the sample departs from the difference in the population.

In this chapter you will use the ttest command to explore and apply inferential statistics. First you will use ttest (pronounced "t-test") to obtain confidence intervals for a sample mean. The 95 percent confidence interval will tell you the boundaries within which there is a .95 probability that the true population mean falls. You also will find the 90 percent confidence interval, which is applied in testing hypotheses at the .05 level of significance. You then will learn to tailor the ttest command to test for statistically significant differences between two sample means. Another Stata command, robvar, plays an important supporting role in significance testing. Results obtained from robvar (which derives its name from the term "robust variance") will tell you whether to override a Stata default on the ttest command.

DESCRIBING A SAMPLE MEAN

To gain insight into the properties and application of inferential statistics, we will work through an example using gss2006. The dataset contains science_quiz, which was created from 10 true-false questions testing respondents' knowledge of basic scientific facts. You analyzed science_quiz in a Chapter 2 exercise. Recall that the values of science_quiz range from 0 (the respondent did not answer any of the questions correctly) to 10 (the respondent answered all 10 correctly). First we will use our old standbys, codebook and summarize, to obtain basic information about science_quiz. Open gss2006. In the Command window, type "codebook science_quiz" and press Enter. Then type "sum science_quiz, detail" and press Enter:

```
codebook science_quiz

─────────────────────────────────────────────────────────────────────
science_quiz
─────────────────────────────────────────────────────────────────────

                  type:  numeric (float)

                 range:  [0,10]              units:  1
         unique values:  11             missing .:  2652/4510

                  mean:  5.87352
              std. dev:  2.40638

           percentiles:       10%      25%      50%      75%      90%
                               2        4        6        8        9

. sum science_quiz, detail

                      10-item science test
─────────────────────────────────────────────────────────────────────
          Percentiles      Smallest
 1%           0              0
 5%           2              0
10%           2              0           Obs                  1858
25%           4              0           Sum of Wgt.          1858

50%           6                          Mean             5.87352
                          Largest        Std. Dev.        2.406381
75%           8             10
90%           9             10           Variance         5.790672
95%          10             10           Skewness        -.2524598
99%          10             10           Kurtosis         2.445919
```

Among the 1,858 respondents, scores on science_quiz range from 0 to 10. The mean value of science_quiz is 5.87352 (which rounds to 5.87), with a standard deviation of 2.406381, or 2.41.[1] How closely does the mean of 5.87 reflect the true mean in the population from which this sample was drawn? If we had measured science_quiz for every U.S. adult and calculated a population mean, how far off the mark would our sample estimate of 5.87 be?

The answer depends on the standard error of the sample mean. The standard error of a sample mean is based on the standard deviation and the size of the sample. To calculate the standard error of a sample mean, you would divide the standard deviation by the square root of the sample size. For science_quiz, the standard error is the standard deviation, 2.41, divided by the square root of 1,858. Performed with a hand calculator: $2.41 / sqrt(1858) = 2.41 / 43.105 \approx .056$, or .06.

This number, .06, tells us the extent to which the sample mean of 5.87 departs by chance from the population mean. The standard error is the essential ingredient for making inferences about the population mean. But let's get Stata to help us make these inferences. Specifically, we will use the ttest command to do three things: find the 95 percent confidence interval of the mean, calculate the 90 percent confidence interval of the mean, and test a hypothetical claim about the population mean using the .05 level of significance.

By default, the ttest command will give us the 95 percent confidence interval. The barebones ttest syntax is as follows:

ttest *varname* = *test_value*

The ttest procedure is naturally designed to run what Stata calls a *one-sample t test*. The one-sample t test will compare the mean of a variable, supplied by the user in "varname," with a hypothetical mean value, provided by the user in "test_value." The test will then determine if random error could account for the difference. (We will discuss this calculation below.) For now, our goal is simpler. We want to know the 95 percent confidence interval of science_quiz. This can be accomplished by substituting any number for "test_value" in the ttest command. Click in the Command window and type "ttest science_quiz=0":

```
. ttest science_quiz=0

One-sample t test
```

Variable	Obs	Mean	Std. Err.	Std. Dev.	[95% Conf. Interval]	
scienc~z	1858	5.87352	.0558267	2.406381	5.76403	5.98301

```
    mean = mean(science_quiz)                                t = 105.2100
Ho: mean = 0                               degrees of freedom =      1857

      Ha: mean < 0              Ha: mean != 0                Ha: mean > 0
 Pr(T < t) = 1.0000     Pr(|T| > |t|) = 0.0000       Pr(T > t) = 0.0000
```

Stata's results repeat several facts about science_quiz that we already knew: its mean (5.87), its standard deviation (2.41), and the number of respondents on which the computations are based (1,858). In addition, Stata has provided the standard error of science_quiz's mean, .06 (which, reassuringly, is the same number we arrived at by hand). The values appearing beneath the label "[95% Conf. Interval]", 5.76 and 5.98, define the lower and upper boundaries of the 95 percent confidence interval.

Now, we are trying to determine how much confidence to invest in our sample mean of 5.87. Is the true population mean right around 5.87? The 95 percent confidence interval provides a probabilistic—not a definitive—answer. There is a high probability, a 95 percent probability, that the true population mean lies in the region between 5.76 at the low end and 5.98 at the high end. If we were to take a very large number of random samples from the population and calculate, for each sample, the mean of science_quiz, 95 percent of those calculated means would fall in the interval between 5.76 and 5.98. To be sure, there is random "noise" in each random sample. Yet 95 percent of the time, that noise will give us a sample mean within the bandwidth of 5.76 to 5.98. On uncommon occasions—5 percent of the time—we would obtain a sample mean that falls outside those boundaries, below 5.76 or above 5.98. Therefore, we can infer that there is a 95 percent chance that the true population mean is in the 5.76 to 5.98 range and a 5 percent probability that the population mean lies outside these boundaries—a 2.5 percent chance that the population mean is less than 5.76 and a 2.5 percent chance that it is greater than 5.98. You might be wondering where the "2.5 percent chance" came from. Aren't we discussing the 95 percent confidence interval? Shouldn't the statement instead say "5 percent chance"? The "2.5 percent" terminology is correct. This is an understandable confusion, so let's pause and clear things up.

Figure 6-1 shows a bell-shaped curve. The gss2006 sample mean, 5.87, is in the center of the distribution, bisecting the curve, with half of the distribution of possible sample means falling in the negative tail, below 5.87, and half falling in the positive part of the tail, above 5.87. Now consider the two shorter lines, one in the negative tail, drawn at 5.76, and one in the positive tail, at 5.98. These numbers, as we have seen, define the 95 percent confidence interval. Because the 95 percent confidence interval brackets 95 percent of all possible sample means, the remaining 5 percent must fall below 5.76 *or* above 5.98. Furthermore, because the curve is symmetrical, one-half of the remaining 5 percent (2.5 percent) will fall in the negative tail, below 5.76, and one-half (the other 2.5 percent) will fall in the positive tail, above 5.98.

Suppose someone made the (weak) hypothetical claim that the true population mean was *different from* 5.87. This person didn't say whether they thought the true mean was greater than 5.87 or less than 5.87. Just different from 5.87. Such a claim—a claim that the real population mean is different from the observed sample mean—requires a two-tailed test of statistical significance. Because we don't know the direction of the hypothetical difference, we would apply the 95 percent confidence interval and use a .05 two-tailed test. We would simply say that there is a 95 percent chance that the population mean falls between 5.76 and 5.98 and a 5 percent chance that it falls above or below these numbers.

Most hypothesis testing in political science uses a one-tailed test, not a two-tailed test. Why? Because any properly constructed hypothesis communicates the direction of a relationship. A gender-gap hypothesis, for example, would not ambiguously suggest that women and men will have different means on

Figure 6-1 The Normal Curve

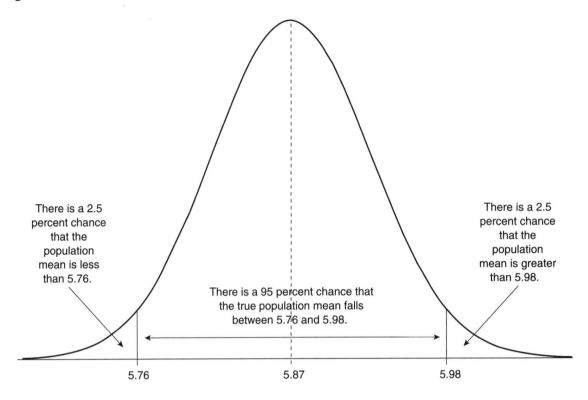

There is a 2.5 percent chance that the population mean is less than 5.76.

There is a 2.5 percent chance that the population mean is greater than 5.98.

There is a 95 percent chance that the true population mean falls between 5.76 and 5.98.

| 5.76 | 5.87 | 5.98 |

science_quiz. The hypothesis will tell you that the female mean on science_quiz should be found to be higher (or lower) than the male mean on science_quiz. Because hypothetical relationships imply direction, only one-half of the bell-shaped curve (either the half with the negative tail or the half with the positive tail) comes into play in testing the hypothesis. For this reason, the 95 percent confidence interval provides a stringent .025 one-tailed test of statistical significance for hypothetical claims about the population mean.

Let's apply this one-tailed logic. Suppose someone were to suggest that science_quiz's population mean is 6.00 and that we obtained a sample mean of 5.87 by chance when we drew the sample. Notice that this hypothetical assertion, 6.00, locates the population mean above the observed sample mean of 5.87, out in the positive region of the curve. For the purposes of testing this claim, then, we ignore the negative tail and use the positive tail. Return your attention to Figure 6-1, focusing only on the upper half, the half with the line drawn at 5.98, the upper boundary of the 95 percent confidence interval. Ask yourself this question: If the unseen population mean is equal to the observed sample mean of 5.87, what is the probability that a random sample would produce a mean of 6.00? As Figure 6-1 illustrates, we know that if we were to draw a large number of random samples from a population in which the true mean is 5.87, only 2.5 percent of those samples would yield sample means of 5.98 *or higher*. Using the stringent .025 standard, then, we would reject the claim that the population mean is 6.00. If the population mean is equal to the observed sample mean of 5.87, then random processes would yield a mean of 6.00 less than 2.5 percent of the time. Naturally, the same logic applies to any hypothetical claim that locates the population mean below the observed sample mean, down in the negative tail of the distribution.

A .025 one-tailed test of statistical significance is conservative—it makes it tougher to reject hypothetical challenges to relationships observed in a sample. Researchers tend to err on the side of caution, and you will never be criticized for using the .025 criterion. However, a somewhat less stringent test, the .05 one-tailed test of statistical significance, is perhaps a more widely applied standard. There are two ways to apply this standard—the confidence interval approach and the P-value approach. In the confidence interval approach, the researcher finds the 90 percent confidence interval of the mean. Why the 90 percent confidence interval? For the same reasons that the 95 percent confidence interval provides a .025 one-tailed test, the 90 percent confidence interval sets the limits of random sampling error in applying the .05 standard.

There is a 90 percent probability that the population mean falls between the lower value of the 90 percent confidence interval and the higher value of the 90 percent confidence interval. There is a 10 percent chance that the population mean falls outside these limits—5 percent *below* the lower boundary and 5 percent *above* the upper boundary.

In the P-value approach the researcher determines the exact probability associated with a hypothetical claim about the population mean. First, let's find the 90 percent confidence interval for science_quiz. Then we will use the P-value approach to evaluate a hypothetical claim about the mean of science_quiz.

We can change ttest's default confidence interval (95 percent) by using the level option and specifying a different value. To change to a 90 percent confidence interval, we will modify the ttest command to read "ttest science_quiz=0, level(90)":

```
. ttest science_quiz=0, level(90)

One-sample t test
```

Variable	Obs	Mean	Std. Err.	Std. Dev.	[90% Conf. Interval]	
scienc~z	1858	5.87352	.0558267	2.406381	5.781647	5.965392

```
     mean = mean(science_quiz)                              t = 105.2100
Ho: mean = 0                            degrees of freedom =        1857

    Ha: mean < 0                Ha: mean != 0                 Ha: mean > 0
 Pr(T < t) = 1.0000      Pr(|T| > |t|) = 0.0000          Pr(T > t) = 0.0000
```

You can be confident, 90 percent confident anyway, that the population mean of science_quiz lies between 5.78 at the low end and 5.97 at the high end. There is a probability of .10 that the population mean lies beyond these limits—a .05 probability that it is less than 5.78 and a .05 probability that it is greater than 5.97.

We can apply this knowledge to the task of testing a hypothetical claim. Suppose you hypothesized that ninth-grade students at a local science fair know more about science than most adults. To test this idea, you ask a group of science fair ninth-graders a series of 10 true-false questions about scientific facts—the same set of questions that appears in the 2006 General Social Survey (GSS). Whereas the 2006 GSS reports a mean value of 5.87 on science_quiz, you find a higher mean value, 5.95, among the young subjects in your study. Thus it would appear that the ninth-graders are, on average, more knowledgeable than are the individuals in the GSS's random sample of U.S. adults. But is this difference, 5.87 versus 5.95, *statistically* significant at the .05 level? No, it is not. Why can we say this? Because the ninth-graders' mean, 5.95, does not exceed the GSS sample's upper confidence boundary, 5.97.

Think about it this way. Imagine a population of U.S. adults in which the true mean of science_quiz is equal to 5.87. Now suppose you were to draw a random sample from this population and calculate the mean of science_quiz. The upper confidence boundary tells you that such a sample would yield a mean of greater than 5.97 *less frequently* than five times out of a hundred. The upper confidence boundary also says that such a sample would produce a mean of less than 5.97 *more frequently* than five times out of a hundred. Since 5.95 is less than 5.97, you must conclude that the ninth-graders' mean is not significantly higher than the GSS mean. Put another way, there is a probability of greater than .05 that the sample of ninth-graders and the GSS's sample of adults were both drawn from the same population—a population in which science_quiz has a mean equal to 5.87.

Confidence interval approaches to statistical significance work fine. Find the 90 percent confidence interval and compare the hypothetical mean to the appropriate interval boundary. If the hypothetical mean falls above the upper boundary (or below the lower boundary), conclude that the two numbers are significantly different at the .05 level. If the hypothetical mean falls below the upper boundary (or above the lower boundary), conclude that the two numbers are not significantly different at the .05 level. Thus the confidence interval approach tells you that a random sample of U.S. adults would produce a sample mean of 5.95 more frequently than 5 percent of the time.

The P-value approach to statistical significance is more precise. The P-value will tell you *exactly* how frequently a sample mean of 5.95 would occur. Supplied with the appropriate information, Stata will calculate the difference between the mean of science_quiz in the GSS sample, 5.87, and the ninth-graders' mean, 5.95. Stata will then report the probability that the two numbers, 5.87 and 5.95, came from the same population. Of course, from the confidence interval approach, we already know that this probability is greater than .05. But this time we are after a more precise probability.

Let's again modify the ttest command to obtain the information we need to determine the P-value associated with the ninth-graders' mean of 5.95. Click the ttest command back into the Command window. For this run, we will replace the "=0" part of the command with a test value, the ninth-graders' mean of 5.95: "ttest science_quiz=5.95, level(90)":

```
. ttest science_quiz=5.95, level(90)
```

One-sample t test

Variable	Obs	Mean	Std. Err.	Std. Dev.	[90% Conf. Interval]	
scienc~z	1858	5.87352	.0558267	2.406381	5.781647	5.965392

```
    mean = mean(science_quiz)                                     t =  -1.3700
Ho: mean = 5.95                               degrees of freedom =      1857

   Ha: mean < 5.95                 Ha: mean != 5.95                 Ha: mean > 5.95
   Pr(T < t) = 0.0854         Pr(|T| > |t|) = 0.1709           Pr(T > t) = 0.9146
```

For this run, we will need to focus on the information in the bottom part of the Results window, beneath the "science~z" row of tabular entries. Here is how Stata proceeds. First it calculates the difference between the sample mean and the test value by subtracting the test value from the sample mean: sample mean – test value. In the current example, Stata subtracted the ninth-graders' mean from the GSS sample mean: 5.87 – 5.95. This calculation, of course, results in a negative number, –.08. So, as hypothesized, the GSS sample mean is lower than the ninth-graders' mean. (Weirdly, even for Stata, the –.08 mean difference is not reported anywhere.) Stata then calculates a Student's t-test statistic, or t-ratio: the mean difference, –.08, divided by science_quiz's standard error, .06. If you performed the precise calculation by hand—that is, if you calculated the mean difference using the nonrounded value of the GSS mean (5.87352 – 5.95 = –.07648) and divided the mean difference by the nonrounded value of the standard error (–.07648/.0558267)—you would arrive at t = –1.37, which is the value of t that Stata reports, to the right and just beneath the tabular entries. Thus science_quiz's mean falls 1.37 standard errors below the ninth-graders' mean.

If, in the population of U.S. adults, the GSS mean and the ninth-graders' mean really are the same, how often would random processes produce a t-ratio of –1.37? Imagine a bell-shaped curve, centered on zero, and tapering off gradually and symmetrically into a skinnier and skinner tail above zero (positive values of t) and into a skinnier and skinner tail below zero (negative values of t). If the GSS mean and the ninth-graders' mean were the same, then the calculated value of t would be equal to zero, give or take random sampling error. Sampling error would produce t-ratios that are close to zero, the fat and tall part of the curve, where most random events reside. As the gap between the GSS mean and the ninth-graders' mean widens, the t-ratio grows in size—into positive numbers if the test value is lower than the sample mean, and into negative numbers if the test value is higher than the sample mean. How about our t-statistic of –1.37? How often would random error produce a t-ratio that reaches 1.37 standard errors into the negative tail of the curve?

About 8.5 percent of the time. How do we know this? Let's direct our attention to the bottom row of results, where Stata has reported three P-values, labeled "Pr" and followed (in parentheses) by a logical expression. Depending on the direction of the hypothesis you are testing, you will either want the P-value on the far right or the P-value on the far left. If you hypothesize that the test value is less than the sample mean (a positive value of t), then you will want to refer to the P-value on the right. If, as in the current example, you hypothesize that the test value is greater than the sample mean (a negative value of t), then you will want to refer to the P-value on the left. What does the relevant expression, "Pr(T < t) = 0.0854", mean? It means this: ".0854 of the curve lies below (<) the calculated value of t, –1.37." Thus, if the GSS mean and the ninth-graders' mean really are the same, random processes would produce a t-ratio of –1.37 about 8.5 percent of the time. From the confidence interval approach we already knew that there is a probability of greater than .05 that the ninth-graders' mean and the GSS sample mean came from the same population. We can now put a finer point on this probability. We now can say that, if the ninth-graders' mean and the GSS mean came from the same population, the observed difference between them would occur, by chance, .0854 of the time. Since .0854 exceeds the .05 threshold, we would again conclude that the test subjects' mean is not significantly higher than the population mean.

Before proceeding, let's review the procedure for obtaining a P-value from the ttest command. This is also the appropriate place to introduce a useful template for writing an interpretation of your results. If your hypothesis suggests that the t-ratio should be positive, then look for the P-value on the right-hand side of the Results window. If your hypothesis suggests that the t-ratio should be negative, then look for the P-value on the left-hand side of the Results window. Use the P-value to fill in the blank of the following template:

"If in the population there is no difference between the mean of [the sample variable] and [the test value], then the observed t-ratio of _____ would occur _____ of the time by chance."

Of course, you can embellish the template to make it fit the hypothesis you are testing. For the science_quiz example, you could complete the sentence this way: "If in the population there is no difference between the GSS mean of science_quiz and the ninth-graders' mean of 5.95, then the observed difference of −.08 would occur .0854 of the time by chance." It is also acceptable to express the P-value as a percentage, as in: "would occur 8.5 percent of the time by chance." The .05 benchmark is the standard for testing your hypothesis. If the P-value is less than or equal to .05, you can infer that the test value is significantly greater than (or less than) the mean of the sample variable. If the P-value is greater than .05, you can infer that the test value is not significantly greater than (or less than) the mean of the sample variable.

TESTING THE DIFFERENCE BETWEEN TWO SAMPLE MEANS

P. 127

We now turn to a common hypothesis-testing situation: comparing the sample means of a dependent variable for two groups that differ on an independent variable. Someone investigating the gender gap, for example, might test a series of hypotheses about the political differences between men and women. In the next guided example, we will test two gender gap hypotheses. The first hypothesis compares men and women on gss2006's female-role scale (fem_role), a 13-point metric that measures attitudes toward the role of women in society and politics. Lower scale scores denote more traditional beliefs ("women domestic"), and higher scores denote more egalitarian beliefs ("women in work/politics"). The second hypothesis compares the genders on a gss2006 scale (breadwinner) that measures the percentage of total family income earned by the respondent. Values can range from 0 (zero percent of total family income is earned by the respondent) to 100 (all of the total is earned by the respondent).

Hypothesis 1: In a comparison of individuals, men score lower on the female-role scale than women.

Hypothesis 2: In a comparison of individuals, men earn a higher percentage of total family income than do women.

The first hypothesis suggests that when we divide the sample on the basis of the independent variable, sex, and compare mean values of the female-role scale, the male mean will be lower than the female mean. The second hypothesis suggests that in a similar male-female comparison on the percentage of total family income earned, the male mean will be higher than the female mean.

The researcher always tests his or her hypotheses against a skeptical foil, the *null hypothesis*. The null hypothesis claims that, regardless of any group differences that a researcher observes in a random sample, no group differences exist in the population from which the sample was drawn. How does the null hypothesis explain systematic patterns that might turn up in a sample, such as a mean difference between women and men on the female-role scale? Random sampling error. In essence the null hypothesis says, "You observed such and such a difference between two groups in your random sample. But, in reality, no difference exists in the population. When you took the sample, you introduced random sampling error. Thus random sampling error accounts for the difference you observed." For both hypotheses 1 and 2 above, the null hypothesis says that there are no real differences between men and women in the population, that men do not score lower than women on the female-role scale, and men do not earn higher percentages of total family income than do women. The null hypothesis asserts further that any observed differences in the sample can be accounted for by random sampling error.

The null hypothesis is so central to the methodology of statistical inference that we always begin by assuming it to be correct. We then set a fairly high standard for rejecting it. The researcher's hypotheses—such as the female-role hypothesis and the family income hypothesis—are considered alternative hypotheses. The ttest command permits us to test each alternative hypothesis against the null hypothesis and to decide whether the observed differences between males and females are too large to have occurred by random chance when the sample was drawn. For each mean comparison, the ttest results will give us a P-value: the probability of obtaining the sample difference under the working assumption that the null hypothesis is true.

When we use ttest to evaluate the difference between two sample means, we are performing what Stata calls a *two-sample t test*. A key statistical assumption of the two-sample t test is that the amount of variation in the dependent variable is the same in each of the samples we are comparing. So, by default, Stata will assume that the amount of variance in the female-role scale in the male sample will be equal to the amount of variance in the female-role scale in the female sample. Or, at least, Stata assumes that these two sample variances are so similar that the difference between them is statistically indistinguishable from zero. However, if this assumption does not hold up—if, for example, the female-role scale has significantly more variation among the female sample than among the male sample—then we need to inform Stata of this fact so that it can make appropriate statistical adjustments when it runs the two-sample t test.

It will come as no surprise that Stata has a separate command, robvar, that tests to see if two samples have equal variances on an interval-level variable. The general syntax of the robvar command is as follows:

robvar *varname*, **by**(*group_var*)

Stata will divide the cases on the basis of the values of "group_var" and compare their variances on the variable named in "varname." To find out if the variation in the female-role scale (fem_role) is different for male and female respondents (sex), we would run the command "robvar fem_role, by(sex)":

```
. robvar fem_role, by(sex)
```

Respondent's sex	Summary of Female role: Children, home, politics		
	Mean	Std. Dev.	Freq.
Male	7.1404853	2.5867424	783
Female	7.9034749	2.5980943	1036
Total	7.5750412	2.6198979	1819

W0 = 0.04901627   df(1, 1817)   Pr > F = 0.82480883

W50 = 0.03268872   df(1, 1817)   Pr > F = 0.85654456

W10 = 0.27991336   df(1, 1817)   Pr > F = 0.59682263

Stata compares the two sample variances under several sets of assumptions. Happily, we need to focus on and interpret only one number: the P-value ("Pr") at the end of the row labeled "W0." If this number is less than .05, then the sample variances are significantly different, and you will need to specify "unequal" as an option when you run ttest. If, as in the current example, the value at the end of the W0 row is greater than or equal to .05, then the sample variances are not significantly different and you can run ttest on its defaults.[2]

The robvar command is a necessary preliminary. You will need to run robvar before every two-sample t test that you perform. But armed with the knowledge that the two variances are not significantly different, we can now return to the analysis at hand. The general syntax for the two-sample t test is as follows:

ttest *varname*, **by**(*group_var*) **level**(*#*)

To test for a significant difference in the female-role scale (fem_role) between men and women (sex), using the .05 threshold, we would type "ttest fem_role, by(sex) level(90)": [3]

```
. ttest fem_role, by(sex) level(90)
```

Two-sample t test with equal variances

Group	Obs	Mean	Std. Err.	Std. Dev.	[90% Conf. Interval]	
Male	783	7.140485	.0924426	2.586742	6.98825	7.29272
Female	1036	7.903475	.0807189	2.598094	7.770585	8.036365
combined	1819	7.575041	.0614282	2.619898	7.473949	7.676133
diff		-.7629896	.1227988		-.9650787	-.5609005

```
    diff = mean(Male) - mean(Female)                              t =  -6.2133
Ho: diff = 0                                    degrees of freedom =      1817

    Ha: diff < 0                  Ha: diff != 0                  Ha: diff > 0
 Pr(T < t) = 0.0000        Pr(|T| > |t|) = 0.0000        Pr(T > t) = 1.0000
```

There is a lot of information here to digest, so let's take it a step at a time. According to the results, the 783 males in the sample average 7.14 on the fem_role scale. Among the 1,036 females, the fem_role mean is 7.90. So it would appear that our alternative hypothesis has merit: Men do indeed score lower than women. Notice the protocol that Stata follows in calculating mean differences. It subtracts the mean of the category having the higher numeric code on the independent variable from the mean of the category having the lower numeric code on the independent variable. Since males are coded 1 on sex and females are coded 2, Stata subtracted the female mean from the male mean and recorded the difference, –.7629896 or –.76, in the "diff" row. The null hypothesis claims that this difference is the result of random sampling error and, therefore, that the true male-female difference in the population is zero. Using selected information in the Results window, we will test the null hypothesis against the alternative hypothesis that the male mean is lower than the female mean.

Let's use the 90 percent confidence interval of the mean difference—the confidence interval displayed along the "diff" row—to apply the .05 standard. There are, of course, two boundaries: a lower boundary, –.965, and an upper boundary, –.561. Here is a foolproof method for testing a hypothesis using the confidence interval approach. First, make sure that the direction of the mean difference is consistent with the alternative hypothesis. If the mean difference runs in the direction opposite from the one you hypothesized, then the game is already up—the alternative hypothesis is incorrect. Second, determine whether the confidence interval of the difference—the interval between the lower boundary and the upper boundary—includes zero. If the confidence interval includes zero, then the mean difference is not significant at the .05 level. It would occur by chance more than 5 times out of 100. If the confidence interval does not include zero, then the mean difference is statistically significant at the .05 level. The difference would occur by chance fewer than 5 times out of 100.

In the current example, the difference between men and women on fem_role runs in the hypothesized direction: Males have a lower mean than do females. So the alternative hypothesis is still alive. Does the confidence interval, the interval between –.965 and –.561 include zero? No, it doesn't. Conclusion: If the null hypothesis is correct, the probability of observing a mean difference of –.76 is less than .05. Reject the null hypothesis.

Just as we did earlier, we can arrive at an exact probability of observing a mean difference of –.76 under the assumption that the null hypothesis is correct. Given the way that Stata calculates mean differences— subtracting the mean of the higher coded category, females, from the mean of the lower coded category, males—our alternative hypothesis says that we should obtain a negative value of t. And, in fact, we do find a negative t-value, –6.21, which Stata reports in the Results window. Because we hypothesized a negative t-ratio, we refer to the P-value on the left side of the bottom row: 0.0000. More precise conclusion: If the null hypothesis is correct, then random sampling error would produce a t-ratio of –6.21 zero times out of 10,000. Reject the null hypothesis.

All right, so men score lower than women on the female-role scale. Do men earn a higher percentage of total family income than women, as hypothesis 2 suggests? First, perform the mandatory robvar analysis of breadwinner to check for equality of variances, "robvar breadwinner, by(sex)":

```
. robvar breadwinner, by(sex)
```

Respondent's sex	Summary of Percent of total family $ earned by R		
	Mean	Std. Dev.	Freq.
Male	86.669215	21.327073	1306
Female	77.535691	25.681542	1300
Total	82.112968	24.033444	2606

```
W0  =   89.975495   df(1, 2604)     Pr > F = 0.00000000

W50 =   81.027486   df(1, 2604)     Pr > F = 0.00000000

W10 =   85.565141   df(1, 2604)     Pr > F = 0.00000000
```

In this case, the "W0" row shows a P-value of 0.000, which is less than .05. Therefore, we cannot assume that the variance in the male sample and the variance in the female sample are equal, and we will have to override Stata's ttest default.

In the ttest command for testing the breadwinner-sex hypothesis, we would specify "unequal" as an option, "ttest breadwinner, by(sex) level(90) unequal":

```
. ttest breadwinner, by(sex) level(90) unequal
```

Two-sample t test with unequal variances

Group	Obs	Mean	Std. Err.	Std. Dev.	[90% Conf. Interval]	
Male	1306	86.66922	.5901463	21.32707	85.69782	87.64061
Female	1300	77.53569	.7122778	25.68154	76.36326	78.70812
combined	2606	82.11297	.4707917	24.03344	81.33831	82.88763
diff		9.133525	.9249931		7.611486	10.65556

```
    diff = mean(Male) - mean(Female)                          t =   9.8742
Ho: diff = 0                     Satterthwaite's degrees of freedom = 2514.91

    Ha: diff < 0                  Ha: diff != 0                  Ha: diff > 0
 Pr(T < t) = 1.0000           Pr(|T| > |t|) = 0.0000         Pr(T > t) = 0.0000
```

On average, men earn 86.67 percent of total family income, compared with 77.54 percent for women, a mean difference of 9.13. Is this difference significant at the .05 level? Use the confidence interval approach. Does the 90 percent confidence interval, from 7.61 to 10.66, include zero, the null's talisman? No, the confidence interval brackets values greater than zero. Thus we know that the mean difference would occur by chance fewer than 5 times out of 100. Indeed, things do not look good for the null hypothesis. The large t-ratio, 9.87, and relevant P-value, 0.0000, support this inference: If the null hypothesis is correct, we would observe by chance a t-ratio of 9.87 zero times out of ten thousand. Reject the null hypothesis.

Both the female-role example and the income example used sex as the independent variable. Sex has only two coded values, so when we specified "by(sex)" Stata knew exactly what to do—compare the mean values of the dependent variable for the two coded groups, males and females. Often, however, you will want to run ttest using an independent variable that has more than two coded values. Suppose, for example, you hypothesized that independents will score significantly higher on the female-role scale than will Republicans, a perfectly reasonable idea. The problem is that the relevant gss2006 variable, partyid_3, has three codes: Democrat (coded 1 on partyid_3), independent (coded 2), and Republican (coded 3). How can we get Stata to compare only independents and Republicans? By using the if qualifier. As described in Chapter 4 ("A Closer Look," p. 65), the if qualifier instructs Stata to perform a command only for cases that meet the logical restrictions you specify. Consider the following robvar command:

robvar fem_role if partyid_3>1, by(partyid_3)

Because Democrats (whom we do not wish to include) are coded 1, the if qualifier, "if partyid_3>1", will restrict the analysis to respondents coded 2 or 3 on partyid_3, independents and Republicans. Go ahead and type "robvar fem_role if partyid_3>1, by(partyid_3)":

```
. robvar fem_role if partyid_3>1, by(partyid_3)

                   Summary of Female role: Children,
 Party ID: 3              home, politics
        cats       Mean      Std. Dev.         Freq.

  Independe     7.1753846    2.5561612           325
  Republica     7.0954693    2.7509737           618

      Total     7.1230117    2.6843358           943

W0  =  1.1285413    df(2, 975)     Pr > F = 0.32392701

W50 =  1.4441329    df(2, 975)     Pr > F = 0.23645482

W10 =  1.1216560    df(2, 975)     Pr > F = 0.32615989
```

The P-value, .324, gives us the all-clear to assume equal sample variances. Now run ttest, again restricting the analysis to independents and Republicans, "ttest fem_role if partyid_3>1, by(partyid_3) level(90)":

```
. ttest fem_role if partyid_3>1, by(partyid_3) level(90)

Two-sample t test with equal variances

    Group |    Obs        Mean     Std. Err.    Std. Dev.   [90% Conf. Interval]

 Independ |    325     7.175385    .1417903     2.556161    6.941492    7.409278
 Republic |    618     7.095469    .1106604     2.750974    6.913175    7.277763

 combined |    943     7.123012    .087414      2.684336    6.979087    7.266936

     diff |             .0799154    .184011                 -.2230541    .3828849

     diff = mean(Independ) - mean(Republic)                        t =   0.4343
Ho: diff = 0                                    degrees of freedom =      941

    Ha: diff < 0                  Ha: diff != 0                    Ha: diff > 0
 Pr(T < t) = 0.6679       Pr(|T| > |t|) = 0.6642             Pr(T > t) = 0.3321
```

Is the independent mean higher than the Republican mean? Yes, the mean difference is .08. Is the difference statistically significant at the .05 level? No, it isn't. By the confidence interval approach, we can see that the 90 percent confidence interval, from −.223 to .283, includes the null's favorite number, 0. The anemic t-ratio, .43, has an accompanying P-value equal to .3321. Thus, if the null hypothesis is correct that, in the population, independents and Republicans do not differ on fem_role, we would observe a sample difference of .08 about 33 percent of the time by chance. Do not reject the null hypothesis.

EXERCISES

1. (Dataset: gss2006. Variable: spend6.) Dataset gss2006 contains spend6, which records the number of government policy areas in which respondents think spending should be increased. Scores range from 0 (the respondent does not want to increase spending on any of the policies) to 6 (the respondent wants to increase spending on all six policies). The 2006 GSS, of course, is a random sample of U.S. adults. In this exercise you will analyze spend6 using the one-sample t test. You then will draw inferences about the population mean.

   A. The variable spend6 has a sample mean of _____.

   B. There is a probability of .95 that spend6's true population mean falls between a score of _____ at the low end and a score of _____ at the high end.

   C. There is a probability of .90 that spend6's true population mean falls between a score of _____ at the low end and a score of _____ at the high end.

   D. A student researcher hypothesizes that political science majors will score significantly higher than the typical adult on spend6. The student researcher also hypothesizes that business majors will score significantly lower than the average adult on the spend6. Using the same questions asked in the GSS survey, the researcher obtains scores on spend6 from a number of political science majors and a group of business majors. Here are the results: political science majors' mean, 3.65; business majors' mean, 3.55. Using the confidence interval approach to apply the .05 one-tailed test of significance, you can infer that (check one)

   ❑ political science majors do not score significantly higher on spend6 than do U.S. adults.

   ❑ political science majors score significantly higher on spend6 than do U.S. adults.

   Using the confidence interval approach to apply the .05 one-tailed test of significance, you can infer that (check one)

   ❑ business majors do not score significantly lower on spend6 than do U.S. adults.

   ❑ business majors score significantly lower on spend6 than do U.S. adults.

   E. Examine the t-ratio and P-value from your analysis of the business majors' mean. Fill in the blanks: If in the population there is no difference between the mean of spend6 and the business majors' mean, then the observed t-ratio of _____ would occur _____ of the time by chance.

2. (Dataset: gss2006. Variables: spend6, sex.) In discussing the gender gap, two scholars of public opinion observe that there are gender differences "on issues relating to jobs, education, income redistribution, and protection of the vulnerable in society."[4] This idea suggests the following hypothesis: In a comparison of individuals, women will score significantly higher on spend6 than will men.

   A. According to the null hypothesis, in the population from which the sample is drawn, the difference between the mean value of spend6 for men and the mean value of spend6 for women is equal to _____. Any difference observed in the sample was produced by _____ when the sample was drawn.

   B. Run the command "robvar spend6, by(sex)". The robvar P-value is equal to (fill in the blank) _____. The ttest command (circle one)

      will not need to specify "unequal" in options   will need to specify "unequal" in options

C. Run ttest to find out if women score significantly higher on spend6 than do men. Apply the .05 level of significance. Fill in the blanks:

Male mean: _____

Female mean: _____

Mean difference: _____

90 percent confidence interval of the mean difference: between _____ and _____

t-ratio: _____

P-value: _____

D. Which of the following statements are supported by your findings? (check all that apply)

❑ In the population, women probably score higher on spend6 than do men.

❑ There is a .0000 probability that the null hypothesis is correct.

❑ If the null hypothesis is correct, random processes would produce the calculated t-ratio less frequently than 5 times out of 100.

❑ The 90 percent confidence interval contains the null hypothesis's favorite number.

❑ Reject the null hypothesis.

3. (Dataset: gss2006. Variables: childs, attend4.) The role of religion lies at the center of an interesting debate about the future of U.S. partisan politics. Republican presidential candidates do much better among people who frequently attend religious services than among people who are less observant. However, religious attendance has been waning. This growing secularization, according to some observers, portends a weakening of the Republican base and a growing opportunity for the Democratic Party.[5] But we also know that religious beliefs and affiliations (or the lack thereof) are strongly shaped by childhood socialization. Are the less-religious raising and socializing children at the same rate as the more-religious?

In this exercise you will test this hypothesis: In a comparison of individuals, those with lower levels of religiosity will have fewer children than will those with higher levels of religiosity. This hypothesis says that as religious attendance goes up, so will the average number of children. Dataset gss2006 contains childs, the respondent's number of children. This is the dependent variable. The independent variable is attend4, which measures religious attendance by four categories: "Never-<1/yr" (coded 1), "1/yr-sev times/yr" (coded 2), "1/mnth-nrly ev wk" (coded 3), and "Ev wk->1/wk" (coded 4).

A. Exercise a familiar skill you acquired in Chapter 4. Perform a mean comparison analysis, obtaining mean values of childs (and numbers of cases) for each value of attend4. Fill in the following table:

Religious attendance: 4 cats	Summary of Number of Children	
	Mean	Freq.
Never-<1/yr	?	?
1/yr-sev times/yr	?	?
1/mnth-nrly ev wk	?	?
Ev wk->1/wk	?	?
Total	1.9	4,482

B. Do these findings support or not support the childs-attend4 hypothesis? The findings (circle one)

support do NOT support

the hypothesis.

Briefly explain your reasoning. _____

_____

_____

_____

C. Focus your analysis on a comparison between respondents with the lowest attendance ("Never-<1/yr" and coded 1) and respondents with the highest attendance ("Ev wk->1/wk" and coded 4). Run robvar with the if qualifier to test for equal variances on childs for respondents having code 1 or code 4 on attend4.

The robvar P-value is equal to (fill in the blank) _____. The ttest command (circle one)

will need to specify "unequal" in options. will not need to specify "unequal" in options.

D. Run ttest with the if qualifier to find out if high attenders ("Ev wk->1/wk") have significantly more children than do low attenders ("Never-<1/yr"). Apply the .05 level of significance. Fill in the blanks:

Mean for low attenders: _____

Mean for high attenders: _____

Mean difference: _____

90 percent confidence interval of the mean difference: between _____ and _____

t-ratio: _____

P-value: _____

E. Does the statistical evidence support the hypothesis that people who are more religious have significantly more children than do people who are less religious? (check one)

❑ Yes, the statistical evidence supports the hypothesis.

❑ No, the statistical evidence does not support the hypothesis.

4. (Dataset: gss2006. Variables: sibs, relig, authoritarianism, sex.) Here are two bits of conventional wisdom, beliefs that are widely accepted as accurate descriptions of the world. Conventional wisdom 1: Catholics have bigger families than do Protestants. Conventional wisdom 2: Men have stronger authoritarian tendencies than do women. In this exercise you will test these ideas and see how well they stand up to the statistical evidence. Test conventional wisdom 1 by comparing the average number of siblings (gss2006 variable sibs) for Protestants and Catholics (relig). In running robvar and ttest, use the if qualifier to confine the analysis to relig code 1 (Protestant) or code 2 (Catholic). Test conventional wisdom 2 by comparing mean authoritarianism scale scores (authoritarianism) for males and females (sex). The authoritarianism scale

ranges from 0 (low authoritarianism) to 7 (high authoritarianism). Run the analyses. Record the results in the following table:

	Conventional wisdom 1	Conventional wisdom 2
Need to specify "unequal" option? (yes or no)	?	?
Mean difference	?	?
Lower 90 percent confidence boundary of mean difference	?	?
Upper 90 percent confidence boundary of mean difference	?	?
Does the confidence interval contain zero? (yes or no)	?	?
t-ratio	?	?
P-value for t-ratio	?	?
Is the conventional wisdom supported? (yes or no)	?	?

This concludes the exercises for this chapter. After exiting Stata, be sure to take your removable media with you.

NOTES

1. To simplify the presentation of the material in this chapter, all mean values will be rounded to two decimal places.
2. The robvar command performs Levene's test for equality of variances and reports the results in the row labeled "W0." Levene's statistic tests the null hypothesis that the two variances are equal. P-values of greater than or equal to .05 suggest that the null hypothesis should not be rejected. P-values of less than .05 suggest that the researcher should reject the null hypothesis and conclude that the two variances are significantly different. Two proposed alternatives to Levene's statistic are reported in the "W50" and "W10" rows. Some researchers prefer to test for equality of variances using a different Stata command, sdtest. However, sdtest is less robust than robvar; that is, sdtest is more sensitive to departures from normality.
3. Options may be typed in any order. As far as Stata is concerned, the command "ttest fem_role, by(sex) level(90)" is same as the command "ttest fem_role, level(90) by(sex)".
4. Robert S. Erikson and Kent L. Tedin, *American Public Opinion: Its Origins, Content, and Impact*, 7th ed. (New York: Pearson Longman, 2005), 209.
5. John B. Judis and Ruy Teixeira, *The Emerging Democratic Majority* (New York: Scribner, 2002).

7

Chi-square and
Measures of Association

Commands Covered

(tabulate option) chi2	Reports the chi-square test of statistical significance
(tabulate option) V	Reports the value of Cramer's V
somersd *indep_var dep_var*	Reports the value of Somers' d
lambda *dep_var indep_var*	Reports the value of lambda

In the preceding chapter you learned how to test for mean differences on an interval-level dependent variable. But what if we are not dealing with interval-level variables? What if we are doing cross-tabulation analysis, and we are trying to figure out whether an observed relationship between two nominal or ordinal variables mirrors the true relationship in the population? Just as with mean differences, the answer depends on the boundaries of random sampling error, the extent to which our observed results "happened by chance" when we took the sample. Stata's tabulate command, with the right options, can provide the information we need to test the statistical significance of nominal or ordinal relationships. For some situations, tabulate will also provide an appropriate measure of association for gauging the strength of the relationship between an independent and a dependent variable. In other situations, we will need to run an additional Stata command, such as somersd or lambda.

You know how to use the tabulate command to produce cross-tabulations. For analyzing datasets that contain a preponderance of categorical variables—variables measured by nominal or ordinal categories—cross-tabulation is by far the most common mode of analysis in political research. In this section we will revisit tabulate and use the chi2 option to obtain the oldest and most widely applied test of statistical significance in cross-tabulation analysis, the chi-square test. With rare exceptions, chi-square can always be used to determine whether an observed cross-tab relationship departs significantly from the expectations of the null hypothesis. In the first guided example, you will be introduced to the logic behind chi-square, and you will learn how to interpret Stata's chi-square results.

In this chapter you also will learn how to obtain measures of association for the relationships you are analyzing. If one or both variables in the cross-tabulation are nominal level, then you need to obtain lambda. If both are ordinal-level variables, then Somers' d is the appropriate measure of association. Lambda and Somers' d are *asymmetrical* measures. Each reports different measures of the strength of a relationship, depending on whether the independent variable is used to predict the dependent variable or the dependent variable is used to predict the independent variable. Asymmetrical measures of association generally are preferred over *symmetrical* measures, which yield the same value, regardless of whether the independent variable is used to predict the dependent variable or the dependent variable is used to predict the independent variable.[1] Therefore, in this book we will cover lambda for nominal relationships and Somers' d for ordinal relationships.[2]

Both lambda and Somers' d provide proportional reduction in error (PRE) measures of the strength of a relationship. A PRE measure tells you the extent to which the values of the independent variable predict the values of the dependent variable. A value close to zero says that the independent variable provides little predictive leverage; the relationship is weak. Values close to the poles—to –1 for negative associations or to

+1 for positive relationships—tell you that the independent variable provides a lot of help in predicting the dependent variable; the relationship is strong.

Lambda's PRE status stands it in good stead with political researchers because PRE measures are generally preferred over measures that do not permit a PRE interpretation. Even so, lambda tends to underestimate the strength of a relationship, especially when one of the variables has low variation. Therefore, when you are analyzing a relationship in which one or both of the variables are nominal, it is a good practice to request Cramer's V as a tabulate option. Cramer's V, one of a variety of chi-square-based measures, does not measure strength by the PRE criterion. However, it is bounded by 0 (no relationship) and 1 (a perfect relationship).

ANALYZING ORDINAL-LEVEL RELATIONSHIPS

We will begin by using gss2006 to analyze an ordinal-level relationship. Consider this hypothesis: In a comparison of individuals, younger people are more likely to perceive scientific consensus on the causes of global warming than are older people. Dataset gss2006 contains science_gw3, an ordinal variable that measures the extent to which respondents think that "environmental scientists agree among themselves about the existence and causes of global warming." You analyzed science_gw3 in a Chapter 4 exercise. Respondents who think "scientists agree" are coded 1, those taking a middle position are coded 2, and those who think "scientists disagree" are coded 3. Science_gw3 is the dependent variable. One of the variables you created in Chapter 3, cohort3 ("Three generations"), will serve as the independent variable. Cohort3's three value labels are "1949/before" (coded 1949), "1950-1965" (coded 1965), and "1966-1988" (coded 1988).

First we will test the science_gw3-cohort3 hypothesis the old fashioned way—by getting a cross-tabulation and comparing column percentages. Open gss2006. In the Command window, type "tab science_gw3 cohort3, col nokey":

```
. tab science_gw3 cohort3, col nokey
```

Global warming: Do scientists agree? (gwsci)	1949/befo	1950-1965	1966-1988	Total
Scientists agree	103	127	159	389
	42.74	46.01	48.18	45.93
Middle	92	104	120	316
	38.17	37.68	36.36	37.31
Scientists disagree	46	45	51	142
	19.09	16.30	15.45	16.77
Total	241	276	330	847
	100.00	100.00	100.00	100.00

(Header spanning "1949/befo 1950-1965 1966-1988": **Three generations**)

How would you evaluate the science_gw3-cohort3 hypothesis in light of this analysis? Focus on the column percentages in the "Scientists agree" row. According to the hypothesis, as we move along this row, from older to younger, the percentage of respondents thinking that scientists agree should increase. Is this what happens? Well, the percentages increase from 42.74 percent among the oldest cohort, to 46.01 percent among the middle generation, to 48.18 percent for the youngest age group. So there is something on the order of a 5-percentage-point difference between the oldest and youngest respondents—a measurable if not a terribly robust relationship between the independent and dependent variables. Indeed, two political analysts might offer conflicting interpretations of these results. The first analyst might conclude that, yes, younger generations are more likely to perceive scientific agreement than are older generations. The other might declare the relationship too weak to support the science_gw3-cohort3 hypothesis. Inferential statistics, of course, is designed to settle such arguments.

Let's reconsider the science_gw3-cohort3 cross-tabulation in the way that the chi-square test of statistical significance would approach it. Chi-square begins by looking at the "Total" column, which contains the distribution of the entire sample across the values of the dependent variable, the science_gw3. Thus 45.93

percent of the sample thinks that scientists agree, 37.31 percent takes a middle position, and 16.77 percent thinks that scientists disagree. Chi-square then frames the null hypothesis, which claims that, in the population, science_gw3 and cohort3 are not related to each other, that individuals' ages are unrelated to their opinions about environmental science. If the null hypothesis is correct, then a random sample of people who were born in 1949 or earlier would produce the same distribution of opinions as the total distribution: 45.93 percent "scientists agree" / 37.31 percent "middle" / 16.77 percent "scientists disagree." By the same token, a random sample of people born between 1950 and 1965 would yield a distribution that looks just like the total distribution: 45.93 percent "scientists agree" / 37.31 percent "middle" / 16.77 percent "scientists disagree." A random sample of individuals in the youngest cohort, born between 1966 and 1988, would produce the same result: 45.93 percent "scientists agree" / 37.31 percent "middle" / 16.77 percent "scientists disagree." Thus, if the null hypothesis is correct, then the distribution of cases down each column of the table will be the same as the "Total" column. Of course, the null hypothesis asserts that any departures from this monotonous pattern resulted from random sampling error.

Now reexamine the table and make a considered judgment. Would you say that the observed distribution of cases within each category of cohort3 conforms to the expectations of the null hypothesis? For the oldest generation, the distribution is pretty close to the total distribution, with modest departures—for example, a somewhat lower percentage in the "scientists agree" category than the null would expect and a slightly higher percentage in the "scientists disagree" category. The distribution for the 1950–1965 generation corresponds quite well to the total distribution, as does the distribution for the youngest respondents. Thus, for each value of cohort3, there is fairly close conformity to what we would expect to find if the null hypothesis is true. The small departures from these expectations, furthermore, might easily be explained by random sampling error.

Let's rerun the analysis and find out if our considered judgment is borne out by the chi-square test. Click "tab science_gw3 cohort3, col nokey" back into the Command window and add the "chi2" option: "tab science_gw3 cohort3, col nokey chi2".

```
. tab science_gw3 cohort3, col nokey chi2
```

Global warming: Do scientists agree? (gwsci)	Three generations 1949/befo	1950-1965	1966-1988	Total
Scientists agree	103 42.74	127 46.01	159 48.18	389 45.93
Middle	92 38.17	104 37.68	120 36.36	316 37.31
Scientists disagree	46 19.09	45 16.30	51 15.45	142 16.77
Total	241 100.00	276 100.00	330 100.00	847 100.00

Pearson chi2(4) = 2.1850   Pr = 0.702

Stata gives us the cross-tabulation analysis again, and this time it has produced an additional line of statistics, labeled "Pearson chi2." The first computed value in the "Pearson chi2" row, 2.1850, is the chi-square test statistic.[3] If the observed data perfectly fit the expectations of the null hypothesis, this test statistic would be 0. As the observed data depart from the null's expectations, this value grows in size. For the science_gw3 cohort3 cross-tabulation, Stata calculated a chi-square test statistic equal to 2.1850. Is this number, 2.1850, statistically different from 0, the value we would expect to obtain if the null hypothesis is true? Put another way: Under the assumption that the null hypothesis is correct, how often would we obtain a test statistic of 2.1850 by chance? The answer is contained in the right-most entry: "Pr = 0.702," the P-value for the chi-square test statistic. How would you interpret a P-value of .702? Assuming that the null hypothesis is correct in its assertion that there is no relationship between the independent and dependent variables, we will obtain a test statistic of 2.1850, by chance, 70.2 percent of the time. The null hypothesis is on safe inferential ground. From our initial comparison of percentages, we were unsure whether the relationship was strong enough to trump the null hypothesis. Maybe it was or maybe it wasn't. The chi-square test has given us the inferential leverage we needed to make a decision. If the null hypothesis is correct, the observed pattern would occur by chance more frequently than 5 times out of 100. Do not reject the null hypothesis.

Chi-square is a test of statistical significance. It tells you whether random sampling error could plausibly account for the observed results. For ordinal-by-ordinal tables we can augment our analysis with Somers' d, a measure of association that gives a precise reading of the strength of the relationship. You installed the somersd package in Chapter 1. (Before proceeding, find out whether somersd is installed by clicking in the Command window and typing "which somersd". If somersd is not installed, return to Chapter 1 and follow the download and installation instructions.) The general syntax for the somersd command is as follows:

somersd *indep_var dep_var*

Somers' d is an asymmetrical measure of association—that is, it is sensitive to the causal order of the variables. In typing the variables, make sure to type the independent variable first, followed by the dependent variable:[4] "somersd cohort3 science_gw3".

```
. somersd cohort3 science_gw3
Somers' D with variable: cohort3
Transformation: Untransformed
Valid observations: 847

Symmetric 95% CI
```

cohort3	Coef.	Jackknife Std. Err.	z	P>|z|	[95% Conf. Interval]	
science_gw3	−.0423825	.0300947	−1.41	0.159	−.101367	.0166019

Stata returns a Somers' d of −.0423825, or about −.04, for the science_gw3-cohort3 relationship. Ignore for the moment its puny magnitude and consider its negative sign. In our initial evaluation of the relationship, we found a (weak) positive pattern. As we moved across the values of the independent variable, from older to younger, the percentage thinking that "scientists agree" increased by about 5 percentage points. So shouldn't the sign on Somers' d be positive? Indeed, confusion about what the sign means is common in computer analysis. So we need to be clear about what Stata has done.

Stata doesn't know how you framed your hypothesis, and it doesn't care. It only cares about how the variables are coded. If increasing codes on the independent variable are associated with increasing codes on the dependent variable, then Stata calls it a positive relationship and shows a positive value for the Somers' d statistic. If increasing codes on the independent variable are related to decreasing codes on the dependent variable, then Stata calls it a negative relationship and places a minus sign on the Somers' d statistic. Because in our example people with higher codes on cohort3—the higher the code (1949, 1965, 1988), the younger the cohort—are somewhat more likely to fall into lower codes of science_gw3 ("scientists agree"), Stata has reported a negative relationship. Indeed, if we were to recode cohort3 so that the codes run from younger to older (1988, 1965, 1949), Stata would report a positive value for the Somers' d statistic: .04 instead of −.04. By being alert to how the variables are coded, you will know which sign is implied by your hypothesis, a positive sign or a negative sign. Placing that worry aside, you can focus on the magnitude of the Somers' d statistic.

What does the magnitude of Somers' d, .04, tell us about our ability to predict values of the dependent variable based on knowledge of the independent variable? It tells us this: Compared with how well we can predict individuals' global warming opinions without knowledge of their generation, knowledge of their generation improves our prediction by 4 percent. Not much going on there. Let's frame another hypothesis, using different variables, and see if our luck changes.

Here is a hypothesis that sounds more promising: In a comparison of individuals, younger people will be less likely than will older people to think that homosexuality is wrong. For the dependent variable we will use homosex2, which measures attitudes toward homosexuality by two response categories, "Not always wrong" (coded 0) and "Always wrong" (coded 1). The independent variable remains cohort3. Although we did not follow this proviso in the preceding example, it is often a good idea to control for education when testing hypotheses about political opinions in which age is an independent variable. Older people tend to have lower levels of educational attainment than do younger people. And because education might itself be related to opinions about homosexuality—people with more education may be less likely to think that it is wrong—we don't want our analysis to confuse the effects of age with the effects of education. Thus we will include a control variable, educ_3, coded 1 for respondents with high school or less ("12 or fewer yrs"), coded 2 for respondents having 13–15 years of schooling ("13-15 years"), and coded 3 for those with 16 years or more ("16 or more yrs").

For this analysis, we want Stata to produce three ordinal-by-ordinal cross-tabulations—a cross-tab showing the homosex2-cohort3 relationship for each value of educ_3. By including the bysort prefix in the tabulate command, we can obtain the cross-tabulation analyses and the chi-square tests of statistical significance. The somersd command, again combined with the bysort prefix, will give us the appropriate measure of strength for the homosex2-cohort3 relationship separately for respondents at each education level. First obtain the cross-tabs by typing the command "bysort educ_3: tab homosex2 cohort3, col nokey chi2":

```
. bysort educ_3:  tab  homosex2 cohort3, col nokey chi2
```

-> educ_3 = 12 or few

Homosexuality always wrong?	Three generations 1949/befo	1950-1965	1966-1988	Total
Not always wrong	66 22.68	71 32.27	139 46.33	276 34.03
Always wrong	225 77.32	149 67.73	161 53.67	535 65.97
Total	291 100.00	220 100.00	300 100.00	811 100.00

Pearson chi2(2) =   37.2270   Pr = 0.000

-> educ_3 = 13-15 yea

Homosexuality always wrong?	Three generations 1949/befo	1950-1965	1966-1988	Total
Not always wrong	48 36.64	79 41.80	120 51.28	247 44.58
Always wrong	83 63.36	110 58.20	114 48.72	307 55.42
Total	131 100.00	189 100.00	234 100.00	554 100.00

Pearson chi2(2) =   8.1875   Pr = 0.017

-> educ_3 = 16 or mor

Homosexuality always wrong?	Three generations 1949/befo	1950-1965	1966-1988	Total
Not always wrong	78 55.71	121 62.69	131 63.90	330 61.34
Always wrong	62 44.29	72 37.31	74 36.10	208 38.66
Total	140 100.00	193 100.00	205 100.00	538 100.00

Pearson chi2(2) =   2.5853   Pr = 0.275

Do peoples' opinions on homosexuality depend on when they were born? For those in the first two education levels—12 or fewer years and 13–15 years—the answer is yes. For respondents with 16 years or more, the answer is no. The chi-square statistics in the first cross-tabulation (chi-square = 37.2270, P-value =

0.000) and the second (chi-square = 8.1875, P-value = 0.017) easily defeat the null hypothesis. The observed relationship in the third cross-tab, however, does not depart significantly from the null hypothesis' view of the world (chi-square = 2.5853, P-value = 0.275).

Take a closer look at the percentages and figure out what is going on—spuriousness, additive relationships, or interaction. Among the least educated group, a large generation gap exists: 77.32 percent of the oldest cohort say "always wrong," compared with 67.73 for the boomer generation, and 53.67 among the youngest group. Calculated from oldest to youngest, that is a sizable 24-percentage-point decline. We see an attenuated but still statistically significant effect in the middle education category: a 15-point difference between the "always wrong" percentage for the oldest group (63.36 percent) and the youngest (48.72 percent). At the highest education level, however, we find a weak (and statistically insignificant) 8-point difference: 44.29 percent versus 36.10 percent. Because the homosex2-cohort3 relationship persists within at least one value of the educ_3 variable, the relationship is not spurious. Note, as well, that the relationship has the same tendency at all education levels. Older people are more likely to say "always wrong" than are younger people. Yet the strength of the relationship differs across educational levels—strong for less educated respondents and becoming progressively weaker as educated increases. Interaction would seem the best way to describe this set of relationships.

Let's see if this interpretation is supported by Somers' d, which will provide a precise PRE measure of the strength of the homosex2-cohort3 relationship at each value of educ_3. Use the bysort prefix to obtain Somers' d for the homosex2-cohort3 relationship at each level of education: "bysort educ_3: somersd cohort3 homosex2".

```
. bysort educ_3: somersd cohort3 homosex2
```

```
-> educ_3 = 12 or few
Somers' D with variable: cohort3
Transformation: Untransformed
Valid observations: 811

Symmetric 95% CI
```

cohort3	Coef.	Jackknife Std. Err.	z	P>|z|	[95% Conf. Interval]
homosex2	−.1659764	.0266947	−6.22	0.000	−.2182971 −.1136558

```
-> educ_3 = 13-15 yea
Somers' D with variable: cohort3
Transformation: Untransformed
Valid observations: 554

Symmetric 95% CI
```

cohort3	Coef.	Jackknife Std. Err.	z	P>|z|	[95% Conf. Interval]
homosex2	−.0999508	.0347637	−2.88	0.004	−.1680865 −.0318152

```
-> educ_3 = 16 or mor
Somers' D with variable: cohort3
Transformation: Untransformed
Valid observations: 538

Symmetric 95% CI
```

cohort3	Coef.	Jackknife Std. Err.	z	P>|z|	[95% Conf. Interval]
homosex2	−.0494726	.03479	−1.42	0.155	−.1176597 .0187144

Again note the negative signs on the Somers' d statistics. At each education level, as the coded values of cohort3 increase from 1949 (the oldest cohort) to 1988 (the youngest cohort), homosex2's codes decline from 1 ("Always wrong") to 0 ("Not always wrong"). Thus the negative signs are consistent with the hypothesis that younger people will be less likely than older people to think that homosexuality is wrong.

Focus on the Somers' d magnitudes. Somers' d has a magnitude of .1659764 (or .17) for the least educated, .10 for the middle group, and .05 for the most educated. So the values of Somers's d capture the weakening relationship between homosex2 and cohort3 as education increases. Plus, because Somers' d is a PRE measure, we can give a specific answer to the "how strong?" question. For the least educated respondents, we would say that, compared to how well we can predict their opinions about homosexuality without knowing their generation, we can improve our prediction by 17 percent by knowing their generation. The predictive leverage of the independent variable declines to 10 percent for the middle group, and slides to 5 percent for those at the highest level of educational attainment.

ANALYZING NOMINAL-LEVEL RELATIONSHIPS

All the variables analyzed thus far have been ordinal level. Many social and political characteristics, however, are measured by nominal categories—gender, race, region, or religious denomination, to name a few. In this example we will use race to help frame the following hypothesis: In a comparison of individuals, whites are more likely than blacks to favor the death penalty. To make things more interesting, we will control for another variable that might also affect attitudes toward capital punishment: whether the respondent resides in the south. Would the racial difference on the death penalty be the same for southerners and non-southerners? Or might the racial divide be stronger in the south than the non-south? Let's investigate.

Dataset gss2006 contains cappun, coded 1 for respondents who favor the death penalty and coded 2 for those who oppose it. Cappun is the dependent variable. The independent variable is race_2 (whites are coded 0 and blacks are coded 1). For the control variable we will use south, coded 0 for non-southerners and 1 for southerners. The analytic task at hand is, by now, abundantly familiar: Tack the prefix "bysort south:" onto a tabulate run: "bysort south: tab cappun race_2, col nokey chi2 V". The only unfamiliar element to add is a capital "V," which instructs Stata to report, for each cross-tab, the value of Cramer's V.

```
. bysort south: tab cappun race_2, col nokey chi2 V
```

```
-> south = Nonsouth
```

Favor or oppose death penalty for murder	Race of respondent White	Black	Total
Favor	956 70.40	55 40.74	1,011 67.72
Oppose	402 29.60	80 59.26	482 32.28
Total	1,358 100.00	135 100.00	1,493 100.00

```
        Pearson chi2(1) =    49.4023   Pr = 0.000
             Cramér's V =     0.1819
```

```
-> south = South
```

Favor or oppose death penalty for murder	Race of respondent White	Black	Total
Favor	566 78.61	104 43.15	670 69.72
Oppose	154 21.39	137 56.85	291 30.28
Total	720 100.00	241 100.00	961 100.00

```
        Pearson chi2(1) =   107.5285   Pr = 0.000
             Cramér's V =     0.3345
```

Before examining the chi-square and Cramer's V statistics, consider the substantive relationships depicted in the cross-tabulations. Among non-southerners, 70.40 percent of whites favor capital punishment, compared with 40.74 percent of blacks—nearly a 30-percentage-point gap. What happens when we switch to respondents who reside in the south? Among southerners, the percentage of blacks who support the death penalty, 43.15 percent, is only slightly higher than that of non-southern blacks. Among whites there is a larger increase, from 70.40 percent for non-southern whites to 78.61 percent for whites in the south. Thus the racial gap is wider inside the south than outside the south. The cappun-race_2 relationship is stronger for one value of the control (when south = 1) than for the other value of the control (when south = 0). Is interaction going on here?

Consider the statistics. The cappun-race_2 relationship defeats the null hypothesis in the non-south cross-tab (chi-square = 49.4023; P-value = 0.000) and in the south cross-tab (chi-square = 107.5285; P-value = 0.000). Thus it is highly unlikely that either relationship was produced by random sampling error. But notice that Cramer's V returns a larger value in the south cross-tab (.3345) than in the non-south table (.1819). Frequently you will find a relationship that is statistically significant at all values of the control. Further inspection of the percentages and statistics reveals that the relationship is stronger at one value of the control than at a different value of the control. This is a common pattern of interaction—a pattern we found, as well, in the homosex2-cohort3-educ_3 analysis.

As you can see, Cramer's V is a useful tool in interpreting controlled comparisons when you want to get an idea about the relative strength of two or more relationships. For a PRE measure for nominal relationships, however, you must turn to lambda. The basic syntax of the lambda command is as follows:

lambda *dep_var indep_var*

There are two noteworthy differences between the lambda and somersd commands. First, for the lambda command we adhere to the normal Stata protocol of typing the dependent variable first, followed by the independent variable. Second, unlike somersd, lambda does not permit the use of the bysort prefix. To obtain lambda for different values of a control variable, then, you must use the if qualifier. To obtain lambda for the cappun-race_2 relationship among non-southerners, type the following command: "lambda cappun race_2 if south==0".

```
. lambda cappun race_2 if south==0

Favor or
oppose
death
penalty       Race of respondent
for murder     White      Black  |      Total
-----------+-------------------------+----------
     Favor |       956         55  |      1,011
    Oppose |       402         80  |        482
-----------+-------------------------+----------
     Total |     1,358        135  |      1,493

lambda_a       0.0519  ←──
lambda_b       0.0000
lambda         0.0405
```

Stata produces an austere table (of raw frequencies), accompanied by a bumper crop of different lambda statistics: "lambda_a," "lambda_b," and just plain "lambda." Which one is correct? The statistic labeled lambda_a.[5] Thus, compared to how well we can predict capital punishment opinions without knowledge of race, by knowing race we can increase our predictive power by about 5.19 percent. What about southern respondents? Click the previous command back into the Command window and change "if south==0" to "if south==1": "lambda cappun race_2 if south==1".

```
. lambda cappun race_2 if south==1
```

Favor or oppose death penalty for murder	Race of respondent White	Black	Total
Favor	566	104	670
Oppose	154	137	291
Total	720	241	961

```
lambda_a    0.1134
lambda_b    0.0000
lambda      0.0620
```

In reassuring support of our interaction interpretation, the lambda for southern respondents (.1134) is more than twice its magnitude for non-southern respondents. Compared with our ability to predict death penalty opinions without knowing race, by knowing race we can improve our prediction by 11.34 percent.

A PROBLEM WITH LAMBDA

One final example will emphasize an important limitation of lambda. Consider this gender-based hypothesis: In a comparison of individuals, men will be more likely than women to have a gun in their homes. Dataset gss2006 contains owngun2, coded 0 for people who do not have a gun in their homes and coded 1 for those who do. In testing this hypothesis, it seems prudent to control for marital status, measured by the variable married. The following command will show us a cross-tabulation of the relationship between owngun2 and sex, separately for unmarried and married respondents: "bysort married: tab owngun2 sex, col nokey chi2 V".

```
. bysort married: tab owngun2 sex, col nokey chi2 V
```

```
-> married = No
```

Gun in home?	Respondent's sex Male	Female	Total
No	293	496	789
	65.84	82.12	75.21
Yes	152	108	260
	34.16	17.88	24.79
Total	445	604	1,049
	100.00	100.00	100.00

```
        Pearson chi2(1) =   36.4120    Pr = 0.000
           Cramér's V =   -0.1863
```

```
-> married = Yes
```

Gun in home?	Respondent's sex Male	Female	Total
No	228	290	518
	56.30	56.31	56.30
Yes	177	225	402
	43.70	43.69	43.70
Total	405	515	920
	100.00	100.00	100.00

```
        Pearson chi2(1) =    0.0000    Pr = 0.997
           Cramér's V =   -0.0001
```

From the first cross-tab it is clear that the hypothesis has merit, at least for unmarried people. Among unmarried males, 34.16 percent have a gun in their homes, compared with only 17.88 of females, nearly a 17-point gender difference. And according to chi-square (36.4120; P-value = 0.000), we can reject the null hypothesis and infer that, in the population from which the sample was drawn, unmarried men probably are more likely than unmarried women to have a firearm in the house. For married people, however, men and women are equally likely to report gun ownership in the home.[6] This non-relationship is marked dutifully by a vanishingly small chi-square statistic (0.0000) and a gargantuan P-value (0.997).

The following two commands will return lambda for the owngun2-sex relationship at each value of the control variable: "lambda owngun2 sex if married==0" and "lambda owngun2 sex if married==1".

```
. lambda owngun2 sex if married==0
```

Gun in home?	Respondent's sex		Total
	Male	Female	
No	293	496	789
Yes	152	108	260
Total	445	604	1,049

```
lambda_a     0.0000
lambda_b     0.0989
lambda       0.0624
```

```
. lambda owngun2 sex if married==1
```

Gun in home?	Respondent's sex		Total
	Male	Female	
No	228	290	518
Yes	177	225	402
Total	405	515	920

```
lambda_a     0.0000
lambda_b     0.0000
lambda       0.0000
```

Consider the value of lambda for unmarried respondents: lambda_a = 0.0000. This suggests that gender plays no role in predicting gun ownership for unmarried people. What is going on here? Because of the way lambda is computed, it will sometimes fail to detect a relationship that, by all other evidence, clearly exists. Lambda looks at the modal value of the dependent variable for each category of the independent variable. Lambda can detect a relationship only if the mode is different between categories. In our earlier analysis of the cappun-race_2 relationship among southerners, for example, whites and blacks had different modes on the dependent variable—the modal value for whites was "favor" (with 78.61 percent of whites), and the mode for blacks was "oppose" (with 56.85 percent of blacks). So lambda picked up the relationship. In the owngun2-sex cross-tab for unmarried respondents, however, both genders have the same mode, "No," the response category of 65.84 percent of the males and 82.12 percent of the females. Because men and women have the same mode on the dependent variable, lambda returned a value of 0.0000—no relationship detected. In situations like this, which are not uncommon, rely on Cramer's V as a useful gauge of strength. In the current example, Cramer's V registers a magnitude of .1863, indicating a weak to moderate relationship between the independent and dependent variables.

EXERCISES

1. (Dataset: states. Variables: abortlaw3, gunlaw_rank3_rev, cook_index3.) Pedantic pontificator is pondering a potential partisan paradox of public policy:

   "Think about two sorts of policies that figure prominently in cultural debate: laws restricting abortion and laws restricting guns. For both policies, fewer restrictions mean more choices and greater freedom, while more restrictions mean fewer choices and less freedom. Because choice and freedom are the touchstone values, one would think that partisan elites would be consistent in their positions on these policies. If Republicans favor fewer gun restrictions, then they ought to favor fewer abortion restrictions, too. By the same logic, if Democrats favor fewer abortion restrictions, then they should also support less gun control. As a keen observer of state politics, however, it is my impression that Republican-controlled states have less-restrictive gun laws but more-restrictive abortion laws. Democrat-controlled states are just the reverse: less-restrictive abortion laws and more-restrictive gun laws. I am sure that when you analyze the states dataset, you will discover this odd partisan paradox."

The states dataset contains these two policy measures, which will serve as dependent variables: abortlaw3 and gun_rank3_rev. Both variables are identically coded, three-category ordinals. Codes range from 1 (states having fewer restrictions) to 3 (states having more restrictions). Another three-category ordinal, cook_index3, measures states' partisan balance with three codes: 1 (Republican states), 2 (states with even balance), and 3 (Democratic states). This is the independent variable.

A. If pedantic pontificator is correct, as you compare states across increasing values of cook_index3—from Republican states, to even states, to Democratic states—the percentage of states having more-restrictive abortion policies should (circle one)

decrease.   stay the same.   increase.

The percentage of states having more-restrictive gun policies should (circle one)

decrease.   stay the same.   increase.

B. If pedantic pontificator is correct, you should find that states having higher codes on cook_index3 will have (circle one)

lower   higher

codes on abortlaw3. You should also find that states having higher codes on cook_index3 will have (circle one)

lower   higher

codes on gun_rank3_rev.

C. Think about how Stata calculates Somers' d. If pedantic pontificator is correct, the Somers' d statistic for the abortlaw3-cook_index3 relationship will have a (circle one)

negative   positive

sign. The Somers' d statistic for the gunlaw_rank3_rev-cook_index3 relationship will have a (circle one)

negative   positive

sign.

D. Run two tabulate analyses, one for the abortlaw3-cook_index3 relationship and one for the gunlaw_rank3_rev-cook_index3 relationship. Make sure to request chi-square. Obtain Somers' d for both relationships. (*Hint*: Because the somersd command permits the user to specify more than one dependent variable, only one somersd run is required: "somersd cook_index3 abortlaw3 gunlaw_rank3_rev".) Browse the cross-tabulation results. In the table below, enter the percentage of Democratic states, even states, and Republican states having more-restrictive policies. In the abortlaw3 row, for example, record the percentage of states having "9-10" abortion restrictions. For the gunlaw_rank3_rev row, enter the percentage of states in the "More restr" category. For each relationship, record chi-square, chi-square's P-value, and Somers' d.

Dependent variable	More Rep	Even	More Dem	Chi-square	P-value	Somers' d
abortlaw3 % more restrictive	?	?	?	?	?	?
gunlaw_ rank3_rev % more restrictive	?	?	?	?	?	?

E. Consider Somers' d for the gunlaw_rank3_rev-cook_index3 relationship. This value of Somers' d means that, compared to how well we can predict gunlaw_rank3_rev without knowing cook_index3, (complete the sentence) _____

_____.

F. Consider the chi-square P-value for the abortlaw3-cook_index3 relationship. This P-value means that, under the assumption that the null hypothesis is correct, (complete the sentence) _____

_____.

Therefore, you should (circle one)

reject   not reject

the null hypothesis.

G. Consider all the evidence from your analysis. The evidence suggests that pedantic pontificator is (circle one)

correct.   incorrect.

Explain your reasoning. _____

_____

_____

_____

_____

2. (Dataset: gss2006. Variables: abhealth, femrole2, sex.) Interested student has joined pedantic pontificator in a discussion of the gender gap in U.S. politics.

Interested student: "On what sorts of issues or opinions are men and women most likely to be at odds? What defines the gender gap, anyway?"

Pedantic pontificator: "That's easy. A couple of points seem obvious, to me anyway. First, we know that the conflict over abortion rights is the defining gender issue of our time. Women will be more likely than men to take a strong pro-choice position on this issue. Second—and pay close attention here—on more mundane cultural questions, such as whether women should play a role in work and politics, men and women will not differ at all."

A. Pedantic pontificator has suggested the following two hypotheses about the gender gap: (check two)

❑ In a comparison of individuals, women will be less likely than men to think that abortion should "always" be allowed.

❑ In a comparison of individuals, women and men will be equally likely to think that abortion should "always" be allowed.

❑ In a comparison of individuals, women will be more likely than men to think that abortion should "always" be allowed.

❑ In a comparison of individuals, women will be less likely than men to think that women should play a role in work and politics.

❑ In a comparison of individuals, women and men will be equally likely to think that women should play a role in work and politics.

❑ In a comparison of individuals, women will be more likely than men to think that women should play a role in work and politics.

B. Run tabulate to test pedantic pontificator's hypotheses. Gss2006 contains two variables that will serve as dependent variables. The variable abhealth, which measures the number of conditions under which respondents think an abortion should be allowed, ranges from 0 ("Never allow") to 3 ("Allow, 3 conditions"). The variable femrole2, which measures attitudes toward the role of women in work and politics, is coded 1 ("Women domestic") or 2 ("Women in work, politics"). The independent variable is sex, coded 1 for males and 2 for females. Request chi-square. Sex is a nominal variable, so be sure to request Cramer's V. (Lambda may not detect a relationship where one exists, so Cramer's V is a good back-up statistic.) Obtain lambda for each relationship. In the abhealth-sex cross-tabulation, focus on the percentage saying "Allow, 3 conditions." In the femrole2-sex cross-tabulation, focus on the "Work, politics" category. Record your results in the table that follows:

Dependent variable	Male	Female	Chi-square	P-value	Cramer's V	Lambda
Percent "Allow, 3 conds" (abhealth)	?	?	?	?	?	?
Percent "Work politics" (femrole2)	?	?	?	?	?	?

C. Based on these results, you may conclude that (check three)

❑ a statistically significant gender gap exists on abortion opinions.

❑ pedantic pontificator's hypothesis about the femrole2-sex relationship is not supported by the analysis.

❑ under the assumption that the null hypothesis is correct, the abhealth-sex relationship could have occurred by chance more frequently than 5 times out of 100.

❑ pedantic pontificator's hypothesis about the abhealth-sex relationship is supported by the analysis.

❑ a higher percentage of females than males think that women belong in work and politics.

D. The P-value of the chi-square statistic in the femrole2-sex cross-tabulation tells you that, under the assumption that the null hypothesis is correct, (complete the sentence) _____

_____ .

3. (Dataset: gss2006. Variables: polview3, racial_liberal3, social_cons3, spend3.) While having lunch together, three researchers are discussing what the terms *liberal*, *moderate*, and *conservative* mean to most people. Each researcher is touting a favorite independent variable that may explain the way survey respondents describe themselves ideologically.

Researcher 1: "When people are asked a question about their ideological views, they think about their attitudes toward government spending. If people think the government should spend more on important programs, they will respond that they are 'liberal.' If they don't want too much spending, they will say that they are 'conservative.'"

Researcher 2: "Well, that's fine. But let's not forget about social policies, such as abortion and pornography. These issues must influence how people describe themselves ideologically. People with more permissive views on these sorts of issues will call themselves 'liberal.' People who favor government restrictions will label themselves as 'conservative.'"

Researcher 3: "Okay, you both make good points. But you're ignoring the importance of racial issues in American politics. When asked whether they are liberal or conservative, people probably think about their opinions on racial policies, such as affirmative action. Stronger proponents of racial equality will say they are 'liberal,' and weaker proponents will say they are 'conservative.'"

In Chapter 3 you created an ordinal measure of ideology, polview3, which is coded 1 for "Liberal," 2 for "Moderate," and 3 for "Conservative." This is the dependent variable. The gss2006 dataset also contains researcher 1's favorite independent variable, spend3, a three-category ordinal measure of attitudes toward government spending. Spend3 is coded 1 (spend on fewer programs), 2 (middle position), or 3 (spend on more programs). Researcher 2's favorite independent variable is social_cons3, a three-category ordinal measure of attitudes on social issues. Social_cons3 is coded 1 (respondent has the most permissive views on social issues), 2 (middle), or 3 (respondent has the least permissive views). Researcher 3's favorite independent variable is racial_liberal3, also a three-category ordinal variable. Racial_liberal3 is coded 1 (respondent has the least liberal positions on racial policies), 2 (middle), or 3 (respondent has the most liberal positions).

A. Think about how Stata calculates Somers' d. Assuming that each researcher is correct, Stata should report (check all that apply)

❑ a negative sign on Somers' d for the polview3-spend3 relationship.

❑ a positive sign on Somers' d for the polview3-social_cons3 relationship.

❑ a negative sign on Somers' d for the polview3-racial_liberal3 relationship.

B. Run a tabulate analysis for each of the relationships, using polview3 as the dependent variable and spend3, social_cons3, and racial_liberal3 as independent variables. Request chi-square. Obtain Somers's d for each relationship. Summarize your results in the following table. In the first three columns, enter the percent of self-identified "conservatives" on polview3 for each value of the independent variable. For example, from the spend3 cross-tab, record the percentage of conservatives among respondents who want to "spend on fewer" (code 1 of spend3), the percentage of conservatives among respondents taking the "middle" position (code 2 on spend3), and the percentage of conservatives among respondents wanting to "spend on more" (code 3 on spend3). For each relationship, record chi-square, chi-square's P-value, and Somers' d.

	Code on independent variable*			Chi-square	P-value	Somers' d
	1	2	3			
Percent "Conservative" (spend3 cross-tab)	?	?	?	?	?	?
Percent "Conservative" (social_cons3 cross-tab)	?	?	?	?	?	?
Percent "Conservative" (racial_liberal3 cross-tab)	?	?	?	?	?	?

*For spend3, code 1 = "Spend on fewer," code 2 = "Middle", and code 3 = "Spend on More." For social_cons3, code 1 = "Most permissive," code 2 = "Middle," and code 3 = "Least permissive." For racial_liberal3, code 1 = "Least liberal," code 2 = "Middle," and code 3 = "Most liberal."

C. Consider the evidence you have assembled. Your analysis supports which of the following statements? (check three)

❑ As values of spend3 increase, the percentage of respondents describing themselves as conservatives decreases.

❑ As values of social_cons3 increase, the percentage of respondents describing themselves as conservative increases.

❑ The polview3-racial_liberal3 relationship is not statistically significant.

❑ If the null hypothesis is correct, you will obtain the polview3-spend3 relationship less frequently than 5 times out of 100 by chance.

❑ If the null hypothesis is correct, you will obtain the polview3-racial_liberal3 relationship more frequently than 5 times out of 100 by chance.

D. Somers' d for the polview3-social_cons3 relationship is equal to (fill in the blank) _____.
Thus, compared with how well we can predict polview3 by not knowing (complete the sentence)

_____

_____.

E. The three researchers make a friendly wager. The researcher whose favorite independent variable does the worst job predicting values of the dependent variable has to buy lunch for the other two. Who pays for lunch? (circle one)

Researcher 1   Researcher 2   Researcher 3

4. (Dataset: gss2006. Variables: partyid_3, trade_union2, pro_secure, genX.) Certainly you would expect partisanship and attitudes toward trade unions to be related. Unions have been mainstays of Democratic support since the New Deal of the 1930s, so you could hypothesize that people holding pro-union opinions are more likely to be Democrats than are people less favorably disposed toward unions. Yet it also seems reasonable to hypothesize that the relationship between union opinions (independent variable) and party identification (dependent variable) will not be the same for all age groups. It may be that, among an older cohort—those born from the New Deal era through the union heyday of the 1950s—attitudes toward unions will play a stronger role in shaping partisanship than they will among "Generation X," those born during and after the 1960s. Assuming that union opinions do indeed play a weaker role for Generation X, what sorts of issues might play a larger role in defining partisanship among the younger cohort? Perhaps the renewed debate

between those wishing to protect civil liberties and those wanting greater security from terrorist threats figures more prominently in affecting the partisan loyalties of the younger generation.

Let's call this idea the "generational change perspective." According to the generational change perspective: (a) the relationship between union opinions and party identification will be stronger for older people than for younger people, and (b) the relationship between civil liberties opinions and party identification will be stronger for younger people than for older people. In this exercise you will test the generational change perspective.

The gss2006 dataset contains partyid_3, which measures party identification (Democrat, coded 1; independent, coded 2; Republican, coded 3). This is the dependent variable. (For this exercise, treat partyid_3 as an ordinal-level variable, with higher codes denoting stronger Republican identification.) One independent variable is trade_union2, a two-category ordinal measure that gauges opinions toward labor unions. Respondents could "Agree" (coded 1) or "Disagree" (coded 2) with the following statement: "Workers need strong unions to protect their interests." A second independent variable is pro_secure, coded 0 for respondents who favor protecting civil liberties over security, and coded 1 for respondents who favor security over civil liberties. The control variable is genX, which assigns respondents to an older generation (born in 1962 or before, coded 0) or a younger generation (born after 1962, coded 1). Run a tabulate analysis using partyid_3 as the dependent variable, trade_union2 and pro_secure as independent variables, and genX as the control. Request chi-square. Run somersd with the bysort prefix to obtain Somers' d statistics separately for each generation.

A. In the controlled comparison cross-tabulations, focus on the percentages of Democrats across the values of trade_union2 and pro_secure. Fill in the table that follows:

| Generation X | trade_union2 Workers need strong unions | | Chi-square | P-value | Somers' d |
	Agree (% Dem)	Disagree (% Dem)			
Born 1962 or before	?	?	?	?	?
Born after 1962	?	?	?	?	?

| Generation X | pro_secure Civil liberties or security? | | Chi-square | P-value | Somers' d |
	Pro-civil liberties (% Dem)	Pro-security (% Dem)			
Born 1962 or before	?	?	?	?	?
Born after 1962	?	?	?	?	?

B. Which of the following inferences are supported by your analysis? (check all that apply)

❑ For both generations, people with pro-union opinions are more likely to be Democrats than are people with anti-union opinions.

❑ For both generations, people with pro-civil-liberties opinions are more likely to be Democrats than are people with pro-security opinions.

❑ For the older generation, random sampling error would produce the observed relationship between partisanship and civil liberties opinions less frequently than 5 times out of 100.

❑ For the younger generation, the partyid_3-trade_union2 relationship is weaker than the partyid_3-pro_secure relationship.

C. Focus on the value of Somers' d for the younger cohort in the pro_secure cross-tabulation. This value of Somers' d says that, compared to how well you can predict (complete the sentence) _____

_____.

D. Based on your analysis of these relationships, you can conclude that (check one)

❑ the generational change perspective is incorrect.

❑ the generational change perspective is correct.

Explain your reasoning. _____

_____

_____

_____

_____

_____.

5. (Dataset: world. Variables: protact3, gender_equal3, vi_rel3, pmat12_3.) Ronald Inglehart offers a particularly elegant and compelling idea about the future of economically advanced societies. According to Inglehart, the cultures of many postindustrial societies have been going through a value shift—the waning importance of materialist values and a growing pursuit of postmaterialist values. In postmaterialist societies, economically based conflicts—unions versus big business, rich versus poor—are increasingly supplanted by an emphasis on self-expression and social equality. Postmaterialist societies also are marked by rising secularism and elite-challenging behaviors, such as boycotts and demonstrations. In this exercise you will investigate Inglehart's theory.[7]

The world variable pmat12_3 measures the level of postmaterial values by a three-category ordinal measure: low postmaterialism (coded 1), moderate postmaterialism (coded 2), and high postmaterialism (coded 3). Higher codes denote a greater prevalence of postmaterial values. Use pmat12_3 as the independent variable. Here are three dependent variables, all of which are three-category ordinals: gender_equal3, which captures gender equality (1 = low equality, 2 = medium equality, 3 = high equality); protact3, which measures citizen participation in protests (1 = low, 2 = moderate, 3 = high); and vi_rel3, which gauges religiosity by the percentage of the public saying that religion is "very important" (1 = less than 20 percent, 2 = 20–50 percent, 3 = more than 50 percent). Higher codes on the dependent variables denote greater gender equality (gender_equal3), more protest activity (protact3), and higher levels of religiosity (vi_rel3).

A. Using pmat12_3 as the independent variable, three postmaterialist hypotheses can be framed:

Gender equality hypothesis (fill in the blank): In a comparison of countries, those with higher levels of postmaterialism will have _____ levels of gender equality than will countries having lower levels of postmaterialism.

Protest activity hypothesis (fill in the blanks): In a comparison of countries, those with _____ levels of postmaterialism will have _____ levels of protest activity than will countries having _____ levels of postmaterialism.

Religiosity hypothesis (complete the sentence): In a comparison of countries, those with _____

_____.

B. Which of the following measures of association is most appropriate for all three relationships? (circle one)

Lambda   Somers' d

C. Consider how the independent variable is coded and how each dependent variable is coded. In the way that Stata calculates the appropriate measure of association, which one of the three hypotheses implies a negative sign on the measure of association? (check one)

❑ The gender equality hypothesis

❑ The protest activity hypothesis

❑ The religiosity hypothesis

D. Test each hypothesis. Obtain chi-square and the appropriate measure of association. In the table that follows, record the percentages of countries falling into the highest category of each dependent variable. Also, report chi-square statistics, P-values, and measures of association.

Dependent variable	Level of postmaterialism			Chi-square	P-value	Measure of association
	Low	Moderate	High			
Percentage high gender equality	?	?	?	?	?	?
Percentage high protest activity	?	?	?	?	?	?
Percentage high religiosity	?	?	?	?	?	?

E. Which of the following inferences are supported by your analysis? (check all that apply)

❑ The gender equality hypothesis is supported.

❑ Compared with how well we can predict gender equality by not knowing the level of postmaterialism, we can improve our prediction by 20.03 percent by knowing the level of postmaterialism.

❑ The protest activity hypothesis is supported.

❑ If the null hypothesis is correct, the postmaterialism-protest activity relationship would occur, by chance, less frequently than 5 times out of 100.

❑ The religiosity hypothesis is supported.

❑ If the null hypothesis is correct, the postmaterialism-religiosity relationship would occur, by chance, less frequently than 5 times out of 100.

That concludes the exercises for this chapter. After exiting Stata, be sure to take your removable media with you.

NOTES

1. Asymmetry is the essence of hypothetical relationships. Thus one would hypothesize that income causes opinions on welfare policies, but one would not hypothesize that welfare opinions cause income. We would prefer a measure of association that tells us how well income (independent variable) predicts welfare opinions (dependent variable), not how well welfare opinions predict income. Or, to cite Warner's tongue-in-cheek example: "There are some situations where the ability to make predictions is asymmetrical; for example, consider a study about gender and pregnancy. If you know that an individual is pregnant, you can predict gender (the person must be female) perfectly. However, if you know that an individual is female, you cannot assume that she is pregnant." Rebecca M. Warner, *Applied Statistics* (Los Angeles: Sage, 2008), 316.

2. Somers' d may be used for square tables (in which the independent and dependent variables have the same number of categories) and for nonsquare tables (in which the independent and dependent variables have different numbers of categories). Because of its other attractive properties, some methodologists prefer Somers' d to other measures, such as gamma, Kendall's tau-b, or Kendall's tau-c. See George W. Bohrnstedt and David Knoke, *Statistics for Social Data Analysis*, 2nd ed. (Itasca, Ill: Peacock Publishers, 1988), 325.

3. Stata reports degrees of freedom in parentheses. The science_gw3 cohort3 table has 4 degrees of freedom, which is displayed in the label, "Pearson chi2(4)."

4. The somersd command pairs the first-named variable (the independent variable) with each succeeding variable (modeled as dependent variables) and returns the value of Somers' d for each pair. Thus the command "somersd x y1 y2" will report values of Somers' d for the x-y1 relationship and for the x-y2 relationship.

5. The lambda_a statistic is the value of lambda in which the variable appearing first in the lambda command is the dependent variable and the variable appearing second is the independent variable. The lambda_b statistic is the value of lambda in which the variable appearing first is independent and the variable appearing second is dependent. The plain lambda is a symmetrical version of the statistic—that is, a generic measure of association that can be used when the researcher is not proposing a causal relationship between the variables.

6. As you might expect, married women are much more likely than married men to report that the in-home gun is not theirs. Analysis of another gss2006 variable, owngun3, reveals that of the married women who report having a gun in the house, 70.67 percent say that the firearm is not theirs. This compares with only 4.52 percent of men.

7. Inglehart has written extensively about cultural change in postindustrial societies. For example, see his *Culture Shift in Advanced Industrial Society* (Princeton: Princeton University Press, 1990).

8

Correlation and Linear Regression

Correlation and regression are powerful and flexible techniques used to analyze interval-level relationships. Pearson's correlation coefficient (Pearson's r) measures the strength and direction of the relationship between two interval-level variables. Pearson's r is not a proportional reduction in error (PRE) measure, but it does gauge strength by an easily understood scale—from –1, a perfectly negative association between the variables, to +1, a perfectly positive relationship. A correlation of 0 indicates no relationship. Researchers often use correlation techniques in the beginning stages of analysis to get an overall picture of the relationships between interesting variables.

Regression analysis produces a statistic, the regression coefficient, that estimates the effect of an independent variable on a dependent variable. Regression also produces a PRE measure of association, R-squared, which indicates how completely the independent variable (or variables) explains the dependent variable. In regression analysis the dependent variable is measured at the interval level, but the independent variable can come in any variety—nominal, ordinal, or interval. Regression is more specialized than correlation. Researchers use regression analysis to model causal relationships between one or more independent variables and a dependent variable.

In this chapter you will learn to perform correlation analysis using the correlate command. You will run bivariate regression and multiple regression using the regress command. Bivariate regression uses one independent variable to predict a dependent variable, whereas multiple regression uses two or more independent variables to predict a dependent variable. Using the graph twoway command, you will learn to overlay a scatterplot with a regression prediction line. These graphic techniques will help you interpret your findings and will greatly enhance the presentation of your results.

THE CORRELATE COMMAND AND THE REGRESS COMMAND

Suppose that a student of state politics is interested in the gender composition of state legislatures. Running the summarize command on a states dataset variable (womleg), this student finds that state legislatures range from 8.8 percent female to 37.8 percent female. Why is there such variation in this variable? The student researcher begins to formulate an explanation. Perhaps states with lower percentages of college graduates have lower percentages of women legislators than do states with more college-educated residents. And maybe a cultural variable, the percentage of Christian adherents, plays a role. Perhaps states with higher percentages of Christian residents have lower percentages of female lawmakers. Correlation analysis would give this researcher an overview of the relationships among these variables.

Open the states dataset. First we will use correlate to get a general idea about the direction and strength of the relationships among three variables: the percentage of Christian adherents (christad), the percentage of college graduates (college), and the percentage of female state legislators (womleg). Stata commands don't get much simpler than correlate. The user types "correlate" (or "cor" for short) and then types or clicks the variables into the Command window: "cor christad college womleg".

```
. cor christad  college womleg
(obs=50)

             |  christad  college   womleg
-------------+---------------------------------
    christad |   1.0000
     college |  -0.1250   1.0000
      womleg |  -0.4458   0.5799   1.0000
```

Stata produces a table, called a correlation matrix, which shows the correlation of each variable with each of the other variables—it even shows the correlation between each variable and itself! The correlation between christad and womleg is –.4458, or about –.45, which tells us that increasing values of one of the variables is associated with decreasing values of the other variable. So as the percentage of Christian adherents goes up, the percentage of female legislators goes down. How strong is the relationship? We know that Pearson's r is bracketed by –1 and +1, so we could say that this relationship is a moderately strong negative association. The correlation between college and womleg, at about .58, indicates a positive relationship: As states' percentages of college graduates increase, so do their percentages of women legislators. This is a fairly strong association—stronger than the womleg-christad relationship. Finally, christad and college, with a Pearson's r of –.125, are weakly related. This value for Pearson's correlation coefficient suggests that the relationship has no clear, systematic pattern.

Correlation analysis is a good place to start when analyzing interval-level relationships. Even so, a correlation coefficient is agnostic on the question of which variable is the cause and which is the effect. Does an increase in the percentage of college graduates somehow cause higher percentages of women in state legislatures? Or do increasing percentages of women in state legislatures somehow cause states to have higher percentages of college graduates? Either way, correlation analysis reports the same measure of association, a Pearson's r of .58.

Regression is more powerful than correlation, in part because it helps the researcher investigate causal relationships—relationships in which an independent variable is thought to affect a dependent variable. Regression analysis will (1) reveal the precise nature of the relationship between an independent and a dependent variable, (2) test the null hypothesis that the observed relationship occurred by chance, and (3) provide a PRE measure of association between the independent variable and the dependent variable. To illustrate these and other points, we will run two separate bivariate regressions. First we will examine the relationship between christad and womleg, and then we will analyze the relationship between college and womleg.

The general syntax of the regress command is as follows:

regress *dep_var indep_var(s)*

Using the permissible command abbreviation "reg," we would analyze the effect of christad on womleg by typing "reg womleg christad":

```
. reg womleg christad

      Source |       SS       df       MS              Number of obs =      50
-------------+------------------------------           F(  1,    48) =   11.90
       Model | 522.218159       1   522.218159         Prob > F      =  0.0012
    Residual | 2105.80664      48   43.8709717          R-squared     =  0.1987
-------------+------------------------------           Adj R-squared =  0.1820
       Total | 2628.0248       49   53.6331592          Root MSE      =  6.6235

------------------------------------------------------------------------------
      womleg |      Coef.   Std. Err.      t    P>|t|     [95% Conf. Interval]
-------------+----------------------------------------------------------------
    christad |   -.303706    .088027    -3.45   0.001    -.4806961   -.1267158
       _cons |   37.92915   4.357105     8.71   0.000     29.1686    46.68969
------------------------------------------------------------------------------
```

In the bottom-most table, Stata reports values ("Coef.") for the y-intercept or constant, _cons, and for the regression coefficient on the independent variable, christad. According to these coefficients, the regression equation for estimating the effect of christad on womleg is

Percent of state legislators who are women = 37.93 – 0.30*christad.

The constant, 37.93, is the estimated value of Y when X equals 0. If you were using this equation to estimate the percentage of women legislators for a state, you would start with 37.93 percent and then subtract .30 for each percentage of the state's population who are Christian adherents. So your estimate for a state with, say, 50 percent Christian adherents would be $37.93 - .30*(50) = 37.93 - 15.0 \approx 23$ percent female legislators. The main statistic of interest, then, is the regression coefficient, –.30, which estimates the average change in the dependent variable for each unit change in the independent variable. A regression coefficient of –.30 tells us that, for each one-unit increase in the percentage of Christian adherents, there is a .30-unit decrease in the percentage of female legislators. So a 1-percentage-point increase in christad is associated with a .30-percentage-point decrease in womleg.[1]

What would the null hypothesis have to say about all this? Of course, we are not analyzing a random sample here, since we have information on the entire population of 50 states. But let's assume, for illustrative purposes, that we have just analyzed a random sample and that we have obtained a sample estimate of the effect of christad on womleg. The null hypothesis would say what it always says: In the population from which the sample was drawn, there is no relationship between the independent variable (in this case, the percentage of Christian adherents) and the dependent variable (the percentage of female legislators). In the population the true regression coefficient is equal to 0. Furthermore, the regression coefficient that we obtained, -.30, occurred by chance.

In Stata regression results, you test the null hypothesis by examining two columns in the bottom table—the column labeled "t," which reports t-ratios, and the column labeled "P>| t |," which reports P-values. Informally, to safely reject the null hypothesis, the researcher generally looks for t-ratios with magnitudes (absolute values) of 2 or greater. According to the results of our analysis, the regression coefficient for christad has a t-ratio of –3.45, well above the informal 2-or-greater rule. A P-value, which tells you the probability of obtaining the results if the null hypothesis is correct, helps you to make more precise inferences about the relationship between the independent variable and the dependent variable. If "P>| t |" is greater than .05, then the observed results would occur too frequently by chance, and you must not reject the null hypothesis. By contrast, if "P>| t |" is equal to or less than .05, then the null hypothesis represents an unlikely occurrence and may be rejected. The t-ratio for christad has a corresponding P-value of .001. If the null is correct, it is highly unlikely that we would obtain these results.[2] Reject the null hypothesis. It depends on the research problem at hand, of course, but for most applications you can ignore the t-ratio and P-value for the constant.[3]

How strong is the relationship between christad and womleg? The answer is provided by the R-squared statistics, which appear on the right-hand side of the results, above the table of coefficients, t-ratios, and P-values. Stata reports two values, one labeled "R-squared," and one labeled "Adj R-squared." Which one should you use? Most research articles report the adjusted value, so let's rely on "Adj R-squared" to provide the best overall measure of the strength of the relationship. (See "A Closer Look" for a discussion of the

 **Closer Look** **R-squared and Adjusted R-squared:**
What's the Difference?

Most data analysis programs, Stata included, provide two values of R-squared—a plain version, which Stata labels "R-squared," and an adjusted version, "Adj R-squared." Adjusted R-squared is often about the same as (but is always less than) plain R-squared. What is the difference? Just like a sample mean, which provides an estimate of the unseen population mean, a sample R-squared provides an estimate of the true value of R-squared in the population. And just like a sample mean, the sample R-squared is equal to the population R-squared, give or take random sampling error. However, unlike the random error associated with a sample mean, R-squared's errors can assume only positive values—squaring any negative error, after all, produces a positive number—introducing upward bias into the estimated value of R-squared. This problem, which is more troublesome for small samples and for models with many independent variables, can be corrected by adjusting plain R-squared "downward." For a sample of size N and a regression model with k predictors, adjusted R-squared is equal to $1 - (1 - R\text{-squared})[(N - 1)/(N - k - 1)]$.

See Barbara G. Tabachnick and Linda S. Fidell, *Using Multivariate Statistics*, 3rd ed. (New York: HarperCollins, 1996), 164-165.

difference between R-squared and adjusted R-squared.) Adjusted R-squared is equal to .182. What does this mean? R-squared communicates the proportion of the variation in the dependent variable that is explained by the independent variable. Like any proportion, R-squared can assume any value between 0 and 1. Thus, of all the variation in womleg between states, .182, or 18.2 percent, is explained by christad. The rest of the variation in womleg, 81.8 percent, remains unexplained by the independent variable.

So that you can become comfortable with bivariate regression—and to address a potential source of confusion—let's perform another regression analysis, this time using college as the independent variable. Press the Page Up key to return "reg womleg christad" to the Command window. Replace "christad" with "college" and press Enter:

```
. reg womleg college

    Source |       SS       df       MS              Number of obs =      50
-----------+------------------------------           F(  1,    48) =   24.32
     Model |  883.778597     1   883.778597          Prob > F      =  0.0000
  Residual |   1744.2462    48   36.3384626          R-squared     =  0.3363
-----------+------------------------------           Adj R-squared =  0.3225
     Total |   2628.0248    49   53.6331592          Root MSE      =  6.0281

------------------------------------------------------------------------------
    womleg |      Coef.   Std. Err.      t    P>|t|     [95% Conf. Interval]
-----------+------------------------------------------------------------------
   college |   .9382839   .1902593     4.93   0.000     .555742    1.320826
     _cons |  -1.002885   4.990791    -0.20   0.842    -11.03754    9.031772
------------------------------------------------------------------------------
```

What is the regression line for the effect of college on womleg? It is

Percent of state legislators who are women = −1.00 + 0.94*college.

As is sometimes the case with regression, the constant, −1.00, represents an "unreal" situation. For states in which 0 percent of residents have college degrees, the estimated percentage of female legislators is a *minus* 1 percent. Of course, the smallest value of college in the actual data is substantially higher than 0.[4] However, for the regression line to produce the best estimates for real data, the regression procedure has anchored the line at a y-intercept. The regression coefficient, .94, says that for each percentage-point increase in college, there is an average increase of .94 of a percentage point in the percentage of female legislators. Again, increase the percentage of college graduates by 1, and the percentage of women legislators goes up by almost 1, on average. In the population, could the true value of the regression coefficient be 0? Probably not, according to the t-ratio (4.93) and the P-value (.000). Also, according to the adjusted R-squared, the independent variable does a fair amount of work in explaining the dependent variable. About 32 percent of the variation in womleg is explained by college. As bivariate regressions go, that's not too bad.

CREATING A SCATTERPLOT WITH A LINEAR PREDICTION LINE

A familiar command, twoway, adds a visual dimension to correlation and regression and, thus, can help you to paint a richer portrait of a relationship. Consider Figure 8-1, which overlays two graphic forms: a scatterplot (scatter) and a linear prediction or linear fit line (lfit). The scatterplot displays the states in a two-dimensional space according to their values on the two variables. The horizontal axis is defined by the independent variable, college, and the vertical axis is defined by a dependent variable, womleg. We know from our correlation analysis that Pearson's r for this relationship is .58. We can now see what the correlation "looks like." Based on the figure, states with lower percentages of college graduates tend to have lower percentages of women legislators, with values on the y-axis that range from 10 percent to about 25 percent or so. The percentages of women legislators for states at the higher end of the x-axis, furthermore, fall between 15–20 percent and around 35 percent. So as we move from left to right along the x-axis, values on the y-axis generally increase, just as the positive correlation coefficient suggested. The dots have been overlaid by the linear prediction line obtained from the analysis we just performed: Estimated percentage of women legislators = −1.00 + .94*college. Thanks to this visual depiction, we can see that the linear summary of the relationship, while reasonably coherent, is far from perfect. Obviously, this graph adds depth and interest to our

Figure 8-1 Scatterplot with Linear Prediction Line

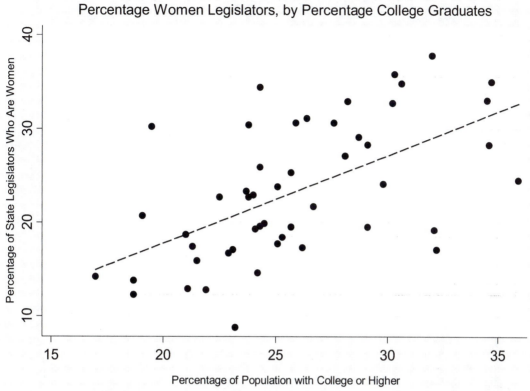

Source: states dataset

description of the relationship. How was it created? A stripped-down twoway command constructed the basics. An excursion into the Graph Editor added detail. First, the twoway command:

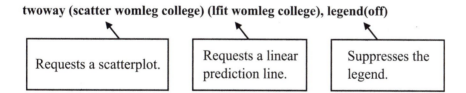

The first parenthetical, "scatter womleg college", creates the scatterplot. The second parenthetical, " lfit womleg college", overlays a linear prediction line. In accordance with Stata's rules, the dependent variable or y-axis variable (womleg) is named first, and the independent variable or x-axis variable (college) is named second. Unless instructed otherwise, Stata will include a legend that distinguishes the different plotted elements in its graphic overlays. For the kind of straightforward plotting we are doing here—a scatter plus a linear prediction line—a legend adds unnecessary clutter. The option, "legend(off)", ensures a tidier display. Type "twoway (scatter womleg college) (lfit womleg college), legend(off)" and press Enter. We're off to yet another good start (Figure 8-2).

What enhancements and edits does Figure 8-2 require? Using Figure 8-1 as a benchmark, you will need to make five changes: (1) change the x-axis title; (2) add a y-axis title; (3) add a source note; (4) add a chart title; and (5) change the pattern (and perhaps the color) of the linear prediction line. Given your prior experience with the Graph Editor, these tasks require little coaching. Figure 8-3 provides a basic refresher. For text objects, such as a chart title, select the desired chart element in the Object Browser and then enter the desired text in the text box that opens along the main menu bar. For plot objects, such as the linear prediction line, select the desired plot region in the Object Browser and use the main-menu drop-downs to make changes. When things are to your liking, be sure to save the graph.

Figure 8-2   Scatterplot with Linear Prediction Line (unedited)

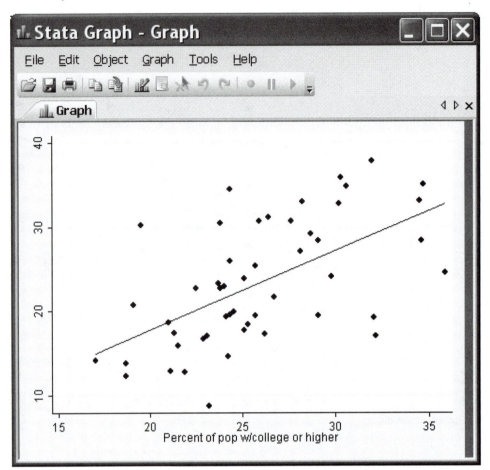

Figure 8-3   Editing a Scatterplot with a Linear Prediction Line

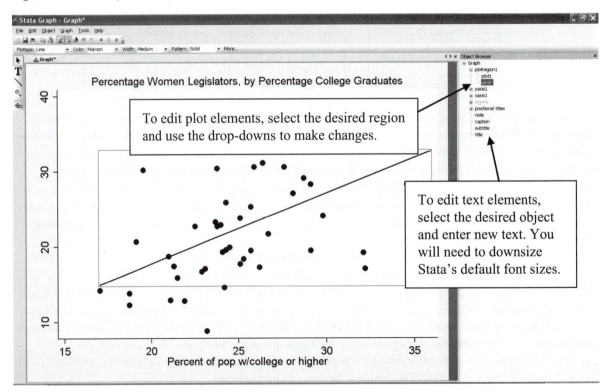

EXPLORING MULTIVARIATE RELATIONSHIPS WITH REGRESSION

Suppose a policy researcher is investigating factors causally related to motor vehicle deaths in the states. One such factor might be a simple characteristic of states: how densely populated they are. Residents of sparsely populated states, the policy researcher reasons, would typically drive longer distances at higher speeds than would residents of more densely populated states. Plus, a car accident in a thinly populated state would be more likely to be fatal, because "both Good Samaritans and hospitals are more scattered in thinly populated states compared to the denser states."[5] So as density goes up, we should find that fatalities go down. Another variable might be demographic: the proportion of young people in the population. As every insurance agent knows—and as many premium-paying parents will attest—younger drivers are more likely to be involved in automobile accidents than are older drivers. Thus, as the proportion of younger people goes up, fatalities should be found to go up, too.

The states dataset contains three variables: carfatal, the number of motor vehicle deaths per 100,000 residents; density, state population per square mile; and pop_18_24, the percentage of the population between 18 and 24 years of age. To get an idea of the relationships among these variables, run the command "cor carfatal density pop_18_24":

```
. cor carfatal density pop_18_24
(obs=50)
```

	carfatal	density	pop_1~24
carfatal	1.0000		
density	-0.5739	1.0000	
pop_18_24	0.3882	-0.4778	1.0000

Note the correlation between each independent variable and the dependent variable. The correlation between density and carfatal is negative, indicating that as density increases, motor vehicle fatalities decrease ($r = -.57$). The relationship between pop_18_24 and carfatal, as the policy researcher suspected, is positive: As the percentage of young people increases, fatalities also increase ($r = .39$). But notice, too, that the two independent variables are themselves moderately related ($r = -.48$). This correlation is negative, suggesting that densely populated states have lower percentages of young people than do sparsely populated states. (This relationship becomes important later on.)

First, let's run a simple regression, using carfatal as the dependent variable and density as the independent variable. Type "reg carfatal density":

```
. reg carfatal density
```

Source	SS	df	MS
Model	531.277234	1	531.277234
Residual	1082.04277	48	22.5425576
Total	1613.32	49	32.924898

Number of obs =	50
F(1, 48) =	23.57
Prob > F =	0.0000
R-squared =	0.3293
Adj R-squared =	0.3153
Root MSE =	4.7479

carfatal	Coef.	Std. Err.	t	P>|t|	[95% Conf. Interval]	
density	-.0127797	.0026325	-4.85	0.000	-.0180726	-.0074868
_cons	19.93871	.8361094	23.85	0.000	18.2576	21.61982

Consider the Coef. column, which reports the y-intercept (_cons) and the regression coefficient on density. According to these values, the y-intercept is equal to 19.94, and the regression coefficient is −.01. The regression equation for the effect of density on carfatal, therefore, is

Motor vehicle fatalities per 100,000 pop. = 19.94 − .01*Population per square mile.

What do these coefficients mean? In terms of its magnitude, for example, the regression coefficient seems to be an incredibly small number, and its meaning is not intuitively obvious. Remember to keep the substantive relationship in mind—and focus on the units of measurement. Very thinly populated states will have an estimated fatality rate close to the intercept, or about 20 fatalities per 100,000 population. Alaska, for example, has a population density of just more than 1 person per square mile. So its estimated fatality rate would be close to the intercept of about 20. The regression coefficient tells us that, for each additional *person* per square mile, the motor vehicle fatality rate drops by .01. New Jersey, for instance, is a very densely populated state, with a density of about 1,200 people per square mile. So New Jersey's estimated fatality rate would be $20 - .01*1200$, which is equal to $20 - 12$, or about 8 fatalities per 100,000 population. Thus, as density increases, by one person at a time, fatalities decrease by .01 of a fatality per 100,000 population. According to the t-ratio (-4.85) and accompanying P-value (.000), we can safely reject the null hypothesis. Stata reports an adjusted R-squared of .3153. Thus, of all the variation among states in automobile fatality rates, about 32 percent is explained by population density.

Now let's run another bivariate regression. We will keep carfatal as the dependent variable, but this time we'll use the percentage of the population aged 18–24 (pop_18_24) as the independent variable. Modify the previous regression command to read, "reg carfatal pop_18_24":

```
. reg carfatal pop_18_24
```

Source	SS	df	MS
Model	243.15653	1	243.15653
Residual	1370.16347	48	28.5450723
Total	1613.32	49	32.924898

Number of obs =	50
F(1, 48) =	8.52
Prob > F =	0.0053
R-squared =	0.1507
Adj R-squared =	0.1330
Root MSE =	5.3428

carfatal	Coef.	Std. Err.	t	P>|t|	[95% Conf. Interval]	
pop_18_24	2.729226	.9351086	2.92	0.005	.8490638	4.609388
_cons	-10.10208	9.494206	-1.06	0.293	-29.19146	8.987302

According to the estimated coefficients, the regression line for the effect of pop_18_24 on carfatal is

Motor vehicle fatalities per 100,000 pop. $= -10.10 + 2.73*$Percent age 18–24.

Again we have a y-intercept depicting an unreal situation, so let's focus on the regression coefficient, 2.73. This says that for each percentage point increase in pop_18_24, there is a 2.73-unit increase in the motor vehicle fatality rate—2.73 additional fatalities per 100,000 population. As the percentage of younger people in the population increases, so too does the fatality rate. In the population, could the true value of the regression coefficient be 0? Probably not, according to the t-ratio (2.92) and the P-value (.005). Also, the adjusted R-squared, .1330, tells us that about 13 percent of the variation in carfatal is explained by pop_18_24.

Let's review what we have found so far. In the first bivariate regression, we found that population density has a statistically significant negative effect on motor vehicle fatalities. Low-density states have higher fatality rates than do high-density states. In the second bivariate regression, we found that the percentage of younger people has a significant positive effect on motor vehicle fatalities. States with lower percentages of young people have lower fatality rates than do states with higher percentages of young people. But recall the initial correlation matrix. There we found that the two independent variables are related: As density goes up, the percentage of younger people goes down. So when we compare states with lower percentages of young people with states with higher percentages of young people, we are also comparing high-density states with low-density states. Perhaps states with higher percentages of young people have higher fatality rates not because they have more young people, but because they have lower population densities. Thus the relationship between pop_18_24 and carfatal might be spurious. Then again, it might not be. Unless we reexamine the pop_18_24-carfatal relationship, controlling for density, there is no way to tell.

Multiple regression is designed to estimate the partial effect of an independent variable on a dependent variable, controlling for the effects of other independent variables. Stata's reg command easily allows the researcher to run multiple regression analysis. Let's do such an analysis, again using carfatal as the dependent variable and specifying *both* density and pop_18_24 as independent variables. Click the last regression command back into the Command window. Modify it to read, "reg carfatal pop_18_24 density":

```
. reg carfatal pop_18_24 density
```

Source	SS	df	MS
Model	558.471141	2	279.235571
Residual	1054.84886	47	22.4435927
Total	1613.32	49	32.924898

Number of obs =	50
F(2, 47) =	12.44
Prob > F =	0.0000
R-squared =	0.3462
Adj R-squared =	0.3183
Root MSE =	4.7375

carfatal	Coef.	Std. Err.	t	P>|t|	[95% Conf. Interval]	
pop_18_24	1.038959	.9438627	1.10	0.277	-.8598478	2.937766
density	-.0112072	.00299	-3.75	0.000	-.0172224	-.0051921
_cons	9.125956	9.858423	0.93	0.359	-10.70663	28.95855

The Coef. column provides the information we need to isolate the partial effect of each independent variable on the dependent variable. The multiple regression equation is

$$\text{Motor vehicle fatalities per 100,000 pop.} =$$
$$9.13 + 1.04 * (\text{Percent age 18-24}) - .01 * (\text{Population per square mile}).$$

Let's focus on the regression coefficients for each of the independent variables. The coefficient for pop_18_24, 1.04, tells us the effect of pop_18_24 on carfatal, controlling for density. Recall that in the bivariate analysis, a 1-percentage-point increase in pop_18_24 was associated with about a 2.73-unit increase in the fatality rate. When we control for density, however, we find a substantial reduction in this effect—to about a 1-unit increase in the fatality rate. What is more, the regression coefficient for pop_18_24, with a P-value of .277, is not statistically significant. Density, on the other hand, retains much of its predictive power. The regression coefficient, −.011, is essentially the same effect we found earlier when we investigated the bivariate relationship between carfatal and density. With a P-value of .000, we can say that, controlling for the percentage of young residents, population density is significantly related to motor vehicle fatalities. It would appear, then, that the carfatal-pop_18_24 relationship is a spurious artifact of differences between states in population density.

In multiple regression, adjusted R-squared communicates how well all the independent variables explain the dependent variable. So by knowing two things about states—the percentage of younger people and the population density—we can account for about 32 percent of the variation in motor vehicle death rates. But notice that this value of adjusted R-squared is practically the same as the adjusted R-squared we found before, using density by itself to explain carfatal. Clearly, density does the lion's share of explanatory work in accounting for the dependent variable.

EXERCISES

1. (Dataset: states. Variables: demnat, demstate, union.) Consider a plausible scenario for the relationships between three variables: The percentages of a state's U.S. House and U.S. Senate delegations who are Democrats, the percentage of state legislators who are Democrats, and the percentage of workers in the state who are unionized. One could hypothesize that, compared with states with few Democrats in their state legislatures, states having larger percentages of Democratic legislators would also have greater proportions of Democrats in their U.S. congressional delegations. Furthermore, because unions tend to support Democratic candidates, one would also expect more heavily unionized states to have higher percentages of Democratic legislators at the state and national levels. The states dataset contains three variables: demnat, the percentage of House and Senate members who are Democrats; demstate, the percentage of state legislators who are Democrats; and union, the percentage of workers who are union members.

A. Run correlate to find the Pearson's correlation coefficients among demnat, demstate, and union. Next to the question marks, write in the two missing correlation coefficients in the correlation matrix:

		Percent U.S. House and Senate Democratic (demnat)	Percent of state legislators who are Democrats (demstate)	Percent workers who are union members (union)
Percent U.S. House and Senate Democratic (demnat)	Pearson's Correlation	1		

(continues)

		Percent U.S. House and Senate Democratic (demnat)	Percent of state legislators who are Democrats (demstate)	Percent workers who are union members (union)
Percent of state legislators who are Democrats (demstate)	Pearson's Correlation	.6412	1	
Percent workers who are union members (union)	Pearson's Correlation	?	?	1

B. According to the correlation coefficient, as the percentage of unionized workers increases, the percentage of Democratic U.S. representatives and U.S. senators (circle one)

increases.   decreases.

C. According to the correlation coefficient, as the percentage of unionized workers decreases, the percentage of Democratic U.S. representatives and U.S. senators (circle one)

increases.   decreases.

D. Which two of the following statements describe the relationship between the percentage of unionized workers and the percentage of state legislators who are Democrats? (check two)

❑ The relationship is negative.

❑ The relationship is positive.

❑ The relationship is stronger than the relationship between the percentage of unionized workers and the percentage of Democratic U.S. representatives and U.S. senators.

❑ The relationship is weaker than the relationship between the percentage of unionized workers and the percentage of Democratic U.S. representatives and U.S. senators.

2. (Dataset: states. Variables: conpct_m, cons_hr.) Two congressional scholars are discussing the extent to which members of the U.S. House of Representatives stay in touch with the voters in their states.

Scholar 1: "When members of Congress vote on important public policies, they are closely attuned to the ideological make-up of their states. Members from states having lots of liberals will tend to cast votes in the liberal direction. Representatives from states with mostly conservative constituencies, by contrast, will take conservative positions on important policies."

Scholar 2: "You certainly have a naïve view of congressional behavior. Once they get elected, members of Congress adopt a 'Washington, D.C., state of mind,' perhaps voting in the liberal direction on one policy and in the conservative direction on another. One thing is certain: The way members vote has little to do with the ideological composition of their states."

Think about an independent variable that measures the percentage of self-described "conservatives" among the mass public in a state, with low values denoting low percentages of conservatives and high values denoting high percentages of conservatives. And consider a dependent variable that gauges the degree to which the state's House delegation votes in a conservative direction on public policies. Low scores on this dependent variable tell you that the delegation tends to vote in a liberal direction, and high scores say that the delegation votes in a conservative direction.

A. Below is an empty graphic shell showing the relationship between the independent variable and the dependent variable. Draw a regression line inside the shell that depicts what the relationship should look like if Scholar 1 is correct.

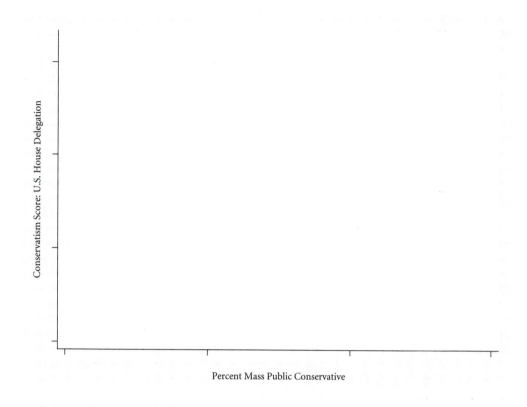

B. Below is another graphic shell showing the relationship between the independent variable and the dependent variable. Draw a regression line inside the shell that depicts what the relationship should look like if Scholar 2 is correct.

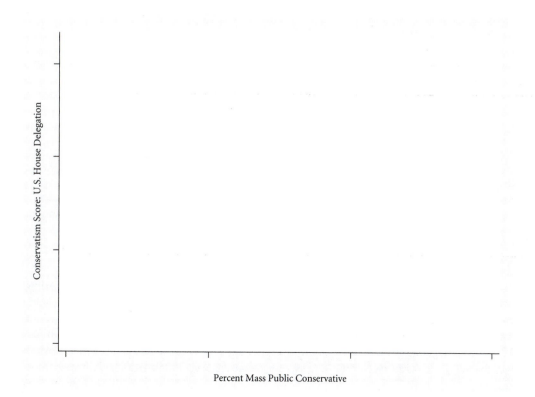

C. The states dataset contains the variable conpct_m, the percentage of the mass public calling themselves conservative. This is the independent variable. The dataset also contains cons_hr, a measure of conservative votes by states' House members. Scores on this variable can range from 0 (low conservatism) to 100 (high conservatism). This is the dependent variable. Run regress.

According to the regression equation, a 1-percentage-point increase in conservatives in the mass public is associated with (check one)

❑ about a 42-point decrease in House conservatism scores.

❑ about a 3-point increase in House conservatism scores.

❑ about a 7-point increase in House conservatism scores.

D. If you were to use this regression to estimate the mean House conservatism score for states having 30 percent conservatives, your estimate would be (circle one)

a score of about 45.   a score of about 65.   a score of about 85.

E. The adjusted R-squared for this relationship is equal to _____. This tells you that about _____ percent of the variation in cons_hr is explained by conpct_m.

F. Run twoway to obtain a scatterplot with a linear prediction overlay. Remember that cons_hr is the y-axis variable and conpct_m is the x-axis variable. Suppress the legend. Make the following changes in the Graph Editor: (i) add a y-axis title ("Conservatism Score, House Delegation"); (ii) add a source note ("Source: states dataset"); (iii) add a chart title ("House Conservatism, by Percent Mass Public Conservative"); and (iv) change the pattern of the linear prediction line. Print the graph.

G. Based on your inspection of the regression results, the scatterplot and linear prediction line, and adjusted R-squared, which congressional scholar is more correct?

❑ Scholar 1 is more correct because _____

_____.

❑ Scholar 2 is more correct because _____

_____.

3. (Dataset: states. Variables: to_0408, obama08). An article of faith among Democratic Party strategists (and a source of apprehension among Republican strategists) is that high voter turnout helps Democratic candidates. Why should this be the case? According to the conventional wisdom, Democratic electorates are less likely to vote than are Republican voters. Thus low turnouts naturally favor Republican candidates. As turnouts push higher, the reasoning goes, a larger number of potential Democratic voters will go to the polls, creating a better opportunity for Democratic candidates. Therefore, as turnouts go up, so should the Democratic percentage of the vote.[6]

A. Use the regress command to test this conventional wisdom. The states dataset contains to_0408, the percentage-point change in presidential election turnout between 2004 and 2008. States in which turnout declined between 2004 and 2008 have negative values on to_0408, while states in which turnout increased have positive values on to_0408. (For example, North Carolina's turnout increased from 57.8 percent to 65.8 percent, giving North Carolina a value of 8.0 on to_0408. Utah's turnout dropped from 58.9 percent to 53.3 percent, giving it a value of −5.6 on to_0408.) To_0408 is the independent variable. Another variable, obama08, the percentage of the vote cast for Democratic candidate Barack Obama, is the dependent variable.

Based on your results, the regression equation for estimating the percentage voting for Obama is (put the constant, _cons, in the first blank)

_____ + _____*to_0408.

B. The P-value for the regression coefficient on to_0804 is _____, and the adjusted R-squared

is _____.

C. Consider your findings in A and B. One may conclude that

❑ the conventional wisdom is correct because _____

_____.

❑ the conventional wisdom is incorrect because _____

_____.

4. (Dataset: states. Variables: abortlaw, permit.) As you are no doubt aware, in its momentous decision in *Roe v. Wade* (1973), the U.S. Supreme Court declared that states may not outlaw abortion. Even so, many state legislatures have enacted restrictions and regulations that, while not banning abortion, make an abortion more difficult to obtain. Other states, however, have few or no restrictions. What factors might explain these differences in abortion laws among the states? We know that the mass public remains divided on this issue. Public opinion in some states is more favorable toward permitting abortion, while in other states public opinion is less favorable. Does public opinion guide state policy on this issue?

The states dataset contains abortlaw, which measures the number of abortion restrictions a state has enacted into law. Values on abortlaw range from 0 (least restrictive) to 10 (most restrictive). This is the dependent variable. The dataset also has the variable permit, the percentage of the mass public saying that abortion should "always" be permitted. This is the independent variable.

A. If you were to use regression analysis to test the idea that public opinion on abortion affects state abortion policy, you would expect to find (check one)

❑ a negative sign on permit's regression coefficient.

❑ a positive sign on permit's regression coefficient.

B. Using regression, analyze the abortlaw-permit relationship. According to the results, the regression equation for estimating the number of abortion restrictions is (fill in the blanks)

_____   _____ *permit.
   (constant)   (regression coefficient)

C. The P-value for the regression coefficient is _____. The adjusted R-squared is _____.

D. According to states, about 44 percent of Colorado residents believe that abortion should "always" be permitted. In Louisiana, by contrast, only about 14 percent of the public holds this view. Based on the regression equation (fill in the blanks),

you would estimate that Colorado would have about _____ abortion restrictions.

you would estimate that Louisiana would have about _____ abortion restrictions.

E. Run twoway to obtain a scatterplot with a linear prediction overlay. In the Graph Editor, use the following titles and notes: (i) y-axis title, "Number of Abortion Restrictions"; (ii) title, "Number of Abortion Restrictions, by Percent Public Supporting Abortion"; and (iii) note, "Source: states dataset". Also, (iv) change the color and pattern of the linear prediction line. Print the graphic.

5. (Dataset: states. Variables: demstate, dempct_m, libpct_m.) In Exercise 2 you analyzed the connection between mass political attitudes and congressional voting, and in Exercise 4 you examined the link between public opinion and public policy. In this exercise you will use correlation and multiple regression to examine a set of relationships between mass attitudes and the partisan make-up of state legislatures. State legislatures are remarkably varied in this regard—ranging in partisan composition from about 25 percent Democratic to over 88 percent Democratic. What accounts for this variation? Consider two plausible independent variables: The percentage of a state's citizens who are self-identified Democrats, and the percentage of citizens who are self-described "liberals." Each of these variables should have a positive relationship with the percentage of Democrats in the state legislature.

A. The states dataset contains these three variables: demstate, the percentage of state legislators who are Democrats; dempct_m, the percentage of Democrats in the mass electorate; and libpct_m, the percentage of self-described liberals in the mass public. Find the Pearson's correlation coefficients among demstate, dempct_m, and libpct_m. Write the correlation coefficients next to the question marks in the following matrix:

		Percent of state legislators Democratic (demstate)	Percent of mass public Democratic (dempct_m)	Percent of mass public Liberal (libpct_m)
Percent of state legislators Democratic (demstate)	Pearson's Correlation	1		
Percent of mass public Democratic (dempct_m)	Pearson's Correlation	?	1	
Percent of mass public Liberal (libpct_m)	Pearson's Correlation	?	?	1

B. According to the correlation coefficients, as the percentage of liberals in the mass public increases, the percentage of Democratic state legislators (circle one)

increases.   decreases.

C. Suppose someone were to make this claim: "Being a Democrat and being a liberal are practically synonymous. The relationship between the percentage of Democratic identifiers and the percentage of liberals, therefore, will be positive and strong." According to the correlation coefficient, this claim is

❏ correct because _____

_____.

❏ incorrect because_____

_____.

D. Run regression analysis to obtain multiple regression estimates for the partial effects of dempct_m and libpct_m on demstate. Demstate is the dependent variable, and dempct_m and libpct_m are the independent variables. Based on your results, the multiple regression for estimating the percentage of Democratic state legislators is

−24.94 + _____*dempct_m + _____*libpct_m.

E. The P-value for the regression coefficient on dempct_m is _____, and the P-value for the regression coefficient on libpct_m is _____.

F. As you may know, Nebraska's state legislature is unique in two ways—it is unicameral (all other state legislatures are bicameral) and it is nonpartisan. Candidates do not run for the state legislature using party labels, and the legislature is not organized on the basis of party. Thus, Nebraska has a missing value on the variable demstate, and it was not included in the regression analysis you just performed. However, if you were to peruse the states dataset, you would find that 29.03 percent of Nebraskans are Democrats and 16.44 percent are self-described liberals. For the sake of speculation, assume that Nebraska decided that all members of the state legislature should declare a partisan allegiance. Based on you regression model, about what percentage would be Democrats? (circle one)

About 25 percent   About 40 percent   About 55 percent

G. Based on your interpretation of the multiple regression output, you can conclude that (check three)

❑ controlling for the percentage of the mass public who are liberal, a 1-percentage-point increase in the percentage of Democrats in the mass public is associated with about a 5.8-percent increase in the percentage of Democratic state legislators.

❑ controlling for the percentage of the mass public who are Democratic, a 1-percentage-point increase in the percentage of liberals in the mass public is associated with about a 2.3-percentage-point increase in the percentage of Democratic state legislators.

❑ both independent variables are significantly related to the dependent variable.

❑ the relationship between dempct_m and demstate is spurious.

❑ taken together, both independent variables explain about one-half of the variation in the dependent variable.

6. (Dataset: gss2006. Variables: civlibs, educ, exploit3, pol_trust, polviews.) In recent years there has been much public debate about the "civil liberties tradeoff." To what extent is the public's belief in free speech and association counterbalanced by a desire for more security against terrorist activity? What factors determine whether a person is pro–civil liberties or pro-security? Certainly such attitudes have more than one source. According to Darren W. Davis and Brian D. Silver, people with higher levels of education will be more reluctant than the less educated to trade civil liberties for security, and liberals will be more pro–civil liberties than will conservatives. Interestingly, Davis and Silver theorize that two sorts of trust—political trust and interpersonal trust—will pull in opposite directions. People harboring greater trust in political authorities will be more pro-security. However, as faith in fellow citizens goes up—as interpersonal trust increases—individuals will be more pro–civil liberties. Thus, "higher interpersonal trust might partly compensate for the effect of higher trust in government."[7] In this exercise you will test the Davis-Silver model of support for civil liberties.

In Chapter 3 you created civlibs, a scale that ranges from 0 (the strongest pro-security position) to 9 (the strongest pro-civil-liberties position). The gss2006 variable educ measures education by the number of years of formal schooling (from 0 to 20 years). Self-described ideology is captured by polviews, which runs from 1 ("Extremely liberal") to 7 ("Extremely conservative"). The variable pol_trust uses a 5-point scale, "strongly disagree" (coded 1) through "strongly agree" (coded 5), to elicit the level of agreement with the statement

"Most government administrators can be trusted." Higher scores denote higher political trust. Finally, exploit3 measures interpersonal trust by asking respondents whether they agree (coded 0), neither agree nor disagree (coded 1), or disagree (coded 2) with the following statement: "If you are not careful, other people will take advantage of you." Higher codes on exploit3 mean higher interpersonal trust.

A. Imagine running a multiple regression using civlibs as the dependent variable and educ, exploit3, pol_trust, and polviews as independent variables. According to the Davis-Silver idea, which of the following variables will have a positive relationship with civlibs? (circle two)

$$educ \quad exploit3 \quad pol\_trust \quad polviews$$

Which of the following variables will have a negative relationship with civlibs? (circle two)

$$educ \quad exploit3 \quad pol\_trust \quad polviews$$

B. Run the regression analysis. Which of the following variables have a positive and statistically significant relationship with civlibs? (circle two)

$$educ \quad exploit3 \quad pol\_trust \quad polviews$$

Which of the following variables have a negative and statistically significant relationship with civlibs? (circle two)

$$educ \quad exploit3 \quad pol\_trust \quad polviews$$

C. Use the regression equation to estimate the civil liberties scale score for the typical respondent, which we will define as a person having the median values of all the independent variables. Run summary with the detail option to obtain the median values for each independent variable. Write the medians in the table that follows (the median of educ already appears in the table):

	educ	exploit3	pol_trust	polviews
Median	13	?	?	?

D. When you use the median values to estimate the civil liberties score for the typical person, you obtain an estimate equal to (fill in the blank) _____.

E. Now let's get an idea of the importance of political trust in shaping civil liberties beliefs, controlling for educ, exploit3, and polviews. Assuming median values for educ, exploit3, and polviews, the estimated civil liberties score for people having the lowest level of political trust is equal to (fill in the blank) _____.

Again assuming median values for educ, exploit3, and polviews, the estimated civil liberties score for people having the highest level of political trust is equal to (fill in the blank) _____.

F. Suppose you witnessed two nonviolent but vociferous groups of demonstrators outside the halls of Congress. One side carries signs indicating that they strongly favor an expansion of civil liberties. The other side's signs advocate just the opposite: more government power to detain people and gather information about citizens. You administer a questionnaire to individuals from both sides, obtaining information on educational attainment, social trust, political trust, and ideology. Before you can administer the civlibs questions, however, the demonstrators disperse. When you examine your incomplete dataset, you find that both groups average 13 years of schooling. On the other variables, though, the groups are starkly different. The pro-civil-liberties demonstrators have the highest level of interpersonal trust, the lowest level of political trust, and they are all "extremely liberal." The pro-security crowd has the lowest level of interpersonal trust, the highest level of political trust, and they are all "extremely conservative."

Based on your regression analysis, the pro-civil-liberties demonstrators would have what score on the civlibs scale? A score of (fill in the blank) _____.

Based on your regression analysis, the pro-security demonstrators would have what score on the civlibs scale? A score of (fill in the blank) _____.

That concludes the exercises for this chapter. After exiting Stata, be sure to take the media containing your datasets with you.

NOTES

1. Regression analysis on variables measured by percentages can be confusing. Always stay focused on the exact units of measurement. One percentage point would be 1.00. So if christad increases by 1.00, then womleg decreases, on average, by .30, or .30 of a percentage point.
2. Stata reports two-tailed P-values, not one-tailed P-values. The expression "P>| t |" means, "the area of the curve above the absolute value of t." This includes the region below a negatively signed t and above a positively signed t. Strictly speaking, then, you may correctly apply the .05 standard by rejecting the null hypothesis for any reported P-value of .10 or less. However, in this book we will follow the more conservative practice of rejecting the null hypothesis for P-values of .05 or less.
3. The t-ratio for the y-intercept permits you to test the null hypothesis that, in the population, the y-intercept is 0. In this case we have no interest in testing the hypothesis that states having 0 Christian adherents have 0 percent women in their state legislatures.
4. If you do a quick summarize run, you will find that the lowest value of college is 17 percent.
5. Edward R. Tufte, *Data Analysis for Politics and Policy* (Englewood Cliffs, N.J.: Prentice Hall, 1974), 21. Tufte uses regression analysis to evaluate the effectiveness of motor vehicle inspections, controlling for population density.
6. See Michael D. Martinez and Jeff Gill, "The Effects of Turnout on Partisan Outcomes in U.S. Presidential Elections 1960–2000," *Journal of Politics* 67 (Nov. 2005): 1248–1274. Martinez and Gill find that the Democratic advantage from higher turnouts has declined over time.
7. Darren W. Davis and Brian D. Silver, "Civil Liberties vs. Security: Public Opinion in the Context of the Terrorist Attacks on America," *American Journal of Political Science* 48 (Jan. 2004): 28–46; this quote, p. 31.

9

Dummy Variables and Interaction Effects

With Stata, you can easily adapt regression analysis to different research situations. In one situation you might have nominal or ordinal independent variables. Provided that these variables are dummy variables, you can run a regression analysis, using categorical variables to predict values of an interval-level dependent variable. In this chapter you will learn how to use dummy variables in regression analysis. In a second research situation you might suspect that the effect of one independent variable on the dependent variable is not the same for all values of another independent variable—that is, interaction is going on in the data. Provided that you have computed an interaction variable, Stata will run multiple regression to estimate the size and statistical significance of interaction effects. In this chapter you will learn how to perform and interpret multiple regression with interaction effects.

REGRESSION WITH DUMMY VARIABLES

A dummy variable can take on only two values, 1 or 0. Each case being analyzed either has the characteristic being measured (a code of 1) or does not have it (a code of 0). For example, a dummy variable for gender might code females as 1 and males as 0. Everybody who is coded 1 has the characteristic of being female, and everybody who is coded 0 does not have that characteristic. To appreciate why this 0-or-1 coding is the essential feature of dummy variables, consider the following regression model, which is designed to test the hypothesis that women will give Democratic presidential nominee Barack Obama higher feeling thermometer ratings than will men:

$$\text{Obama feeling thermometer} = a + b(\text{female}).$$

In this formulation, gender is measured by a dummy variable, female, which is coded 0 for males and coded 1 for females. Since males are scored 0 on the dummy, the constant or intercept, a, will tell us the average Obama rating among men. Why so? Substituting 0 for the dummy yields: a + b*0 = a. In the language of dummy variable regression, males are the "omitted" category, the category whose mean value on the dependent variable is captured by the intercept, a. The regression coefficient, b, will tell us how much to adjust the intercept for women—that is, when the dummy switches from 0 to 1. Thus, just as in any regression, b will estimate the average change in the dependent variable for a unit change in the independent variable. Since in this case a unit change in the independent variable is the difference between men (coded 0 on female) and women (coded 1 on female), the regression coefficient will reflect the mean difference in Obama ratings between males and females. It is important to be clear on this point: The coefficient, b, does not communicate the mean Obama rating among females. Rather, it estimates the mean *difference* between males and females. (Of course, an estimated value of the dependent variable among females can be easily arrived at by summing a and b: a + b*1 = a + b.) As with any regression coefficient, we can rely on the coefficient's t-ratio and P-value to test the null hypothesis that there is no statistically meaningful gender difference in thermometer ratings of Obama.

Let's open nes2008 and figure out how to use gender as an independent variable in a regression analysis of Obama thermometer ratings. We'll use obama_therm as the dependent variable. The independent variable, gender, is a nominal-level measure, coded 1 for males and 2 for females. Because of the way it is currently coded, gender could not be used in regression analysis. How can we create a variable coded 0 for males and 1 for females? One solution is to run tabulate and use the generate option to compute a set of indicator variables, one of which could become our 0/1 female dummy.[1]

Stata programmers, however, have come up with a better solution—the xi: prefix. As applied to regression analysis, the general syntax of the xi: prefix is as follows:

xi: regression *dep_var* **i.***indep_var*

You type "xi:", followed by the regression command and the name of the dependent variable. You then type "i.", followed immediately (without a space) by the name of the independent variable. The variable prefix, "i.", tells Stata to create a set of dummy variables from the independent variable. By default, the lowest-coded value of the independent variable is treated as the omitted category and assigned a value of 0 on the dummy. Because males have the lower numeric code on gender (code 1), the xi: prefix will create a dummy variable that codes males 0 and females 1.

The xi: prefix is best understood firsthand. In our example, the basic command would be typed, "xi: reg obama_therm i.gender". Because we are analyzing nes2008, we must also include the weight, "[aw=w]":

xi: reg obama_therm i.gender [aw=w]

```
. xi: reg obama_therm i.gender [aw=w]
i.gender           _Igender_1-2       (naturally coded; _Igender_1 omitted)
(sum of wgt is     2.3026e+03)
```

Source	SS	df	MS		
Model	4748.24819	1	4748.24819		
Residual	1846274.51	2291	805.881497		
Total	1851022.76	2292	807.601553		

```
                                        Number of obs =      2293
                                        F( 1,  2291) =      5.89
                                        Prob > F     =    0.0153
                                        R-squared    =    0.0026
                                        Adj R-squared =   0.0021
                                        Root MSE     =    28.388
```

obama_therm	Coef.	Std. Err.	t	P>|t|	[95% Conf. Interval]
_Igender_2	2.891247	1.191116	2.43	0.015	.5554684 5.227026
_cons	56.27424	.8815562	63.84	0.000	54.54551 58.00297

Stata automatically created a dummy variable, _Igender_2, coded 0 for men and 1 for women. How can we be sure that women, not men, are coded 1 on _Igender_2? The numeric suffix "_2" tells us that cases coded 2 on the original variable, gender, are coded 1 on the new dummy. Stata plugged the dummy into the analysis and arrived at estimates for the constant and regression coefficient:

$$\text{Obama feeling thermometer} = 56.274 + 2.891 * \_Igender\_2.$$

How would we interpret these estimates? As always, the constant estimates the value of the dependent variable when the independent variable is 0. Because males have a value of 0 on _Igender_2, the mean thermometer rating of Barack Obama for males is 56.274, the intercept. The regression coefficient on_Igender_2 communicates the mean change in the dependent variable for each unit change in the independent variable. So when the dummy switches from 0 to 1, the Obama rating goes up, on average, about 2.9 degrees. We can use this value to estimate the mean rating for females: 56.274 + 2.891 = 59.165. So men rated Obama at about 56 and women rated him at about 59. Was this gender difference produced by random sampling error? Not according to the P-value, which equals .015. Do gender differences account for a big chunk of the variation in Barack Obama thermometer ratings? Not exactly. According to adjusted R-squared, gender alone accounts for about two-tenths of one percent of the variation in the dependent variable. Clearly, other variables "out there" must contribute to the explanation of Obama's ratings. Let's expand the model.

We would expect partisanship to have a big effect on the Obama thermometer scale. Democrats should score higher on the dependent variable than do independents or Republicans. Plus, we know that women are more likely than men to be Democrats, so the obama_therm-_Igender_2 relationship might be the spurious result of partisan differences, not gender differences. The nes2008 dataset contains partyid3, which codes Democrats as 1, independents as 2, and Republicans as 3. Partyid3 is a categorical variable, so we cannot use it in a regression—not in its present form, anyway. But we can use partyid3 to create a dummy variable for partisanship.

We actually need to create not one but two dummy variables from partyid3. Why two? Here is a general rule about dummy variables: If the variable you want to "dummy-ize" has K categories, then you will need K − 1 dummies to measure the variable. Because partyid3 has three categories, we will need two dummy variables. We will ask Stata to create a Democrat dummy, which will be coded 1 for Democrats and 0 for Republicans and independents. We will also create a Republican dummy, coded 1 for Republicans and 0 for Democrats and independents. Independents, then, will be the omitted category—uniquely identified by their code of 0 on the Democrat dummy and their code of 0 on the Republican dummy.

By seeking to make independents the omitted category, we find ourselves at odds with a Stata default. Because Democrats have the lowest numeric code on partyid3 (code 1), the xi: prefix will create dummies for independents (coded 2 on partyid3) and Republicans (coded 3 on partyid3), and it will assign Democrats a code of 0 on both, making Democrats the omitted category. This default does not suit our purpose. Happily, we can use the char command to tell Stata how we want things done. The general format of the char command is as follows:

char *varname* [**omit**] #

We would replace "varname" with the variable name (partyid3) and replace "#" with the numeric code of the category we want Stata to treat as omitted (code 2). So the command would be "char partyid3 [omit] 2".

Stata silently makes the requested change.[2] All right. Now enter the following command, which will produce a dummy variable regression that uses gender and partisanship to predict Obama thermometer ratings: "xi: reg obama_therm i.gender i.partyid3 [aw=w]".

```
. char partyid3 [omit] 2

. xi: reg obama_therm i.gender i.partyid3 [aw=w]
i.gender          _Igender_1-2       (naturally coded; _Igender_1 omitted)
i.partyid3        _Ipartyid3_1-3     (naturally coded; _Ipartyid3_2 omitted)
(sum of wgt is    2.2807e+03)

      Source |       SS       df       MS              Number of obs =    2264
-------------+------------------------------           F(  3,  2260) =  341.99
       Model |  571894.062     3  190631.354           Prob > F      =  0.0000
    Residual |  1259754.58  2260  557.413532           R-squared     =  0.3122
-------------+------------------------------           Adj R-squared =  0.3113
       Total |  1831648.64  2263   809.38959           Root MSE      =   23.61

-----------------------------------------------------------------------------
 obama_therm |     Coef.   Std. Err.      t    P>|t|     [95% Conf. Interval]
-------------+---------------------------------------------------------------
  _Igender_2 |  1.049861   1.003041     1.05   0.295    -.9171161    3.016838
 _Ipartyid3_1|  16.34317   1.161857    14.07   0.000     14.06475    18.62159
 _Ipartyid3_3| -25.07067   1.255029   -19.98   0.000     -27.5318   -22.60954
       _cons |  58.18489    .923372    63.01   0.000     56.37414    59.99563
-----------------------------------------------------------------------------
```

Again Stata created a gender dummy, _Igender_2, coded 0 for males and 1 for females.[3] Stata also created two partisanship dummies, one having the numeric suffix "_1" and one having the suffix "_3". In the wa·

A Closer Look   **The test Command**

In dummy variable regression, all the effects are gauged relative to the constant or intercept—the mean value of the dependent variable for the omitted category. For any given regression coefficient, you can determine how much to adjust the intercept. And by enlisting the t-ratio and P-value you can tell if the adjusted mean is significantly different from the intercept. For dummy-ized categorical variables having more than two values, you may also want to know whether two non-omitted categories have effects that are significantly different from each other.

Consider the nes2008 variable deathpen, a four-category ordinal measure of opinions about capital punishment.[1] This variable is coded 1 ("Favor strongly"), 2 ("Favor not strongly"), 3 ("Oppose not strongly"), or 4 ("Oppose strongly"). The following xi: regression analyzes the effect of deathpen on Obama thermometer ratings:

```
. xi: reg obama_therm i.deathpen [aw=w]
i.deathpen         _Ideathpen_1-4      (naturally coded; _Ideathpen_1 omitted)
(sum of wgt is   2.1537e+03)
```

Source	SS	df	MS		
Model	145480.426	3	48493.4754	Number of obs =	2110
Residual	1572680.11	2106	746.761683	F(3, 2106) =	64.94
				Prob > F =	0.0000
				R-squared =	0.0847
				Adj R-squared =	0.0834
Total	1718160.53	2109	814.680195	Root MSE =	27.327

obama_therm	Coef.	Std. Err.	t	P>|t|	[95% Conf. Interval]	
_Ideathpen_2	7.181318	1.614044	4.45	0.000	4.01603	10.34661
_Ideathpen_3	19.14377	2.057019	9.31	0.000	15.10977	23.17777
_Ideathpen_4	19.06658	1.571397	12.13	0.000	15.98492	22.14823
_cons	50.44025	.8266394	61.02	0.000	48.81913	52.06136

The constant records the mean value for the omitted category ("Favor strongly," coded 1 on deathpen), a chilly 50.440 degrees. The coefficient on _Ideathpen_2 makes the adjustment for respondents saying "Favor not strongly," telling us to adjust the constant upward by 7.181 degrees. The coefficient on_ Ideathpen_3 shows the effect among those taking the "Oppose not strongly" position (add 19.144 to the constant); and _Ideathpen_4's coefficient estimates the relative effect for respondents holding the "Oppose strongly" opinion (add 19.067 to the constant). According to the t-ratios and P-values, each of these effects is significantly greater than 0. Thus, respondents coded 2, 3, or 4 on the deathpen variable gave Obama significantly higher ratings than did respondents who strongly favor capital punishment. But are these effects significantly different from each other? For example, do respondents in code 3 ("Oppose not strongly") rate Obama significantly higher than do respondents in code 2 ("Favor not strongly")? The test command provides the answer.

(continued)

that the xi: prefix names new variables, _Ipartyid3_1 is the Democrat dummy (since Democrats are coded 1 on the original variable) and _Ipartyid_3 is the Republican dummy (coded 3 on the original variable). Let's write out the regression equation and have a closer look at the estimates. To enhance readability, we will substitute "Female" for _Igender_2, "Democrat" for _Ipartyid3_1, and "Republican" for _Ipartyid3_3:

Obama thermometer rating = 58.185 + 1.050*Female + 16.343*Democrat – 25.071*Republican.

First, get oriented by using the constant, 58.185, as a point of reference. Again, because this value estimates the dependent variable when all the independent variables are 0, 58.185 is the mean Obama rating for males

A Closer Look   **The test Command**   *(continued)*

The test command is one of more than a dozen post-estimation commands, procedures that use most-recently estimated parameters to adjust predictions, create new variables, or test hypotheses.[2] Applied to the problem of determining whether two regression coefficients are significantly different from each other, the test command syntax is as follows:

test *varname1* = *varname2*

To test the difference between _Ideathpen_2 and _Ideathpen_3, we would type, "test_Ideathpen_ 2 = _Ideathpen_3":

```
. test _Ideathpen_2 = _Ideathpen_3

 ( 1)  _Ideathpen_2 - _Ideathpen_3 = 0

       F(  1,  2106) =    26.16
            Prob > F =     0.0000
```

Stata tests the null hypothesis that the two coefficients are not statistically different from each other and returns a P-value for this test, labeled "Prob > F =". If, as in the current example, this P-value is less than or equal to .05, then you may infer that the two coefficients are significantly different. If the P-value is greater than .05, then you can conclude that the two coefficients are not significantly different from each other. Thus, moving from code 2 ("Favor not strongly") to code 3 ("Oppose not strongly") occasions a significant increase in Obama ratings. Given their nearly identical magnitudes, it is a safe bet that the "Oppose not strongly" coefficient, 19.144, and the "Oppose strongly" coefficient, 19.067, are not significantly different. But let's ask Stata to confirm that bet:

```
. test _Ideathpen_3 = _Ideathpen_4

 ( 1)  _Ideathpen_3 - _Ideathpen_4 = 0

       F(  1,  2106) =     0.00
            Prob > F =     0.9733
```

Sure enough. With a P-value of .9733, we can infer that respondents who are most strongly opposed to the death penalty do not rate Obama significantly more favorably than do respondents falling into code 3 on the death penalty measure.

---

[1] Deathpen is based on 2008 ANES variable V083163x.

[2] Stata retains in memory the estimates from the most recently estimated model. However, by using the estimates command, you can save the results for any model and replay them later. The test command has four different syntactical forms, only one of which is described here. A related command, testparm, may also be of interest.

---

who are independents. Why so? Because all the dummies are switched to 0: Female is 0 (that's the "male" part of the intercept) and both the Democrat dummy and the Republican dummy are 0 (that's the "independent" part of the intercept). The regression coefficient on Female tells us how much to adjust the "male" part of the intercept, controlling for partisanship. The regression coefficients on the partisanship dummies tell us how much to adjust the "independent" part of the intercept, controlling for gender. Thus, compared with independents, Democrats average 16 degrees higher—and Republicans score 25 degrees lower—on the Obama thermometer. The partisan coefficients are large and statistically significant, with huge t-ratios and miniscule P-values. These results suggest that Democrats are significantly different from independents— and that Republicans, too, are significantly different from independents—on the Obama thermometer.

And, because the coefficient on Democrat is so large and positive and the coefficient on Republican is so large and negative, in this case it would make little sense to ask whether the two effects, +16.343 and −25.071, are significantly different from each other. Obviously they are. (Sometimes it makes a great deal of sense to ask whether two effects are significantly different from each other. The test command is designed for this purpose. See "A Closer Look" on pages 178–179 for a discussion of the test command.)

What about the effect of gender? The coefficient on Female, 1.050, tells us that women, on average, score only about 1 degree higher on the Obama scale, controlling for partisanship. This weak effect fails to trump the null hypothesis (t = 1.05 with P-value = .295). In the earlier regression, using the female dummy alone, we found a gender difference of nearly 3 degrees. That regression, of course, didn't account for the fact that women are more likely than men to be Democrats. After taking party differences into account, the gender difference fades to insignificance.

Overall, however, the model performs fairly well. The adjusted R-squared of .3113 tells us that all the independent variables, taken together, account for about 31 percent of the variation in the dependent variable. So the "glass is 31 percent full." A skeptic would point out, of course, that the "glass is still 69 percent empty." Before going on to the next section, you may want to exercise your new skills by getting the xi: prefix to create new dummies and further expanding the model.

INTERACTION EFFECTS IN MULTIPLE REGRESSION

Multiple regression is a linear and additive technique. It assumes a linear relationship between the independent variables and the dependent variable. It also assumes that the effect of one independent variable on the dependent variable is the same for all values of the other independent variables in the model. In the regression we just estimated, for example, multiple regression assumed that the effect of being female is the same for all values of partisanship—that Democratic females are about 1 degree warmer toward Barack Obama than are Democratic males and that Republican females and independent females also are 1 degree warmer than are their male counterparts. This assumption works fine for additive relationships. However, if interaction is taking place—if, for example, the gap between male and female ratings is significantly larger among Republicans than among Democrats or independents—then multiple regression will not capture this effect. Before researchers model interaction effects by using multiple regression, they have usually performed preliminary analyses that suggest such effects are occurring in the data.

Consider an interesting theory in American public opinion. According to this perspective, which we will call the "polarization perspective," political disagreements are often more intense among people who are interested in and knowledgeable about public affairs than they are among people who are disengaged or who lack political knowledge.[4] For example, it seems reasonable to hypothesize that individuals who think that "protecting the environment is not as important as maintaining jobs and our standard of living" would give the Republican Party higher ratings than would individuals who believe that "it is important to protect the environment, even if it costs some jobs or otherwise reduces our standard of living." So if we were to compare ratings on a Republican Party feeling thermometer for pro-jobs and pro-environment respondents, we should find a higher mean among the pro-jobs group. According to the polarization perspective, however, this relationship will be weaker for people with low political knowledge than for people with higher political knowledge. Among people with lower political knowledge, the mean difference in Republican ratings may be modest at best, with pro-jobs respondents giving the Republican Party somewhat higher average ratings than do pro-environment respondents. As political knowledge increases, however, this mean difference should increase, reflecting greater polarization between the pro-environment and pro-jobs camps. Thus, the strength of the relationship between environmental attitudes and evaluations of the Republican Party will depend on the level of political knowledge.

The nes2008 dataset contains rep_therm, which records respondents' feeling thermometer ratings of the Republican Party. Another variable, enviro_jobs, is a 3-point gauge of respondents' environmental attitudes, coded 0 (pro-environment), 1 (middle), or 2 (pro-jobs). A third variable, know_scale3, measures each respondent's political knowledge by three values: 0 (low knowledge), 1 (medium knowledge), or 2 (high knowledge).[5]

A preliminary analysis will reveal whether the polarization perspective has merit. The following command will produce a breakdown table reporting mean values of rep_therm for each combination of enviro_jobs and know_scale3: "tab know_scale3 enviro_jobs [aw=w], sum(rep_therm) nost noobs".

```
. tab know_scale3 enviro_jobs [aw=w], sum( rep_therm) nost noobs
```

Means and Frequencies of Feeling Thermometer: Republican Party

RECODE of know_scale	Environment vs. jobs tradeoff			Total
	Environ	Middle	Jobs	
Low	49.54	50.15	54.89	51.21
	70.5476	63.822	50.2208	184.5904
Med	42.81	47.86	53.13	48.07
	133.6011	116.8745	143.7686	394.2442
High	36.26	46.26	59.56	48.35
	96.0343	80.0321	118.5682	294.6346
Total	42.30	47.93	55.85	48.83
	300.183	260.7286	312.5576	873.4692

In the way that the table is set up, we would assess the effect of the environmental attitudes variable, at each level of political knowledge, by reading from left to right. Examine the low-knowledge row. As we move from pro-environment to pro-jobs, do mean Republican ratings increase? Not by much. The Republicans are rated at 49.54 degrees among pro-environment respondents, 50.15 among those taking the middle position, and 54.89 among pro-jobs respondents. End to end, this a barely discernible 5-degree increase. The relationship is substantially stronger, however, at medium and high levels of political knowledge. For people with medium knowledge, Republican ratings rise from 42.81 to 53.13, a 10-point increase. And the relationship is stronger still for individuals at the highest knowledge level, for whom the data show about a 23-point difference in ratings of the Republican Party, from 36.26 at the pro-environment end to 59.56 at the pro-jobs end. So it looks like the rep_therm-enviro_jobs relationship does indeed strengthen as political knowledge increases. How would we use regression analysis to estimate the size and statistical significance of these relationships?

We would begin in a familiar way, by estimating the effects of each independent variable, enviro_jobs and know_scale3, on the dependent variable, rep_therm:

$$\text{Republican rating} = a + b1*\text{enviro\_jobs} + b2*\text{know\_scale3}.$$

This is a simple additive model. The constant, a, estimates rep_therm for respondents who have a value of 0 on both independent variables—pro-environment respondents who have low political knowledge. The parameter b1 estimates the effect of each unit increase in enviro_jobs, from 0 to 2. The parameter b2 tells us the effect of each unit increase in know_scale3, from 0 to 2.

Think about why the simple additive model does not adequately represent the complex relationships we discovered in the mean comparison analysis. For low-knowledge respondents, for whom know_scale3 is equal to 0, the model reduces to

$$\text{Republican rating} = a + b1*\text{enviro\_jobs}.$$

Our previous analysis revealed that, for low-knowledge people, Republican ratings increase from 49.54 (among pro-environment respondents) to 54.89 (among pro-jobs respondents), a weak positive effect. Based on those results, we know that the constant, a, will be equal to about 50 and that the coefficient, b1, will be a small number. Now consider how the simple model would estimate the effect of enviro_jobs for medium-knowledge respondents, for whom know_scale3 is equal to 1:

$$\text{Republican rating} = a + b1*\text{enviro\_jobs} + b2*1,$$

which is the same as

$$\text{Republican rating} = (a + b2) + b1*\text{enviro\_jobs}.$$

The coefficient, b2, adjusts the constant. If b2 is positive, we can say that higher-knowledge people give the Republican Party higher ratings, on average, than do lower-knowledge people. A negative sign on b2 will mean that higher-knowledge people give the Republican Party lower average ratings than do lower-knowledge people. That's fine. But notice that, in the simple additive model, b1 remains unaffected as knowledge goes up. Yet the mean comparison analysis clearly showed that the effect of enviro_jobs on Republican ratings—estimated by b1—strengthens as knowledge increases. We need to add an adjustment to the regression, an adjustment that permits b1 to change as know_scale3 increases.

In multiple regression, this adjustment is accomplished by including an interaction variable as an independent variable. To create an interaction variable, you multiply one independent variable by the other independent variable. Consider how we would create an interaction variable for the problem at hand: enviro_jobs*know_scale3. All respondents who are coded 0 on know_scale3 will, of course, have a value of 0 on the interaction variable. As political knowledge increases, however, so will the magnitude of the interaction variable. Let's include this term in the model just discussed and see what it looks like:

$$\text{Republican rating} = a + b1^*\text{enviro\_jobs} + b2^*\text{know\_scale3} + b3(\text{enviro\_jobs}^*\text{know\_scale3}).$$

The simple additive model did not permit b1 to change as knowledge increased. Consider how the interaction term, "enviro_jobs*know_scale3," remedies this situation. Using medium-knowledge respondents (know_scale3 equals 1) to illustrate, the interaction model would be

$$\text{Republican rating} = a + b1^*\text{enviro\_jobs} + b2(1) + b3(1^*\text{enviro\_jobs}),$$

which is the same as

$$\text{Republican rating} = (a + b2) + (b1+b3)^*\text{enviro\_jobs}.$$

As in the simple model, b2 tells us by how much to adjust the constant as knowledge increases. The key difference is the role of b3, which tells us by how much to adjust the *effect* of enviro_jobs as knowledge increases. Because the positive relationship between rep_therm and enviro_jobs gets stronger as know_scale3 increases, we are expecting a positive sign on b3. The t-ratio and P-value on b3 will allow us to test the null hypothesis that the effect of enviro_jobs on rep_therm is the same at all levels of political knowledge.

Let's work through the research problem and get Stata to estimate the model for us. Use generate to calculate the interaction variable. The expression for creating the variable, which we will name "interact" is "gen interact = enviro_jobs * know_scale3". Now we're set to estimate our model. Type "reg rep_therm enviro_jobs know_scale3 interact [aw=w]" and press Enter:

```
. gen interact = enviro_jobs * know_scale3
(1478 missing values generated)

. reg rep_therm enviro_jobs know_scale3 interact [aw=w]
(sum of wgt is    8.7347e+02)
```

Source	SS	df	MS			
Model	35475.8405	3	11825.2802	Number of obs =	825
Residual	477087.728	821	581.105637	F(3, 821) =	20.35
				Prob > F =	0.0000
				R-squared =	0.0692
				Adj R-squared =	0.0658
Total	512563.568	824	622.043166	Root MSE =	24.106

rep_therm_~e	Coef.	Std. Err.	t	P>|t|	[95% Conf. Interval]	
enviro_jobs	1.21356	1.89153	0.64	0.521	-2.499244	4.926363
know_scale3	-6.694495	1.783578	-3.75	0.000	-10.1954	-3.193586
interact	4.937208	1.389016	3.55	0.000	2.210768	7.663648
_cons	49.26417	2.343195	21.02	0.000	44.66481	53.86353

The regression equation for estimating Republican thermometer ratings (rep_therm) is shown below (To simplify the discussion, coefficients are rounded to one decimal. Also, the interaction term is represented by its computational expression, "enviro_jobs * know_scale3."):

$$\text{rep\_therm} = 49.3 + 1.2^*\text{enviro\_jobs} - 6.7^*\text{know\_scale3} + 4.9^*(\text{enviro\_jobs} * \text{know\_scale3}).$$

Again use the constant, 49.3, to get oriented. This is the estimated mean of rep_therm for respondents who have values of 0 on all the independent variables: pro-environment individuals (code 0 on enviro_jobs) with low political knowledge (a value of 0 on know_scale3). So, this group averages about 49 on the dependent variable. Now consider the small and statistically insignificant coefficient on enviro_jobs, 1.2. This coefficient estimates the effect of enviro_jobs when all the other coefficients are 0—that is, at low levels of knowledge. For respondents taking the middle position on the environmental question, the model returns a predicted Republican rating of 49.3 + 1.2*1 = 50.5. For low-knowledge/pro-jobs respondents: 49.3 + 1.2*2 = 51.7. Thus, predicted ratings increase slightly, from 49.3 to 51.7. Just as the mean comparison analysis suggested, at low levels of knowledge, environmental opinions have no statistically meaningful effect on ratings of the Republican Party.

Now switch know_scale3 to 1 and light up the coefficients on know_scale3 and the interaction term. The coefficient on know_scale3, –6.7, tells us to subtract 6.7 degrees from the intercept. Perform the arithmetic: 49.3 – 6.7 = 42.6. This number, 42.6, is the estimated mean of rep_therm for pro-environment respondents (enviro_jobs = 0) with medium knowledge (know_scale3 = 1):

$$49.3 + 1.2*0 - 6.7*1 + 4.9*(0*1) = 49.3 - 6.7 = 42.6.$$

A thermometer rating of 42.6 is pretty cold. Do medium-knowledge individuals (know_scale3 = 1) with the strongest pro-jobs opinions (enviro_jobs = 2) have a warmer response to the Republicans? Yes, they do, according to the significant positive coefficient on the interaction term, 4.9. As we did with staunch environmentalists, begin by adjusting the intercept downward: 49.3 – 6.7 = 42.6. Now add the (paltry) base effect of enviro_jobs, multiplied by 2, the strongest pro-jobs opinion: 1.2*2 = 2.4. So far, we have: 42.6 + 2.4 = 45.0. Here is where the coefficient on the interaction variable, 4.9, comes into play. This number tells by how much to boost the effect of enviro_jobs as political knowledge goes up. For medium-knowledge, pro-jobs respondents, the boost is equal to 4.9 * (2 * 1) = 9.8. Adding the interaction effect: 42.6 + 2.4 + 9.8 = 54.8. For medium-knowledge respondents, then, the model's estimates range from 42.6 for pro-environment respondents to 54.8 for pro-jobs respondents. These estimates are a fairly accurate fit to the actual data, which range from 42.8 to 53.1. If you were to work out the estimates for high-knowledge individuals (know_scale3 = 2), you would arrive at 35.9 for pro-environment respondents and 57.9 for pro-jobs respondents, which closely match the data (36.3 and 59.6). Thus, our regression model has captured the interaction effect quite nicely.

GRAPHING LINEAR PREDICTION LINES FOR INTERACTION RELATIONSHIPS

A point emphasized throughout this book is that visual representations can often help to simplify and clarify complex relationships. This is again illustrated by Figure 9-1, which shows the relationship between environmental opinions (x-axis) and predicted values of the Republican feeling thermometer (y-axis) for each value of know_scale3. The visual signature of interaction is evident here. The line depicting the relationship at the lowest level of knowledge slopes upward mildly, from 49.3 at the pro-environment end to about 51.7 at the pro-jobs end. (These are, of course, the same endpoint estimates that we hand-calculated above.) At medium levels of knowledge the line rakes upward more steeply, signaling the strengthening of the relationship as political knowledge moves up a notch. And the high-knowledge line is the steepest of the three, connecting endpoint 35.9 degrees for pro-environment respondents with endpoint 57.9 degrees for pro-jobs respondents. It is quite clear from the graphic that, although the direction of the rep_therm-enviro_jobs relationship is the same at all three values of know_scale3, the relationship gets stronger as political knowledge increases.

Linear prediction overlays like Figure 9-1 are not difficult to create. First, use the regression model's estimates to generate a predicted value of the dependent variable, rep_therm, for each respondent. Second, run twoway to graph predicted values of rep_therm (y-axis) across values of enviro_jobs (x-axis), using the if qualifier to request a separate line for each level of know_scale3. The first step is accomplished with the predict command, which works with the estimates of the most-recently run regression model. (Are the model's estimates still there? Click in the Command window. Type "estimates" and press Enter. Stata will return the results of the most recent model.) The syntax of the predict command follows:

predict *newvar*

Just as we did in our hand calculations, Stata will generate a new variable containing predicted Republican ratings for respondents having different values of enviro_jobs and know_scale3. If we wanted to name the new variable rep_therm_pred, we would type "predict rep_therm_pred":

```
. predict rep_therm_pred
(option xb assumed; fitted values)
(1478 missing values generated)
```

Stata is uncharacteristically chatty. The term "xb" means "linear prediction," which Stata has fitted using the model's coefficients. (Only about a third of all respondents were asked the environment-jobs tradeoff question. That's why there are so many missing values on rep_therm_pred.)

Now create the basic graph with twoway:

```
twoway (line rep_therm_pred enviro_jobs if know_scale3==0, sort)

(line rep_therm_pred enviro_jobs if know_scale3==1, sort)

(line rep_therm_pred enviro_jobs if know_scale3==2, sort), legend(off)
```

Type "twoway", followed by the first parenthetical, which specifies the low-knowledge line ("if know_scale3==0"). Copy/paste the first parenthetical to the end of the command line, changing "know_scale3==0" to know_scale3==1". Copy/paste again, requesting the line for "know_scale3==2". In options, specify "legend(off)". (For ease of presentation, the command is shown here in three separate lines. Make sure to type it as one continuous line.) In terms of unedited graphic output, it's déjà vu all over again (Figure 9-2). You have acquired all the editing skills you need to transform the graph shown in Figure 9-2 into the one shown in Figure 9-1. Figure 9-3 may help refresh some of those skills.

Figure 9-1 Linear Prediction Lines for Interaction Relationships

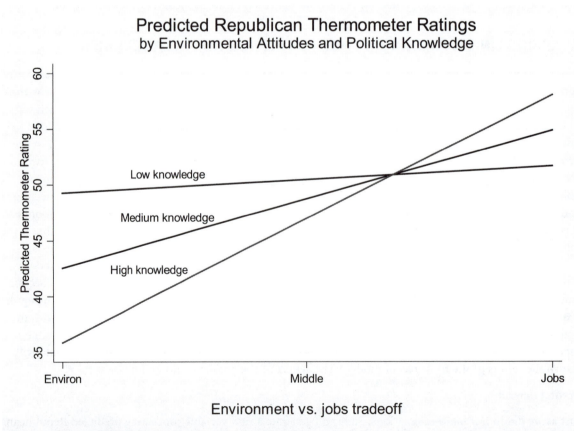

Figure 9-2 Linear Prediction Lines for Interaction Relationships (unedited)

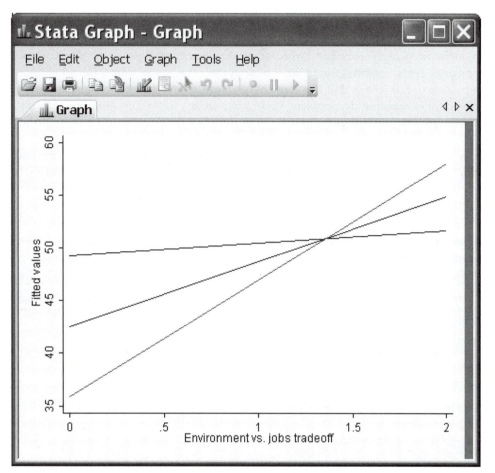

Figure 9-3 Editing a Linear Prediction Overlay

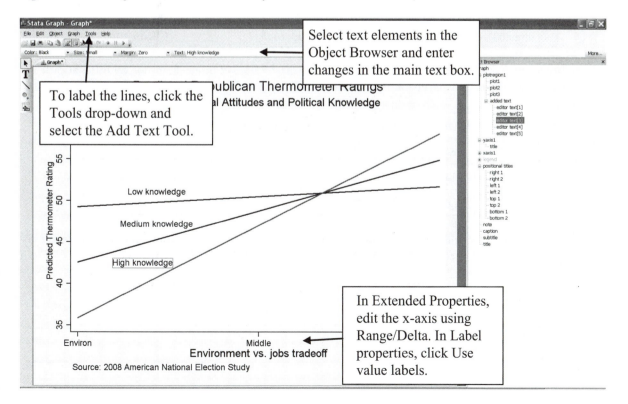

EXERCISES

1. (Dataset: world. Variables: fhrate08_rev, gdp_cap3.) In a Chapter 5 exercise, you used world to investigate the relationship between economic development and democracy. In this exercise, you will use xi: regression to analyze a similar relationship—one between economic development and political rights. The world dataset contains fhrate08_rev, an interval-level measure of democracy that ranges from 0 (fewest political rights) to 12 (most political rights). The dataset also contains gdp_cap3, a three-category ordinal measure of per capita GDP, an indicator of economic development. Codes range from 1 (low-GDP countries), through 2 (middle-GDP countries), to 3 (high-GDP countries).

   A. Imagine running the following xi: regression command: "xi: reg fhrate08_rev i.gdp_cap3". Stata would create a set of dummies from gdp_cap3 and use them as variables in the following model:

   $$\text{Political rights score} = a + b1*\_Igdp\_cap3\_2 + b2*\_Igdp\_cap3\_3.$$

   Complete the matching exercise below by drawing a line connecting the desired estimate on the left to the appropriate coefficient (or combination of coefficients) on the right:

Your estimate of the . . .	Would be provided by (the) . . .
mean difference between countries with the lowest gdp and the highest gdp . . .	constant
mean of the dependent variable for the highest gdp countries. . .	b1
mean of the dependent variable for the lowest gdp countries . . .	constant + b2
mean difference between the lowest gdp and the middle gdp countries . . .	b2

   B. Run "xi: reg fhrate08_rev i.gdp_cap3". The regression equation for estimating fhrate08_rev is (fill in the blanks, putting the constant in the first blank)

   fhrate08_rev = _____ + _____*_Igdp_cap3_2 + _____*_Igdp_cap3_3.

   C. Use the regression coefficients to arrive at estimated mean values of fhrate08_rev for countries at each level of per capita GDP. Write the estimates in the following table:

GDP per capita	Estimated mean on political rights scale
Low	?
Middle	?
High	?

   D. Examine the t-ratio and P-value on _Igdp_cap3_2. Do the middle-GDP per capita countries score significantly higher on fhrate08_rev than do the lowest-GDP per capita countries? (circle one)

   No   Yes

   Briefly explain. _____

   _____

E. Examine the t-ratio and P-value on _Igdp_cap3_3. Do the highest-GDP per capita countries score significantly higher on fhrate08_rev than do the lowest-GDP per capita countries? (circle one)

No   Yes

Briefly explain. _____

_____

_____

F. Run the test command. Do the highest-GDP per capita countries score significantly higher on fhrate08_rev than do the middle-GDP per capita countries? (circle one)

No   Yes

Briefly explain. _____

_____

_____

G. According to adjusted R-squared, GDP per capita accounts for _____ percent of the variation in fhrate08_rev.

2. (Dataset: world. Variables: gini08, hi_gdp, democ_regime, rich_democ.) As a country becomes richer, do more of its citizens benefit economically? Or do economic resources become inequitably distributed across society? The answer may depend on the type of regime in power. Democratic regimes, which need to appeal broadly for votes, may adopt policies that redistribute wealth. Dictatorships, by contrast, are less concerned with popular accountability, and so might hoard economic resources among the ruling elite, creating a less equitable distribution of wealth. This explanation suggests a set of interaction relationships. It suggests that, when we compare poorer democracies with richer democracies, richer democracies will have a *more equitable* distribution of wealth. However, it also suggests that, when we compare poorer dictatorships with richer dictatorships, richer dictatorships will have a *less equitable* distribution of wealth. In this exercise you will investigate this set of relationships.

The world dataset contains the variable gini08, which measures the extent to which wealth is inequitably distributed in society. Gini08 can take on any value between 0 (equal distribution of wealth) and 100 (unequal distribution of wealth). So, lower values of gini08 denote less economic inequality and higher values of gini08 denote greater economic inequality. Gini08 is the dependent variable. The dataset also has a dummy variable, hi_gdp, that classifies each country as low-gdp (coded 0) or high-gdp (coded 1). Hi_gdp will serve as the measure of the independent variable, level of wealth. Another dummy, democ_regime, which categorizes each country as a dictatorship (coded 0 on democ_regime) or a democracy (coded 1 on democ_regime), is the control variable.

A. Exercise a skill you learned in Chapter 5. To see whether interaction is occurring, obtain a breakdown table that shows the relationship between gini08 and hi_gdp, controlling for democ_regime. Write the mean values of gini08 next to the question marks in the table that follows:

Is regime a democracy?	Low GDP	High GDP
No	?	?
Yes	?	?

B. Examine the table in part A. It would appear that interaction (circle one)

is   is not

occurring in the data. Explain your reasoning. _____

_____

_____

_____

_____

C. World contains rich_democ, an interaction variable computed by the expression hi_gdp*democ_regime. Rich_democ takes on the value of 1 for high-gdp democracies and the value of 0 for all other countries. Run regression, using gini08 as the dependent variable and hi_gdp, democ_regime, and rich_democ as independent variables. The regression equation for estimating gini08 is as follows (fill in the blanks, putting the constant in the first blank):

gini08 = _____ + _____*hi_gdp + _____*democ_regime + _____*rich_democ.

D. Suppose someone claimed that, from the standpoint of statistical significance, low-GDP dictatorships have a significantly more equitable distribution of wealth than do low-GDP democracies.

This claim is (circle one)

correct   incorrect

because _____

_____

_____.

E. Suppose someone claimed that, as gdp increases, wealth becomes distributed significantly more equitably in democracies but not in dictatorships.

This claim is (circle one)

correct   incorrect

because _____

_____

_____.

F. Using the predict command, generate a new variable, gini_pred, which contains predicted values of gini08. Use twoway to obtain a line graph that shows the relationship between gini_pred (y-axis) and hi_gdp (x-axis) separately for democracies and dictatorships. Specify the legend(off) option. In the Graph Editor, make these changes: Add a title and a subtitle; add a source note; change the y-axis title; edit the x-axis values so that they use hi_gdp's value labels; and use the Add Text Tool to label the lines. Print the graph.

3. (Dataset: gss2006. Variables: abortion, reliten2, educ.) The abortion issue is a perennially conflictual debate in U.S. politics. What factors divide people on this issue? Because opposition to abortion is often deeply rooted in religious convictions, you could hypothesize that individuals having strong religious ties will be more likely to oppose abortion than will those with weaker affiliations. (If this hypothesis seems too commonplace to test, be patient. It gets more interesting below.) Gss2006 contains the variable abortion, a scale that records the number of conditions under which respondents believe an abortion should be allowed. Scores can range from 0 (abortion should be allowed under none of the conditions) to 6 (abortion should be allowed under all conditions). So higher scale scores denote a stronger pro-abortion stance. Gss2006 also has the dummy variable reliten2, scored 0 for respondents with weak (or no) religious affiliations and 1 for those with strong ties. If the reliten2-abortion hypothesis is correct, then respondents who are coded 0 on reliten2 will have higher scores on the abortion variable than will respondents who are coded 1 on reliten2.

A. Run the regression command to test the hypothesis that people with strong religious affiliations will be more likely to oppose abortion than will those with weak religious affiliations. Abortion is the dependent variable and reliten2 is the independent variable. Examine the results, and fill in the blanks below.

The constant (or intercept) is equal to _____, and reliten2's regression coefficient is equal to _____. Reliten2's regression coefficient has a P-value of _____, and adjusted R-squared is equal to _____.

B. Based on your analysis, you can conclude that (check all that apply)

❑ people with weaker religious affiliations score about 4 on the abortion scale.

❑ people with stronger religious affiliations score about 1 on the abortion scale.

❑ reliten2 is significantly related to abortion opinions.

❑ reliten2 explains more than 25 percent of the variation in abortion scores.

C. A critic, upon examining your results, might reasonably ask, "Did you control for education? It could be that individuals with strong religious ties have lower levels of education than do the weakly affiliated. If education is also related to abortion opinions, then you might be confusing the effect of religious attachment with the effect of education."

Gss2006 contains educ, which measures the number of years of formal education for each respondent, from 0 (no formal schooling) to 20 (20 years of formal schooling). Run the regression again, using abortion as the dependent variable and reliten2 and educ as independent variables. Based on your results, you may conclude that (check all that apply)

❑ controlling for education, the relationship between reliten2and abortion is spurious.

❑ controlling for education, individuals with strong religious ties score more than 1 point lower on the abortion scale than do individuals with weaker religious ties.

❑ according to the regression estimates, strongly affiliated individuals with no formal schooling would score about 1 on the abortion scale.

❑ education is significantly related to abortion opinions.

❑ both independent variables together explain more than 30 percent of the variation in the dependent variable.

4. (Dataset: gss2006. Variables: abortion, reliten2, educ.) One of the examples in this chapter discussed the polarization perspective–the idea that political conflict is more pronounced among people who are more knowledgeable

about politics than it is among less knowledgeable people. Perhaps the same pattern applies to the relationship between strength of religious attachment and abortion opinions. That is, it could be that religious commitment has a strong effect on abortion attitudes among politically knowledgeable people but that this effect is weaker for people who have lower knowledge about politics. We can use respondents' years of education (educ) as a surrogate for political knowledge because we can reasonably assume that people with more education will be more politically knowledgeable than will less-educated people. In this exercise you will compute an interaction variable. You will then run and interpret a multiple regression that includes the interaction variable you created.

A. Use generate to create a new variable, relhi_educhi, by multiplying reliten2 by educ. (The numeric expression will be reliten2*educ.) Think about relhi_educhi, the interaction variable you computed. A respondent with a weak religious affiliation (coded 0 on reliten2) has what value on relhi_educhi? (circle one)

      a value of 0   a value of 1   a value equal to his or her years of education

A respondent with a strong religious affiliation (coded 1 on relint2) has what value on the interaction variable? (circle one)

      a value of 0   a value of 1   a value equal to his or her years of education

B. Run regression, using abortion as the dependent variable and reliten2, educ, and relhi_educhi as the independent variables. According to the results, the multiple regression equation for estimating scores on the abortion scale is as follows (fill in the blanks, putting the constant in the first blank):

    _____ + _____*reliten2 + _____*educ + _____*relhi_educhi.

C. Consider the regression coefficients. Suppose you were to use this regression to estimate the effect of religious commitment on abortion opinions among people with no formal education, that is, for people with a value of 0 on educ. First use the regression to estimate the mean abortion score for respondents who have 0 years of education and weak religious affiliations (coded 0 on reliten2). These respondents score (fill in the blank) _____ on the abortion scale.

Now use the regression to estimate the mean abortion score for respondents who have 0 years of education and strong religious affiliations (coded 1 on reliten2). These respondents score (fill in the blank) _____ on the abortion scale.

D. Suppose you were to use this regression to estimate the effect of religious commitment on abortion opinions among people with 20 years of education, that is, for people with a value of 20 on educ. First use the regression to estimate the mean abortion score for respondents who have 20 years of education and weak religious affiliations (coded 0 on reliten2). These respondents score (fill in the blank) _____ on the abortion scale.

Now use the regression to estimate the mean abortion score for respondents who have 20 years of education and strong religious affiliations (coded 1 on reliten2). These respondents score (fill in the blank) _____ on the abortion scale.

E. Think about the polarization perspective. Does the analysis support the idea that, as education increases, religious commitment plays a larger role in defining conflict on the abortion issue?

                               Yes   No

Briefly explain your reasoning. _____

_____

_____

_____

5. (Dataset: gss2006. Variables: polviews, race_2, homosex2). If one were trying to predict ideological self-identification on the basis of opinions on social issues, such as homosexuality, one would expect most African Americans to be conservatives. Indeed, blacks are considerably more likely to oppose homosexuality than are whites. According to the gss2006 data, for example, over 70 percent of blacks say that homosexuality is "always wrong," compared with 50 percent of whites. Yet only about 25 percent of blacks call themselves "conservative," compared with over a third of whites. Why? A commonly accepted view is that social issues lack *salience* for African Americans. Issues such as homosexuality may matter for whites—white opponents of homosexuality are more likely to be self-described conservatives than are white non-opponents—but they have no effect for blacks. According to this argument, blacks who think homosexuality is wrong are no more likely to call themselves conservatives than are blacks who do not think homosexuality is wrong. Or so the familiar argument goes. Is this idea correct? More research needs to be done on this question.[6]

You can model salience with interaction variables. Consider the 7-point ideological scale (polviews) as a dependent variable, ranging from "Extremely liberal" at 1 to "Extremely conservative" at 7. Now bring in two independent variables: a dummy variable for race (race_2, with blacks scored 1 and whites scored 0) and a dummy variable gauging opposition to homosexuality (homosex2, scored 1 if the respondent said homosexuality is "always wrong" and 0 for "not always wrong"). Finally, think about (but don't generate yet) an interaction variable, black_wrong, created by multiplying race_2 and homosex2. Examine the regression model that follows:

$$\text{polviews} = a + b1^*\text{race\_2} + b2^*\text{homosex2} + b3^*\text{black\_wrong}.$$

A. The interaction variable, black_wrong, will take on a value of 1 for (check one)

   ❑ blacks who think that homosexuality is "always wrong."

   ❑ blacks who think that homosexuality is "not always wrong."

   ❑ all respondents.

B. To gauge the effect of homosex2 among whites, you would need to compare values of polviews for "not always wrong" whites and "always wrong" whites. Which of the following will estimate polviews for "not always wrong" whites? (circle one)

a   a + b1   a + b2

   Which of the following will estimate polviews for "always wrong" whites? (circle one)

a   a + b1   a + b2

C. Remember that higher scores on polviews denote stronger "conservative" self-identifications. If the salience argument is correct—the idea that heightened opposition to homosexuality leads to stronger conservative ideological leanings among whites but not blacks—then the sign on the coefficient b2 will be (circle one)

negative.   positive.   zero.

   If the salience argument is correct, then the sign on the coefficient b3 will be (circle one)

negative.   positive.   zero.

D. Use generate to create black_wrong. The multiplicative expression is homosex2*race_2. Run regression to obtain estimates for the model. The regression equation for estimating polviews is as follows (fill in the blanks, putting the constant in the first blank):

   polviews = _____ + _____*race_2 + _____*homosex2 + _____*black_wrong.

E. Which of the variables in the model have statistically significant effects on polviews? (check all that apply)

❑ race_2

❑ homosex2

❑ black_wrong

F. Use the model to estimate polviews for "not always wrong" whites and "always wrong" whites. For "not always wrong" whites you obtain _____, and for "always wrong" whites you obtain _____.

G. Use the model to estimate polviews for "not always wrong" blacks and "always wrong" blacks. For "not always wrong" blacks you obtain _____, and for "always wrong" blacks you obtain _____.

H. Using the predict command, generate a new variable, polviews_pred, which contains predicted values of polviews. Use twoway to obtain a line graph that shows the relationship between polviews_pred (y-axis) and homosex2 (x-axis) separately for whites and blacks. Specify the legend(off) option. In the Graph Editor, make these changes: Add a title and a subtitle; add a source note; change the y-axis title; edit the x-axis values so that they use homosex2's value labels; and use the Add Text Tool to label the lines. Print the graph.

I. Consider all the evidence you have adduced. Based on the evidence, the salience idea appears to be (circle one)

correct. incorrect.

Explain your answer. _____

_____

_____

_____

That concludes the exercises for this chapter. After exiting Stata, make sure to take your removable media with you.

NOTES

1. The following command would create two indicator variables, gendum1 and gendum2: "tab gender, gen(gendum)". Since females are coded 2 on gender, the second indicator variable, gendum2, would be coded 0 for males and 1 for females.
2. The changes made with the char command (which stands for "characteristics") remain in effect while the dataset is open and are preserved when the dataset is saved. The following command resets the default: "char *varname* [omit]".
3. Stata retains the most recently created xi: variables, but subsequent xi: runs automatically to overwrite any previously created xi: variables. Run "drop _I*" to delete any existing xi: variables that you do not want to save.
4. See John R. Zaller's influential work, *The Nature and Origins of Mass Opinion* (New York: Cambridge University Press, 1992).
5. Enviro_jobs is based on 2008 ANES variable V083154, a 7-point scale that gauges opinion from 1 ("Protect environment, even if it costs jobs and standard of living") to 7 ("Jobs and standard of living more important than environment"). Enviro_jobs recodes points 1–3 ("Environment"), point 4 ("Middle"), and points 5–7 ("Jobs"). Know_scale is based on respondents' ability to recognize the offices held by Nancy Pelosi (V085120a), Dick Cheney (V085121a), Gordon Brown (V085122a), and John Roberts (V085123a). Each failure was coded 0 and each success coded 1. The 0–4 scale, created by summing responses, was recoded as follows: 0 ("Low"), 1–2 ("Med"), and 3–4 ("High").
6. See Quentin Kidd, Herman Diggs, Mehreen Farooq, and Megan Murray, "Black Voters, Black Candidates, and Social Issues: Does Party Identification Matter?" *Social Science Quarterly* 88 (Mar. 2007): 165–176.

10

Logistic Regression

Commands Covered

logit *dep_var indep_var(s)*	Reports logistic regression coefficients and maximum likelihood iteration history for logistic regression models
logistic *dep_var indep_var(s)*, [coef]	Reports odds ratios for logistic regression models. With coef option, reports logistic regression coefficients
estimates store *name*	Stores estimates from the most recent analysis
lrtest *name*, force	Compares two logistic regression models and determines if one provides significantly better predictions
adjust *indep_var1*, by (*indep_var2*) pr gen(*newvar*)	Creates a new variable containing predicted probabilities of the dependent variable for each value of the independent variable, calculated at the sample-wide means or user-specified values of other independent variables
quietly	Command prefix that asks Stata to perform a command but not to display the output in the Results window
tabstat *dep_var1 dep_var2*, by(*indep_var*)	Displays means of one or more dependent variables for each value of an independent variable

You now have an array of data analysis skills that enable you to perform the appropriate analysis for just about any situation you will encounter. To analyze the relationship between two categorical variables—variables measured at the nominal or ordinal level—you would enlist the tabulate command. If the dependent variable is an interval-level scale and the independent variable is categorical, then tabulate with the summarize option would be one way to go. Alternatively, you might run xi: regression to estimate the effect of a dummy variable (or variables) on the dependent variable. Finally, if both the independent and the dependent variables are interval level, then the regress command would be the appropriate technique. There is, however, a common research situation you are not yet equipped to tackle.

In its most specialized application, logistic regression is designed to analyze the relationship between an interval-level independent variable and a *binary* dependent variable. A binary variable, as its name suggests, can assume only two values. Binary variables are just like the indicator variables or dummy variables you have created and analyzed in this book. A case either has the attribute or behavior being measured or it does not. Voted/did not vote, married/not married, favor/oppose gay marriage, South/non-South, are all examples of binary variables.

Consider a binary dependent variable that is of keen interest to students of political behavior, whether people voted in an election. This variable, of course, has only two values: individuals either voted (coded 1 on the binary variable) or they did not vote (coded 0). Now think about an interval-level independent variable often linked to turnout, years of education. As measured by the General Social Survey, this variable ranges from 0 (no formal schooling) to 20 (20 years of education). One would expect a positive relationship between the independent and dependent variables. As years of education increase, the probability of voting should increase as well. So people with fewer years of schooling should have a relatively low probability of voting, and this probability should increase with each additional year of education. Now, we certainly can conceptualize this relationship as positive. However, for statistical and substantive reasons, we may not assume that it is linear—that is, we cannot assume that a 1-year change in education occasions a consistent increase in the probability of voting. Because ordinary least squares (OLS) regression assumes linearity between the independent and dependent variables, we may not use the regress command to analyze this relationship. But as luck and statistics would have it, the researcher may assume a linear relationship between education and the *logged odds* of voting. Let's put the relationship into logistic regression form and discuss its special properties:

$$\text{Logged odds (voting)} = a + b(\text{years of education}).$$

This logistic regression model is quite OLS-like in appearance. Just as in OLS regression, the constant or intercept, a, estimates the dependent variable (in this case, the logged odds of voting) when the independent variable is equal to 0—that is, for people with no formal education. And the logistic regression coefficient, b, will estimate the change in the logged odds of voting for each 1-year increase in education. What is more, the analysis will produce a standard error for b, permitting us to test the null hypothesis that education has no effect on turnout. Finally, Stata output for logistic regression will provide an R-squared-type measure, giving us an idea of the strength of the relationship between education and the likelihood of voting. In all these ways, logistic regression is comfortably akin to linear regression.

However, logistic regression can be more difficult to interpret than OLS. In ordinary regression, the coefficients of interest, the constant (a) and the slope (b), are expressed in actual units of the dependent variable. If one were to use OLS to investigate the relationship between years of education (X) and income in dollars (Y), the regression coefficient on education would communicate the dollar-change in income for each 1-year increase in education. With OLS, what you see is what you get. In the logistic regression model, by contrast, the coefficients of interest are expressed in terms of the logged odds of the dependent variable. The constant (a) will tell you the logged odds of voting when education is 0, and the regression coefficient (b) will estimate the change in the logged odds for each unit-change in education. Logged odds, truth be told, have no intuitive appeal. Thus the researcher often must translate logistic regression results into language that makes better intuitive sense.

THE LOGIT COMMAND AND THE LOGISTIC COMMAND

Two Stata commands perform binary logistic regression: the logit command and the logistic command. The logit command provides estimates for the coefficients in the logistic regression model. Applied to the education-voting equation, the logit command would display estimates for the constant, a, and the coefficient, b—both of which are expressed in terms of the logged odds of the dependent variable. The logistic command runs the same analysis as the logit command. However, the logistic command will express the coefficients either as odds ratios or, by specifying the coef option, as logged odds. Odds ratios, as we will see, are easier to interpret than are logged odds coefficients.

Because the logistic command, at the user's discretion, will report odds ratios or logistic regression coefficients, this book focuses mostly on the logistic command. However, output from the logit command provides information that will help you to understand how logistic regression works. For our first analysis, then, we will illustrate the use of the logit command and the logistic command.

The syntax of the logit command is as follows:

logit *dep_var indep_var(s)*

The syntax of the logistic command is identical except, of course, for the command name:

logistic *dep_var indep_var(s)*

Let's run the voting-education analysis and learn how to interpret Stata's output. The dataset gss2006 contains voted04, coded 0 for respondents who did not vote in the 2004 election and coded 1 for those who did vote. The dataset also has educ, which records the number of years of schooling for each respondent. First run logit and then run logistic. Type "logit voted04 educ" and press Enter. Then type "logistic voted04 educ" and press Enter:

```
. logit voted04 educ

Iteration 0:   log likelihood = -2377.7759
Iteration 1:   log likelihood =  -2184.398
Iteration 2:   log likelihood = -2180.2709
Iteration 3:   log likelihood = -2180.2633
Iteration 4:   log likelihood = -2180.2633

Logistic regression                          Number of obs   =      4118
                                              LR chi2(1)      =    395.03
                                              Prob > chi2     =    0.0000
Log likelihood = -2180.2633                   Pseudo R2       =    0.0831
```

voted04	Coef.	Std. Err.	z	P>|z|	[95% Conf. Interval]	
educ	.2478197	.0138205	17.93	0.000	.220732	.2749075
_cons	-2.214701	.1804077	-12.28	0.000	-2.568293	-1.861108

```
. logistic voted04 educ

Logistic regression                          Number of obs   =      4118
                                              LR chi2(1)      =    395.03
                                              Prob > chi2     =    0.0000
Log likelihood = -2180.2633                   Pseudo R2       =    0.0831
```

voted04	Odds Ratio	Std. Err.	z	P>|z|	[95% Conf. Interval]	
educ	1.281229	.0177073	17.93	0.000	1.246989	1.316409

First consider the output from the logit command. Just as in the output from Stata's regression command, the numbers in the column labeled "Coef." are the estimates for the constant and the regression coefficient. Plug these estimates into our model:

$$\text{Logged odds (voted04)} = -2.215 + .248(educ).$$

What do these coefficients tell us? Again, the constant says that, for people with no education, the estimated logged odds of voting is equal to −2.215. The logistic regression coefficient on educ says that the logged odds of voting increases by .248 for each 1-year increase in education. So, as expected, as the independent variable increases, the likelihood of voting increases, too. Does education have a statistically significant effect on the likelihood of voting? In OLS regression, Stata determines statistical significance by calculating a t-statistic and an accompanying P-value. In logistic regression, Stata calculates a z-statistic and reports a (two-tailed) P-value. Interpretation of this P-value, displayed in the column labeled "P>|z|," is directly analogous to ordinary regression.[1] If the P-value is greater than .05, do not reject the null hypothesis. Conclude that the independent variable does not have a significant effect on the dependent variable. If the P-value is less than or equal to .05, then reject the null hypothesis and infer that the independent variable has a significant relationship with the dependent variable. In our output, the P-value for educ is .000, so we can conclude that, yes, education has a significant effect on voting turnout.

Now turn your attention to the output for the logistic command and consider how Stata has made educ's regression coefficient more meaningful. Note the entry next to educ in the column labeled "Odds Ratio." Here Stata has reported the value 1.281229 (which rounds to 1.28) for the independent variable, educ. From where did this number originate? Stata obtained this number by raising the natural log base e (approximately equal to 2.72) to the power of the logistic regression coefficient, .248. This procedure translates the logged odds regression coefficient into an odds ratio. An odds ratio tells you by how much the odds of the dependent variable change for each unit change in the independent variable. An odds ratio of less than 1 says that the odds decrease as the independent variable increases (a negative relationship). An odds ratio equal to 1 says that the odds do not change as the independent variable increases (no relationship). And an odds ratio of greater than 1 says that the odds of the dependent variable increase as the independent variable increases (a positive relationship). An odds ratio of 1.28 means that respondents at a given level of education are 1.28 times more likely to have voted than are respondents at the next lower level of education. So people with, say, 10 years of education are 1.28 times more likely to have voted than are people with 9 years of education, people with 14 years are 1.28 times more likely to have voted than people with 13 years, and so on.

The value of the odds ratio is often used to obtain an even more understandable estimate, the *percentage change in the odds* for each unit change in the independent variable. Mercifully, simple arithmetic accomplishes this task. Subtract 1 from the odds ratio and multiply by 100. In our current example: $(1.28 - 1) * 100 = 28$. So we can now say that each 1-year increment in education increases the odds of voting by 28 percent. As you can see, when the relationship is positive—that is, when the logistic regression coefficient is greater than 0 and the odds ratio is greater than 1—figuring out the percentage change in the odds requires almost no thought. Just subtract 1 from the odds ratio and move the decimal point two places to the right. But be alert for negative relationships, when the odds ratio is less than 1. (In the exercises at the end of this chapter you will interpret negative relationships.) Suppose, for example, that the odds ratio were equal to .28, communicating a negative relationship between the independent variable and the probability of the dependent variable. The percentage change in the odds would be equal to $(.28 - 1) * 100 = -72.0$, indicating that a one-unit change in the independent variable decreases the odds of the dependent variable by 72 percent.

How strong is the relationship between years of education and the likelihood of voting? It is here that the "Iteration" lines of the logit results become especially instructive. In figuring out the most accurate estimates for the model's coefficients, logistic regression uses a technique called maximum likelihood estimation (MLE). When it begins the analysis, MLE finds out how well it can predict the observed values of the dependent variable *without* using the independent variable as a predictive tool. So MLE first determined how accurately it could predict whether individuals voted by not knowing how much education they have. The log likelihood in the "Iteration 0" line, equal to -2377.7759, summarizes this initial, know-nothing prediction. MLE then brings the independent variable into its calculations, running the analysis again—and again and again—to find the best possible predictive fit between years of education and the likelihood of voting. According to the logit output, MLE ran through five iterations, finally deciding that it had maximized its ability to predict voting by using education as a predictive instrument. The log likelihood in the "Iteration 4" line, -2180.2633, summarizes this final-step prediction.

In logistic regression, you can get an idea of how well a model performs by comparing the initial log likelihood with the final log likelihood. Obviously, if using education to predict voting worked about as well as not using education to predict voting, then the final log likelihood would be about the same as the initial log likelihood. If, by contrast, education greatly improved the model's predictive power, then the two log likelihoods would be very different—the final log likelihood would be much closer to 0 than the initial log likelihood.[2] Stata's logit and logistic commands return two measures that gauge the strength of the relationship between the independent variable(s) and the likelihood of the dependent variable: the likelihood ratio (labeled "LR chi2") and pseudo R-squared ("Pseudo R2"). Both of these statistics are based on the difference between the initial log likelihood and the final log likelihood.

Stata arrives at the likelihood ratio by subtracting the final-iteration log likelihood from the initial log likelihood and multiplying the result by -2. By way of illustration, we can perform this calculation by hand for the voted04-educ model:

$$-2*(\text{initial log likelihood} - \text{final log likelihood}) = -2*(-2377.7759 - (-2180.2633)) = 395.03.$$

This is precisely the number appearing in the logit and logistic results next to the label "LR chi2." The likelihood ratio, which could be more accurately labeled "Change in -2 log likelihood," is a chi-square test statistic.[3] The likelihood ratio may be interpreted as a measure of the amount of predictive leverage gained over the know-nothing model by including the independent variables as predictors. Directly beneath this test statistic, Stata reports its P-value ("Prob > chi2"), which in this case is equal to .0000. Conclusion: Compared to how well we can predict voting without knowing education, including education as a predictor significantly enhances the predictive performance of the model.

OLS researchers are quite fond of R-squared, the overall measure of strength that gauges the amount of variation in the dependent variable that is explained by the independent variable(s). Because of the statistical foundations of logistic regression, however, the notion of "explained variation" has no direct analog in logistic regression. Even so, methodologists have proposed various "pseudo R-squared" measures that seek to communicate the strength of association between the dependent and independent variables. Stata reports the measure suggested by McFadden:[4]

$$(\text{initial log likelihood} - \text{final log likelihood}) / (\text{initial log likelihood}).$$

For the voted04-educ model, we would have

$$(-2377.7759 - (-2180.2633)) / -2377.7759 = -197.5126 / -2377.7759 = .0831.$$

Stata's logit and logistic results record this value next to "Pseudo R2." With a value of about .08, one would conclude that education, though related to voting, by itself provides a less-than-complete explanation of it.

By now you are aware of the interpretive challenges presented by logistic regression analysis. In running good old regression, you had a mere handful of statistics to report and discuss: the constant, the regression coefficient(s) and accompanying P-value(s), and R-squared. That's about it. With logistic regression, there are more statistics to record and make sense of. Below is a tabular summary of the results of the voted04-educ analysis. You could use this tabular format to report the results of any logistic regressions you perform:

Model estimates and Model summary: Logged odds (voting) = a + b(education)				
Model estimates	Coefficient	P-value	Odds Ratio	Percentage change in odds
Constant	−2.215			
Education	.248	.0000	1.28	28.0
Model summary	Statistic	P-value		
Likelihood ratio*	395.03	.0000		
Pseudo R-squared	.0831			
* Alternatively, this row could be labeled "Change in −2 Log likelihood."				

LOGISTIC REGRESSION WITH MULTIPLE INDEPENDENT VARIABLES

The act of voting might seem simple, but we know that it isn't. Certainly, education is not the only characteristic that shapes the individual's decision whether to vote or to stay home. Indeed, we have just seen that years of schooling, although clearly an important predictor of turnout, returned a so-so pseudo-R squared, indicating that other factors might also contribute to the explanation. Age, race, marital status, strength of partisanship, political efficacy—all these variables are known predictors of turnout. What is more, education might itself be related to other independent variables of interest, such as age or race. Thus one might reasonably want to know the partial effect of education on turnout, controlling for the effects of these other independent variables. When performing OLS regression, the researcher can enter multiple independent variables into the model and estimate the partial effects of each one on the dependent variable. Logistic regression, like OLS regression, can accommodate multiple predictors of a binary dependent variable. Consider this logistic regression model:

$$\text{Logged odds (voting)} = a + b_1(\text{educ}) + b_2(\text{age}).$$

Again we are in an OLS-like environment. As before, educ measures number of years of formal education. The variable age measures each respondent's age in years, from 18 to 89. From a substantive standpoint, we would again expect educ's coefficient, b_1, to be positive: As education increases, so too should the logged odds of voting. We also know that older people are more likely to vote than are younger people. Thus we should find a positive sign on age's coefficient, b_2. Just as in OLS, b_1 will estimate the effect of education on voting, controlling for age, and b_2 will estimate the effect of age on the dependent variable, controlling for the effect of education. Finally, the measures of strength—the likelihood ratio and pseudo R-squared—will give us an idea of how well both independent variables explain turnout.

Let's see what happens when we add age to our model. Because we want coefficients and odds ratios for the independent variables, we will again enter two commands. You can run the logit command to obtain the coefficients and then run the logistic command to obtain the odds ratios. Alternatively, you can run the

logistic command with the coef option ("logistic voted04 educ age, coef"), followed by the logistic
command without the coef option ("logistic voted04 educ age"):

```
. logistic voted04 educ age, coef

Logistic regression                              Number of obs   =       4103
                                                 LR chi2(2)      =     636.70
                                                 Prob > chi2     =     0.0000
Log likelihood = -2050.7253                      Pseudo R2       =     0.1344
```

voted04	Coef.	Std. Err.	z	P>|z|	[95% Conf. Interval]	
educ	.297939	.0152076	19.59	0.000	.2681326	.3277454
age	.0364694	.0024989	14.59	0.000	.0315716	.0413672
_cons	-4.554714	.2522394	-18.06	0.000	-5.049094	-4.060334

```
. logistic voted04 educ age

Logistic regression                              Number of obs   =       4103
                                                 LR chi2(2)      =     636.70
                                                 Prob > chi2     =     0.0000
Log likelihood = -2050.7253                      Pseudo R2       =     0.1344
```

voted04	Odds Ratio	Std. Err.	z	P>|z|	[95% Conf. Interval]	
educ	1.34708	.0204859	19.59	0.000	1.30752	1.387836
age	1.037143	.0025917	14.59	0.000	1.032075	1.042235

Plug these coefficient estimates into our model:

Logged odds (voting) = −4.555 + .298(educ) + .036(age).

Interpretation of these coefficients follows a straightforward multiple regression protocol. The coefficient on educ, .298, tells us that, controlling for age, each additional year of education increases the logged odds of voting by .298. Notice that, controlling for education, age is positively related to the likelihood of voting. Each 1-year increment in age produces an increase of .036 in the logged odds of voting. According to the z-statistics and accompanying P-values, each independent variable is significantly related to the dependent variable.

Now consider Stata's helpful translations of the coefficients, from logged odds to odds ratios, which are displayed in the odds ratio column of the second set of results. Interestingly, after controlling for age, the effect of education is stronger than its uncontrolled effect, which we analyzed earlier. When we take respondents' age differences into account, each additional year of schooling increases the odds ratio by 1.347 and boosts the odds of voting by about 35 percent: (1.347 − 1) * 100 = 34.7.[5] For age, too, the odds ratio, 1.037, is greater than 1, again communicating the positive relationship between age and the likelihood of voting. If one were to compare two individuals having the same number of years of education but who differed by 1 year in age, the older person would be 1.037 times more likely to vote than the younger person. Translating 1.037 into a percentage change in the odds: (1.037 − 1) * 100 = 3.7. Conclusion: Each additional year in age increases the odds of voting by about 4 percent.[6]

Overall, how does the voted04-educ-age model perform? According to the pseudo R-squared (.134), adding age to the model increased its explanatory power, at least when compared with the simple analysis using education as the sole predictor, which returned a pseudo R-squared of .083. And the likelihood ratio, 636.70, defeats the null hypothesis (P-value = .0000) and suggests that, compared to the know-nothing model, both independent variables significantly improve our ability to predict the likelihood of voting. Finally, you may have noticed that the final-iteration log likelihood for the voted04-educ-age model, −2050.7253, represents an improvement over the simpler voted04-educ model, which converged at a final-iteration log likelihood of −2180.2633. Clearly, both models outperform the know-nothing model, in which neither independent variable is used to predict the likelihood of voting. But is the voted04-educ-age model significantly better than the more parsimonious voted04-educ model? Yes, it is. (To find out how to compare the performance of different logistic regression models, see "A Closer Look.")

The estimates Command and the lrtest Command

Does knowing the independent variables offer significant predictive leverage—compared, that is, with not knowing the independent variables? For any logistic regression model, as we have seen, this question is answered by the likelihood ratio, a test statistic that compares the model's final log likelihood with its initial log likelihood. However, you may wish to compare two models, one of which (the "full" model) uses more independent variables than does a more austere counterpart (the "reduced" model). Two commands, the estimates command and the lrtest command, will help you make these model-to-model comparisons.

Suppose we want to compare the full voted04-educ-age model with the reduced voted04-educ model. After running the logit command or the logistic command to obtain estimates for the reduced model ("logistic voted04 educ"), we would store the model's estimates using the estimates command. The relevant syntax of the estimates command is as follows:

estimates store *name*

In this command syntax, *name* is a user-supplied name for the model. Applied to our example, we would type, "estimates store educ_model". Next we would run the full-model logistic regression, including age as a predictor: "logistic voted04 educ age". (We could store the full model's estimates, too, but we really don't need to, because Stata retains in memory the estimates from the most recently fitted model.) We then would enter the lrtest command, comparing the full model's likelihood ratio with the reduced model's likelihood ratio. The syntax of the lrtest command is as follows:

lrtest *name*, force

In this command, *name* is the model name used in the estimates command. The force option directs Stata to perform the command, even if it doesn't want to.[1] Thus we would type, "lrtest educ_model, force". Stata will assume (correctly) that we wish to compare the most recently estimated model, the full model, with the model named "educ_model," the reduced model. Here are the results from all the commands:

```
. logistic voted04 educ

Logistic regression                          Number of obs   =      4118
                                             LR chi2(1)      =    395.03
                                             Prob > chi2     =    0.0000
Log likelihood = -2180.2633                  Pseudo R2       =    0.0831
```

voted04	Odds Ratio	Std. Err.	z	P>|z|	[95% Conf. Interval]	
educ	1.281229	.0177073	17.93	0.000	1.246989	1.316409

```
. estimates store educ_model

. logistic voted04 educ age

Logistic regression                          Number of obs   =      4103
                                             LR chi2(2)      =    636.70
                                             Prob > chi2     =    0.0000
Log likelihood = -2050.7253                  Pseudo R2       =    0.1344
```

voted04	Odds Ratio	Std. Err.	z	P>|z|	[95% Conf. Interval]	
educ	1.34708	.0204859	19.59	0.000	1.30752	1.387836
age	1.037143	.0025917	14.59	0.000	1.032075	1.042235

```
. lrtest educ_model, force

Likelihood-ratio test                        LR chi2(1)  =    259.08
(Assumption: educ_model nested in .)         Prob > chi2 =    0.0000
```

(continued)

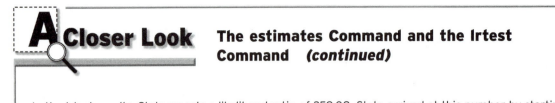

In the Irtest results, Stata reports a likelihood ratio of 259.08. Stata arrived at this number by starting with the log likelihood of the reduced model (-2180.2633), subtracting the log likelihood of the full model (-2050.7253), and then multiplying the result by -2: -2*(-2180.2633 - (-2050.7253)) = 259.08. Just as with any likelihood ratio, this number is a chi-square test statistic.[2] With a P-value of .0000, we can conclude that, compared with using education alone, adding age as an independent variable significantly improves the predictive power of the model.

---

[1] Why might Stata refuse to run Irtest? If the two models are estimated using different numbers of cases (Ns), Stata will not run Irtest. Perhaps Stata is being overly sensitive on this point. In analyzing survey data, we almost always reduce the valid N when we add predictors—any cases included in the reduced-model analysis that have missing values on the added variable(s) will be dropped from the full-model analysis. For the voted04-educ model, N = 4,118. For the voted04-educ-age model, N = 4,103.

[2] Degrees of freedom are equal to the number of predictors in the full model minus the number of predictors in the reduced model.

WORKING WITH PREDICTED PROBABILITIES: MODELS WITH ONE INDEPENDENT VARIABLE

You now know how to perform basic logistic regression analysis, and you know how to interpret the logistic regression coefficient in terms of an odds ratio and in terms of a percentage change in the odds. No doubt, odds ratios are easier to comprehend than are logged odds. And percentage change in the odds seems more understandable still. Having said this, most investigators prefer to think in terms of probabilities. One might reasonably ask, "What is the effect of a 1-year increase in education on the probability of voting?" Inconveniently, with logistic regression the answer is always, "It depends."

In the first analysis we ran, which examined the education-voting relationship, logistic regression assumed that a linear relationship exists between years of education and the logged odds of voting. This linearity assumption permitted us to arrive at an estimated effect that best fits the data. However, the technique also assumed a nonlinear relationship between years of education and the probability of voting. That is, it assumed that for people who lie near the extremes of the independent variable—respondents with either low or high levels of education—a 1-year increase in education will have a weaker effect on the probability of voting than will a 1-year increase for respondents in the middle range of the independent variable. People with low education are unlikely to vote, so a 1-year change should not have a huge effect on this likelihood. Ditto for people with many years of schooling. They are already quite likely to vote, and a one-unit increase should not greatly enhance this probability. It is in the middle range of the independent variable that education should have its most potent marginal impact, pushing individuals over the decision threshold from "do not vote" to "vote." So the effect of a 1-year change in education is either weaker or stronger, depending on where respondents "are" on the education variable.

In logistic regression models having more than one independent variable, such as the voted04-educ-age analysis, working with probabilities becomes even more problematic. The technique assumes that the independent variables have additive effects on the logged odds of the dependent variable. Thus for any combination of values of the independent variables, one obtains an estimated value of the logged odds of the dependent variable by adding up the partial effects of the predictor variables. However, logistic regression also assumes that the independent variables have interactive effects on the probability of the dependent variable.

For example, in the case of younger respondents (who have a lower probability of voting), the technique might estimate a large effect of education on the probability of voting. For older respondents (who have a higher probability of voting), logistic regression may find a weaker effect of education on the probability of voting. So the effect of each independent variable on the probability of the dependent variable will depend on the values of the other predictors in the model.

Let's explore these issues one at a time, beginning with the simple model that used education alone to predict voting. Even though we cannot identify a single coefficient that summarizes the effect of education on the probability of voting, we can use Stata to calculate a predicted probability of voting for respondents at each level of education. How does this work? Recall the logistic regression equation Stata estimated in our first analysis:

$$\text{Logged odds (voting)} = -2.147 + .248(\text{years of education}).$$

By enlisting the predict command, we would ask Stata to use this logistic regression model to obtain an estimated logged odds of voting for each respondent. Stata would plug in each respondent's education level, do the math, and calculate an estimated value of the dependent variable, the logged odds of voting. Stata would then use the following formula to convert the estimated logged odds of voting into a predicted probability of voting:

$$\text{Probability of voting} = \text{Exp(Logged odds of voting)} / (1 + \text{Exp(Logged odds of voting)}).$$

According to this formula, you retrieve the probability of voting by first raising the natural log base e to the power of the logged odds of voting. You then divide this number by the quantity 1 plus e raised to the power of the logged odds of voting.[7] Clear as mud.

Here is an example of how Stata calculates predicted probabilities from a logistic regression model. Consider respondents who have a high school education, 12 years of schooling. Using the logistic regression equation obtained in the first guided example, we find that the logged odds of voting for this group would be $-2.215 + .248(12) = -2.215 + 2.976 = .761$. What is the predicted probability of voting for people with 12 years of education? It would be $\text{Exp}(.761) / (1 + \text{Exp}(.761)) = 2.140 / 3.140 = .682$. So for respondents with a high school education, the estimated probability of voting is .682.

The predict command, covered in chapter 9, will produce predicted probabilities for respondents at each value of education. Recall that predict makes its calculations using the most recently fitted model. So first we'll need to rerun "logistic voted04 educ". Then we can run predict, choosing a descriptive name for the predicted probabilities: "predict educ_pred".

```
. logistic voted04 educ
```

Logistic regression				Number of obs	=	4118
				LR chi2(1)	=	395.03
				Prob > chi2	=	0.0000
Log likelihood = -2180.2633				Pseudo R2	=	0.0831

voted04	Odds Ratio	Std. Err.	z	P>|z|	[95% Conf. Interval]	
educ	1.281229	.0177073	17.93	0.000	1.246989	1.316409

```
. predict educ_pred
(option pr assumed; Pr(voted04))
(11 missing values generated)
```

Stata's parenthetical remark, "option pr assumed; Pr(voted04)," informs us that our new variable, educ_pred, will contain the estimated probability of voting ("option pr") and will be labeled "Pr(voted04)."

In what ways can this new variable, educ_pred, help us to describe changes in the estimated probability of voting as education increases? Remember, Stata now has a predicted probability of voting for respondents at each value of the education variable, from 0 years to 20 years. One way to describe the relationship between education and educ_pred is to ask Stata to calculate the mean values of educ_pred (dependent variable) for each value of educ (independent variable). This would show us by how much the estimated probability of voting increases between groups of respondents having different numbers of years of schooling. Using tabulate with the summarize option (and suppressing standard deviations), the appropriate command is "tab educ, sum(educ_pred) nost":

```
. tab educ, sum(educ_pred) nost
```

Highest year of school completed	Summary of Pr(voted04) Mean	Freq.
0	.09843811	22
1	.1227243	4
2	.15199213	28
3	.18675399	13
4	.22733484	11
5	.2737653	23
6	.32568157	69
7	.38226095	32
8	.44222352	85
9	.50391912	127
10	.56549567	152
11	.62511498	215
12	.68116611	1204
13	.73242396	422
14	.77812541	628
15	.81796122	212
16	.85200512	687
17	.8806116	167
18	.90430963	208
19	.92371124	78
20	.93944252	112
Total	.72545324	4499

The values of educ appear in ascending order down the left-hand column, and mean predicted probabilities of Pr(voted04) are reported (somewhat distractingly, to 8-decimal point precision) in the column labeled "Mean." What happens to the predicted probability of voting as education increases? Notice that, in the lower range of the independent variable, between 0 years and about 5 years, the predicted probabilities are quite low (between .10 and about .27) and these probabilities increase on the order of .02 to .05 for each increment in education. Now shift your focus to the upper reaches of education and note much the same thing. Beginning at about 13 years of schooling, the estimated probability of voting is at or above about .73—a high likelihood of turning out—and so increments in this range have weaker effects on the probability of voting. In the middle range, from 8 to 12 years, the probabilities increase at a "faster" marginal rate.

Although most political researchers like to get a handle on predicted probabilities, as we have just done, there is no agreed-upon format for succinctly summarizing logistic regression results in terms of probabilities. One commonly used approach is to report the so-called full effect of the independent variable on the probability of the dependent variable. The full effect is calculated by subtracting the probability associated with the lowest value of the independent variable from the probability associated with the highest value of the independent variable. According to our tabulate analysis, the predicted probability of voting for people with no formal schooling is about .10, and the predicted probability for those with 20 years of education is .94. The full effect would be .94 − .10 = .84. So, measured across its full range of observed values, education boosts the probability of voting by a healthy .84.

Another way of summarizing a relationship in terms of probabilities is to report the interval of the independent variable that has the biggest impact on the probability of the dependent variable. Suppose that you had to pick a 1-year increment in education that has the largest impact on the probability of voting. What would that increment be? Study the results and think about the phenomenon you are analyzing.

Figure 10-1 A Logistic Regression Curve

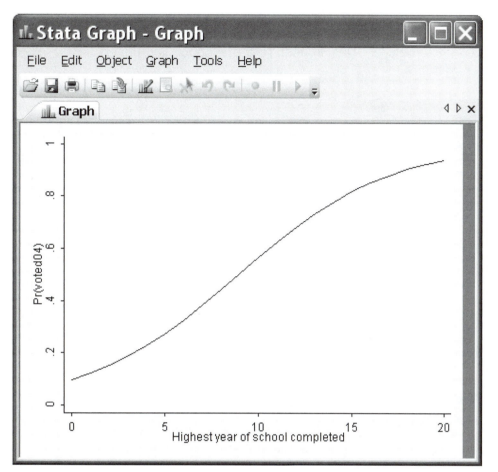

Remember that voting is an up or down decision. A person either decides to vote or she decides not to vote. But between which two values of education does a "vote" decision become more likely than a "do not vote" decision? You may have noticed that, between 8 and 9 years, the predicted probabilities increase from .442 to .504, a difference of .062 and the largest marginal increase in the data. It is between these two values of education that, according to the analysis, the binary decision shifts in favor of voting—from a probability of less than .50 to a probability of greater than .50. The interval between 8 and 9 years is the "sweet spot"—the interval with the largest impact on the probability of voting, and the interval in which the predicted probability switches from less than .50 to more than .50.[8]

As we have seen throughout this book, Stata's graphics can add visual clarity and elegance to the description of relationships. Figure 10-1, which was obtained by typing "twoway (line educ_pred educ, sort)", clearly shows the nonlinear relationship between education, recorded along the x-axis, and the predicted probability of voting, shown on the y-axis. A little quality time in the Graph Editor produces the customary enhancements (Figure 10-2).

WORKING WITH PREDICTED PROBABILITIES: MODELS WITH MULTIPLE INDEPENDENT VARIABLES

Saving predicted probabilities with the predict command works fine for simple models with one independent variable. By examining these predicted probabilities, we are able to summarize the full effect of the independent variable on the dependent variable. Furthermore, we can describe the interval of the independent variable having the largest impact on the probability of the dependent variable. Of course, you can also use the predict command to save predicted probabilities for logistic regression models having more than

Figure 10-2 A Logistic Regression Curve (edited)

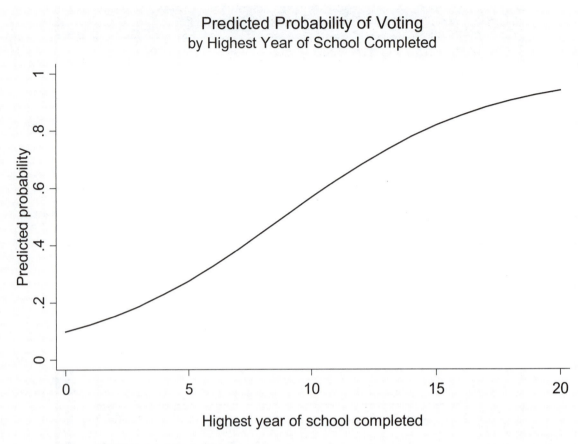

Predicted Probability of Voting
by Highest Year of School Completed

Source: 2006 General Social Survey

one independent variable. However, these predicted probabilities are not very useful for summarizing the effect of each independent variable on the probability of the dependent variable, controlling for the other independent variables in the model. As noted earlier, although logistic regression assumes that the independent variables have an additive effect on the logged odds of the dependent variable, the technique also assumes that the independent variables have an interactive effect on the probability of the dependent variable. Thus the effect of, say, education on the probability of voting will be different for younger people than for older people. And the effect of age will vary, depending on the level of education being analyzed. How can we summarize these interaction effects?

In dealing with logistic regression models with multiple independent variables, many researchers use the *sample averages method* for presenting and interpreting probabilities. In the sample averages approach, the analyst examines the effect of each independent variable while holding the other independent variables constant at their sample means. For example, we would ask and answer these questions: "For people of 'average' age, what effect does education have on the probability of voting?" "For respondents with 'average' levels of education, what effect does age have on the probability of voting?" In this way, we can get an idea of the effect of each variable on individuals who are "average" on all the other variables being studied.

One of Stata's post-estimation commands, the adjust command, will calculate (and, at the user's discretion, save) predicted probabilities of the dependent variable for each value of an independent variable, while holding all other variables constant at their sample means. Because adjust is a post-estimation command, we first must re-run the voted04-educ-age analysis: "logistic voted04 educ age". With the most recent estimates in memory, we are ready to run adjust. The general syntax of the adjust command is as follows:

adjust *indep_var1*, **by**(*indep_var2*) **pr gen**(*newvar*)

Let's say that we want to calculate predicted probabilities for people with different numbers of years of education, holding age constant at its sample mean. We also want Stata to save these estimates in a new variable called "age_mean." We would type, "adjust age, by(educ) pr gen(age_mean)".

Note the syntax. The name of the "control variable" goes after the adjust command and the name of the "variable we are allowing to vary" goes in parentheses after the by option. By default, adjust will return linear predictions, so to get probabilities we must specify the pr option.[9] Finally, the generate option tells Stata to create a new variable containing the estimated probabilities. After running "logistic voted04 educ age", run "adjust age, by(educ) pr gen(age_mean)":

```
. adjust age, by(educ) pr gen(age_mean)
```

```
         Dependent variable: voted04     Equation: voted04     Command: logistic
           Created variable: age_mean
     Covariate set to mean: age = 47.138108
```

Highest year of school completed	pr
0	.05543
1	.073259
2	.096239
3	.125451
4	.161941
5	.206538
6	.259613
7	.320812
8	.388861
9	.461535
10	.535882
11	.608668
12	.67692
13	.738385
14	.791754
15	.836645
16	.873405
17	.902854
18	.926033
19	.944024
20	.957838

```
         Key:  pr  =  Probability
```

Stata's preliminary comment, "Covariate set to mean: age = 47.138108," tells us that predicted probabilities for different values of educ were calculated while holding age constant at its sample mean, which is about 47 years of age.

Let's examine those probabilities. What is the full effect of education? Notice that people with 0 years of education have a probability of voting equal to .055 (or about .06), compared with a probability of .96 for individuals with 20 years of education. Thus, holding age constant at its sample mean, the full effect of education is equal to .96 − .06 = .90. You might also note that education's largest marginal effect, a boost of nearly .08 in the probability of voting, occurs between 9 and 10 years of schooling.

As you can see, the sample averages method is a convenient way of summarizing the effect of an independent variable on the probability of a dependent variable. A more sophisticated approach, the *probability profile method*, affords a closer and more revealing look at multivariate relationships. In the probability profile method, we compare the effects of one independent variable at two (or more) values of another independent variable. Such comparisons can provide a clearer picture of the interaction relationships between the independent variables and the probability of the dependent variable. In estimating the voted04-educ-age model, for example, logistic regression assumed that the effect of education on the probability of voting is not the same for people of all ages. But just how much does the effect of education vary across age groups? If we were to estimate and compare the effects of education among two groups of respondents—those who are, say, 26 years of age, and those who are 65 years of age—what would the comparison reveal? The adjust command, properly specified, allows us to construct probability profiles showing the relationship between education and the probability of voting for respondents of different ages. Consider the following two commands:

quietly adjust age=26, by(educ) pr gen(age_26)

quietly adjust age=65, by(educ) pr gen(age_65)

The first command will estimate the probability of voting at each value of education, while holding age constant at 26 years. And it will save these predictions in a new variable, "age_26." The second command estimates the probability of the dependent variable at each value of education, holding age constant at 65 years, and it too will save a new variable, "age_65." The command prefix, quietly, asks Stata to run the commands normally, but to suppress any output. (Below we introduce a new command that will redisplay the results in a more readable format.) As requested, running the commands elicits no response from Stata:

```
quietly adjust age=26, by(educ) pr gen(age_26)
quietly adjust age=65, by(educ) pr gen(age_65)
```

To view a side-by-side comparison of age_26 and age_65—the estimated probability of voting, at each value of education, for 26 year olds and for 65 year olds—we can enlist the tabstat command. The relevant syntax of the tabstat command is as follows:

tabstat *dep_var1 dep_var2*, **by(***indep_var***)**

Because we want to examine age_26 and age_65 for each value of educ, we would type "tabstat age_26 age_65, by(educ)":

```
. tabstat age_26 age_65, by(educ)

Summary statistics: mean
  by categories of: educ (Highest year of school completed)
```

educ	age_26	age_65
0	.026429	.1011783
1	.0352784	.1316713
2	.0469479	.16962
3	.0622286	.2157879
4	.0820546	.2704295
5	.1074733	.3330315
6	.1395689	.4021375
7	.1793237	.475363
8	.2274095	.5496635
9	.2839284	.6218129
10	.3481641	.6889445
11	.4184401	.7489703
12	.4921904	.8007625
13	.566282	.8440934
14	.6375247	.8794196
15	.7031986	.9076174
16	.7614262	.9297479
17	.811296	.9468872
18	.8527573	.9600248
19	.8863846	.9700158
20	.9131145	.977568
Total	.5796331	.8228088

Consider the dramatically different effects of education for these two age groups. To be sure, the full effect of education is essentially the same for 26 year olds (.91 − .03 = .88) and 65 year olds (.98 − .10 = .88). But the patterns of marginal effects are not the same at all. For younger people with low levels of education (between 0 and 8 years of schooling) the probability of voting is extraordinarily low, in the .03 to .23 range. Indeed, the educational increment with the largest marginal effect—the increment in which the probability of voting switches from less than .50 to more than .50—occurs beyond high school, between 12 and 13 years of schooling. Compare the probability profile of younger respondents—sluggish marginal effects in the lower range of education, a high "switchover" threshold—with the probability profile of older respondents. Does education work the same way as we read down the column labeled "age_65"? Here the probabilities start at a higher level (about .10) and build quite rapidly, in increments of .03 to .06, crossing the .50 threshold at a fairly low level of education, between 7 and 8 years of schooling. So 65 year olds with 8 years of education are about as likely to vote as are 26 year olds with 13 years of education.[10]

When you use the probability profile method to explore complex relationships, you will want to complement your analyses with appropriate graphic support. Consider the raw-to-refined transition that has become a staple of this book: Figure 10-3 (raw) and Figure 10-4 (refined). With the exception of an optioned request for a y-axis reference line, drawn at a probability of .5, the command that created Figure 10-3 is abundantly familiar: "twoway (line age_26 educ, sort) (line age_65 educ, sort), legend(off) yline(.5)". Getting from Figure 10-3 to Figure 10-4 is, by this point, a labor of love—or perhaps at least a labor of like.

Figure 10-3 Two Logistic Regression Curves

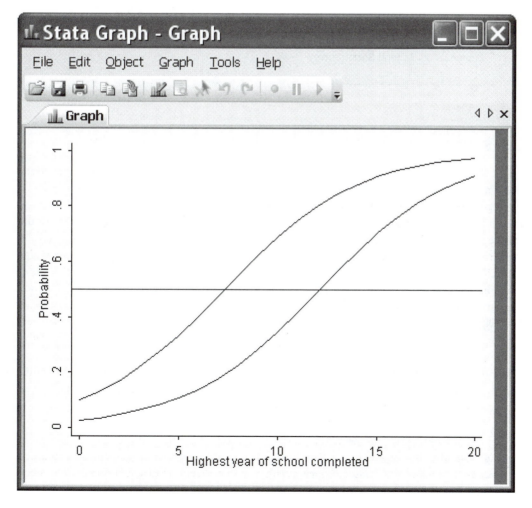

Figure 10-4 Two Logistic Regression Curves (edited)

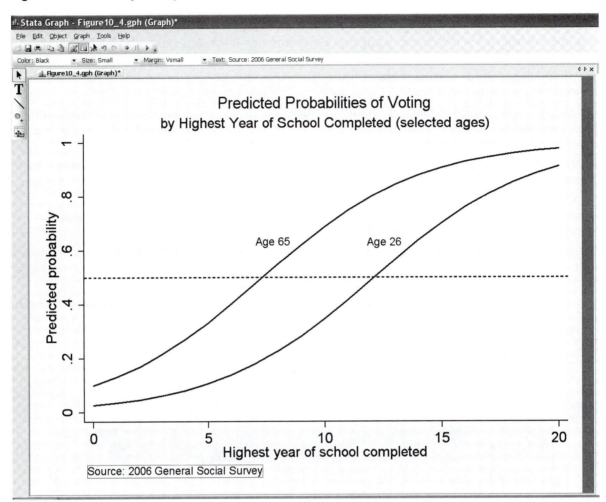

EXERCISES

1. (Dataset: states. Variables: obama_win08, attend_pct, gunlaw_rank.) As you know, presidential elections in the United States take place within an unusual institutional context. Naturally, candidates seek as many votes as they can get, but the real electoral prizes come in winner-take-all, state-sized chunks: The plurality-vote winner in each state receives all the electoral college votes from that state. Cast in logistic regression terms, each state represents a binary outcome—it goes either Democratic or Republican. What variables shape this outcome? As a candidate for the Democratic nomination, Barack Obama pointed toward several plausible variables. During a campaign appearance, Obama suggested that many voters, frustrated by the disappearance of economic opportunities, "cling to guns or religion or antipathy to people who aren't like them or anti-immigrant sentiment or anti-trade sentiment as a way to explain their frustrations." Obama said that these factors helped explain why his electoral support was weaker in certain geographical areas of the country.[11] These remarks were controversial, to be sure. Controversy aside, was candidate Obama onto something?

   Consider the following hypothesis: In a comparison of states, those with higher percentages of residents who frequently attend religious services were less likely to have been won by Obama than were states having lower percentages of residents who frequently attend religious services.

   The states dataset contains obama_win08, a binary variable coded 1 if the state's electoral votes went to Democratic candidate Barack Obama in 2008, and coded 0 if the votes went to Republican John McCain. This is the dependent variable. The dataset also has attend_pct, the percentage of state residents who frequently attend religious services. Attend_pct is the independent variable.[12]

A. Run "logistic obama_win08 attend_pct, coef". Run "logistic obama_win08 attend_pct". The following table contains seven question marks. Write the correct value next to each question mark.

Model estimates	Coefficient	Odds Ratio	P-value
Constant	?		
attend_pct	?	?	?
Model summary	Statistic		P-value
Likelihood ratio	?		?
Pseudo R-squared	?		

Before proceeding to part B, review the procedure for converting an odds ratio into a percentage change in the odds for negative relationships.

B. After converting the odds ratio to a percentage change in the odds of an Obama win, you can say that a one-unit increase in attend_pct decreases the odds of an Obama win by _____ percent.

C. Run the predict command to create a new variable containing predicted probabilities of an Obama win. (Choose a descriptive name for the new variable, such as "attend_pred.") Run tabulate with the summarize option to obtain mean predicted probabilities for each value of attend_pct.

For the state having the lowest percentage of frequent church attenders, the predicted probability of an Obama win is equal to _____. For the state having the highest percentage of frequent attenders, the predicted probability of an Obama win is equal to _____. What is the full effect of attend_pct on the probability of obama_win08? The full effect is equal to _____. (*Hint*: Because the probability of an Obama win decreases as attend_pct increases, the full effect will be a negative number.)

D. A Democratic strategist must decide in which states to concentrate her limited campaign resources. To achieve maximum effect, this strategist should concentrate her campaign on (check one)

❑ a state in which 31 percent of its residents frequently attend religious services.

❑ a state in which 41 percent of its residents frequently attend religious services.

❑ a state in which 50 percent of its residents frequently attend religious services.

E. Briefly explain your reasoning in part D. _____

_____

_____

_____

Suppose you want to improve the predictive performance of the obama_win08-attend_pct model by adding a second independent variable, the Brady campaign's ranking of states' gun laws (gunlaw_rank). Higher scores on gunlaw_rank denote fewer restrictions on firearms ownership. You reason that the full obama_win08-attend_pct-gunlaw_rank model will produce significantly better predictions than the simple obama_win08-attend_pct model. However, a critic plausibly suggests that the two independent variables, attend_pct and gunlaw_rank, are themselves related—states with many frequent churchgoers will have fewer gun restrictions than will states with fewer frequent churchgoers. This critic argues that adding gunlaw_rank to the model will not significantly enhance your ability to predict electoral outcomes.

F. Run estimates store to save the estimates from the obama_win08-attend_pct model. (Choose a descriptive name for the model, such as "attend_model.") Now run the logistic command for the full model. Obtain odds ratios, not coefficients.

Refer to the odds ratios for the obama_win08-attend_pct-gunlaw_rank model. Controlling for attend_pct, a 1-point increase in gunlaw_rank decreases the odds of an Obama win by about (circle one)

79 percent.   21 percent.   15 percent.

G. Run lrtest to find out whether adding gunlaw_rank to the model provides significantly improved predictions of obama_win08. The lrtest has a likelihood ratio equal to _____ and a P-value equal to _____. Based on this information, may you infer that using two independent variables, attend_pct and gunlaw_rank, yields significantly better predictions of an Obama win than does using attend_pct by itself? (check one)

❑ No, adding gunlaw_rank to the model does not provide significantly better predictions.

❑ Yes, adding gunlaw_rank to the model does provide significantly better predictions.

2. (Dataset: world. Variables: democ_regime, frac_eth, gdp_10_thou.) In Chapter 5, you tested this hypothesis: In a comparison of countries, those with lower levels of ethnic heterogeneity are more likely to be democracies than are those with higher levels of ethnic heterogeneity. This hypothesis says that, as heterogeneity goes up, the probability of democracy goes down. You then reran the analysis, controlling for a measure of countries' economic development, gross domestic product per capita. For this independent variable, the relationship is thought to be positive: As economic development increases, so does the likelihood that a country will be democratic. In the current exercise, you will reexamine this set of relationships, using a more powerful method of analysis, logistic regression.

The world dataset contains democ_regime, frac_eth, and gdp_10_thou. The democ variable is coded 1 if the country is a democracy and coded 0 if it is not a democracy. This is the dependent variable. One of the independent variables, frac_eth, can vary between 0 (denoting low heterogeneity) and 1 (high heterogeneity). The other independent variable, gdp_10_thou, measures gross domestic product per capita in units of $10,000.

A. Run "logistic democ_regime frac_eth gdp_10_thou, coef". Run "logistic democ_regime frac_eth gdp_10_thou". The following table contains nine question marks. Write the correct value next to each question mark.

Model estimates	Coefficient	Odds Ratio	P-value
Constant	.842		
frac_eth	?	?	?
gdp_10_thou	?	?	?
Model summary	Statistic		P-value
Likelihood ratio	?		?
Pseudo R-squared	?		

B. Use the odds ratios to calculate a percentage change in the odds. Controlling for gdp_10_thou, a one-unit change in frac_eth, from low heterogeneity to high heterogeneity (check one)

❑ increases the odds of democracy by about 20 percent.

❑ decreases the odds of democracy by about 20 percent.

❑ decreases the odds of democracy by about 80 percent.

Controlling for frac_eth, each $10,000 increase in per capita gross domestic product (check one)

❑ increases the odds of democracy by about 104 percent.

❑ increases the odds of democracy by about 204 percent.

❑ increases the odds of democracy by about 40 percent.

Run the adjust command to calculate the estimated probability of democracy at each value of frac_eth, holding gdp_10_thou constant at its mean. (Make sure to specify the pr option. It is not necessary, however, to generate a new variable containing the probabilities.)

C. As an empirical matter, the most homogeneous country in world has a value of 0 on frac_eth, and the most heterogeneous country has a value of .93 on frac_eth. The predicted probability of democracy for a highly homogeneous country (frac_eth = 0) with an average level of gdp_10_thou is equal to _____. The predicted probability of democracy for a highly heterogeneous country (frac_eth = .93) with an average level of gdp_10_thou is equal to _____.

D. As frac_eth increases, from low heterogeneity to high heterogeneity, the predicted probability of democracy (circle one)

decreases.   does not change.   increases.

E. At mean levels of gdp_10_thou, the full effect of frac_eth (from 0 to .93) on the probability of democracy is equal to _____.

3. (Dataset: gss2006. Variables: homosex_ok, attend, educ.) What factors affect individuals' attitudes toward homosexuality? Certainly, one would expect frequency of religious attendance to play a big role, in that infrequent churchgoers should be more likely than regular attenders to believe that homosexuality is not wrong. A major demographic attribute, level of education, may have an effect as well, with more educated individuals more likely than the less educated to approve of homosexuality. Interestingly, religiosity and education are themselves positively related—as education goes up, religious attendance increases.[13] How do these variables work together in explaining beliefs about homosexuality? The gss2006 dataset contains homosex_ok, coded 0 for respondents who think homosexuality is "wrong" and coded 1 for respondents who believe it is "not wrong". The attend variable measures religious attendance in nine categories, from 0 ("never") to 8 ("more than once a week"). The dataset also has educ, which gauges respondents' number of years of formal schooling, from 0 to 20.

A. Run "logistic homosex_ok attend educ, coef". Run "logistic homosex_ok attend educ". Write the correct values next to the question marks in the following table:

Model estimates	Coefficient	Odds Ratio	P-value
Constant	?		
attend	?	?	?
educ	?	?	?
Model summary	Statistic		P-value
Likelihood ratio	?		?
Pseudo R-squared	?		

B. Based on your analysis in part A, you may conclude that (check all that apply)

❑ a model that uses attend and educ to predict the likelihood of approving homosexuality performs significantly better than the know-nothing model.

❑ each one-unit increase in education increases the odds of approving homosexuality by about 24 percent.

❑ each one-unit increase in religious attendance decreases the odds of approving homosexuality by about 25 percent.

❑ both independent variables are significantly related to the dependent variable.

Next you are going to see how education affects the probability of approval for people having different levels of religious attendance: people who never attend (coded 0 on attend), people who attend several times a year (coded 3 on attend), and people who attend more than once a week (coded 8 on attend). You will need to run three adjust commands and create three new variables. Name the new variables "attend_low," "attend_mid," and "attend_high." *Hint*: The following command will create attend_low, the predicted probability of approving homosexuality for each value of education, holding attend constant at 0: "quietly adjust attend=0, by (educ) pr gen (attend_low)".

C. Run "tabstat attend_low attend_mid attend_high, by(educ)". Examine the effects of education at each level of religious attendance. For example, for respondents who never attend, and who have 0 years of education, the probability of approving of homosexuality is .104. For respondents who never attend, and who have 20 years of schooling, the probability is .902. For nonattenders, then, education increases the probability of approval by .798. Fill in the missing values in the following table:

	Probability at 0 years of education	Probability at 20 years of education	Full effect of education
attend_low	.104	.902	.798
attend_mid	?	?	?
attend_high	?	?	?

D. Based on your tabstat analysis and the table in part C, you may infer that (check all that apply)

❑ the full effect of education on approval of homosexuality is about the same for people who never attend (attend_low) as for people who attend several times a year (attend_mid).

❑ people with mid-level attendance (attend_mid) and 14 years of education are about as likely to approve as are low-attenders with 10 years of education.

❑ education has its weakest effect among people who attend more than once a week (attend_high).

❑ high-attenders (attend_high) with 20 years of education are more likely not to approve of homosexuality than to approve of homosexuality.

E. Use twoway to create a line graph showing predicted probabilities of approving homosexuality for low-, mid-, and high-attenders. *Hint:* The following statement will create the low-attender line: "(line attend_low educ, sort)". Include a y-axis reference line, drawn at a probability of .5. Suppress the legend. In the Graph Editor, label the lines using the Add Text tool. Add a title, a subtitle, and a source note. Make any other desired changes or enhancements. Print the graph you created.

That concludes the exercises for this chapter. After exiting Stata, make sure to take your removable media with you.

NOTES

1. As noted in Chapter 8, because Stata reports two-tail P-values, you may correctly apply the .05 standard by reject-ing the null hypothesis for any reported P-value of .10 or less. However, many researchers follow the more stringent practice of rejecting the null hypothesis for two-tailed P-values of .05 or less. In this book, we follow the more conservative approach.

2. Because likelihoods can vary between 0 and 1, the logs of likelihoods can vary between large negative numbers (any likelihood of less than 1 has a negatively signed log) and 0 (the log of 1 is equal to 0). As a model's predictive power improves, therefore, log likelihoods approach 0.

3. Stata reports degrees of freedom in bold typeface within the parentheses next to "LR chi2." Degrees of freedom is equal to the number of independent variables in the model. Because the model in our current example has one independent variable, the likelihood ratio is labeled "LR chi2(1)".

4. Daniel McFadden, "Conditional Logit Analysis of Qualitative Choice Behavior," in Paul Zarembka (ed.), *Frontiers in Econometrics* (New York: Academic Press, 1974): 105–142. See especially pp. 120–121.

5. Why is the controlled effect of education (a 35 percent increase in the odds of voting) greater than its uncontrolled effect (a 28 percent increase in the odds of voting)? Running "corr age educ" provides an important clue: educ and age are negatively correlated ($r = -.06$). Thus in the earlier analysis, in which we compared respondents having less education with respondents having more education (but in which we did not control for age), we were also comparing older respondents (who, on average, have fewer years of schooling) with younger respondents (who, on average, have more years of schooling). Since younger people are less likely to vote than are older people, the uncontrolled effect of age worked to weaken the zero-order relationship between educ and voted04. In a situation like this, age is said to be a *suppressor variable*, because it acts to suppress or attenuate education's true effect on turnout.

6. When using interval-level independent variables with many values, you will often obtain logistic regression coefficients and odds ratios that appear to be quite close to null hypothesis territory (coefficients close to 0 and odds ratios close to 1) but that nonetheless trump the null hypothesis. Remember that logistic regression, like OLS, estimates the marginal effect of a one-unit increment on the logged odds of the dependent variable. In the current example, logistic regression estimated the effect of a 1-year change in age (from, say, an age of 20 years to 21 years) on the logged odds of voting. The investigator may describe the relationship in terms of larger increments. Thus, if a 1-year increase in age (from 20 years to 21 years) increases the odds of voting by an estimated 4 percent, then a 10-year increase in age (from 20 years to 30 years) would produce a 40 percent increase in the odds of voting.

7. The expression "Exp(Logged odds of voting)" translates logged odds into odds: Exp(Logged odds of voting) = Odds of voting. One gets from an odds to a probability by dividing the odds by the quantity one plus the odds: Probability of voting = Odds of voting / (1 + Odds of voting). Thus the formula for the probability of voting, "Exp(Logged odds of voting) / (1 + Exp(Logged odds of voting))," is equivalent to the formula "Odds of voting / (1 + Odds of voting)."

8. The largest marginal effect of the independent variable on the probability of the dependent variable is sometimes called the *instantaneous effect*. In our example, the instantaneous effect is equal to .06, and this effect occurs between 9 and 10 years of education. The effect of a one-unit change in the independent variable on the probabil-ity of the dependent variable is always greatest for the interval containing a probability equal to .5. The instanta-neous effect, calculated by hand, is equal to $b * .5 * (1 - .5)$, in which b is the value of the logistic regression coeffi-cient. For a discussion of the instantaneous effect, see Fred C. Pampel, *Logistic Regression: A Primer*, Sage University Papers Series on Quantitative Applications in the Social Sciences, series no. 07-132 (Thousand Oaks, Calif.: Sage Publications, 2000), 24–26.

9. When you run predict after logistic, Stata assumes that you want probabilities. However, when you run adjust after logistic, Stata assumes that you want linear predictions (xb), not probabilities.

10. See Raymond E. Wolfinger and Steven J. Rosenstone's classic study of turnout, *Who Votes?* (New Haven: Yale University Press, 1980). Using probit analysis, a technique that is very similar to logistic regression, Wolfinger and Rosenstone explore the effects of a range of demographic characteristics on the likelihood of voting.

11. Obama reportedly made this remark at a fundraising event in San Francisco on April 6, 2008. See http://thepage .time.com/transcript-of-obamas-remarks-at-san-francisco-fundraiser-sunday/.

12. The attend_pct variable, which is drawn from the Pew Forum on Religion and Public Life, is one of the four factors Pew uses in its measure of secularism. See http://pewforum.org/docs/?DocID=504. The states dataset contains the Pew secularism scale.

13. A tabulated analysis of attend3 and educ_3 reveals that the percentage of respondents attending nearly every week or more frequently rises from 29 percent (high school or less), to 31 percent (13–15 years of education), to 35 percent (16 or more years of education).

11

Doing Your Own Political Analysis

In working through the guided examples in this book, and in performing the exercises, you have developed some solid analytic skills. The datasets that you have analyzed could, of course, become the raw material for your own research. You would not be disappointed, however, if you were to look elsewhere for excellent data. High-quality social science data on a variety of phenomena and units of analysis—individuals, census tracts, states, countries—are increasingly accessible via the Internet and might serve as the centerpiece for your own research. Your school, for example, may be a member of the Inter-university Consortium for Political and Social Research (ICPSR), the premier organizational clearinghouse for datasets of all kinds.[1] In this chapter, we will take a look at various sources of available datasets and provide practical guidance for inputting them into Stata. In the process, we will also cover situations in which you are confronted with raw, uncoded data—perhaps from an original questionnaire you developed and administered—that you need to code and analyze.

To get you thinking about doing your own research, we begin by laying out the stages of the research process and by offering some manageable ideas for original analysis. We then consider different data sources and procedures for inputting the data into Stata's Data Editor. Finally, we will describe a serviceable format for an organized and presentable research paper.

FIVE DOABLE IDEAS

Let's begin by describing the five stages of an ideal research procedure and then discuss some practical considerations and constraints. In an ideal world you would

1. Observe an interesting behavior or relationship and frame a research question about it
2. Develop a causal explanation for what you have observed and construct a hypothesis
3. Read and learn from the work of other researchers who have tackled similar questions
4. Collect and analyze the data that will address the hypothesis
5. Write a research paper or article in which you present and interpret your findings

In this scenario the phenomenon that you observe in stage 1 drives the whole process. First, think up a question, then research it and obtain the data that will address it. As a practical matter, the process is almost never this clear cut. Often someone else's idea or assertion may pique your interest. For example, you might read articles or attend lectures on a variety of topics—democratization in developing countries, global environmental issues, ideological change in the Democratic or Republican Party, the effect of election laws on turnout and party competition, and so on—that suggest hypotheses you would like to examine. In that case, you may begin the process at stage 3, then return to stage 1 and refine your own ideas. Furthermore, the availability of relevant data, considered in stage 4, almost always plays a role in the sorts of questions you address. Suppose, for example, that you want to assess the organizational efforts to mobilize African

Americans in your state in the last presidential election. You want precinct-level registration data, and you need to compare these numbers with the figures from previous elections. You would soon become an expert in the bureaucratic hassles and expense involved in dealing with county governments, and you might have to revise your research agenda. Indeed, for professional researchers and academics, data collection in itself can be a full-time job. For students who wish to produce a competent and manageable project, the so-called law of available data can be a source of frustration and discouragement.

A doable project often requires a compromise between stage 1 and stage 4. What interesting question can you ask, given the available data? Fortunately, this compromise need not be as restrictive as it sounds. Consider five possibilities: political knowledge, economic performance and election outcomes, state courts and criminal procedure, electoral turnout in comparative perspective, and Congress.

Political Knowledge

As you may have learned in other political science courses, scholars continue to debate the levels of knowledge and political awareness among ordinary citizens. Do citizens know the length of a U.S. senator's term of office? Do they know what constitutional protections are guaranteed by the First Amendment? Do people tend to know more about some things—Internet privacy or abortion policy, for example—and less about other things, such as foreign policy or international politics? Political knowledge is a promising variable because the researcher is likely to find some people who know a lot about politics, some who know a fair amount, and others who know very little. One could ask, "What causes this variation?" Imagine constructing a brief questionnaire that asks eight or ten multiple-choice questions about basic facts and is tailored to the aspects of political knowledge you find most thought provoking.[2] After including questions that gauge some potentially important independent variables (partisanship, gender, liberalism/conservatism, college major, class standing), you could conduct an exploratory survey among perhaps 50 or 100 of your fellow students.

Economic Performance and Election Outcomes

Here is one of the most widely discussed ideas in political science: The state of the economy before an election has a big effect on the election result. If the economy is strong, the candidate of the incumbent party does well, probably winning. If the economy is performing poorly, the incumbent party's nominee pays the price, probably losing. This idea has a couple of intriguing aspects. For one thing, it works well—but not perfectly. (The 2000 presidential election is a case in point.) Moreover, the economy-election relationship has several researchable layers. Focusing on presidential elections, you can imagine a simple two-category measure of the dependent variable—the incumbent party wins or the incumbent party loses. Now consider several stints in the reference section of the library, collecting information on some potential independent variables for each presidential election year: inflation rates, unemployment, economic growth, and so on. Alternatively, you could look at congressional or state-level elections, or elections in several different countries. Or you could modify and refine the basic idea, as many scholars have done, by adding additional noneconomic variables you believe to be important. Scandal? Foreign policy crises? With some hands-on data collection and guidance from your instructor, you can produce a well-crafted project.

State Courts and Criminal Procedure

To what extent does a justice's partisanship (or political ideology) affect his or her ruling in a case? This is a perennial question in the annals of judicial research. Again, the 2000 election comes to mind. The U.S. Supreme Court based its pivotal decision on judicial principles, but the Court split along partisan lines. And, given the level of partisan acrimony that accompanies the nominations of would-be federal judges, members of the U.S. Senate behave as if political ideology plays a role in judicial decision making. Original research on judicial proceedings, particularly at the federal level, is among the most difficult to conduct, even for seasoned scholars. But consider state judicial systems. Using an online resource available through most university servers, you could collect information about a large number of, say, criminal cases heard on appeal by the highest court in your state.[3] You could record whether the criminal defendant won or lost, and then determine the party affiliations of the justices. Additionally, you might compare judicial decision making in two states—one in which judges are appointed and one in which they are elected. You could make this comparison at the individual justice level at one point in time. Or you could look at the same set of courts over time, using aggregate units of analysis.

Electoral Turnout in Comparative Perspective

The record of voter turnout in American presidential elections, while showing encouraging reversals in 2004 and 2008, is relatively low. The situation in other democratic countries is strikingly different. Turnouts in some Western European countries average well above 70 percent. Why? More generally, what causes turnout to vary between countries? Some scholars have focused on legal factors. Unlike the United States, some countries may not require their citizens to register beforehand, or they may penalize citizens for not voting. Other scholars look at institutional differences in electoral systems. Many countries, for example, have systems of proportional representation in which narrowly focused parties with relatively few supporters nonetheless can gain representation in the legislature. Are citizens more likely to be mobilized to vote under such institutional arrangements? Using data sources available on the Internet,[4] you could gather information on a number of democratic countries. You could then look to see if different legal requirements and institutional arrangements are associated with differences in turnout. This area of research might also open the door for some informed speculation on your part. What sort of electoral reforms, if instituted in the United States, might enhance electoral turnout? What other (perhaps unintended) consequences might such reforms have?

Congress

Political scholars have long taken considerable interest in questions about the U.S. Congress. Some researchers focus on internal dynamics: the role of leadership, the power of party ties versus the pull of constituency. Others pay attention to demographics: Has the number of women and minorities who serve in Congress increased in the recent past? Still others look at ideology: Are Republicans, on average, becoming more conservative and Democrats more liberal in their congressional voting? The great thing about Congress is the rich data that are available. The U.S. House and the U.S. Senate are among the most-studied institutions in the world. Several annual or biannual publications chronicle and report a large number of attributes of members of the House and Senate.[5] And the Internet is rife with information about current and past Congresses. Liberal groups, such as Americans for Democratic Action, conservative groups, such as the American Conservative Union, and nonpartisan publications, such as the *National Journal,* regularly rate the voting records of elected officials and post these ratings on their Internet sites.[6]

INPUTTING DATA

Each of these five possibilities represents a practical compromise between posing an interesting question, obtaining available data, and using Stata to perform the analysis. However, as you will no doubt discover, data sources vary in their "input friendliness"—some data are easy to input into Stata, and other data require more typing. This section reviews different data sources and input procedures.

Stata-Formatted Datasets

The least labor-intensive sources provide Stata datasets that are ready to download and analyze. One such source, the ICPSR's data clearinghouse at the University of Michigan, was mentioned at the beginning of this chapter. But many other sites exist, often maintained by scholars, academic departments, and private foundations. For example, if you are interested in comparative politics or international relations topics, visit Pippa Norris's Web site at Harvard's John F. Kennedy School of Government.[7] Planning a project on the U.S. Supreme Court? You will want to download Lee Epstein's (Northwestern University) Stata dataset, which contains information on every Supreme Court nominee since John Jay.[8] For links to a number of Stata datasets having a particular emphasis on Latino politics, see Prof. Matt A. Barreto's site at the University of Washington.[9] Are you interested in the political beliefs and civic behavior of young people? The Center for Information and Research on Civic Learning and Engagement (CIRCLE) provides excellent data in Stata format.[10] More generally, the University of California–Berkeley's Survey Documentation and Analysis (SDA) Web site—a clearinghouse for the General Social Surveys, the American National Election Studies, and Census Microdata—allows you to download customized datasets and codebooks in a variety of formats, including Stata.[11]

Microsoft Excel Datasets

Much Internet data is not Stata-ready but, rather, is available in spreadsheet form, predominately Microsoft Excel format. In these situations, you can copy/paste the data from Excel into the Stata Data Editor. There are a few caveats to keep in mind, however. To illustrate, consider a typical U.S. Census site, which links an Excel dataset that records consumer complaints of fraud and identity theft, by state (Figure 11-1).[12] This set provides an instructive example of a common "gotcha" in transferring data from Excel to Stata.

Figure 11-1 Opening an Excel Dataset and Evaluating Its Stata-Friendliness

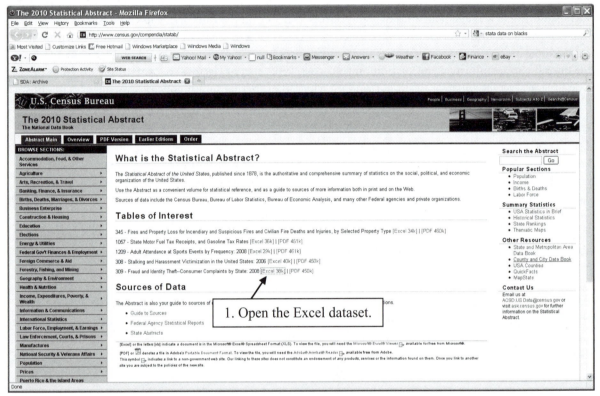

Figure 11-2   Removing Commas from Data Values Using Excel

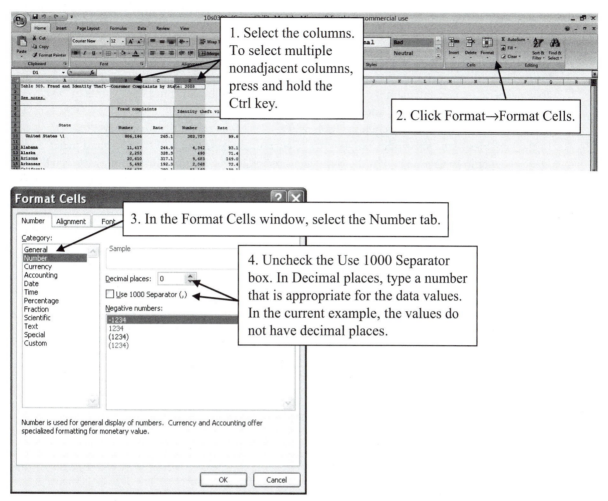

Stata recognizes two basic forms of data, numeric and string. Numeric data contain only numbers, including numbers with decimals. String data contain letters, words, symbols, or commas. Although some string data are essential—case identifiers, such as state or country names, are obvious examples—Stata much prefers to analyze numerics, not strings. In the current example, the data in the "Rate" columns of the fraud and identity theft dataset are numeric. But note that the data in the two "Number" columns contain commas and, so, will be recognized by Stata as strings. Stata would be happy to let you paste these values into the Data Editor, but it would not be at all happy to analyze them for you. To remove the commas, and thereby convert the data from string to numeric, follow these steps, which are illustrated in Figure 11-2:

1. Select the columns you wish to edit by clicking the column header. To select multiple nonadjacent columns, select the first column, press and hold the Ctrl key, and then select the second column.
2. On Excel's main menu bar, click Format→Format Cells.
3. In the Category pane of the Format Cells window, select the Number tab.
4. In the Number tab, you will always want to uncheck the Use 1000 Separator box. Depending on the exact character of the data, you may want to modify the value in the Decimal places box. If the data contain decimals, then specify the number of decimal places. In the current example, the numbers in the edited columns do not contain decimals, so we would type "0" in the Decimal places box.

To copy/paste the edited Excel data into the Stata Data Editor, follow these steps, which are described in Figure 11-3:

1. Select the Excel data rows that you want to paste into Stata. Make sure that the selection is square—that is, ensure that each row contains the same number of columns. Avoid selecting column headers and labels. Also, do not use Excel's row-number markers to make the selection. (This copies the

desired columns, plus a number of empty columns.) Rather, select the data by clicking inside the matrix. In the current example, we would begin the selection by clicking on "Alabama," selecting the four columns to the right, and selecting down through the last state, "Wyoming." After completing the selection, click the Copy icon on the Excel menu bar.

2. On the Stata menu bar, click the Data Editor (Edit) icon.

3. In the Data Editor, click the Paste icon. Stata pastes the data into the Data Editor, giving each variable a generic name. State names are contained in "var1," number of fraud complaints in "var2," fraud complaint rate in "var3," and so on.

4. Change the variable names by clicking Tools→Variables Manager on the main menu bar.

5. In the Variables Manager window, highlight the current variable name in the left-hand panel, and make changes in the Name box in the right-hand panel. In the current illustration, with "var1" highlighted, we would click in the Name box, type "state," and press Enter or click Apply. By Stata's rules, a variable name may be from 1 to 32 characters in length, although 8–12 characters are usually adequate. Characters may be letters, numbers, and underscores. You may begin a name with an underscore, although Stata recommends that you not do this, because many of Stata's reserved names begin with underscores. Stata is case sensitive, so "State" is different from "state."

Figure 11-3 Copy/Pasting from Excel into Stata's Data Editor

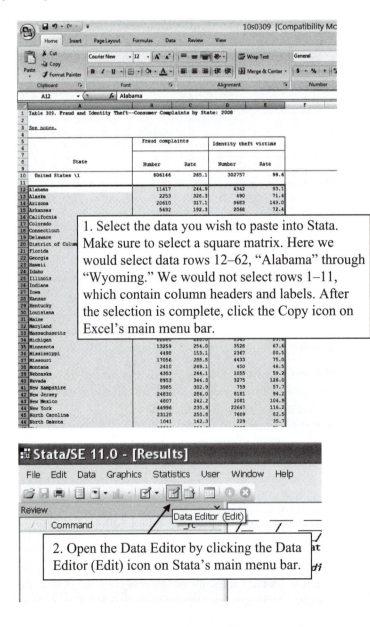

Figure 11-3 Copy/Pasting from Excel into Stata's Data Editor (continued)

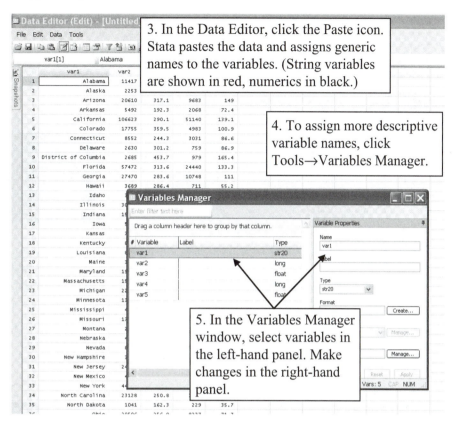

3. In the Data Editor, click the Paste icon. Stata pastes the data and assigns generic names to the variables. (String variables are shown in red, numerics in black.)

4. To assign more descriptive variable names, click Tools→Variables Manager.

5. In the Variables Manager window, select variables in the left-hand panel. Make changes in the right-hand panel.

As we have just seen, if the data are available in Excel format, it is a relatively simple matter to copy/paste into Stata. If the data are in HTML format, it is a relatively simple matter to copy/paste into Excel. Note that the HTML-to-Excel procedure works with Internet Explorer, but it will not work with Mozilla Firefox. By way of illustration, consider the *National Journal*'s data on members of the U.S. House.[13] As shown in Figure 11-4, we would select the data and then copy it to the clipboard. Once in Excel (see Figure 11-5), inspect the data values for unwanted strings. In the current example, each House member's party affiliation is recorded as a "D" or an "R". Numeric codes are preferred—such as code 1 for Democrat and code 2 for Republican. To make the change, select the column, and then use Find/Replace to replace the Ds with 1s and the Rs with 2s. Once you are satisfied that things look okay, select the dataset, copy it to the clipboard, and dump it into Stata's Data Editor. (Refer to Figure 11-5.) Again, we would want to use the Variables Manager to supply useful names for the variables.

PDF Format or Hand-coded Data

How do you proceed when your data are in paper-and-pencil form (a stack of completed questionnaires, for example), or are downloadable in print-only format, such as in a PDF file? You could code the data into Excel and copy/paste into Stata. Better still, you could enter the data directly into the Stata Data Editor. Figure 11-6 displays a partial Web page from the Americans for Democratic Action (ADA) site, which reports ratings of the 2009 Senate. The ADA is a liberal group that uses a series of key votes to rate members of Congress, awarding a plus sign (+) for a liberal vote and a minus sign (-) for a conservative vote. In 2009, the ADA monitored 20 key votes, denoted by the unhelpful numbers 1 through 20 on the Web page. Elsewhere on the ADA site we find that the first key vote involved wage discrimination legislation, which the ADA supported. Any senator who voted for the legislation is coded as "+," and those opposed are coded "-." To the right of the page we find ADA's overall liberalism score for 2009, under the heading "LQ," which stands for "Liberal Quotient." ADA arrives at the Liberal Quotient by determining the percentage of votes on which the senator supported ADA's position. Scores can range from 0% (most conservative) to 100% (most liberal). How would you take the information from this site and put it into a form that Stata can analyze?

Figure 11-4 Data in HTML Format

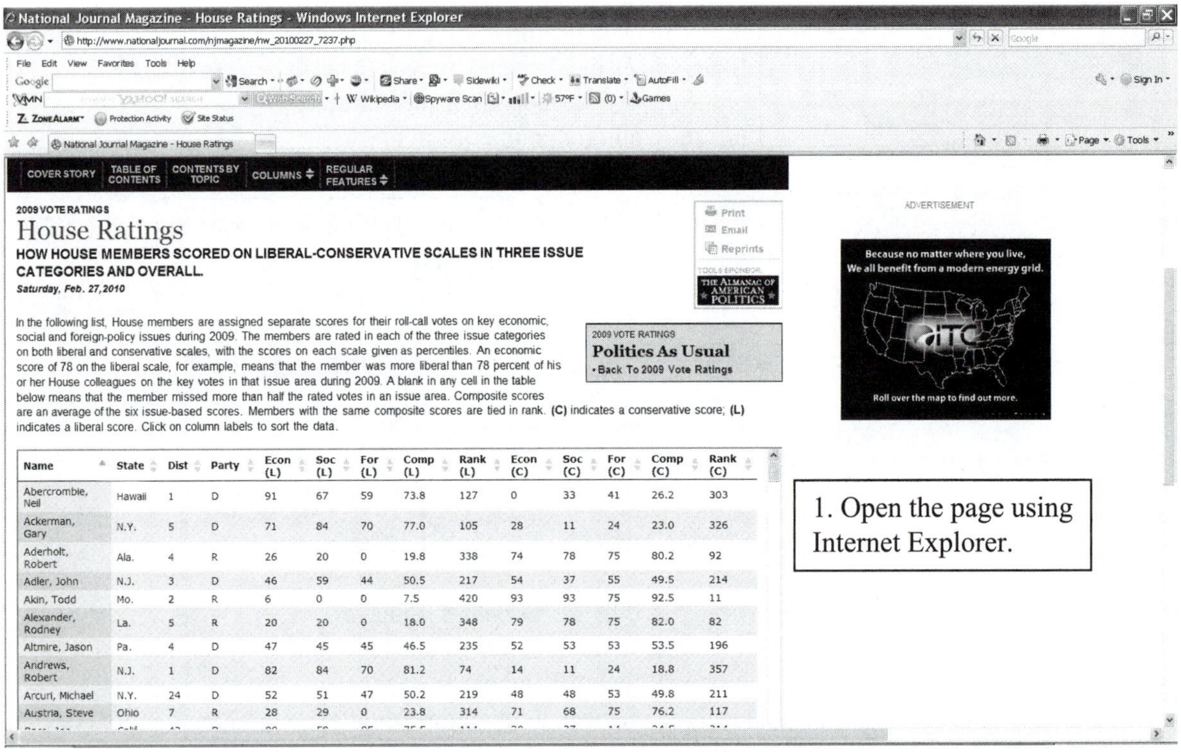

1. Open the page using Internet Explorer.

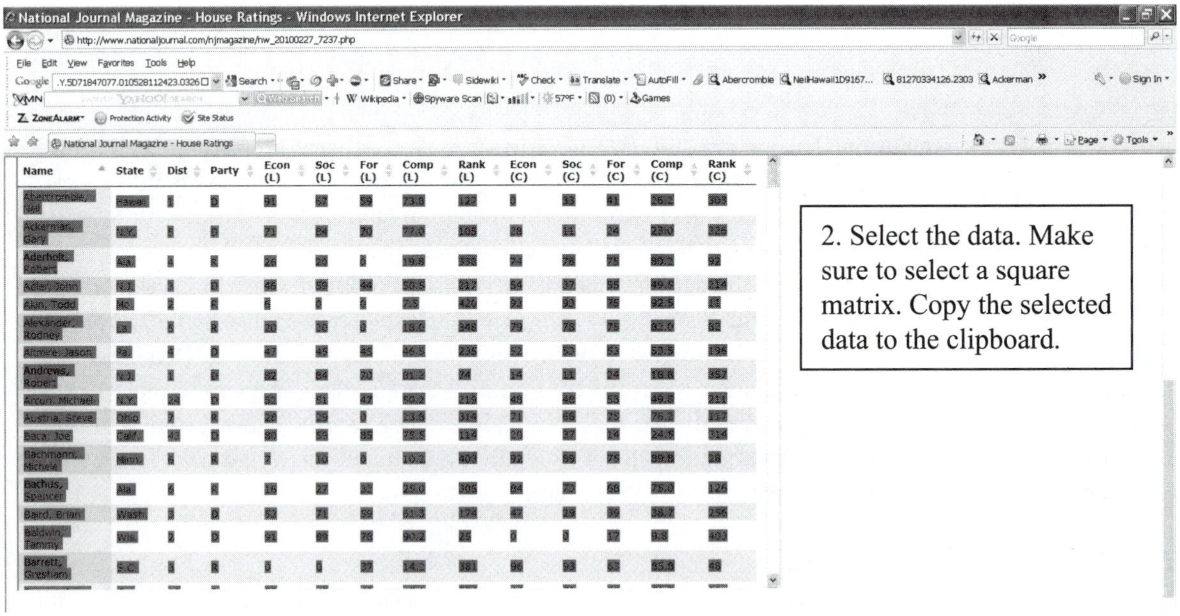

2. Select the data. Make sure to select a square matrix. Copy the selected data to the clipboard.

Here, in raw form, is the first data line, for Senator Sessions of Alabama:

Sessions. (R) - - - - - - - - - - - - - - - - - - + - 5%

Every data value in this line of code is a string. If you were coding this data into Stata, you would first need to convert all the values, except the senators' names, to numerics. An intuitive scheme might be to code party affiliation as 1 for Democrats and 2 for Republicans, to code minus signs as zeros and plus signs as 1s, and to remove the string symbol "%" from the LQ scores. Here is Senator Sessions's information, converted to numerics:

Sessions 2 0 0 0 0 0 0 0 0 0 0 0 0 0 0 0 0 0 0 1 0 5

Figure 11-5 Copying HTML Data from Excel to Stata

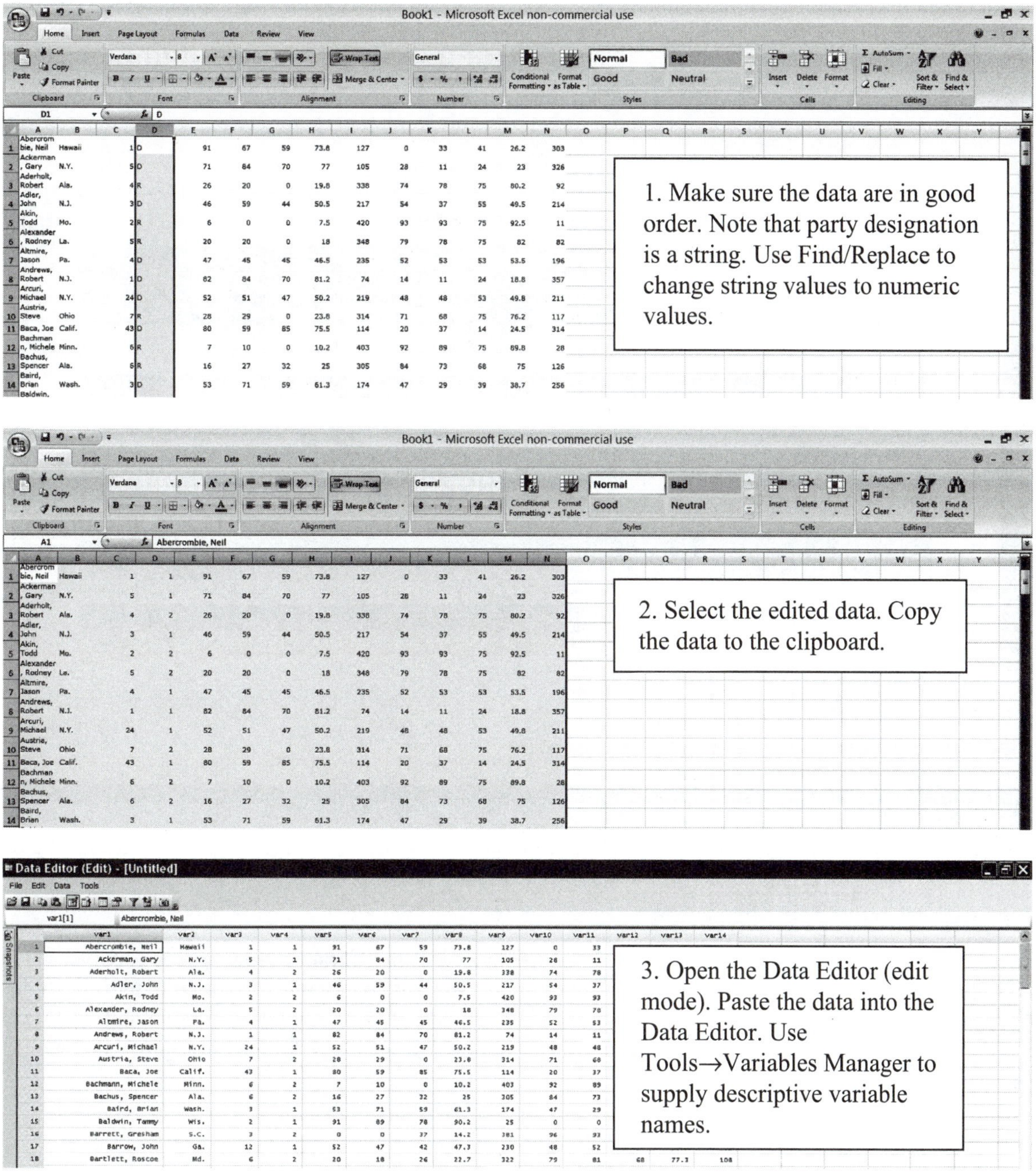

Once the coding protocol is established, it is a simple (if tedious) matter to type the data directly into the Stata Data Editor (see Figure 11-7). Type the code directly into each cell, using the arrow keys to navigate between cells. Use the Variables Manager to supply more descriptive variable names. Also, make good use of the Variable Manager's label box, which permits longer and more detailed variable descriptions. And don't forget to click the Save File icon frequently.

WRITING IT UP

Several of the datasets described thus far would provide great raw material for analysis. After inputting your data, you can let the creative juices flow—describing the variables, performing cross-tabulation and mean comparison analyses, running linear regression and logit models. Rewarding findings are guaranteed. Yet at some point the analysis ends, and the writing must begin. It is at this point, as well, that two contradictory

Figure 11-6 Data in PDF Format

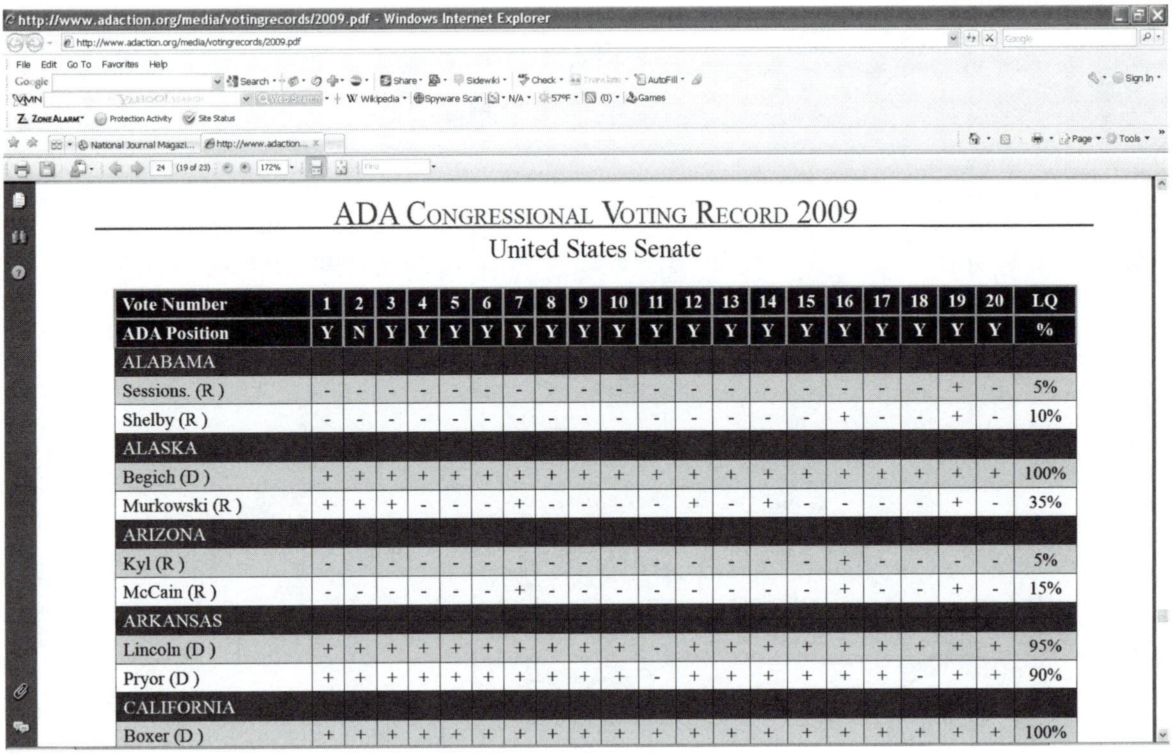

ADA CONGRESSIONAL VOTING RECORD 2009

United States Senate

Vote Number	1	2	3	4	5	6	7	8	9	10	11	12	13	14	15	16	17	18	19	20	LQ
ADA Position	Y	N	Y	Y	Y	Y	Y	Y	Y	Y	Y	Y	Y	Y	Y	Y	Y	Y	Y	Y	%
ALABAMA																					
Sessions. (R)	-	-	-	-	-	-	-	-	-	-	-	-	-	-	-	-	-	-	+	-	5%
Shelby (R)	-	-	-	-	-	-	-	-	-	-	-	-	-	-	-	+	-	-	+	-	10%
ALASKA																					
Begich (D)	+	+	+	+	+	+	+	+	+	+	+	+	+	+	+	+	+	+	+	+	100%
Murkowski (R)	+	+	+	-	-	-	+	-	-	-	-	+	-	+	-	-	-	-	+	-	35%
ARIZONA																					
Kyl (R)	-	-	-	-	-	-	-	-	-	-	-	-	-	-	-	+	-	-	-	-	5%
McCain (R)	-	-	-	-	-	-	+	-	-	-	-	-	-	-	-	+	-	-	+	-	15%
ARKANSAS																					
Lincoln (D)	+	+	+	+	+	+	+	+	+	+	-	+	+	+	+	+	+	+	+	+	95%
Pryor (D)	+	+	+	+	+	+	+	+	+	+	-	+	+	+	+	+	+	-	+	+	90%
CALIFORNIA																					
Boxer (D)	+	+	+	+	+	+	+	+	+	+	+	+	+	+	+	+	+	+	+	+	100%

Figure 11-7 Entering Data Directly into the Data Editor

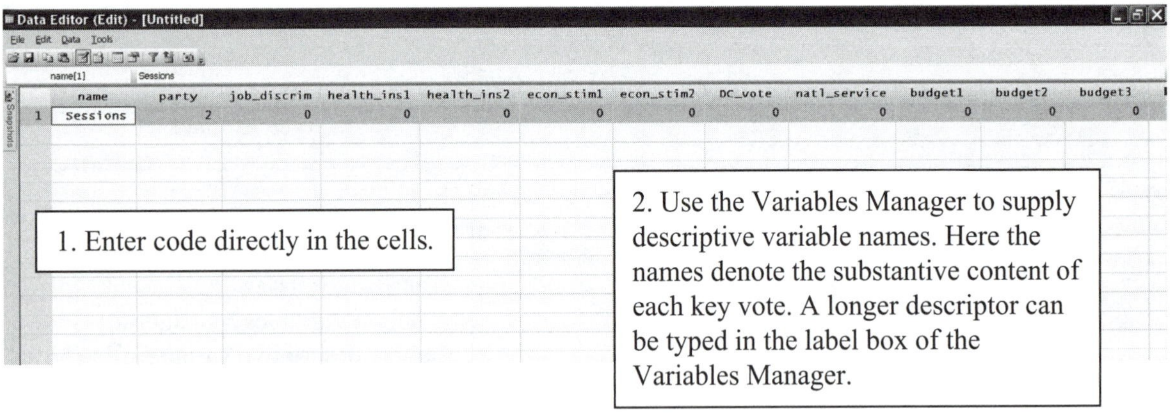
Data Editor (Edit) - [Untitled]
name party job_discrim health_ins1 health_ins2 econ_stim1 econ_stim2 DC_vote natl_service budget1 budget2 budget3
1 Sessions 2 0 0 0 0 0 0 0 0 0 0
1. Enter code directly in the cells.
2. Use the Variables Manager to supply descriptive variable names. Here the names denote the substantive content of each key vote. A longer descriptor can be typed in the label box of the Variables Manager.

considerations often collide. On one hand, you have an embarrassment of riches. You have worked on your research for several weeks, and you know the topic well—better, perhaps, than does anyone who will read the paper. There may be a large amount of material that you want to include in your paper. On the other hand, you want to get it written, and you do not want to write a book.

Viewed from an instructor's perspective, the two questions most frequently asked by students are, "How should my paper be organized?" and "How long should it be?" (The questions are not necessarily asked in this order.) Of course, different projects and instructors might call for different requirements. But here is a rough outline for a well-organized paper of 16–24 double-spaced pages (in 12-point font).

I. The research question (3–4 pages)
   A. Introduction to the problem (1 page)
   B. Theory and process (1–2 pages)
   C. Propositions (1 page)

II. Previous research (2–4 pages)
    A. Descriptive review (1–2 pages)
    B. Critical review (1–2 pages)
III. Data and hypotheses (3–4 pages)
    A. Data and variables (1–2 pages)
    B. Measurement (1 page)
    C. Hypotheses (1 page)
IV. Analysis (5–8 pages, including tables)
    A. Descriptive statistics (1–2 pages)
    B. Bivariate comparisons (2–3 pages)
    C. Controlled comparisons (2–3 pages)
V. Conclusions and implications (3–4 pages)
    A. Summary of findings (1 page)
    B. Implications for theory (1–2 pages)
    C. New issues or questions (1 page)

The Research Question

Because of its rhetorical challenges, the opening section of a paper is often the most difficult to write. In this section you must both engage the reader's interest and describe the purpose of the research. Here is a heuristic device that may be useful: In the first page of the write-up, place the specific research problem in the context of larger, clearly important issues or questions. For example, suppose your research is centered on the landmark healthcare legislation passed by Congress in 2010. A narrowly focused topic? Yes. A dry topic? Not at all. The opening page of this paper could frame larger questions about the sometimes-conflicting roles of congressional party leadership and constituency interests in shaping the behavior of representatives and senators. Thus your analysis will advance our knowledge by illuminating one facet of a larger, more complex question.

Following the introduction, you begin to zero in on the problem at hand. The "theory and process" section describes the logic of the relationships you are studying. Many political phenomena, as you have learned, have competing or alternative explanations. You should describe these alternatives, and the tension between them, in this section. Although a complete description of previous research does not appear in this section, you should give appropriate attribution to the most prominent work. These references tie your work to the scholarly community, and they raise the points you will cover in a more detailed review.

You should round out the introductory section of your paper with a brief statement of purpose or intent. Think about it from the reader's perspective. Thus far you have made the reader aware of the larger context of the analysis, and you have described the process that may explain the relationships of interest. If this process has merit, then it should submit to an empirical test of some kind. What test do you propose? The "Propositions" page serves this role. Here you set the parameters of the research—informing the reader about the units of analysis, the concepts to be measured, and the type of analysis to be performed.

Previous Research

Here you provide an intellectual history of the research problem, a description and critique of the published research on which the analysis is based. You first would describe these previous analyses in some detail. What data and variables were used? What were the main findings? Did different researchers arrive at different conclusions? Political scientists who share a research interest often agree on many things. Yet knowledge is nourished through criticism, and in reviewing previous work you will notice key points of disagreement—about how concepts should be measured, what are the best data to use, or which variables need to be controlled. In the latter part of this section of the paper, you would review these points and perhaps contribute to the debate. A practical point: The frequently asked question "How many articles and books should be reviewed?" has no set answer. It depends on the project. However, here is an estimate: A well-grounded yet manageable review should discuss at least four references.

Data, Hypotheses, and Analysis

Together, the sections "Data and Hypotheses" and "Analysis" form the heart of the project, and they have been the primary concerns of this book. By now you are well versed in how to describe your data and variables and how to frame hypotheses. You also know how to set up a cross-tabulation or mean comparison table, and you can make controlled comparisons and interpret your findings.

In writing these sections, however, you should bear in mind a few reader-centered considerations. First, assume that the reader might want to replicate your study—collect the data you gathered, define and measure the concepts as you have defined and measured them, manipulate the variables just as you have computed and recoded them, and produce the tables you have reported. By explaining precisely what you did, your write-up should provide a clear guide for such a replication. Second, devote some space to a statistical description of the variables. Often you can add depth and interest to your analysis by briefly presenting the frequency distributions of the variables, particularly the dependent variable. Finally, exercise care in constructing readable tables. You can select, copy, and paste the tables generated by Stata directly into a word processor, but they always require further editing for readability.

Conclusions and Implications

No section of a research paper can write itself. But the final section comes closest to realizing this optimistic hope. Here you discuss the analysis on three levels. First, you provide a condensed recapitulation. What are the main findings? Are the hypotheses borne out? Were there any unexpected findings? Second, you describe where the results fit in the larger fabric of scholarly research on the topic. In what ways are the findings consistent with the work of previous researchers? Does your analysis lend support to one scholarly perspective as opposed to another? Third, research papers often include obligatory "suggestions for further research." Indeed, you may have encountered some methodological problems that still must be worked out, or you might have unearthed a noteworthy substantive relationship that could bear future scrutiny. You should describe these new issues or questions. Here, too, you are allowed some room to speculate—to venture beyond the edge of the data and engage in a little "What if?" thinking. After all, the truth is still out there.

NOTES

1. You can browse ICPSR's holdings at www.icpsr.umich.edu.
2. For excellent guidance on the meaning and measurement of political knowledge, see Michael X. Delli Carpini and Scott Keeter, "Measuring Political Knowledge: Putting First Things First," *American Journal of Political Science* 37 (Nov. 1993): 1179–1206.
3. The cases are available from LexisNexis at www.lexis-nexis.com/academic/universe/Academic/. See also the National Center for State Courts, Court Statistics Project, at www.ncsconline.org/d_research/csp/CSP_Main_Page .html.
4. Pippa Norris of Harvard's John F. Kennedy School of Government has compiled excellent comparative and international data, which are available to the general public. These datasets are available in several formats, including Stata. See www.pippanorris.com.
5. Examples include three books published by CQ Press: *Who's Who in Congress*, offered twice a year through 2001; *CQ's Politics in America*, ed. Brian Nutting and H. Amy Stern, published every two years; and *Vital Statistics on American Politics*, by Harold W. Stanley and Richard G. Niemi, which also appears every two years. *Vital Statistics* is an excellent single-volume general reference on American politics.
6. See www.adaction.org, www.conservative.org, and www.nationaljournal.com/njonline.
7. See www.pippanorris.com.
8. See http://epstein.law.northwestern.edu/research/justicesdata.html.
9. See http://faculty.washington.edu/mbarreto/data/index.html.
10. See www.civicyouth.org/research/products/data.htm.
11. See http://sda.berkeley.edu/archive.htm.
12. See www.census.gov/compendia/statab/.
13. See www.nationaljournal.com/njmagazine/nw_20100227_7237.php.

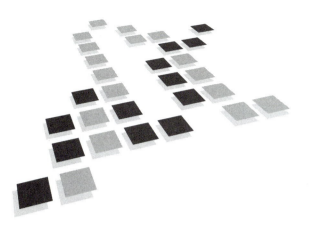

Appendix

Table A-1 Descriptions of Constructed Variables in gss2006

Variable name and label	Source variables, GSS 1972-2006 cumulative data file*	Notes on construction of variable
authoritarianism Authoritarianism scale	thnkself obey	thnkself minus obey (thnkself-obey), rescaled: 0 (low authoritarianism) to 7 (high authoritarianism). Measure based on Karen Stenner, *The Authoritarian Dynamic* (Cambridge, Mass.: Cambridge University Press, 2005).
breadwinner Percent of total family $ earned by R	rincom06 income06	(rincom06 / income06) x 100.
dogmatism Religious dogmatism scale	punsin blkwhite rotapple permoral	Variables coded in "more dogmatic" direction, summed, and rescaled: 0 (low dogmatism) to 12 (high dogmatism). Based on Ted G. Jelen and Clyde Wilcox, "Religious Dogmatism among White Christians: Causes and Effects," *Review of Religious Research* 33 (September 1991): 32–46.
econ_liberalism Economic liberalism scale	cutgovt lessreg	Variables summed and rescaled: 0 (most conservative) to 8 (most liberal).
fem_role Female role: Children, home, politics	fechld fepresch fefam fepol	Variables coded in "liberal" direction, summed, and rescaled: 0 (women domestic) to 12 (women in work/politics).
gun_control Gun control scale	gunsales gunsdrug semiguns guns911 rifles50 gunlaw	Number of pro-control responses summed: 0 (oppose control) to 6 (favor control).

(continued)

Table A-1   Descriptions of Constructed Variables in gss2006   *(continued)*

Variable name and label	Source variables, GSS 1972-2006 cumulative data file*	Notes on construction of variable
job_autonomy How much autonomy does R have in job?	wkfreedm lotofsay	Variables summed and recoded in "more autonomy" direction: 1 (low autonomy) to 7 (high autonomy).
policy_know R's self-assessed knowledge: foreign / economic policy	knwforgn knwecon	Variables summed, recoded, and rescaled: 0 (low knowledge) to 8 (high knowledge).
pro_secure Civil liberties or security?	Based on gss2006 variable civlibs	civlibs recoded: 0–4 = 1; 5–9 = 0.
racial_liberal Racial liberalism scale	affrmact wrkwayup natrace	Variables collapsed; "most liberal" responses summed: 0 (least liberal) to 3 (most liberal).
science_quiz 10-item science test	hotcore boyorgrl electron bigbang condrift evolved earthsun radioact lasers viruses	Number of correct responses summed.
social_connect Social connectedness	socrel socommun socfrend socbar	Variables recoded and summed. Final scale collapsed: 0 (low connectedness) to 2 (high connectedness).
social_cons Social conservatism scale	abany grass cappun homosex pornlaw	Variables recoded; "least permissive" responses summed: 0 (most permissive) to 5 (least permissive).
spend6 Government increase $ on how many programs?	natcity natdrug nateduc natenvir natfare natheal	Number of "increase spending" responses summed.
suicide Incurable patient/incurable disease: suicide permissible?	letdie1 suicide1	Number of "yes" responses summed.

Table A-1 *(continued)*

Variable name and label	Source variables, GSS 1972-2006 cumulative data file*	Notes on construction of variable
sz_place	xnorcsiz	Source variable recoded using this protocol: 1–2 = 1; 5–7 = 1; 3–4 = 2; 8–10 = 3. sz_place categories: 1 = city; 2 = suburb; 3 = rural.
Size of place where R resides		
tol_communist	libcom spkcom	Variables coded 0/1 in more tolerant direction and summed: 0 (least tolerant) to 2 (most tolerant).
Tolerance twrd communists		
tol_racist		
	librac	
Tolerance twrd racists	spkrac	
trust_gov	confed conjudge	Variables summed and recoded: 1 (low trust) to 7 (high trust).
Level of trust in government	conlegis	
trust_media	conpress contv	Variables summed and recoded: 1 (low trust) to 4 (high trust).
Level of trust in media		
trust_social	helpful trust	Number of "trusting" responses summed: 0 (low trust) to 3 (high trust).
Level of social trust	fair	

*To find source variable question wording, see the University of California–Berkeley's Survey Documentation and Analysis (SDA) Web site, http://sda.berkeley.edu/archive.htm.

Table A-2   Descriptions of Variables in the states Dataset

Variable name and label	Description	Source and notes
abortion Abortions per 1000 women	Number of legal abortions per 1,000 women aged 15–44, 2000.	Alan Guttmacher Institute, www.guttmacher .org
		Lawrence B. Finer and Stanley K. Henshaw. 2003. "Abortion Incidence and Services in the United States in 2000," *Perspectives on Sexual and Reproductive Health* 35(1): 6–15.
abortlaw Number of restrictions on abortion	Five variables coded separately and summed: (i) parental involvement = 2, none = 0; (ii) partial birth banned = 2, not = 0; (iii) counseling and waiting period = 2, counseling or waiting period = 1, neither = 0; (iv) public funding limited to life-endangerment/rape/incest = 2, exceptions for health reasons = 1, funding for all or most medically necessary = 0; (v) private insurance coverage limited to life endangerment = 2, providers may refuse to participate = 1, no restrictions = 0. Final variable: 0 (least restrictive) to 10 (most restrictive).	Guttmacher Institute, "State Policies in Brief: An Overview of Abortion Laws." As of November 1, 2007. http://www.guttmacher.org/statecenter/ spibs/spib_OAL.pdf *Note:* All provisions enacted into law, including legally enjoined provisions, are counted as restrictions.
attend Percent frequent church attenders	Percentage attending religious services every week" or "almost every week."	Pooled National Election Study, 1988–2002. Percentage coded 1 ("every week") or 2 ("almost every week") on question #vcf0130. *Note:* Thirteen states have fewer than 30 cases and were set to missing values on attend.
attend_pct % freq attend relig serv (Pew)	Pew Research Center's Forum on Religion & Public Life, polling data, December 21, 2009.	Pew Forum on Religion and Public Life, http://pewforum.org/How-Religious-Is-Your-State-.aspx.
battle04 Battleground state	Coded 1 for 2004 battleground states, coded 0 for non–battleground states.	U.S. Department of State, http://usinfo.state. gov/dhr/Archive/2004/Jul/12-250886.html.
blkleg Percent of state legislators who are black	Percent of state legislators who are black, 2003.	National Conference of State Legislatures, www.ncsl.org/programs/legismgt/about/ afrAmer.htm.
blkpct Percent black	Percent black or African American, 2004.	U.S. Census Bureau, http://www.census.gov/ compendia/smadb/SMADBstate.html.

Table A-2 *(continued)*

Variable name and label	Description	Source and notes
bush00 Percent voting for Bush 2000 gore00 Percent voting for Gore 2000 nader00 Percent voting for Nader 2000	Number of votes cast for Bush [Gore, Nader] as a percentage of all votes cast.	Federal Election Commission, www.fec.gov/pubrec/fe2000/2000presge.htm.
bush04 Percent voting for Bush 2004 kerry04 Percent voting for Kerry 2004	Number of votes cast for Bush [Kerry] as a percentage of all votes cast.	Federal Election Commission, www.fec.gov/pubrec/fe2004/federalelections2004.shtml.
carfatal Motor vehicle fatalities (per 100,000 pop)	Motor vehicle fatalities per 100,000 population, 2002.	U.S. Census Bureau, www.census.gov/compendia/smadb/TableA-13.pdf.
christad Percent of pop who are Christian adherents	Percentage of population who are Christian adherents, 2000.	U.S. Census Bureau, www.census.gov/compendia/statab/tables/07s0075.xls. Dale E. Jones, Sherri Doty, Clifford Grammich, James E. Horsch, Richard Houseal, John P. Marcum, Kenneth M. Sanchagrin, and Richard H. Taylor, *Religious Congregations and Membership in the United States: 2000* (Nashville, Tenn.: Glenmary Research Center, 2002), www.glenmary.org/grc.
Cigarettes Packs bimonthly per adult pop	Bimonthly pack sales per adult population, 2003.	University of California–San Diego, Social Sciences Data Collection, http://ssdc.ucsd.edu/tobacco/sales/.
cig_tax cig_tax_3 Cigarette tax per pack	Cigarette tax per pack, 2007.	Campaign for Tobacco-Free Kids, http://tobaccofreekids.org.
college Percent of pop w/college or higher	Percentage of population 25 years and over who have college degrees or higher.	U.S. Census Bureau, www.census.gov/compendia/smadb/TableA-22.pdf.
cons_hr Conservatism score, US House delegation	Mean American Conservative Union rating of state's delegation to House of Representatives, 2006.	American Conservative Union, http://acuratings.com.
cook_index Cook Partisan Voting Index	Higher scores = more Democratic.	http://www.cookpolitical.com/node/4201.

(continued)

Table A-2   Descriptions of Variables in the states Dataset   *(continued)*

Variable name and label	Description	Source and notes
defexpen Federal defense expenditures per capita	Federal defense expenditures per capita, 2003.	U.S. Census Bureau, http://www.census.gov/compendia/smadb/TableA-84.pdf.
demnat % US House and Senate Democratic	Number of Democratic House and Senate members as a percentage of total House and Senate delegations, 2006.	American Conservative Union, http://acuratings.com.
dempct_m Percent mass public Democratic reppct_m Percent mass public Republican indpct_m Percent mass public Independent libpct_m Percent mass public Liberal modpct_m Percent mass public Moderate conpct_m Percent mass public Conservative	Pooled CBS News/*New York Times* poll party identification and ideology estimates, 1977–1999.	Gerald C. Wright, Indiana University. Data used with permission. Robert S. Erikson, Gerald C. Wright, and John P. McIver, *Statehouse Democracy* (Cambridge, U.K.: Cambridge University Press, 1993).
demstate Percent state legislators Democratic	Number of Democratic state house and senate members as a percentage of total house and senate members, 2006 post-election/2007 pre-election.	National Conference of State Legislatures, www.ncsl.org/statevote/partycomptable2007.htm.
density Population per square mile	Population per square mile, 2005.	U.S. Census Bureau, www.census.gov/compendia/smadb/TableA-01.pdf.
gay_policy Billman's policy scale	Higher scores = more conservative.	Jeffrey Billman, "Marriage for Some: Understanding Variation of Gay Rights and Gay Marriage Policies in the United States," University of Central Florida, M.A. thesis, 2010.
gay_support Lax-Phillips opinion index	Public support for gay rights (higher scores more supportive).	Jeffrey R. Lax and Justin Phillips, "Gay Rights in the States: Public Opinion and Policy Responsiveness," *American Political Science Review* 103 (August 2009).
gb_win00 Did Bush win electoral vote, 2000?	0=Gore win / 1=Bush win.	Federal Election Commission, www.fec.gov.

Table A-2 *(continued)*

Variable name and label	Description	Source and notes
gb_win04 Did Bush win electoral vote, 2004?	0=Kerry win / 1= Bush win.	Federal Election Commission www.fec.gov.
gunlaw_rank Brady Campaign rank gunlaw_scale Brady Campaign score	Brady Campaign ranking (higher scores = fewer gun restrictions) and Brady scale score (higher scores = more gun restrictions).	Brady Campaign 2008 State Scorecard, www.bradycampaign.org/xshare/bcam/stategunlaws/scorecard/StateRatings.pdf.
hispanic Percent hispanic	Percentage of population Hispanic, 2004.	U.S. Census Bureau, www.census.gov/compendia/smadb/TableA-05.pdf.
hs_or_more Percent of pop w/HS or higher	Percentage of population 25 years and over with high school degree or higher.	U.S. Census Bureau, www.census.gov/compendia/smadb/TableA-22.pdf.
mccain08 Percent vote for McCain obama08 Percent vote for Obama	Percent total vote for candidate.	Dave Leip's Atlas of U.S. Presidential Elections, www.uselectionatlas.org.
over64 Percent of pop age 65 or older	Percentage of population aged 65 or older, 2004.	U.S. Census Bureau, www.census.gov/compendia/smadb/TableA-04.pdf
permit Percent public "Always allow" abortion	Percentage responding that abortion should "always" be permitted.	Pooled National Election Study, 1988–2002.
pop_18_24 Percent age 18-24	Percentage of population aged 18 to 24, 2004.	U.S. Census Bureau, www.census.gov/compendia/smadb/TableA-04.pdf.
pot_policy Legalization policies	State legalization policy: none, pending, enacted.	"Slowly, Limits on Pot Are Fading," *USA Today*, March 9, 2010.
prcapinc Per capita income	Income per capita, 2004.	U.S. Census Bureau, www.census.gov/compendia/smadb/TableA-43.pdf.
relig_import Percent religion "A great deal of guidance"	Percentage responding that religion provides "a great deal of guidance" in life.	Pooled National Election Study, 1984–2004; percentage coded 3 on question #vcf0847. *Note:* Twelve states have fewer than 30 cases and were set to missing values on relig_import.
religiosity Relig-observance belief scale (Pew) secularism Secularism scale (Pew)	Pew index of religiosity (secularism). Religiosity scale is reversal of secularism scale.	Pew Forum on Religion and Public Life, http://pewforum.org/How-Religious-Is-Your-State-.aspx.

(continued)

Table A-2 Descriptions of Variables in the states Dataset *(continued)*

Variable name and label	Description	Source and notes
turnout00 turnout04 Turnout in 2000 [2004] presidential election	Number of voters as a percentage of 2000 [2004] voting age population.	Committee for the Study of the American Electorate, press release, November 4, 2004, http://american.edu/ia/cdem/csae/pdfs/csae041104.pdf.
unemploy Unemployment rate	Percent unemployed of the civilian labor force, 2004.	U.S. Census Bureau, www.census.gov/compendia/smadb/TableA-29.pdf.
union Percent workers who are union members	Percentage of workers who are members of a labor union, 2004.	U.S. Census Bureau, www.census.gov/compendia/smadb/TableA-33.pdf.
urban Percent urban pop	Percentage of population in urban areas, 2000.	U.S. Census Bureau, http://www.census.gov/compendia/smadb/TableA-02.pdf.
vep00_turnout vep04_turnout vep08_turnout Turnout in 2000 [2004, 2008] presidential election	Percent turnout of voting eligible population 2000 [2004, 2008].	Michael McDonald, United States Election Project, http://elections.gmu.edu/index.html.
Womleg Percent of state legislators who are women	Percentage of state legislators who are women, 2007.	Center for American Women and Politics, www.cawp.rutgers.edu/Facts/Officeholders/stleg.pdf.

Table A-3 Descriptions of Variables in the world Dataset*

Variable name	Variable label	Source and notes
colony	Colony of what country?	*CIA World Factbook*, www.cia.gov.
confidence	Confidence in institutions scale	Based on Global Indicators variable v52, Confidence in state institutions early-mid 1990s; World Values Survey (1995–2000 waves), wvs.isr.umich.edu (WVS).
decentralization decentralization4	Decentralization scale	Based on the sum of Global Indicators variables Political, Fiscal, and Admin. See A. Schneider, "Who Gets What From Whom? The Impact of Decentralisation on Tax Capacity and Pro-Poor Policy," Institute of Development Studies Working Paper, No. 179 (Brighton: University of Sussex, 2003).
dem_other dem_other5	Percentage of other democracies in region	Calculated by author from region and democ_regime.
district_size3	Average # of members per district	Based on Global Indicators variable dm, mean district magnitude.
durable	Number of years since the last regime transition	Polity IV Project (2000), www.cidcm.umd.edu/polity/data/.
effectiveness	Government effectiveness scale	Kaufmann Governance indicators (2002), www.worldbank.org/wbi/governance/govdata2002/.
enpp_3	Effective number of parliamentary parties, june 2000 (Agora) (Banded)	Based on Global Indicators variable enpp (2000).
enpp3_democ	Effective number of parliamentary parties	Variable enpp3, restricted to democracies.
eu	EU member state (yes/no)	
fhrate04_rev fhrate08_rev	Freedom House rating of democracy (reversed) fhrate04_rev (0-7) fhrate08_rev (0-12)	Freedom House, Gastil index, Annual to 2004, www.freedomhouse.org.
frac_eth frac_eth3	Ethnic fractionalization (combined linguistic and racial)	See Alberto Alesina, Arnaud Devleeschauwer, William Easterly, Sergio Kurlat, and Romain Wacziarg, "Fractionalization," *Journal of Economic Growth* 8 (June 2003): 155–194, www.stanford.edu/~wacziarg/papersum.html.

(continued)

Table A-3 Descriptions of Variables in the world Dataset*   *(continued)*

Variable name	Variable label	Source and notes
free_business free_corrupt free_finance free_fiscal free_govspend free_invest free_labor free_monetary free_overall free_property free_trade	Heritage Foundation ratings, 2010 (higher scores more free)	Heritage Foundation. See www.heritage.org/index/Explore.aspx and www.heritage.org/index/FAQ.aspx.
gdp08	GDP (billions)	World Bank Development Indicators, www.worldbank.org (WB).
gdp_10_thou	GDP per capita in 10K US$	United Nations Development Programme (UNDP), 2004, www.undp.org. Income data are from 2002.
gdp_cap2	GDP per capita (US$): 2 cats	UNDP.
gdp_cap3	GDP per capita (US$): 3 cats	UNDP.
gender_equal3	Gender empowerment measure	Based on Global Indicators variable GEMValue2004; UNDP, 2004. See http://hdr.undp.org/en/statistics/faq/question,81,en.html.
gini04 gini08	gini coefficient, 2004 [2008]	UNDP, 2004 [2008].
indy	Year of independence	*CIA World Factbook.*
old06 old2003	Population ages 65 and above (% of total) 2006 [2003]	WB, 2007 [2004].
pmat12_3	Post-materialism	Based on Global Indicators variable pmat12, postmaterialism 12 cat; WVS, 1995.
pop03 pop08	Population 2003 [2008]	World Bank, DPI2000 Database of political institutions. See http://econ.worldbank.org/.
popcat3	Size of country by population (3-categories)	UNDP.
pr_sys	PR system?	Based on Global Indicators variable elecpr; IDEA, Voter turnout since 1945, www.idea.int.
protact3	Protest activity	Based on Global Indicators variable protact, summary mean protest activity; WVS, 1995.
regime_type3	Regime types	Based on Global Indicators variable Cheibub4Type (2000). Author set mixed systems to missing.
typerel	Predominant religion	*CIA World Factbook.*
unions	Union density	ILO, 1995.

Table A-3 Descriptions of Variables in the world Dataset*   *(continued)*

Variable name	Variable label	Source and notes
urban03 urban06	Urban population (% of total) 2003 [2006]	WB.
vi_rel3	Percent saying religion "very" important	Based on Global Indicators variable vi_rel, Percent religion 'very' important; WVS, 1995.
votevap00s votevap90s	Vote/vap most recent election in 2000s Vote/vap during 1990s	IDEA.
women05 women09	Percent women in lower house of parliament, 2005 [2009]	Inter-Parliamentary Union (IPU), www.ipu.org. Author restricted this measure to democracies only.
womyear	Year women first enfranchised	IPU.
yng2003 young06	Population ages 0-14 (% of total) 2003 [2006]	WB, 2004 [2007].

*All variables used in the world dataset were compiled and made available by Pippa Norris, John F. Kennedy School of Government, Harvard University, www.pipanorris.com. Professor Norris's dataset, Global Indicators Shared Dataset V2.0 (Updated Fall 2005 [September 13, 2005]), may be accessed at http://ksghome.harvard.edu/~pnorris/Data/Data.htm.